P9-DMF-934

READING WITH MEANING

WITHDRAWN

READING WITH MEANING

STRATEGIES•FOR•COLLEGE•READING

FIFTH EDITION

Dorothy Grant Hennings

Kean University

WITHDRAWN

Prentice
Hall

Upper Saddle River, New Jersey 07458

Library of Congress Cataloging-in-Publication Data

Hennings, Dorothy Grant.
  Reading with meaning : strategies for college reading / Dorothy Grant Hennings.—5th ed.
    p. cm.
  ISBN 0-13-040418-7
  1. Reading (Higher education)—United States. 2. College readers. I. Title.

LB2395.3 .H46 2001
428.4′071′1—dc21

00-068816

Editor in Chief: LEAH JEWELL
Acquisitions Editor: CRAIG CAMPANELLA
Editorial Assistant: JOAN POLK
Director of Production and Manufacturing: BARBARA KITTLE
Managing Editor: MARY ROTTINO
Production Editor: KATHLEEN SLEYS
Production Assistant: ELIZABETH BEST
Prepress and Manufacturing Manager: NICK SKLITSIS
Prepress and Manufacturing Buyer: BENJAMIN SMITH
Marketing Manager: RACHEL FALK
Marketing Assistant: CHRISTINE MOODIE
Interior Image Specialist: BETH BOYD
Image Permissions Coordinator: CHARLES MORRIS
Creative Design Director: LESLIE OSHER
Senior Art Director: XIMENA TAMVAKOPOULOS
Interior and Cover Designer: ANNE DEMARINIS
Cover Art: STANLEY MARTUCCI/STOCK ILLUSTRATION SOURCE, INC.

For permission to use copyrighted material, grateful acknowledgment
is made to the copyright holders listed on pages 327–328, which are considered
an extension of this copyright page.

This book was set in 10/12 New Baskerville by Interactive Composition Corp.
and was printed and bound by Courier Companies, Inc.
Covers were printed by Phoenix Color Corp.

© 2002, 1999, 1996, 1993, 1990 by Pearson Education, Inc.
Upper Saddle River, New Jersey 07458

All rights reserved. No part of this book may be
reproduced, in any form or by any means,
without permission in writing from the publisher.

Printed in the United States of America
10 9 8 7 6 5 4 3 2 1

ISBN 0-13-040418-7

WITHDRAWN

Prentice-Hall International (UK) Limited, *London*
Prentice-Hall of Australia Pty. Limited, *Sydney*
Prentice-Hall Canada Inc., Toronto
Prentice-Hall Hispanoamerica, S.A., *Mexico*
Prentice-Hall of India Private Limited, *New Delhi*
Prentice-Hall of Japan, Inc., *Tokyo*
Pearson Education Asia Pte. Ltd., *Singapore*
Editora Prentice-Hall do Brasil, Ltda., *Rio de Janeiro*

To my sister, Barbara M. Grant

CONTENTS

Preface xiii

PART ONE   INTRODUCTION TO READING

1 Getting Ready to Read   1

Getting Ready to Read   1

SELECTION 1:   *A Nation on the Move: America Moves West* (HISTORY)   *6*

SELECTION 2:   *For Heaven's Sakes, Choose a Job You Enjoy!*
(CAREER PLANNING)   *11*

SELECTION 3:   *The Signs of Life* (BIOLOGY)   *14*

SELECTION 4:   *Child Development* (PSYCHOLOGY)   *17*

Extending What You Have Learned   20

PART TWO   VOCABULARY AND READING

2 Unlocking the Meaning of Words: Using Context Clues   23

Unlocking the Meaning of Unfamiliar Words   23

Applying CDC   24

SELECTION 1:   *On Geology* (EARTH SCIENCE)   *27*

SELECTION 2:   *A Chance Event or Not? Anecdote, Common Sense,
and Statistics in Science* (BIOLOGY/MATHEMATICS)   *29*

SELECTION 3:   *Prenatal Development* (DEVELOPMENTAL PSYCHOLOGY)   *32*

Reviewing Chapter Vocabulary   35

Extending What You Have Learned   38

**3 Unlocking the Meaning of Words: Understanding
Word Elements   39**

Unlocking the Meaning of Words   39

Common Word-Building Elements   41

Common Prefixes   45

Common Suffixes   47

Compound Words   48

Syllable Segments   48

SELECTION 1:   *Cohabitation* (SOCIOLOGY)   *49*

SELECTION 2:   *The Internet in Postindustrial Society* (TECHNOLOGY)   *52*

SELECTION 3:   *Food Chains* (ECOLOGY)   *55*

Extending What You Have Learned   58

PART THREE   COMPREHENSION

4   **Grasping the Main Idea of a Paragraph**   **61**

Grasping the Main Idea   61

Identifying the Topic   61

Distinguishing Between General and Specific Points   62

Identifying Topics and General Statements: Marriage Customs   63

Grasping the Main Idea: Deductive, Inductive, and
   Linear Paragraphs   66

SELECTION 1:   *Three States of the United States: Florida, Nevada,
               and Illinois* (GEOGRAPHY)   *71*

SELECTION 2:   *The Color of Money: Being Rich in Black and
               White* (SOCIOLOGY)   *76*

SELECTION 3:   *Thomas Jefferson and His Presidency* (HISTORY)   *78*

Extending What You Have Learned   82

5   **Grasping the Thesis, or Main Idea, of an Entire Selection**   **83**

Grasping the Thesis, or Main Idea, of an Entire Selection   83

SELECTION 1:   *Doing Something About Osteoporosis
               While You Are Young* (HEALTH AND FITNESS)   *85*

SELECTION 2:   *Time Management: A Guide for
               Personal Planning* (MANAGEMENT SCIENCE)   *89*

SELECTION 3:   *The Meaning of Democracy* (POLITICAL SCIENCE)   *93*

Extending What You Have Learned   97

6   **Relating Main Ideas and Details**   **98**

Thinking About Details   98

Identifying Significant Details   98

Approximating Numerical Details   91

SELECTION 1:   *Great Constructions of the Past: The Biggest
               and Greatest* (HISTORY)   *100*

SELECTION 2:   *He's My Son!* (SOCIOLOGY)   *102*

SELECTION 3:   *What Does McDonald's Pay?* (ECONOMICS)   *104*

SELECTION 4:   *The Dream at Panama* (GEOGRAPHY AND HISTORY)   *105*

Extending What You Have Learned   114

7   **Using Clue Words to Anticipate an Author's Thoughts**   **115**

Using Clue Words   115

Paragraphs of Enumeration   115

Paragraphs with Examples   116

Paragraphs with Additional Information: A Continuation of
   or Change in the Topic   118

Paragraphs with Comparisons and Contrasts   120

Paragraphs with Conditional Relationships
   ("What-Then?" Paragraphs)   122

Cause and Effect Paragraphs   124

SELECTION 1:   Forming a Friendship (HUMAN SEXUALITY)   *126*

SELECTION 2:   The Sun Disappears: A Solar Eclipse (ASTRONOMY)   *129*

SELECTION 3:   Elements Known to Ancient Civilizations
   (PHYSICAL SCIENCES)   *134*

Extending What You Have Learned   139

8 Critical Thinking: Applying, Comparing, Inferring, Concluding, and Judging   140

Applying, Comparing, Inferring, Concluding, Judging   140

Applying   140

Comparing   141

Inferring   143

Concluding   146

Judging   147

Thinking and Reading   147

*SELECTION 1:   Eat, Drink, but the Dietary Doom-Sayers Won't Let You
                Be Merry* (NEWSPAPER EDITORIAL)   *148*

SELECTION 2:   Moral Power or Gun Power (SOCIOLOGY)   *151*

*SELECTION 3:   Native American Myths and Legends: The White River
                Sioux and the Cheyenne* (LITERATURE—LEGEND)   *154*

Extending What You Have Learned   161

PART FOUR   STUDY READING

9 Understanding and Studying for College Tests: SQ3R, Highlighting, Charting, Webbing, Outlining, Summarizing, and Remembering   163

Understanding and Studying for College Tests   163

Understanding Objective and Subjective Tests   163

Studying Texts: SQ3R   167

SELECTION 1:   The Child's Experience of Divorce (PSYCHOLOGY)   *168*

Studying Texts: Highlighting and Note-Taking in a Textbook   170

Studying Texts: Charting, Webbing, and Outlining   172

*SELECTION 2:   African-American Folk Music, the Blues,
                and African-American Spirituals* (MUSIC)   *173*

Studying Texts: Writing Summaries 176

Studying Material Without Headings 176

SELECTION 3:   *The Achievement of Desire*
(LITERATURE—AUTOBIOGRAPHY) *177*

Remembering for Tests 178

Extending What You Have Learned 180

10 Adjusting Your Concentration Level and Reading Rate 181

Adjusting Your Concentration and Reading Rate 181

SELECTION 1:   *One Writer's Beginnings*
(LITERATURE—AUTOBIOGRAPHY) *187*

SELECTION 2:   *Big Brother Is Watching You*
(PERSONAL FINANCE) *189*

SELECTION 3:   *Language and Communication* (BIOLOGY) *191*

SELECTION 4:   *Love Isn't Easy* (LITERATURE—ESSAY) *192*

Extending What You Have Learned 194

11 Interpreting Tables, Graphs, and Diagrams 195

Tables, Graphs, and Diagrams 195

Tables 195

SELECTION 1:   *The Fifty States of the United States* (GEOGRAPHY) *199*

Pictographs 203

Circle (or Pie) Graphs 204

Bar Graphs 206

SELECTION 2:   *Immigration to the United States* (HISTORY) *207*

Line Graphs 209

SELECTION 3:   *Age at First Marriage* (SOCIOLOGY) *209*

SELECTION 4:   *Weather in New Delhi and Santiago*
(CLIMATOLOGY) *210*

Line Drawings 211

SELECTION 5:   *Television Viewing, Reading, and School
Achievement* (POPULAR PSYCHOLOGY) *213*

Extending What You Have Learned 215

PART FIVE   SPECIALIZED READING

12 Understanding Opinions and Persuasive Writing 217

Understanding Opinions 217

Detecting Opinion and Bias 217

Clarifying the Opinion, Assessing the Proof, and Formulating Your
Own Opinion: O/P/O 219

SELECTION 1:   *The Eight Best Presidents—and Why*
(LITERATURE—ESSAY)   *220*

SELECTION 2:   *The Genius of Mark Twain: Discovery of Huck Finn*
"Draft" Underlines Author's Greatness
(NEWSPAPER COLUMN)   *224*

SELECTION 3:   *School Thoughts from* I Know Why the Caged
Bird Sings (LITERATURE—AUTOBIOGRAPHY)   *228*

Extending What You Have Learned   *232*

13 **Understanding Definitions and Explanations   233**

Reading Definitions and Explanations   *233*

Definitions   *233*

SELECTION 1:   *Diffusion and Osmosis* (BIOLOGY)   *237*

SELECTION 2:   *Understanding Whole Numbers* (MATHEMATICS)   *239*

Explanations   *240*

SELECTION 3:   *Pavlov's Conditioning Experiments*
(EXPERIMENTAL PSYCHOLOGY)   *243*

SELECTION 4:   *Daydreaming* (PSYCHOLOGY)   *246*

Extending What You Have Learned   *251*

14 **Understanding Descriptions and Narratives   253**

Reading Descriptions and Narratives   *253*

Description   *253*

SELECTION 1:   *Florence the Magnificent: The City of Dante and David,*
Michelangelo and Machiavelli, the Medicis,
Guccis, and Puccis (ART)   *257*

Narration   *262*

SELECTION 2:   *Muhammad the Prophet* (RELIGION)   *267*

Extending What You Have Learned   *275*

15 **Interpreting Style, Tone, and Mood   276**

Style   *276*

Tone and Mood   *278*

SELECTION 1:   *Fatherhood: Because It's There* (LITERARY ESSAY)   *279*

SELECTION 2:   *Address at the Dedication of the Gettysburg National*
Cemetery (SPEECH)   *282*

SELECTION 3:   *She Sat Still* (LITERARY ESSAY)   *284*

SELECTION 4:   *The New Colossus* (AMERICAN LITERATURE—POETRY)   *287*

Extending What You Have Learned   *289*

Summation: Reading with Meaning   290

Appendix A: An Extended Section of a College Text   291

Appendix B: Calculating Your Reading Rate: Reading Rate Tables and Explanations   309

Glossary   312

Credits   327

Index   329

PREFACE

Reading experts define reading as an active process of thinking. To read is to develop relationships between ideas. Reading experts also explain that what you bring to the reading of a selection is as important to your understanding of it as what the author has put into it. To the reading of a text, you bring knowledge of and attitudes toward the sciences, social sciences, and humanities. You bring a purpose for reading. You bring understanding of vocabulary, your ability to figure out meanings, and your attitudes toward reading.

PURPOSE OF THE TEXT

Maintaining the thrust of the first four editions, the fifth edition of *Reading with Meaning: Strategies for College Reading* incorporates this interactive constructive view of reading. It emphasizes the following:

- Active reading, in which you respond while reading. As you read the selections in this book, you will talk and write as you construct meaning.
- Strategic reading, in which you learn specific strategies for understanding the kinds of materials you read in college. For example, you will learn to preview before reading; brainstorm what you know before reading; set purposes for reading; talk to yourself in your mind; distinguish main from supporting ideas; use clue words to follow the author's train of thought; think critically by applying, comparing, inferring, concluding, and judging; and study for tests.
- Vocabulary development, in which you expand your vocabulary through reading. As you read, you will learn to use the context and word elements to unlock the meanings of unfamiliar words and monitor your understanding by checking a dictionary.
- Strategies that are especially helpful as you study assigned readings for college courses.
- Expansion of your core knowledge so that future reading is more meaningful.

Based on the idea that you learn college reading strategies by reading and responding to meaningful content, *Reading with Meaning: Strategies for College Reading* contains selections similar to ones assigned in sociology, psychology, history, English, biology, earth science, and other college subjects, rather than short paragraphs that drill you on specific skills out of the context of real reading. Generally, too, you must construct your own meaning by talking or writing. In a few testlike activities, you may respond by selecting from multiple-choice items or marking items true or false. These activities provide practice in taking tests of these kinds, but on the whole you will be responding as you must do when studying an assigned text: You must wrestle your own meanings out of the text. The primary purpose of this book is to prepare you to read the kinds of materials you will have to read in your courses—textbooks, other books, journals, and newspapers—and to help you succeed in college.

NEW DIRECTIONS

The fifth edition of *Reading with Meaning: Strategies for College Reading* provides significantly expanded coverage of two fundamental skill areas. First, in this new edition you will find more attention to main idea, a pivotal comprehension area for those who find reading college textbooks difficult. Whereas in previous editions the material on identifying the main idea of a paragraph and the thesis of a complete selection—such as an article or chapter of a textbook—was presented in one chapter, in this edition there are two chapters. Chapter 4 deals with the main idea and structure of a paragraph and provides two new selections in which readers practice their main idea–making strategy. Chapter 5 deals with thesis development in longer selections and provides two new selections for practicing a thesis-making strategy. The result is that in this new edition, you will find a comprehensive three-chapter block that focuses on main idea:

- Chapter 4: Grasping the Main Idea of a Paragraph
- Chapter 5: Grasping the Thesis, or Main Idea, of an Entire Selection
- Chapter 6: Relating Main Ideas and Details

This heightened attention to main idea and thesis is in response to reviewers' stated belief that being able to get the gist of passages is a fundamental reading skill that contributes to success in college.

Second, again in response to reviewers' suggestions, this edition of *Reading with Meaning* provides greater coverage of vocabulary and gives more attention to the Greek and Latin elements that make up words. Researchers such as David Corson (*The Lexical Bar*, Oxford: Pergamon Press, 1985) contend that students who grow up in home environments where they hear and use few words derived form the Greek and Latin languages are at a disadvantage as they approach university studies. They must " jump a lexical bar" that young people who have grown up in families where Greek- and Latin-based words are commonly spoken do not have to surmount. As a result, developmental English studies must emphasize vocabulary growth. To help students jump the lexical bar, this edition provides new strategies—word towers and webs—that help students become aware of and visualize word elements; additional margin notes that highlight prefixes, suffixes, and roots at the point where students are encountering these elements in words; and a comprehensive chart of word elements on the inside back cover for easy reference.

Third, although Chapter 9 continues to focus on test-taking and related study strategies, students learn ways to approach test questions in early chapters and apply those techniques throughout the text. Starting in Chapter 2, they learn to use the process of elimination to narrow their options as they complete multiple-choice and fill-in-the blanks questions. They are reminded to apply this test-taking strategy as they respond to test questions in chapters that follow.

Fourth, in the new edition, specific reading strategies have been set off more clearly from the running text. This enables students to check back and review strategies as the need arises. Also, workshop activities have been set off more distinctly from the running text. In this respect, the fifth edition is far more user-friendly that prior editions.

Fifth, users of previous editions of *Reading with Meaning* will notice that a few selections have been deleted, about eight selections have been added, a few selections have been moved to new locations to teach different skills, and the data in some charts and graphs have been updated for accuracy. However, most of the selections remain as in the fourth edition, making it easy for past users to move up to the fifth edition. Also, the principle behind the ordering of the selections within the chapters and the ordering of the chapters within the text remains the same: The early selections in a chapter tend to be less sophisticated than those later in a chapter; the early chapters in the book tend to be more basic. This arrangement makes it possible for instructors who are working with students who need more basic instruction to concentrate attention on the materials at the beginning of the chapters and of the book and to skip the more difficult selections. In the same way, instructors of second level courses in developmental or study reading may concentrate on the selections at the end of the chapters and of the text, giving less attention to basic comprehension strategies and more to specialized strategies that are important in reading the sophisticated selections that characterize college study in the social sciences, natural sciences, and humanities.

Instructors of the course will also find some changes in the instructional materials that accompany the text. Accompanying the fifth edition is an annotated instructor's guide that makes lesson preparation less time-consuming. In addition, there is a booklet of tests and teaching masters that go along with the individual chapters of *Reading wih Meaning*. Those who have used earlier editions of *Reading with Meaning* will notice that the tests have been revised to bring them more closely in line with the skills taught in the text; they will notice that many of the masters have been revised in form and substance.

ORGANIZATION OF *READING WITH MEANING*

You should take time to study the table of contents and the preface before beginning to read this book, which you should do before reading any college text. The table of contents of most books is really a broad outline of major topics to be covered. The preface typically explains the purpose of the book and describes its organization. In the case of *Reading with Meaning*, you will discover that the text starts with basic reading strategies, including vocabulary development, and then moves into more advanced strategies for comprehension, study reading, and specialized reading.

Think about . . .

Look over the table of contents, this preface, the appendices, the glossary, and the index. What function does each of these parts of a book serve? What do you learn from each?

Part I has one chapter that helps you learn a strategy, useful in preparing to read.

Part II focuses on vocabulary. It has two chapters. The first chapter teaches you how to use the surrounding words in a sentence to unlock the meaning of an unfamiliar word; the second teaches you how to use word elements to figure out word meanings, especially the meanings of technical terms important in college textbooks.

Part III helps you understand what you read. The five chapters in this part teach you how to (1) find the main idea of a paragraph, (2) identify the thesis of a selection, (3) make sense out of details, (4) use clue words to follow an author's train of thought, and (5) think critically about what you read.

Part IV deals with study reading. The first chapter in this part focuses on test taking and teaches strategies such as SQ3R, data charting, webbing, highlighting and note-taking, outlining, summarizing, and remembering, which are important as you prepare to take tests. The second chapter shows you how to vary your concentration level and reading rate. The third chapter introduces strategies for reading tables, graphs, and diagrams. Any one of these three chapters can be read earlier in a course if students and their instructor prefer to do so.

Part V helps you understand the specialized materials you will be assigned in college courses. First you will find a chapter that provides practice in reading opinions and persuasive writing, a kind of writing you will encounter in history and the humanities as well as in newspapers and magazines. Next you will find a chapter on comprehending definitions and explanations, which are common aspects of college texts in the natural and social sciences. Then there is a chapter that introduces strategies for comprehending descriptions and narratives, which are commonly found in humanities and science texts. A fourth chapter in Part V helps you handle style, tone, and mood, elements most important in the novels, short stories, plays, poems, and essays you will read in college English.

Following Part V is a concluding page that provides an opportunity for you to summarize the strategies developed in the book.

At the end of *Reading with Meaning* are the appendices and the glossary. Appendices typically provide supplementary material. In this case, Appendix A contains a lengthy segment of a chapter from a sociology text, with activities that enable you to read the segment for a variety of purposes and in a variety of ways. Appendix B provides a chart to enable you to calculate your reading rate. As in most textbooks, the glossary presents the words featured in the text. It provides a pronunciation guide and an explanation of how to use it. You can use the glossary as a dictionary, checking the meanings and pronunciation of unfamiliar words just as you would use the glossary of any college textbook.

ORGANIZATION OF THE CHAPTERS

Very often there is a pattern to the development of chapters in a college text. It generally helps to identify that pattern before you start to read. To this end, turn to Chapter 4 and identify the component parts of a chapter in this book.

In *Reading with Meaning*, each chapter begins with a statement of what you should learn in the chapter: the objective. Next comes an introductory discussion of the strategy to be taught in the chapter and practice in using the strategy.

Following this instructional segment are three or more selections in which you apply what you have learned in the opening segments of the chapter. Accompanying most selections are two activities to do before reading: "Expanding Your Vocabulary" and "Getting Ready to Read." "Expanding Your Vocabulary" features vocabulary from the selection so that you get continued practice in using your understanding of context and word structure clues to unlock the meaning of unfamiliar words. "Getting Ready to Read" encourages you to look over a selection before reading. You can complete these activities by yourself or with class members during workshop time.

Next is a reading selection. The selections are from magazines, books, and textbooks. Exercises follow that you can use to monitor your comprehension. These exercises are either short answer or short essay. In each case, you must apply the strategies learned earlier in the chapter. Additionally, as you read, you will often be asked to record points as margin notes or to circle or underline parts of the text—something you should do in college reading. In some instances, you will find the number of words within a selection written at the end. To calculate your reading rate on a selection, you can use that number and the reading rate chart in Appendix B.

At the ends of selections, you will find activities for reviewing featured vocabulary. In many cases, the activities include sentences using the featured words; they provide practice in using sentence clues to unlock the meaning of words.

At the ends of selections, too, you will find suggestions for writing. Sometimes you will be asked to write using knowledge gained from the selection. Sometimes you will write using the same writing approaches used by the author of the selection. Research shows that writing is a good way to learn content.

A final segment of each chapter provides an opportunity for extending your understanding of the content and vocabulary and for practicing the strategies taught in the chapter.

ACKNOWLEDGMENTS

I want to thank the reviewers who read the manuscript for this book in each of its drafts and who provided suggestions that proved invaluable. Barbara Fowler, Longview Community College; Veronica Wardall, De Vry Institute of Technology; Helen Sabine, El Camino College.

I am grateful, too, for the careful attention to the manuscript by Kathleen Sleys, the project editor; for the suggestions of Craig Campanella, acquisitions editor; for the general helpfulness of Joan Polk, editorial assistant at Prentice Hall; and for the thoughtful attention to details by Carol Anne Peschke, copyeditor.

I also thank George Hennings, helpmate and husband, who contributed by compiling the glossary, criticizing the manuscript, and providing encouragement when the work load became heavy.

Dorothy Grant Hennings

SUPPLEMENTS

SUPPLEMENTS FOR INSTRUCTORS

Annotated Instructor's Edition   Written by the author, the AIE provides instructors with the answers to all the exercises directly in the margin. In addition, the author has provided numerous teaching tips in the margins of the AIE to help instructors get the most out of their classes. Bound directly into the back of the AIE is a 31-page Instructor's Guide, complete with more detailed instructional suggestions for each chapter. **Free to instructors: ISBN: 0-13-041252-X.**

Exams and Transparency Masters   Also written by the author, the Exams and Transparency Masters supplement provides instructors with ready-to-copy chapter tests for each of the fifteen chapters in the fifth edition. Reproducible transparency masters help instructors illustrate key points. **Free to instructors upon adoption. ISBN: 0-13-041240-6.**

Prentice Hall Reading Skills Test Bank   Prepared by Michael Coker at Southeastern Oklahoma State University, the Prentice Hall Reading Skills Test Bank contains 100 questions on each of 11 different reading skills. Skills covred include word analysis, context clues, stated main idea, implied main idea, tone and bias, details, major vs. minor details, style, study reading, reading rate, and visual aids. Question are multiple choice, matching or true/false. The test bank is available in printed format or electronically. **Free to instructors upon adoption. ISBN (printed): 0-13-041249-X. Contact your Prentice Hall representative to request the electronic version.**

SUPPLEMENTS FOR STUDENTS

Companion Website   This text-specific, one stop study and practice resource for college reading students includes:

- Chapter objectives and overviews
- Additional online readings with comprehension and vocabulary quizzes.
- Chapter quizzes to help reinforce the concepts presented in the text.
- Internet activities for each chapter which challenge students to visit existing websites and apply what they have learned.

Free to students at all times. Visit www.prenhall.com/hennings

Online Course   Prentice Hall now offers dynamic media and online content for *Reading with Meaning*, Fifth Edition through course management systems, including CourseCompass, Blackboard and WebCT. Our pre-assembled content gives instructors a head start in creating online components to their courses—whether they are on campus or taught solely online.

To view a demonstration of the content available, visit **www.prenhall.com/cms**.

Free Dictionary Offer   Your students can receive a **FREE** *New American Webster Handy College Dictionary* packaged with their text when you adopt the fifth edition of Hennings, *Reading with Meaning*. This dictionary has over 1.5 million Signet copies in print and over 115,000 definitions, including current phrases, slang, and scientific terms. It offers more than 1,500 new words, with over 200 not found in any competing dictionary, and features boxed inserts on etymologies and language. Includes foreign words and phrases and an international gazetteer with correct place-name pronunciations. This dictionary is available free to your students when packaged with *Reading with Meaning*, Fifth Edition. Please use package **ISBN 0-13-042467-6** for your book orders.

READING WITH MEANING

PART ONE
INTRODUCTION TO READING

CHAPTER 1 Getting Ready to Read

 1

Getting Ready to Read

OBJECTIVE

In this chapter, you will develop strategies for getting ready to read. Specifically, you will learn to

1. Make a general survey, or preview, of a selection before reading to predict what it is about and how it is organized;
2. Consider what you know about the subject and how that subject relates to you;
3. Set your purpose for reading a textbook chapter or selection; and
4. Gauge the difficulty, or reading load, of the text for you and estimate the time you will need to understand it.

You will develop the habit of talking to yourself in your mind before and while you read college assignments as a way to check your comprehension. You will also learn to make a data chart and a web and to use the structure of a textbook to help you as you read.

GETTING READY TO READ

Reading is a thinking process that sets two people in action together—an author and a reader. The author has a purpose in writing and a message to get across. In writing, the author chooses the facts and ideas to include, chooses the words to express those facts and ideas, and organizes them in a clear way. In doing this, the author draws on his or her knowledge and feelings about the subject. Obviously, what the author writes in a text determines what you learn from it.

But what you get from reading also depends on what you bring to the reading of a selection and your purpose for reading it (Figure 1.1). One thing you may bring to the reading of a selection is a set of facts about the subject. You have a lot of knowledge that you have built up through firsthand experience and prior reading. As you read, you connect what is in the text to what you already know about the topic. The more connections you make, the more you get out of a selection when you read.

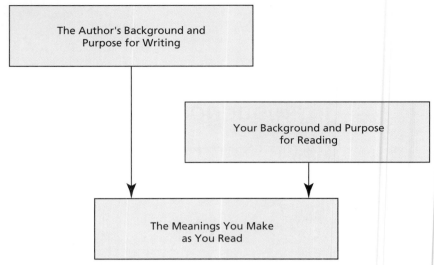

FIGURE 1.1   Reading with Meaning

Because what you get out of a text depends on what you already know about the subject, take four steps before reading college textbook assignments:

**GETTING-READY-TO-READ
STRATEGY**

→ Preview the assigned material to find out what it is about and how it is organized.

→ Think about what you already know about the topic and how that topic relates to you.

→ Set your purpose for reading.

→ Gauge the difficulty, or reading load, of the material for you and estimate how long it will take you to study it.

These steps are important when you read a textbook and your purpose is to prepare for class discussion and tests. In contrast, when you read novels or general magazines and your purpose is enjoyment, a thorough preview is not essential, although you may preview by reading the cover blurb or thumbing through the pages before you decide to read or buy.

Step 1.   Previewing Before Reading

The first step in reading a textbook chapter or an assigned selection is to look through it to build a framework for understanding the material. Your reason for previewing is to predict what the section is about and how the author has organized the topics. To preview, think about these elements of a text:

- Think about the **title.** It often provides a clue to the topic, or subject, of the material you are going to read.

- Think about the **subheadings** that divide a chapter or a selection into sections. The subheadings provide clues to the subtopics to be covered; they also provide clues to the organization. Some college textbooks list the subtopics discussed in a chapter at the beginning of the chapter.

- Run your eyes over and think about the **terms that the author repeats at the beginning of subsections or the terms that are in italics or bold print.** These words are clues to the topic, the subtopics, and the way that the subsection is put together.

Before reading an assigned chapter or selection, also do the following:

- Skim the **introductory** and **concluding paragraphs.** In introductory paragraphs, look for sentences that are clues to where the author is going—sentences that begin, "This chapter includes information on . . . ," or "This section provides four points," or "We will first consider . . . . Then we will consider."
- Study the **illustrations:** the photographs, maps, and charts that accompany the written text. Illustrations can help you figure out the major focus of a chapter or selection. Sometimes the illustrations also are a clue to the order in which the author will explain the subtopics.
- Preview any **margin notes** or **footnotes.** They sometimes contain definitions of key terms, which are clues to what the selection is about.

Use your preview to predict what the selection is about and how the author has organized it.

WORKSHOP: PREVIEWING

Collaborating with a partner or working alone,* apply the previewing strategy to the first chapter of this reading textbook. If you have not read the section of the Preface on the parts of a book, study them before continuing.

1. Think about the title of this chapter, "Getting Ready to Read." What does that title tell you about the topic of the chapter? _____

   _____

   _____

2. Think about the Objective at the beginning of the chapter. What clues does that section give you about the topic of the chapter? _____

   _____

   _____

3. Look over the system of headings and subheadings in this chapter. The first heading after the Objectives is "GETTING READY TO READ." It is a main heading. What kind of print is used for this main heading? To help you see the organization of the chapter, highlight each of the main headings in the chapter in the same way; for example, highlight them with a red marker.

   Locate the subheadings. A subheading under the first main heading is "Step 1. Previewing Before Reading." What kind of print is used in this book for subheadings? Working collaboratively or independently, highlight the subheadings in a different way from the main headings.

   Think about the system of main and subheadings that you have highlighted. What have you learned about the organization of the first chapter of your textbook? How is this chapter organized? How can you use the system of main headings and

---

*Most activities in *Reading with Meaning* can be completed collaboratively or independently. Your instructor will tell you how to proceed.

subheadings to figure out the organization of any college textbook?

_____

_____

4. What words does the author of this book repeat on pages 2–5? _____

_____

Why does the author do this? _____

_____

For what purpose does the author use bold print? _____

5. Look at the introductory and concluding paragraphs of this chapter. What kind of information do they give you? _____

_____

_____

6. Look at the figures in this chapter. What kind of information do they provide?

_____

_____

7. Predict: What do you think you will be learning to do as you read Chapter 1 of this textbook? _____

_____

_____

Step 2. Thinking About What You Already Know and How the Topic Relates to You

A second step to take before reading a chapter of a college text is to ask yourself two questions: "What do I already know about the topic? How does this material relate to me?" To answer, picture in your mind the objects covered in the selection that you already know something about. For example, if you are to read about cathedral building and you have seen pictures of cathedrals or have been in one, you might visualize a cathedral in your mind. If an article is on living cells and you have an idea of what a cell looks like, you might draw a rough sketch of a cell on paper.

To get yourself ready to read, also talk to yourself in your mind. Tell yourself what you already know about the content. For example, if you are going to read a Greek myth for a humanities course, you might say to yourself before beginning, "A myth—that's a story in which ancient people tried to explain happenings in nature. The Greeks told stories about their gods and goddesses." If you are going to read about the American Constitution, you might say to yourself, "Yes, I know that the Constitution set up the structure of government in the United States."

When preparing to read an assigned chapter, you may find it helpful to jot down words that come to mind about the topic. What you are doing at this stage is brainstorming. In brainstorming, you write down words and thoughts that come to mind about the topic on which you will be reading. The topic of Chapter 1 of _Reading with Meaning_ is what to do to get yourself ready to read. Collaborating with a partner or thinking on your own, jot down some things you already know about this topic.

_____

_____

Step 3. Setting Your Purpose for Reading

The third step in previewing is to set your purpose for reading. At this point, knowing what the topic is and what you already know about it, you ask, "What do I expect to learn by reading this material?"

With books you choose for personal reading, you usually know what you hope to get from your reading before you start. But in college you may be dealing with assigned textbook readings. You will read these assignments to learn more about the subject and prepare for class discussions and tests. In this case, it pays to make up questions before reading to guide you as you read. Answering your own questions becomes your purpose for reading. Some textbook authors provide before-reading questions at the beginning of chapters or sections of text. Answering those questions may also become your purpose for reading.

Step 4. Gauging the Reading Difficulty or Load

The fourth step before reading assigned material is to estimate its difficulty and the time necessary for you to master it. Your preview gives you ways to gauge the reading load: You can predict whether it will be light or heavy for you. "Light" means that you bring knowledge to the reading; you know a lot about the topic already. "Light" also means that there are only a few technical terms that are new to you. In contrast, "heavy" means that you know very little about the topic before you start and that the text is loaded with technical terms. When facing a text with a light load, you recognize that you can breeze through it. When facing a text with a heavy load, you know that you must read deliberately, even going back to reread several times. In the latter case, you decide that you will need more time to read your assignment.

The length of a chapter or section of a textbook that you must read obviously determines how long it will take you to study it. Some college students check the length of the assigned material before reading. They start with a rough idea of how much time they will need to complete the reading assignment. See Figure 1.2 for a checklist of pre-reading strategies that include this step.

1. I preview the selection to predict the topic and see how the chapter or selection is put together. I do this by
   • Thinking about the title, the author, and the subheadings;
   • Thinking about terms that are repeated at the beginnings of paragraphs or that are printed in italics or bold type;
   • Reading the first and last paragraphs;
   • Studying the illustrations;
   • Looking over any margin notes or footnotes;
   • Asking continuously, "What is this selection about? How has the author organized the selection?"

2. I review what I know about the subject. I do this by
   • Asking, "What do I already know about the topic? How does it relate to me?"
   • Visualizing, or picturing, what I know;
   • Telling myself what I know;
   • Brainstorming words and thoughts that come to mind.

3. I set a purpose to guide my reading. I ask, "What do I expect to learn from reading this chapter or selection?"

4. I gauge the difficulty of the text for me (the reading load). I ask, "Is it heavy? Light? Is the selection long? Short? Must I be deliberate in my reading, perhaps rereading? Can I breeze through it?"

Think about . . . What do you usually do when you start to read an assigned chapter in a textbook. Which of these strategies do you already use? How do you use them? Which do you think will help in your college reading? Why?

FIGURE 1.2 A Checklist for Analyzing Preview Strategies

SELECTION 1

A Nation on the Move: America Moves West (HISTORY)

A Reading Workshop

Getting Ready to Read

Suppose you are sitting in a history class on the first day of the semester. Your instructor holds up the textbook. It is *The Great Nation: A History of the United States,* by Henry Graff. On the cover is an eagle and a portion of the American flag. The instructor explains that the author, Dr. Graff, is a college professor who is well respected for his studies in American history.

Think
about . . .

What does the word *expectations* mean? How do your expectations influence your everyday activities? How do they influence your reading?

1. Preview the selection. Collaborating with a workshop partner or thinking independently, decide what you would expect to find discussed in this history book. Write your expectations here, including your reaction to that kind of material.

   _____

   _____

   The title of the twelfth chapter of *The Great Nation* is "The Developing Nation." The first main heading in Chapter 12 is "A Nation on the Move." In this textbook, there are introductory questions at the start of each subsection. The questions under "A Nation on the Move" are

   • Why were new means of transporting people and goods necessary after the War of 1812?

   • Why was the invention of the railroad important?

   Alone or with your workshop partner, decide what kind of information you would expect to find in this subsection of Chapter 12. What specific topic or topics do you expect Dr. Graff to cover? In your own words, write your expectations here.

   _____

   _____

2. Review what you already know. What do you already know about the topic that Professor Graff discusses in this subsection? Jot down a few points that come to mind.

   _____

   _____

3. Preview the entire selection to find out in greater detail what it is about and how it is organized. To do this, turn to pages 8–9. Quickly glance over, or skim, the main heading and the subheadings. Read the first paragraph. Look at the photographs. Then return to this section and answer the related questions in the space provided.

   • What is the main topic of the selection? (What is the selection about?) _____

   _____

   • What subtopics does the selection cover? _____

   _____

   • In what order are these subtopics covered? _____

   • What clues did you use to determine the topic and subtopics? _____

   _____

- What kind of information would you expect to find under each subheading? Jot your expectations in the middle column of the following table, or data chart.

Subheading	What You Predict That the Section Is About	What You Already Know About the Subject
1. The National Road		
2. Canals		
3. Steamboats		
4. Railroads		

Think
about . . .

To make this table, where did the author of your text find the labels for the rows? How would you go about making a similar table based on a section of a textbook?

4. Think about what you already know about the subtopics. How did Americans travel west in the early 1800s? Before reading the entire selection, tell yourself or a partner what comes to your mind about westward travel in the 1800s. Talk about such questions as these: How did people travel? How did the trip differ from a similar trip today? How long did it take? Was it an easy journey? Would I have wanted to make the trip? Why or why not? Then jot down whatever you know about the topics identified by the subheadings in the right-hand column of the table. If you know nothing about a subtopic, leave the space blank.

5. Set your purpose for reading. Talking about the westward migration, you may have discovered that you know only a little about some aspect of the topic. What areas will you have to emphasize in your reading? What do you want to find out through reading the selection? What do you expect to learn? In this case, questions that you may try to answer through your reading are, What was the National Road? When was it built? Where was it built? Why was it built?

Before reading, write at least four questions that you expect to answer through reading—one to go with each subheading. Write your questions in the space provided here. Good questions begin with words such as *what, when, where,* and *why*. By writing questions, you are setting a purpose for reading. You read to answer your questions.

Questions that I hope to answer through reading:

_____

_____

_____

_____

6. Gauge the difficulty of the selection for you: light, average, or heavy.

Reading with Meaning

Read the selection. When you find an answer to one of the *what, when, where,* or *why* questions that you wrote before reading, jot it in the margin.

A Nation on the Move:
America Moves West
Henry Graff

After the War of 1812, Americans turned their attention from the problems of Europe to the promise of a growing nation. Vast changes had begun to take place. One of the most exciting of these was the migrating of people into the region between the Appalachians and the Mississippi. One visitor to the United States said in wonder, "America seems to be breaking up and moving westward."

A problem that faced every family deciding to move west was how to go. There was no easy, direct route to follow. Recognizable roads either did not exist or were in such poor condition that after a heavy rain, wagons and horses simply bogged down in the mud.

The National Road

In 1811 the construction of a road, called the Cumberland or National Road, began. This road would stretch from Cumberland, Maryland, to Wheeling, a town in western Virginia. When the road opened seven years later, people by the thousands traveled on it, seeking a new life farther west. Conestogas, or covered wagons, filled with goods bound for market used the road in both directions.

Canals

In the early 1800s shipping goods from one section of the country to another was expensive. The National Road had helped to lower this cost. Still, American businesspeople searched for ways to move freight across the country even more cheaply. A way truly to link the East and the West had to be found. The answer, some thought, was the *canal*, a waterway dug across land for ships to sail through.

FIGURE 1.3   The National Road
As each part of the National Road was finished, hundreds of families in Conestoga wagons moved farther west. The road is now called United States Highway 40. (Collection of the Maryland Historical Society, Baltimore)

FIGURE 1.4 The Erie Canal
Boys walked alongside boats in the Erie Canal, guiding them with ropes to keep them from hitting the banks. (I. N. Phelps Stokes Collection, Miriam and Ira D. Wallach Division of Art, Prints and Photographs, the New York Public Library, Astor, Lenox, and Tilden Foundations). For a chronology of events relative to the Canal, check the web at www.pg1.com/pittsford/erie_canal.html.

DeWitt Clinton, the governor of New York, began in 1817 to push for the construction of a canal linking the Great Lakes with the Atlantic Ocean. Many people considered Clinton's "Big Ditch," as the project was nicknamed, doomed to failure. Finally the massive project got underway. Eight years later the canal stretched from Buffalo, New York, to Albany, New York, on the Hudson River. The Erie Canal, costing $7 million, paid for itself within nine years. Its immense success encouraged other states to begin canal projects.

Steamboats

Americans had always used the natural waterways to transport themselves and their goods from one place to another. When a boat was forced to sail against the current of a river, however, it was impossible to be sure how long the trip would take.

Several Americans worked on an invention—the steamboat—that would greatly aid river travel. They believed that a boat powered by steam engines would be able to move upstream readily against a strong current. When Robert Fulton's *Clermont* sailed up the Hudson River from New York City to Albany in 1807, a new age in travel and transport was born. What was also needed was a faster means of transportation across land.

Railroads

Some Americans were convinced that steam engines could also be used to move wagons faster on land. In 1828 investors in the city of Baltimore began to build a railroad to the Ohio River. The first spadeful of earth was turned by Charles Carroll, the last surviving signer of the Declaration of Independence. The merchants of Baltimore hoped that the railroad would give faster, cheaper service to the West than was then available.

By the 1840s railroad building was going on everywhere. During the 1850s, the amount of railroad track in the United States increased from 9021 miles (14,434 kilometers) to 30,626 miles (49,002 kilometers). The East Coast was now joined to the land beyond the Appalachian Mountains by the iron rails.   [594 words]

Monitoring Comprehension and Writing in Response

1. Make a data web based on the selection you just read. A web is a visual that shows relationships among ideas. To make a web, first ask "What is the subject of the selection?" The title is your clue to the subject. Write the subject in the oval in the middle of the web in Figure 1.5. Then ask, "What are the subtopics covered in the selection?" Write one of the four subtopics in each box. On the lines extending from each box, write facts (or details) about the subtopic that you learned from reading the selection. Remember to think in terms of what, when, where, and why. Try the activity with a workshop partner.

2. On the map in Figure 1.6, circle the following sites: Cumberland, Maryland; Wheeling, West Virginia; the Great Lakes; Buffalo, New York; Albany, New York; New York City; and Baltimore, Maryland. Label the Appalachian Mountains, which extend from West Virginia into Pennsylvania, and the Atlantic Ocean. Label the Hudson River, which runs from Albany to New York City. Plot the locations of the Erie Canal and the National Road. Refer back to the selection to help you plot the locations.

3. Study the places you have circled on the map. Then use what you have learned from the selection and your map study to answer this question: Why was each of the following important to the growth of the United States? Use complete sentences.

   a. National Road _____

   _____

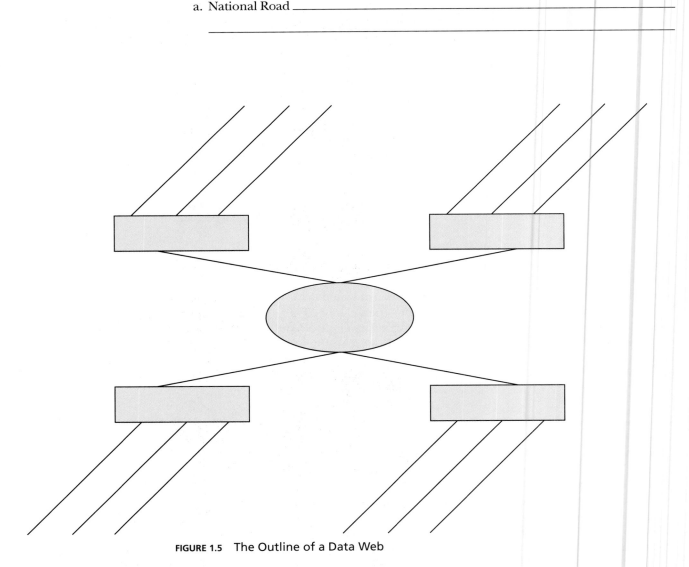

FIGURE 1.5 The Outline of a Data Web

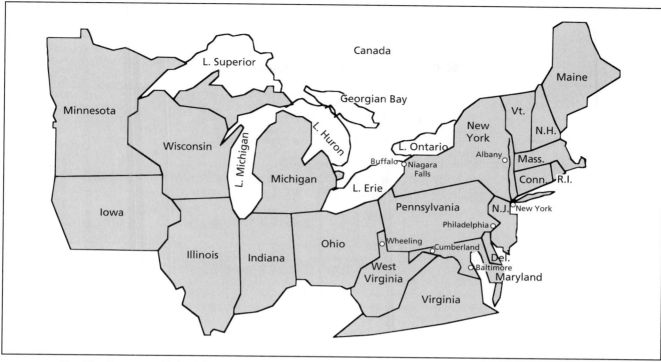

FIGURE 1.6 The Northeastern United States

b. Erie Canal _____

_____

c. Steamboat _____

_____

d. Railroad across the Appalachians _____

_____

4. Which do you think was the biggest accomplishment: the building of the National Road, the building of the Erie Canal, or the building of the railroad between Baltimore and Wheeling, West Virginia? In your notebook, write a paragraph giving your reasons.

SELECTION 2

For Heaven's Sakes, Choose a Job You Enjoy! (CAREER PLANNING)

A Reading Workshop

Getting Ready to Read

1. Preview the selection that follows to figure out what it is about and how it is organized. Glance over the title and the first paragraph. Read the subheadings. Read the concluding paragraph. Think about the footnote information. Then return to this section and answer the questions that follow.

• What is the main topic of the article? (What is it about?) _____

_____

Think about . . .

How do authors use subheadings? What can you learn from textbook subheadings? How can you use numbered lists in reading a college text?

- What kind of information do you expect to learn from it? _____

_____

- How many tips does the author supply? How do you know?

_____

- What is the author's background?

_____

2. Recall what you already know about the topic. What do you think is important in choosing a job? Before reading the selection, tell yourself or a friend what you already know. Talk about this question: What are some things to keep in mind when you look for a job? Jot down a few thoughts here. _____

_____

_____

3. Set your purpose for reading. Do you have any questions that came to mind as you previewed the article and thought about the topic? Before reading, write several questions to answer through reading. Answering your questions is your purpose for reading.

_____

_____

4. Gauge the difficulty of the selection for you: light, average, or heavy.

Reading with Meaning

Read the selection. Write information that answers your purpose-setting questions directly in the margin. A helpful question to answer through reading is, What are seven tips for finding a job that I enjoy?

For Heaven's Sakes, Choose a Job You Enjoy!
Pat McKinney Sleem*

The Greeks bequeathed to us the wise philosophy *nosce teipsum*, "Know thyself." And since graduating from the Harvard Business School nearly ten years ago, I have become convinced of the absolute necessity to apply that wise counsel in one's job choices.

What do you like to do?

As the co-owner of a leading firm in the résumé preparation/career counseling/ job placement business, I see a number of people daily making dramatic "career transitions." Most of them tell me they feel they have wasted their time by taking and staying in jobs that were the "wrong fit" for them. Although they had the skills to do the job, they say, they weren't in a job doing the things they liked to do. Eventually they came face-to-face with the grim reality that people can truly excel—and be happy—only when they are doing things that interest them.

Don't ignore what you know about yourself.

A fellow classmate of mine comes to mind. He knew he wanted to work for the auto industry. He knew his goal was line management. He *knew* what he liked to do and what

---

*Pat McKinney Sleem is a Harvard MBA (Master of Business Administration) and a partner in the firm Professional Résumé and Employment Placement (PREP). PREP specializes in résumé preparation by mail.

his interests were. But when the consulting companies came courting in the Spring, he got seduced by the big bucks and smitten by the prestige of consulting. When I see him now, he seems dissatisfied. Now, 10 years later, he feels "stuck" and unfulfilled working for a great company in a job he's good at but doesn't particularly enjoy. And the sad part of this story is that even though he knew what his real interests were, he chose a job that didn't "fit" his interests and goals.

Seven Tips for Finding the Job You Enjoy

1. Do some self-assessment.
Your interests can change over time. To figure out what interests you now, ask questions that will lead you in the direction of the right job. What gives you the most satisfaction? What is your greatest achievement? Who are the three people whose careers appeal to you most? Name your talents. List the subjects that interest you so much that you have read quite a lot about them.

2. Forget about money for a moment.
If your main objective in your job hunt is to sell yourself to the highest bidder, you're likely to end up disappointed with your job. Financial reward will be a natural byproduct of excelling in a job you really enjoy. So identify your real interests and you'll find that monetary rewards will happen.

3. Who can you talk to who might be a wise sounding board for your ideas?
Talk to someone who knows you well enough to give you a "second opinion" about what you seem best suited for.

4. Given what you know about yourself, what specific careers hold the most appeal?

5. What is the current job market like in the fields that interest you?

6. Get an effective résumé.
If you decide you want to enter a new field, you may not have the experience required for the job you want. A creative, interest-sparking résumé that "sells" your interests, enthusiasm, and potential will be a necessity.

7. Finally, take a risk if you have to.
Successful executives say that "taking risks" has been critical to their job satisfaction. A sobering statistic: Only 10% of American workers find their jobs meaningful and more important than their leisure time. Leaving the familiar rut requires bravery, a skill not necessarily refined in classrooms.

   In summary, remember too that no job is interesting all the time. A company personnel director told me this once: "Sometimes I think I'd hire someone sight unseen who didn't want a challenging job, because there's lots of unchallenging work to be done around here too!" But take some time to "know yourself" and you *can* find the job that is the "best fit" with your interests.   [690 words]

Monitoring Comprehension

Having read the selection, answer these questions on your own or in collaboration with a partner.

1. What is the subject, or topic, of this article? _____

2. How would you web the important ideas of the selection? What would you put in the

    central oval of your web? _____

    How many lines would you extend out from the central oval? _____

    Why? _____

What would you write at the end of each line? —————————————

Web the topic and supporting ideas in your reading notebook.

3. During your preview, how well did you predict what the author was going to say?

   _____

4. Pat Sleem gives seven tips for finding an enjoyable job. List the three that are the most important to you. For each, give a reason for your choice.

   a. _____

   b. _____

   c. _____

5. List the one tip that is least helpful to you. Explain why it is least helpful. _____

   _____

SELECTION 3

The Signs of Life (BIOLOGY)

A Reading Workshop

Getting Ready to Read

1. Preview the selection that follows to figure out what it is about and how it is put together. Glance over the title, the first paragraph, and the last paragraph. Because there are no subheadings to guide your reading, look over the first lines of the other paragraphs to find words that repeat (which is a good strategy to use when there are no subheadings). Then return to this section and answer these questions.

   • What words do the authors repeat at the beginning of most paragraphs that are

      clues to the topic? _____

   • What is the main topic of the selection? _____

   • How many characteristics of living things are the authors going to discuss? _____

      _____

      How do you know? _____

      _____

Think
about . . .

Why do authors of college texts use words such as *first, second,* and *third*? How can you use these words to guide your reading?

2. Recall what you already know about living things. What makes living things different from nonliving things? Think, in specific terms, about living things you know. This is always more helpful than thinking in very general terms. For example, is a dog a living thing? Why? What does a dog have that all living things have? What can a dog do that all living things can do? Is a rock alive? Why not? In the data chart in Figure 1.7—using what you already know about living things—write down things about a dog that make it a living thing. Then write down why you think a rock is not alive—what it cannot do that a dog can. Make your predictions on your own or by collaborating with a partner or two. There are seven rows in the chart because Curtis and Barnes are going to tell you about seven characteristics. If you cannot fill in the seven rows before reading, do what you can. You will learn the rest by reading the selection.

Characteristics of a Dog That Make It a Living Thing	Characteristics of a Rock That Make It a Nonliving Thing
1.	
2.	
3.	
4.	
5.	
6.	
7.	

FIGURE 1.7 The Outline of a Data Chart

Think about . . .

Why are tables or charts like this a good way to organize data?

3. Set your purpose for reading. Write a question that you expect to answer by reading the selection. To do this, start your question with the words "What are . . . ?" Record your question here:

What are _____?

4. Gauge the difficulty of the selection for you: light, average, or heavy. Will this reading be harder than the previous one? Why or why not?

Reading with Meaning

Read Selection 3 with a pen in hand. You may want to read the selection aloud, taking turns with a workshop partner. Underscore the sentences in the text that tell you the characteristics of living things. You should underscore approximately seven sentences. As you read, put a number in front of each paragraph to indicate the number of the particular characteristic the authors are discussing at that point. For example, put a number 1 next to the paragraph that begins, "The first characteristic of living things . . . ." Doing this will help you organize your reading because there are no subheadings. As you read, also keep relating the information to the dog and the rock we talked about earlier. Although the authors do not mention dogs and rocks, what the authors say applies to them.

The Signs of Life
Helena Curtis and N. Sue Barnes

Biology is the "science of life." But what do biologists mean when they use the word "life"? Actually, there is no simple definition for this common word. Life does not exist in the abstract. There is no "life," only living things. And living things come in a great variety of forms, from tiny bacteria to giant sequoia trees. All of these, however, share certain properties that, taken together, distinguish them from nonliving objects.

The first characteristic of living things is that they are highly organized. In living things, atoms—the particles of which all matter is composed—are combined into a vast number of very large molecules called macromolecules. Each type of macromolecule has a distinctive structure and a specific function in the life of the organism. Some macromolecules are linked with other macromolecules to form the structures of an organism's body. Others participate in the dynamic processes essential for the continuing life of the organism; among the most significant are the large molecules known as enzymes. Enzymes, with the help of a variety of smaller molecules, regulate all of the processes occurring within living matter. The complex organization of both structures and processes is one of the most important properties of living things.

The second characteristic is closely related to the first: Living systems maintain a chemical composition quite different from that of their surroundings. The atoms present in living matter are the same as those in the surrounding environment, but they occur in different proportions and are arranged in different ways. Although living systems constantly exchange materials with the external environment, they maintain a stable and characteristic internal environment.

A third characteristic of living things is the capacity to take in, transform, and use energy from the environment. For example, in the process of photosynthesis, green plants take light energy from the sun and transform it into chemical energy stored in complex molecules. The energy stored in these molecules is used by plants to power their life processes and to build the characteristic structures of the plant body. Animals, which can obtain this stored energy by eating plants, change it into still other forms, such as heat, motion, electricity, and chemical energy stored in the characteristic structures of the animal body.

Fourth, living things can respond to stimuli. Bacteria move toward or away from certain chemical substances; green plants bend toward light; cats pounce on small moving objects. Although different organisms respond to widely varying stimuli, the capacity to respond is a fundamental and almost universal characteristic of life.

Fifth, and most remarkably, living things have the capacity to reproduce themselves so that, generation after generation, organisms produce more organisms like themselves. In each generation, however, there are slight variations between parents and offspring and among offspring.

Most organisms have a sixth characteristic: They grow and develop. For example, before hatching, the fertilized egg of a frog develops into the complex, but still immature, form that we recognize as a tadpole; after hatching, the tadpole continues to grow and undergoes further development, becoming a mature frog. Throughout the world of living things, similar patterns of growth and development occur.

A seventh characteristic of living things is that they are exquisitely suited to their environments. Moles, for instance, are furry animals that live underground in tunnels shoveled out by their large forepaws. Their eyes are small and sightless. Their noses, with which they sense the worm and the other small animals that make up their diet, are fleshy and enlarged. This most important characteristic of living things is known as adaptation.

These characteristics of living things are interrelated, and each depends, to a large extent, on the others. At any given moment in its life, an organism is organized, maintains a stable internal environment, transforms energy, responds to stimuli, and is adapted to its external environment; the organism may or may not be reproducing, growing, and developing, but it possesses the capacity to do so.   [660 words]

Did You KNOW?

Photo- is a word element meaning "light." Another word with that element is *photograph*.

Did You KNOW?

The prefix *im-* on *immature* means "not." Other words that start with the prefix are *immaterial* and *immobile*.

Monitoring Comprehension and Writing in Response

1. Go back to the data chart about the dog and the rock in Figure 1.7. Correct the predictions you made. Add points that you learned through reading so that you have seven reasons why a dog is a living thing and some reasons why a rock is nonliving. Also answer the question you wrote before reading.

2. In collaboration with your workshop partner or on your own, use your data chart to respond to the following items. Decide whether each is a characteristic of living things. Put a check in front of the items that are characteristics of all living things. Be ready to support your decision by reading a sentence from the selection. Do not try to do this from memory. Use the notes in your data chart.

_____ a. Living things are highly organized.

_____ b. They maintain a chemical balance similar to that of their surroundings.

_____ c. They can take in, transform, and use energy from their environment.

_____ d. They transform light energy from the sun into chemical energy.

_____ e. They can respond to stimuli.

_____ f. They respond to the same stimuli.

_____ g. They can reproduce themselves.

_____ h. They produce offspring that do not vary at all from themselves.

_____ i. They are well suited to their environments.

_____ j. They can travel from location to location.

_____ k. They have feelings.

_____ l. They are very happy.

3. In your notebook, write a paragraph in which you explain in your own words one characteristic of living things. Pick the characteristic that to you is the most striking one. You may be asked to read your paragraph to the class and tell why you picked that characteristic as the most striking one.

4. Reading textbooks with technical terms, the reader sometimes has to work on understanding the meanings of those terms. This is especially true when the author does not provide definitions of technical terms in the margins. A good strategy is to make a glossary of terms with definitions to use in study. Write definitions of the following terms directly in the margin in the appropriate location of this selection just as you would in studying a textbook. Refer to the selection in writing your answers:
   a. atoms   b. enzymes   c. macromolecules   d. photosynthesis

5. Predict the meaning of the word *immature* based on its prefix. Answer in your notebook.

SELECTION 4
Child Development (PSYCHOLOGY)

A Reading Workshop

Getting Ready to Read

As you have learned, previewing an assigned chapter of a college textbook before reading helps you build a framework for understanding the material when you read it. Today, textbook authors often list the headings and subheadings of a chapter as an outline at the beginning of it. Studying the outline, you can see what the chapter is about and how the chapter is organized.

In addition, some authors start each chapter with an example or interesting story—a vignette—that grabs your attention and introduces the major ideas. Textbook authors may also begin a chapter by telling you point by point what they intend to cover in the chapter. Similarly, they may begin a section by listing the subsections they are going to discuss.

Figure 1.8 is a copy (or fascimile) of the first two pages of the first chapter of a college textbook on child development. The book is *Child Development,* by Hughes, Noppe, and Noppe; the chapter title is "Introduction: Concepts and Theories." Think for a

vignette
vĭ nyĕt´

facsimile
făx sĭm´ə lē

CHAPTER ONE

Child Development

INTRODUCTION: CONCEPTS AND THEORIES

THE NATURE OF CHILD DEVELOPMENT

WHAT IS CHILD DEVELOPMENT?
REASONS FOR STUDYING CHILDHOOD

THE HISTORY OF CHILD DEVELOPMENT

EARLY GREEK CONCEPTIONS
THE MIDDLE AGES
THE REAWAKENING OF HUMANITY
THE ENLIGHTENMENT
THE AGE OF SCIENCE
THE EARLY TWENTIETH CENTURY
THE MID-TWENTIETH CENTURY

THEORIES OF CHILD DEVELOPMENT

BEHAVIORAL/SOCIAL LEARNING THEORIES
COGNITIVE-DEVELOPMENTAL THEORIES
THE INFORMATION-PROCESSING APPROACH
ETHOLOGICAL THEORY
CONTEXTUAL THEORIES
PSYCHOANALYTIC THEORIES

SUMMARY

KEY TERMS

SUGGESTED READINGS

FIGURE 1.8   A Facsimile of Pages from a Psychology Textbook

2   CHAPTER ONE

WHILE WAITING TO CHECK OUT AT A SUPERMARKET, YOU WITNESS THE FOLLOWING SCENE BETWEEN A MOTHER and her 4-year-old daughter ahead of you in line: The little girl notices a display of candy bars and asks her mother if she can have one. Her mother says no. The child says, "Yes! I want some!" The mother again refuses. Now the child begins to cry and, in a louder voice, again demands a candy bar. Irritated and embarrassed, the mother firmly tells her daughter to be quiet. The child screams, throws herself to the floor, and kicks her legs furiously.

What is your assessment of this incident? Why do you think the child is behaving badly? Do you sympathize with the mother because she has to deal with a difficult child? Or do you blame the mother because she obviously hasn't taught her child to behave properly? Do you find yourself thinking that this scene would never have occurred if the little girl were *your* child? Whether you realize it or not, your analysis of this episode reveals your own theoretical beliefs about children's development, and these beliefs influence the way you interpret children's behavior, in supermarkets or elsewhere, and the way you relate to children. Your theoretical beliefs may also influence the understanding you have of your own behavior.■

THE NATURE OF CHILD DEVELOPMENT

To what extent are children's basic natures determined by heredity? To what extent are growing children influenced by their families, peers, or teachers? A person who argues that parents are solely responsible for all that their children grow up to be ("The woman in the supermarket isn't raising her child properly") must obviously believe that environmental forces influence a child's development. In contrast, a person who argues that parents must work with the raw material nature has provided ("The unfortunate woman has a difficult child") probably believes that biological forces are more influential.

This chapter provides an introduction to the perspectives that underlie contemporary theory and research in child development. First, we attempt to define child development as a field of study. Second, we examine a number of issues critical to an understanding of the whole developmental process. Third, we discuss the reasons why the study of children is important. Fourth, we trace the historical roots of this field from ancient Greece to modern times. Finally, we discuss the major contemporary theories of child development, some of which were forged out of centuries of philosophical speculation.

As you read about the evolution of child development theory, you should realize that theories are not simply abstract principles that are of interest only to

child development professionals. Theories provide all of us who interact with children—parents, educators, social workers, counselors, coaches, and others—with a framework in which to better understand children's behavior: They not only form the basis of our assumptions about what we have seen, and our predictions about what we shall see in the future, but they also influence the questions we ask about children's behavior and the answers we arrive at.

WHAT IS CHILD DEVELOPMENT?

Child development is an interdisciplinary study of the developmental processes involved in human physical, social, emotional, and intellectual change from conception through adolescence, and of the numerous biological and cultural factors that influence those processes. Although this definition encompasses a large number of interrelated elements, you should remember these six important points, all of which will be examined in more detail:

1. Child development is a process characterized by genuine developmental changes and should not be confused with nondevelopmental changes that occur over time.
2. Although often described in terms of norms or averages, child development is an individual process.
3. Although conveniently divided into stages, child development is nevertheless a continuous process.
4. Child development involves a complicated interaction of hereditary and environmental factors.
5. Child development is an interdisciplinary study.
6. Child development occurs within a particular setting or context which can have a definite influence on the process itself.

DEVELOPMENT AND CHANGE   All development involves change, but not every change represents a genuine development. To develop means to grow out of, to evolve from. Thus, a definite sense of evolution is present in the developmental process—a sense of one state of affairs not only following but emerging directly from that which preceded it. Nondevelopmental change, in contrast, is a transition requiring no evolution. One unrelated state of affairs simply follows the state that immediately preceded it.

As an illustration of the difference between developmental and nondevelopmental changes, consider this example from the realm of human learning: A student prepares for an exam by memorizing definitions at the end of his textbook chapters, each week working

FIGURE 1.8   *(Continued) Note the smallness of the print. Small print is common in college textbooks*

minute about both titles. Working with a partner, predict what this chapter is about; record your prediction in your notebook. Next, using the topical outline provided in the facsimile, sketch the rows and columns of a data chart that you could use for studying the chapter. Follow the style of the data chart in Figure 1.7 of this book. Then predict what you anticipate each subsection is about and record your expectations on your data chart. Do this in your reading notebook.

Continuing to work with a partner, add to your chart what you already know (if anything) about the subtopics. Raise some questions that you would expect to answer by reading the chapter. Record these in your notebook.

Reading with Meaning

Study the first page of text given in Figure 1.8, especially the introductory paragraphs in the first column. As you read the introduction, keep asking these questions: What are the authors doing here? How is this material similar to that found in the topical outline? If you had the full chapter in front of you, at this point you would probably thumb through it to get a rough idea of what it is about before reading the rest of the chapter.

Monitoring Comprehension: Becoming More Aware of How Textbook Authors Organize Chapters

Talk out the answers to these questions with your workshop partner in preparation for class discussion. Make notes in your notebook so that you can contribute your ideas to the discussion.

1. In Figure 1.8, put a bracket around the vignette that Hughes, Noppe, and Noppe use to open the chapter. Why do you think the authors start with this vignette? What thoughts went through your head as you read the introductory story?

2. Look at the second paragraph of the introductory segment. How many questions do the authors ask just in that one paragraph? Why do Hughes, Noppe, and Noppe ask so many questions in their introduction?

3. Reread the three paragraphs under the main heading "The Nature of Child Development." Circle the paragraph in this section where the authors tell you the topics they will be covering in the chapter and the order in which they will discuss those topics. What sequencing words do the authors use to tell you that they will cover five main points?

4. Review the section of text under the subheading "What Is Child Development?" Put a check next to the numbered list that shows the subtopics the authors will discuss in this subsection. How many subtopics will they talk about?

5. How does the minor subheading "Development and Change" relate to the numbered list of topics that the authors have just given? Predict what the next five minor subheadings in this section will be.

6. Generalize: What kinds of clues do textbook authors give you at the beginning of a chapter to guide your reading of the chapter? Why is it important for you to pick up on these clues as you begin to read a chapter?

 EXTENDING WHAT YOU HAVE LEARNED

Increasing Your Awareness of Prereading Strategies

Reading experts tell us that to be good readers, we must be aware of the specific steps and strategies we use to understand what we are reading. We must know in our own minds how we go about reading and what works best for us, especially as we study college textbooks. Reading experts call this awareness metacognition.

In this chapter, you have developed increased awareness of steps and strategies important in studying chapters of college textbooks and other assigned readings. Tell yourself in your head the four getting-ready-to-read strategies you have been practicing that can help you become a better reader. Outline them here.

1.

2.

3.

4.

Applying the Strategies to Your Personal Reading

Find a selection that you want to read or a chapter that has been assigned in a course you are taking. Apply the four steps of your getting-ready-to-read strategy. Record your getting-ready-to-read notes in your reading notebook. Your notes are your active reading portfolio; your instructor will use your portfolio as evidence of your reading progress.

PART TWO
VOCABULARY AND READING

CHAPTER 2 Unlocking the Meaning of Words: Using Context Clues

CHAPTER 3 Unlocking the Meaning of Words: Understanding Word Elements

Unlocking the Meaning of Words: Using Context Clues

OBJECTIVE

In this chapter, you will develop strategies for figuring out the meaning of an unfamiliar word through the use of context clues, or the surrounding words in a sentence. Specifically, you will learn how to use

1. Definitions built directly into a sentence or given in a margin note or footnote in a textbook;
2. Synonyms placed near the word;
3. Explanations and descriptions given in the paragraph;
4. Words that express contrasting, or opposite, meanings; and
5. The overall sense, or meaning, of a sentence.

UNLOCKING THE MEANING OF UNFAMILIAR WORDS

As you read college texts, you will meet unfamiliar words. How can you figure out what these words mean so that you understand what you are reading?

When you see an unfamiliar word, you should look at the surrounding words in the sentence, or the **context clues.** You should

- Study definitions, synonyms, and explanations built directly into a sentence or placed in the margin;
- Look for contrasting phrases and words of opposite meaning (antonyms) found close by;
- Study the overall meaning of the sentence in which the word occurs and substitute a word you know for the unfamiliar one to see whether it makes sense there.

If you have read the paragraph in which the unfamiliar word appears and you still can't crack the meaning of the word from the context clues, your next step is to check a dictionary or the glossary at the back of the book for possible definitions. Then try each

Context clues   The surrounding words in the sentence

Synonym   A word with almost the same meaning as another word

Antonym   A word with the opposite meaning from another word

23

dictionary or glossary definition in the context of the original sentence—the sentence you had trouble understanding—to see which definition applies there. This last step is necessary because some words have more than one meaning.

Your word-unlocking strategy has these three steps:

WORD-UNLOCKING STRATEGY: CONTEXT CLUES

→ **Context study.** Use sentence context clues to figure out the meaning of an unfamiliar word you must know to understand what the author is saying.

→ **Dictionary check.** If you cannot unlock the meaning of the new word through context study, check the dictionary or glossary for definitions.

→ **Context fix-up.** Try definitions from the dictionary or glossary within the context of the original sentence. Ask, "Which definition works here?" Reread the paragraph in which the word appears to make sure you understand what the author is saying.

We call this strategy for unlocking word meanings Context/Dictionary/Context (CDC). In the next section, you will learn how to apply CDC.

APPLYING CDC

Sometimes context clues are very explicit. To help you understand the meaning of a word, the author may define it right in the sentence. Or he or she may use a **synonym** (a word with almost the same meaning) near the more difficult word. In textbooks, the author may provide a definition in a footnote or in the margin, as we have done here. If there are definitions in the margin, read them during your preview so that you have some background before you read. If not, you may make your own margin notes of technical terms after reading a paragraph.

Now let's consider some examples of explicit clues. Think about the word *synonym* in the previous paragraph. The phrase "a word with almost the same meaning" defines the term *synonym.* The definition is also in the margin. Similarly, the definition of *context clues* is built into a previous paragraph—"the surrounding words in the sentence." This definition is also in the margin on page 230.

Sometimes context clues are not so clear. You must consider an entire sentence and even surrounding sentences to figure out the meaning of an unfamiliar word. For example, think about the sentence you read earlier: "Sometimes context clues are very explicit." What is the meaning of *explicit?* You get some hints from the next sentences that suggest specific ways that authors embed, or tuck in, clues as to the meaning of a word they use. You say to yourself, "Being explicit means to 'set things out clearly.'"

But there is another clue to the meaning of *explicit* in the text. It is in the sentence "Sometimes context clues are not so clear." Here is a contrasting idea. Thinking about both sentences together, you can figure out that *explicit* means the opposite of "not so clear." *Explicit* means "clearly set forth."

Sometimes the only clue to the meaning of a word is the overall meaning of the sentence. In that case, you should substitute a word that you know for the unfamiliar word to see whether it makes sense. What you are doing is seeing whether a word you know works in that context. If it does, you may have a clue to the meaning of the unfamiliar word.

For example, in the sentence "The thirsty man yearned for a drink of water," you may think: "I can substitute the word *craved* for *yearned.* Therefore, *yearned* may mean the same as *craved.* The thirsty man wanted a drink very much." Figure 2.1 summarizes types of context clues and examples. In each example sentence in Figure 2.1, circle the word or words that help you get at the meaning of the italicized term.

We have been talking so far about ways to wrest meaning from the context in which a word is used. In some instances, context takes you only so far. You are still

The Clue	An Example	Notes About the Example
Definition	*Archaeology* is the scientific study of prehistoric cultures by excavation of their remains.	Definition is given directly in the sentence.
	Through *archaeology,* the scientific study of prehistoric cultures by excavation of their remains, we have learned much about our human ancestors.	Definition is given next to the term, set off by commas.
	Through *archaeology*—the scientific study of prehistoric cultures by excavation of their remains—we have learned much about our human ancestors.	Definition is given next to the term, set off by dashes.
	Through *archaeology* (the scientific study of prehistoric cultures by excavation of their remains), we have learned much about our human ancestors.	Definition is given next to the term, set off in parentheses.
Description	A *paramecium* is a microscopic organism. Made up of one small cell, the paramecium is shaped like a slipper and has a deep groove down its side. It lives in fresh water.	A full description is included that gives a complete picture of the object being defined.
Synonym (word with the same meaning)	Reducing the blood cholesterol has a number of *beneficial* results. One positive outcome is a lessening of the chances of heart attack.	The word *positive* is set near its synonym, *beneficial*. You can relate *beneficial* to *positive* and in that way figure out the meaning of *beneficial.*
Antonym (word with the opposite meaning)	Her taste tends toward *pastels.* In contrast, I prefer sharp colors like bright red or deep purple.	The word *pastels* is set near a phrase with nearly the opposite meaning. Using the words *in contrast,* you can pick up the contrast and reason that pastels are less bright.

FIGURE 2.1 Context Clues

unsure of the author's meaning. Suppose that you read, "The man warned me to be careful of dehydration, because of the intensity of the heat." From context, you know that there is a relationship between dehydration and heat; you know that dehydration is not something good because the man warned against it. To get the exact meaning, you check the dictionary, which states, "loss of moisture or water." That meaning makes sense in the context of the sentence: The warning has to do with losing water from one's body, which can be a problem on a hot day. You need the dictionary to get at the idea of water loss. Notice that having checked the dictionary, you go back and apply the dictionary definition to the sentence you are trying to understand. You apply the final fix-up step of CDC.

WORKSHOP: USING CONTEXT CLUES

Working collaboratively in pairs, use the context of these sentences to figure out the meaning of each italicized word. First, read aloud each sentence, taking turns with your partner and using your vocal intonation to express meaning. Then star the option that is closest in meaning to the italicized one. The first three examples model the way to reason out the meaning.

1. The swimmer took some deep breaths to *alleviate* the nervousness she felt before the race. (*Reasoning from context: During a race, it is important not to be nervous. Therefore, the deep breaths would be taken to lower, or lessen, the nervousness.*)
   a. lessen
   b. motivate
   c. increase
   d. cause

2. The college student *brooded* over the loss of his summer job, asking himself over and over whether anything he said could have made a difference. (*Reasoning from context: I would be upset if I lost my job. I would keep thinking about it and wonder why. That's worrying.*)
   a. forgot
   b. rejoiced
   c. worried
   d. hatched

3. The professor felt *contempt* for people who would not stand up for their beliefs. (*Reasoning from context: People generally think that it is important to stand up for their beliefs and not be weak. Therefore, the professor would be negative about such people and would not respect them.* Scorn *is the closest word.*)
   a. respect
   b. scorn
   c. love
   d. concern

4. She did her exercises each day at the *designated* hour; when she became sick, however, she could not exercise when she was supposed to. (*Clue: Could you exercise at any time? How do you know?*)
   a. that was assigned
   b. that she requested
   c. that was best for her
   d. that was part of her design

5. It's hard to do an *improvisation* in drama class because you have to make up your lines as you go along. (*Clue: What phrase tells you what you would do when you improvise?*)
   a. a bad performance
   b. a good performance
   c. a performance without preparation
   d. a performance done alone

6. The shy college student spoke so softly that his voice was practically *inaudible*. (*Clue: How did the man speak? Speaking that way must make his voice inaudible.*)
   a. unable to be heard
   b. unable to be enjoyed
   c. unable to be seen
   d. without variation

7. We saw the ax neatly *cleave* the board in two. (*Clue: You use an ax to cleave. What does an ax do?*)
   a. make into something else
   b. split
   c. hold up
   d. make clean

8. When the tennis player first began training, she was a *novice* at the sport, and her movements were awkward. (*Clue: At what point does the sentence say she is a novice?*)
   a. an expert
   b. a young woman
   c. a beginner
   d. a helper

9. As the wind grew even stronger, the mountain climber came *perilously* close to losing his grip. (*Clue: What would happen if the climber lost his grip? Would that be a safe thing to happen?*)
   a. dangerously
   b. practically
   c. permanently
   d. ridiculously

10. Because his movements were so *subtle,* I was hardly aware he was moving at all. (*Clue: The sentence says that subtle movements are those that appear as if the person is not moving.*)
    a. clear
    b. slight
    c. extreme
    d. wonderful

11. The paintings in the professor's collection appealed to my *aesthetic* sense. (*Clue: Aesthetic seems to relate to the paintings.*)
    a. philosophical
    b. mathematical
    c. scientific
    d. artistic

12. The cat jumped from one window ledge to the next with amazing *agility;* we were impressed at the ease with which the animal made the difficult jumps. (*Clue: Agility seems to relate to the ease with which the animal jumped.*)
    a. nimbleness
    b. speed
    c. clumsiness
    d. care

13. A feeling of *déjà vu* came over me as I stood before the pyramids. (*Clue: You may want to check the glossary to be sure.*)
    a. sadness
    b. feeling of having experienced something before although one has never done so
    c. dizziness
    d. great elation at being in a historic site for the first time

14. The man lived in a *desolate* area. (*Clue: You may want to check a dictionary and try the different meanings that are given in the context of this sentence.*)
    a. barren
    b. unhappy
    c. deserted, unlived in
    d. forlorn

SELECTION 1

On Geology (EARTH SCIENCE)

A Word Study Workshop

Collaborating in teams, use the context to figure out the meaning of each italicized word. In the space provided, write down the reasoning you used to unlock the meaning of the word. The first two are completed as models.

On Geology
Charles Cazeau, Robert Hatcher, and Francis Siemankowski

1. It is morning and you are having a relaxed breakfast in the kitchen. You test your cup of coffee to see how hot it is and *leisurely* unfold the newspaper.
    "Leisurely—it is breakfast time, morning. It appears that you are getting ready to drink your coffee and are relaxed, since you are going to read the newspaper. 'Leisurely' must mean 'taking your time'—in a relaxed, unhurried way."

2. As usual, you think, there is bad news in the world. An earthquake in Chile has left many dead and thousands homeless. They say the *intensity* of the earthquake was 8.1 on the Richter scale, whatever that means.
    "The Richter scale must be a scale for measuring earthquakes. The intensity on this scale was 8.1. The 8.1 must tell how great the earthquake was—how powerful. 'Intensity' must mean 'strength.'"

3. Hawaii is *bracing* for the arrival of large sea waves triggered by the quake. (*Clue: A large sea wave is not good news. You may need dictionary help.*)

    _____

    _____

    _____

4. Another item catches your eye. "Flooding in the Midwest. Several towns *inundated,* and people paddling boats through the streets." (*Clue: The water is so high that you*

Did You
KNOW?

Inundate comes from
the Latin prefix *in-*,
meaning "into, in, or
within" and the Latin
verb *undare*, meaning
"to flow." We can also
talk about being
inundated with work.

need boats to get through.)

_____

_____

_____

5. At the bottom of the page the newspaper notes that scientists are still observing a new volcano that appeared a few days ago in the north Atlantic. The volcano is *spewing* out ash and cinders amid thunderous explosions.

_____

_____

_____

6. You turn the page and take another sip of coffee. Ah, here are more relevant matters on the local news front. In addition to the *furor* over the severe pollution of the lake, a manufacturer is accused of polluting the groundwater supply by pumping acids and other wastes into a disposal well.

_____

_____

_____

7. In this *hypothetical* situation you started your day, perhaps without realizing it, by reading a series of geological reports. (*Clue: Did this really happen to you?*)

_____

_____

_____

8. All the items noted share one thing in common. They involve geology. *Geology* is the study of the earth. The overall objective of the geologist is to try to answer questions about the earth's physical nature, both past and present.

_____

_____

9. Of equal concern to the geologist is the application of this knowledge to certain problems that beset human beings as they *wrest* from the earth the things that they need (e.g., oil, gas, water, metals, construction materials). (*Clue: Is it easy to get these materials out?*)

_____

_____

_____

10. In attempting to understand the nature of the earth, geologists study the rocks that make up its outer crust. These rocks might be thought of as documents that have survived through millions of years yet carry within them the clues to past events. Geologists seek to unlock these secrets by careful study of rock records, not only in their natural outdoor settings, but by subjecting samples of these rocks to further *scrutiny* in the laboratory.

_____

_____

_____

11. In addition, the geologist must pay close attention to forces *operative* at the earth's surface (e.g., wind, wave, and stream action) and forces *operative* within the earth.

_____

_____

_____

In the next two sections of this chapter, you will read selections from college texts that contain words that may be new to you. Use the context in which these words are used to analyze, or figure out, their meanings.

Think
about . . .
. . . What is the meaning of *analyze*? How do you know from context?

SELECTION 2

A Chance Event or Not? Anecdote, Common Sense, and Statistics in Science (BIOLOGY AND MATHEMATICS)

Independent Word Study

Getting Ready to Read

Scan the next selection by reading the title and the first and last paragraphs. Then answer these prereading questions.

• What is the selection about? _____

• Predict: How do scientists use numbers to help them understand events in the

  natural world? _____

  _____

• How difficult will the selection be for you: light, average, heavy?

Reading with Meaning

Read the selection, keeping this question in mind: What is the meaning of each boldfaced word? Use the context in which a word is found to help you figure out its meaning.

A Chance Event or Not? Anecdote, Common Sense, and Statistics in Science
David Krogh

Valuable as they are, experimental and observational tests often are not enough to provide answers to scientific questions. In countless instances, scientists employ an additional tool in coming to comprehend **reality**—a mathematical tool—as you'll see in the following example.

The evidence that cigarette smoking causes lung cancer (and heart disease and **emphysema** and on and on) has been around for so long that most people have no idea why smoking was looked into as a health **hazard** in the first place. You might think that scientists were suspicious of tobacco decades ago and thus began experimenting with it in the laboratory, but this wasn't the case. Instead, the trail that led to tobacco as a health hazard started with a mystery about disease.

When the lung-cancer pioneer Alton Ochsner was in medical school in 1919, his surgery professor brought both the junior and senior classes in to see an **autopsy** of a man who had died of lung cancer. The disease was then so rare that the professor thought the young medical students might never see another case during their professional lifetimes.

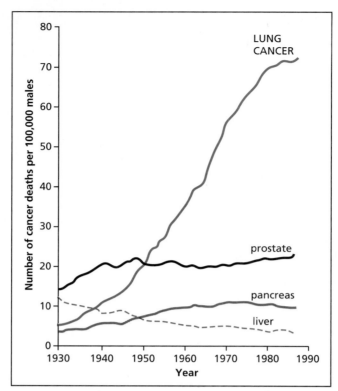

FIGURE 2.2 Rise in Lung-Cancer Mortality in U.S. Males from 1930 Forward

Prior to the 1920s, lung cancer was among the rarest forms of cancer, because cigarette smoking itself was rare before the twentieth century. It did not become the **dominant** form of tobacco use in the United States until the 1920s. This made a difference in lung-cancer rates because cigarette smoke is inhaled, while pipe and cigar smoke generally are not.

If you look at Figure 2.2, you can see the rise in lung-cancer **mortality** in U.S. males from 1930 forward. A graph for women would show a later rise in lung-cancer deaths, because women started smoking *en masse* later. Nevertheless, this trend resulted in lung cancer becoming the most deadly form of cancer among women—a distinction that it retains to this day. (More women contract breast cancer, but more women die of lung cancer.)

Given the lung-cancer **trends** that were apparent by the 1930s, the task before scientists was to explain the alarming increase in this disease. What could the cause of this **scourge** be, medical detectives wondered. The effects of men being gassed in World War I? Increased road tar? Pollution from power plants? Through the 1940s, cigarette smoking was only one suspect among many.

Laboratory experiment eventually would play a part in fingering tobacco as the lung-cancer **culprit,** but the original **indictment** of smoking was written in numbers—in statistical tables showing that smokers were contracting lung cancer at much higher rates than nonsmokers.

It has sometimes been said that "science is measurement," and the phrase is a marvel of compact truth. For centuries, people had an idea that smoking might be causing serious harm, but this information fell into the realm of guessing or of **anecdote,** meaning personal stories. The problem with anecdote is that there is no measurement in it; there is no way of judging the validity of one story as opposed to the next. Related to anecdote is the notion of "common sense," which is valuable in many instances, but which also had us believing for centuries that the sun moved around the Earth. In the case of smoking, it took the extremely careful measurement provided by science—through a discipline called *epidemiology*—to separate truth from fiction.

Did You
KNOW?
The suffix *-logy* means "the study of"; you have seen it on *biology* and *geology*.

Probability in Science

Note that "measurement" in this instance was a matter of calculating *probability,* which is often the case in science. Epidemiologists found a linkage between smoking and lung cancer—in the sense that those who smoked were more likely to get the disease. But, having seen this, scientists then had to ask: Could this result be a matter of pure chance? A person tossing a coin might get heads seven times in a row, and it might be written off to chance. But would it be the same if the person came up with heads *seventy* times in a row? No; at that point there would be justification for assuming that some force other than chance was in operation (such as a rigged coin). When the epidemiologists looked at their statistical tables and saw so many more smokers than nonsmokers getting lung cancer, they had to ask whether this result fell into the realm of seven heads in a row, or seventy. Even in the earliest studies they concluded that more than chance was at work in the results; after many studies, they concluded that smoking was *causing* lung cancer. But how did they judge what was **probable** and what was not in an issue as complicated as this one? The researchers relied on techniques developed in the branch of mathematics called **statistics.**

The importance of probability and statistics to science can hardly be overstated: These tools are used frequently in nearly every scientific discipline.

Monitoring Your Comprehension and Writing with New Words

A. Based on the way these words are used in the selection, hypothesize the meaning of each. Use the process of elimination to help you. Start by crossing out the least likely choice or choices to narrow the field; then respond by starring the most likely one.

1. **reality** (*noun*)
   a. what one can comprehend
   b. what one can measure
   c. what is exceedingly valuable
   d. what actually is

2. **emphysema** (*noun*)
   a. a heart disease
   b. a disease
   c. lung cancer
   d. cigarette smoking

3. **hazard** (*noun*)
   a. source of danger
   b. exciting happening
   c. mysterious occurrence
   d. suspicious happening

4. **autopsy** (*noun*)
   a. injection of medicine to kill pain
   b. injection of medicine to prevent death
   c. surgery performed to prevent death
   d. procedure performed after death

5. **dominant** (*adjective*)
   a. most influential
   b. rarest
   c. most dangerous to the health
   d. most recent to have occurred

6. **mortality** (*noun*)
   a. death rate
   b. length of life
   c. numbers
   d. increase

7. **trends** (*noun*)
   a. things that are apparent
   b. explanations of reality
   c. general directions of movement
   d. causes of events

8. **scourge** (*noun*)
   a. something bringing great trouble
   b. suspicious person
   c. guilty party
   d. happy occurrence

9. **culprit** (*noun*)
   a. medical disaster
   b. suspicious person
   c. guilty party
   d. happy occurrence

10. **indictment** (*noun*)
    a. questioning of
    b. consideration of
    c. fingering as the culprit
    d. study of

11. **anecdote** (*noun*)
    a. guessing
    b. opposite thing
    c. substance used to counteract the effect of poison
    d. personal story

12. **probable** (*adjective*)
    a. problem-like
    b. complicated
    c. issue-oriented
    d. likely

13. **statistics** (*noun*)
    a. branch of mathematics
    b. branch of science
    c. tables or charts
    d. rulers, protractors, and other measuring devices

B. In your notebook, write a paragraph or a couple of sentences about cigarette smoking and lung cancer. Use two or three of the bold-faced words from the selection in your writing.

SELECTION 3

Prenatal Development (DEVELOPMENTAL PSYCHOLOGY)

A Word Study Workshop

Getting Ready to Read

Preview the selection by reading the title, the first paragraph, and the margin notes; then answer these questions.

- What is the selection about? _____

- What do you think contributes to a child's healthy development during the prenatal period? _____
  _____

- Predict: What kind of information will this article give you about the topic?
  _____

- For what purpose does this author use margin notes? _____
  _____

- How heavy is the reading load for you? Is this selection harder or easier than previous ones? _____
  _____

Reading with Meaning

Read this selection from a psychology textbook, thinking about the italicized words as you read and using the context in which the words are used to predict their meaning. The names and dates in parentheses tell whom the author is quoting and when the research quoted was published. This material takes the place of footnotes, which sometimes give this same type of information.

Prenatal Development
Charles Morris

Scientists once thought that the development of the child before birth was simply a process of physical growth. Only at birth, they believed, did experience and learning begin to influence psychological development. Today, we know that the unborn baby is *profoundly* affected by its environment. Some experts, such as psychologist Leni Schwartz, have even gone so far as to say that "the most important time in our lives may well be the time before we were born" (Spezzano, 1981).

The Prenatal Environment

During the earliest period of *prenatal* (before birth) *development,* survival is the most important issue. Immediately after *conception,* the fertilized egg divides many times, beginning the process that will change it from a one-celled organism into a highly complex human being. The cell ball implants itself in the uterus, and around it grows a *placenta,* which carries food to it and waste products from it as the organism grows. In time, the major organ systems and physical features develop. If all goes well, by the end of this stage of development the organism is recognizably human and is now called a *fetus.* The fetal period begins in the eighth week after conception and lasts until birth. (It is usually early in this period that a woman discovers that she is pregnant.) The important role of this period is the preparation of the fetus for independent life.

From the second week after conception until birth, the baby is linked to its mother, and thus to the outside world, through the placenta. Many changes in the mother's body chemistry, whether as a result of nutrition, drugs, disease, or *prolonged* stress or excitement, affect the fetus directly through the placenta. However, the placenta is not merely a *passive* tube connecting mother and fetus; it is an active organ with some ability to select and provide substances that the developing fetus needs. Unfortunately, although it can filter out some harmful substances, it cannot protect the fetus from the *toxic* effects of alcohol, narcotics, medications, and a variety of other chemicals.

Good nutrition is at least as important for the fetus as it is for us. Yet many mothers, especially in developing countries, *subsist* on diets that are not substantial enough to nourish them or their babies properly. Even in the United States, expectant mothers' diets are often inadequate. Malnutrition in the prenatal period can result in seriously deprived babies and often permanent damage. These babies may have smaller brains and bodies and be weak, listless, and disease-prone (Stechler & Halton, 1982). During childhood, they often show *impaired* intellectual functioning that is usually difficult or impossible to improve.

Besides malnutrition, drugs *constitute* a particular threat to the unborn child. If the mother is a heavy drinker, her baby may be born mentally retarded, be unusually small and slow to develop, and suffer from other serious *abnormalities* (Clarren & Smith, 1978). If the mother is a heavy user of drugs, her baby may be born with an addiction and may experience withdrawal symptoms immediately after

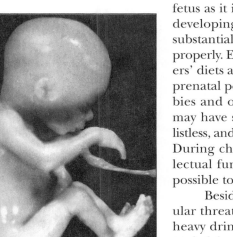

FIGURE 2.3 A Five-Month-Old Human Fetus
(Dr. Landrum Shettles)

Prenatal development Physical and psychological changes in an organism before birth

Placenta Organ that connects the developing fetus to the mother's body, providing nourishment to it and filtering out some harmful substances

Fetus An unborn infant at least eight weeks old

birth. If she smokes, the baby may be premature, underdeveloped, or deformed (Evans, Newcombe, & Campbell, 1979).

Certain diseases can also injure the fetus, particularly early in pregnancy. German measles (rubella) is especially dangerous and leads to eye damage, heart malformations, deafness, and mental retardation. Other diseases, such as syphilis and diabetes, can also produce defects in the fetus.

Moreover, prolonged stress or excitement on the part of the mother can directly affect the health of the fetus. There is some evidence that when pregnant women experience emotional stress, their fetuses move more frequently and forcefully than usual (Sontag, 1964). In one study, it was found that women who were under severe stress (most often from extremely unhappy marriages) gave birth more often to children who were sickly and slow to develop and whose behavior was *abnormal*. Critics of these and similar studies have pointed out, however, that the connection between maternal stress and developmental problems in children is by no means clear. For example, since many of the mothers under stress in their studies were also poor, it may have been that growing up in a deprived household was more responsible for the children's problems than was prenatal stress (Sameroff & Chandler, 1975).

It is possible to detect many fetal disorders before the baby is born, using the technique of *amniocentesis* (the technique of collecting cells cast off by the fetus into the fluid of the womb and testing them for genetic abnormalities). Moreover, it should be kept in mind that despite the hazards to the fetus that we have mentioned, most babies develop normally. If a pregnant woman is careful to eat well, maintain her health, and avoid exposure to harmful substances and communicable diseases, she should not worry about whether stress at home or on the job will harm her child. Young children are *resilient* and with proper care can often recover completely from minor problems related to prenatal development. As human beings, we have a long period of childhood, and most of our development occurs after we have been born.   [847 words]

Monitoring Comprehension and Writing with New Words

A. Underline these terms in the selection and circle the words in the selection that are clues to their meaning. Then star the definition for each highlighted word listed here, first crossing out the choices you know for sure are wrong to narrow the field. Your instructor may use this activity to assess your progress.

1. profoundly
   a. very sincerely
   b. very tenderly
   c. very greatly
   d. very slightly

2. prenatal
   a. related to nations or governments
   b. related to the period before birth
   c. related to a premonition, or prethought
   d. related to natural events

3. conception
   a. point at which a woman becomes pregnant
   b. point at which a ball of cells becomes a fetus
   c. point at which a woman knows she is pregnant
   d. point at which a woman gives birth

4. placenta
   a. the cell ball that implants itself in the uterus
   b. the fertilized egg
   c. a one-celled body
   d. the organ that connects the fetus to the mother's body and provides nourishment to it

Did You KNOW?

The prefix *ab-* means "away from"; the root *norma-* means "rule or pattern." Another word with the prefix is *absorb;* another word with the root is *normalize.*

Did You KNOW?

The prefix *pre-* means "before"; the root *nat-* means "to be born." Another word with the prefix is *preface;* another word with the root is *natural.*

5. fetus
   a. an unborn child
   b. an unborn child at least 3 weeks old
   c. an unborn child at least 8 weeks old
   d. a newly born child

6. prolonged
   a. extended over a period of time   c. personal
   b. slight   d. intense, impossible to endure

7. passive
   a. not active   c. passing materials through
   b. connecting   d. in a position to get excited

8. toxic
   a. alcoholic   c. medical
   b. poisonous   d. chemical

9. subsist
   a. keep alive   c. nourish
   b. continue   d. conceive

10. impaired
    a. impossible   c. improved
    b. damaged   d. thoughtless

11. constitute
    a. threaten   c. make up
    b. cause   d. warn of

12. abnormalities
    a. deviations from the standard
    b. impossible happenings
    c. permanent changes
    d. physical and psychological changes in an organism before birth

13. amniocentesis
    a. the organ that nourishes the developing fetus
    b. abnormalities that appear at birth
    c. the technique of collecting cells cast off by the fetus into the fluid of the womb
       and testing them for genetic abnormalities
    d. physical and psychological changes in an organism before birth

14. resilient
    a. passive   c. residual
    b. underdeveloped   d. able to spring back

B. What does this article say to you as a parent or future parent? What concerns does it
   raise in your mind? Write two or three sentences in response, using some of the words
   you have just studied.

_____

_____

_____

_____

REVIEWING CHAPTER VOCABULARY

A. Put these words into the sentence blanks. Use the context to make your selection.
   Use each option only once. Apply a know-for-sure/process-of-elimination test-taking

strategy. Scan the items for ones you are certain of. Cross out options as you use them. In that way, you leave the difficult items until last and can conquer them through the process of elimination.

bracing	inundated	furor	spewing
hypothetical	leisurely	scrutiny	wrest
intensity	operative		

1. Our trip was a _____ one; we took our time. As a result, we returned home relaxed and full of energy.

2. Because of the _____ that followed the establishment of a harsher grading policy, the administration agreed to reconsider it.

3. The weather reporter predicted a storm of great _____ with much rain and wind.

4. Because the volcano was _____ out lava, we could not go near it.

5. The professor subjected the students' papers to careful _____ before assigning a grade.

6. I tried to _____ the gun from his hand, but I could not get it away.

7. Because we were _____ for a severe storm, we were pleasantly surprised when there was only a little shower.

8. On the exam we had to devise a(n) _____ plan telling what we would have done if we had been there.

9. Near the end of the semester, students often feel _____ with work; so much work comes their way that they do not know where to begin.

10. We studied the forces _____ within society during the Civil War.

B. Write a sentence with a context clue that hints at the meaning of each of the following words. If you have a problem, model your sentences after the ones on pages 26–27 or those in the glossary.

1. alleviate _____

_____

2. brooded _____

_____

3. contempt _____

_____

4. designated _____

_____

5. improvisation _____

_____

6. inaudible _____

_____

7. cleave _____

_____

8. novice _____

_____

9. perilously _____

_____

10. subtle _____

_____

11. aesthetic _____

_____

12. agility _____

_____

13. déjà vu _____

_____

14. desolate (*adjective*) _____

_____

C. Select the word from the list that best fits the context of each sentence. Use each word only once. Use the Know-for-sure/Process-of-elimination test-taking strategy.

abnormalities	passive	resilient
constitutes	profoundly	subsist
impaired	prolonged	toxic

1. Many environmentalists are concerned about the masses of _____ wastes that humankind is producing.

2. Because of the mother's _____ exposure to radioactive materials, the fetus was malformed.

3. The child's vision was _____ because he looked directly into the sun.

4. Children are very _____; they bounce back quickly even after a prolonged illness.

5. There is much controversy over what _____ child abuse.

6. Citizens should not remain _____ onlookers; they should take an active role in the community.

7. I was _____ affected by what I saw; as a result, I now take a less passive role in school activities.

8. Doctors are seeing _____ that are a result of a mother's drug dependency.

9. The explorers had to _____ on berries and roots when they lost all of their supplies.

D. Use each of these technical terms in the appropriate sentence. Apply the Know-for-sure/Process-of-elimination strategy.

amniocentesis	fetus	prenatal
conception	placenta	

1. _____ occurs when the sperm unites with an egg.

2. _____ is a technique for determining genetic abnormalities before the birth of a baby.

3. The _____ period is the period before birth.

4. The _____ is an unborn infant at least 8 weeks old.

5. The _____ is the organ that connects the fetus to its mother.

 ## EXTENDING WHAT YOU HAVE LEARNED

Reviewing Your Understanding of Context Clues

In your notebook, write a brief paragraph in which you present at least three steps to use in understanding new words you meet in reading. Be sure to include something about context clues.

Applying the Strategies to Your Reading

1. Read a column from the editorial page of a newspaper. As you read, underline two or three unfamiliar words. In the margin of the article, jot down the meanings of the words as you figured them out based on the context. Be ready to share your new words with the class and tell how you unlocked the meanings.

2. Starting in Chapter 4, before each reading selection you will find sentences with new words from the selection. Use your understanding of context clues to unlock the meanings of these words as you study the text during the semester.

Unlocking the Meaning of Words: Understanding Word Elements

OBJECTIVE

In this chapter, you will develop strategies for figuring out the meaning of an unfamiliar word through the use of word elements, or the parts that make up the word. Specifically, you will learn how to use

1. Roots (basic word parts, or elements);
2. Affixes (suffixes and prefixes); and
3. Compound word parts.

UNLOCKING THE MEANING OF WORDS

Understanding how words in our language are constructed can help you become a better reader, especially when you deal with content loaded with technical terms. That is so because the English language contains many words built from roots, affixes, and other words. A **root** is a basic unit of meaning in the language. Some English roots—*sing*, for example—can function as words. From that root, or base, we can build *singing* and *singer*. Some word elements come from other languages, such as Latin and Greek; we generally do not use these roots as words in our language, but we make words from them. Affixes include both **prefixes** (meaningful units added to the beginning of words and roots) and **suffixes** (meaningful units added to the end of words and roots). The word towers in Figure 3.1 show how English words are built from prefixes, roots, and suffixes. The roots in this case are *rupt-*, which is from Latin and means "to break," and *port-*, also from Latin and meaning "to carry."

Some English words are the result of **compounding**—putting together two words to form a new word that retains the meaning of the component parts. An example is the word *roommate*, formed from *room* and *mate* and meaning "a friend who rooms, or lives, with you."

As you read unfamiliar words, especially technical terms, you should apply a basic word unlocking strategy:

Think
about . . .
Tell yourself the meaning of *prefix* and *suffix*, using context clues.

WORD-UNLOCKING STRATEGY:
WORD ELEMENTS

→ Look at a word in terms of its component elements: roots, prefixes, suffixes, other words, and syllables.

→ Pronounce the new word by focusing on the elements and syllables.

→ Use the meanings of the elements to figure out the meaning of the new word.

For example, a commonly used Latin root is *astro-*, which means "star." Here are some words formed from *astro-*. Pronounce each word, focusing on the root.

- ***astro****nomy:* scientific study of the heavens
- ***astro****naut:* traveler beyond the earth

	e	rupt			port	
	e	rupt	ion		port	able
		rupt	ure	trans	port	ation
	cor	rupt	ion	trans	port	able
	cor	rupt	able	ex	port	
	cor	rupt	er	ex	port	er
in	cor	rupt	able	im	port	
	dis	rupt		im	port	ation
	dis	rupt	ion	de	port	
	dis	rupt	ive	de	port	able
	inter	rupt		de	port	ment
	inter	rupt	ion	re	port	
				re	port	able
				com	port	

FIGURE 3.1 Word Towers Showing How English Words Are Built from Basic Elements

- *astrology:* pseudoscientific study of the effects of heavenly bodies on people's lives
- *asterisk:* star-shaped symbol (*)
- *aster:* star-shaped flower

Based on your understanding of the root *astro-* and your ability to use context clues, you can figure out the meaning of the italicized word in this sentence: He asked an *astronomically* high price for towing my car to the garage. You might reason, "*Astro-* means 'star.' Stars are very high in the sky. *Astronomically* must mean 'high as the stars.'" That meaning fits the context. An astronomically high price is a very high one. Both a word element and the context help you to unlock the meaning of *astronomically.*

What is the meaning of *astronomer?* Pronounce the word and analyze its structure. You might reason, "*Astro-* means 'star'; *astronomy* is the study of stars and heavenly bodies; *-er* is a suffix that can mean 'a person who.' An *astronomer* is someone who studies the stars and heavenly bodies."

A widely used Greek element is *graph-,* or *grapho-.* It means "drawn or written." Pronounce the italicized words in the next three exercises and predict their meanings, using the meaning of the element and the context as clues.

1. She described the accident in such *graphic* terms that I felt as if I had been there. *Graphic* means
   a. clear or vivid.
   b. terrible.
   c. boastful.
   d. unpleasant.

2. Her brother decided to study *graphic* arts because he could draw well. The *graphic* arts
   a. involve physical activity.
   b. relate to driving a car.
   c. relate to drawing, etching, and painting.
   d. relate to a mathematical graph.

3. Guglielmo Marconi was the inventor of the first successful wireless *telegraph.* The *telegraph* is
   a. a device for sending messages or signals over a distance.
   b. a picture tube.
   c. a computer.
   d. a television set.

In figuring out the meaning of *telegraph,* you may use the meaning of another common Greek element: *tele-*. It means "distant, or sent over a distance." Other words built with *tele-* include *telegram* (a message sent by telegraph), *telescope* (an instrument for making distant objects appear nearer), and *television* (the broadcasting of a moving image over a distance). Think about the meanings of these words: *telethermometer, telepathy, telephone.*

COMMON WORD-BUILDING ELEMENTS

English gets many of its words from the Latin and Greek languages. We say that those English words are derivatives of Latin or Greek words. Sometimes dozens of English words can be traced back to a single root, or base. Recognizing a root in an unfamiliar word can help you crack its meaning. Figure 3.2, for example, is a web that lays out words derived from the Latin verb *vertere,* meaning "to turn." You may already know that the word *reverse* means "to change direction or to turn in the opposite direction," but you may not recognize the meaning of the word *irreversible*. Linking the two and connecting them to the idea of "turning" can help you understand the meaning of the longer word: "not able to be reversed or changed back." Similarly, you may not recognize the word *versus* found on the web. Often we use this word, which comes directly from Latin, in talking

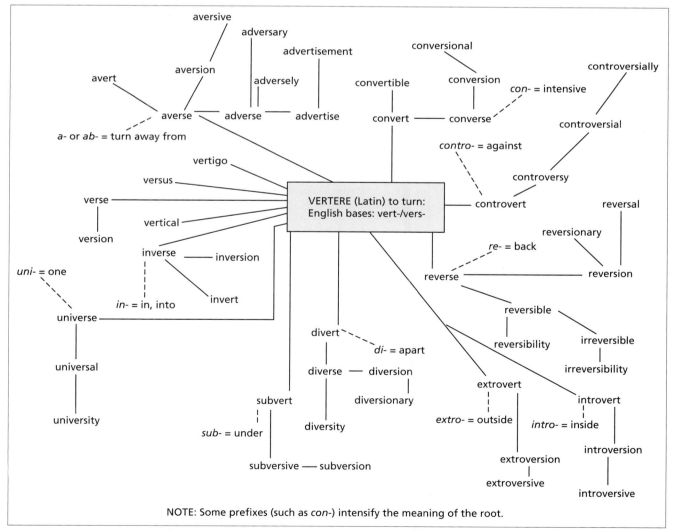

FIGURE 3.2 A Wheel of Words That Trace Their Origins to a Common Root: *Vertere*

about conflicts, as in "Good versus evil," or in talking about court cases, as in "*Roe versus Wade.*" Sometimes in books you will see this written as *Roe vs. Wade.* Using that context and the idea of turning, you can hypothesize that *versus* means "against." Note the number of derivatives on the web; actually there are many more, but they could not fit in the figure.

WORKSHOP 1: HIGHLIGHTING A COMMON ELEMENT WITHIN RELATED WORDS

Two commonly found elements are *bene-* and *mal-*. *Bene-* means "good or well"; *mal-* means just the opposite—"bad." See how those two elements help you to make sense out of this sentence: "One *benefit* of *malpractice insurance* is that the doctor can practice medicine without fear of financial ruin." What is a *benefit*? What is *malpractice insurance*?

Using a dictionary, locate other words that carry *bene-* or *mal-*. For each element, make a word tower like the ones in Figure 3.1. Simply list the words in two towers—one tower of words that contain *bene-*, one tower of words that contain *mal-*. Line up the words in each tower so that the key element (*bene-* or *mal-*) is in a column and the shared element is highlighted. Make your towers in your notebook, working collaboratively with a partner.

WORKSHOP 2: WEBBING WORDS BUILT FROM A COMMON BASE

Two Latin roots, or bases, found in a lot of English words are *dicto-*, meaning "to tell or say," and *scripto-*, meaning "to write." What does a person do when he or she dictates a letter? Why is a dictator called that? Similarly reason out the meaning of *script* in this sentence: "In a theater production, the actors use a script." What is a prescription?

Turning to a dictionary to help you to find examples, make a web of words derived from the root *dicto-*. Simply record the root at the center, or hub, of the web. Then inscribe, or write down, words derived from *dicto-* on spokes extending outward from the hub. Show at least four words. Make a similar web of words derived from *scripto-*. Work alone or collaboratively depending on your professor's instructions.

WORKSHOP 3: WEBBING MORE RELATED WORDS

On the back inside covers of this textbook are lists of roots from which English derives numerous words. Do you recognize any of the roots? Do you recognize any of the exemplar words?

For each of the roots, add one or two more exemplars, or example words. Then working collaboratively, select one root and create a web of English derivatives. You can rely on a dictionary to help you. You can use Figure 3.2 as a model. Your instructor may assign a particular root for your group to work on so that each group in your class is working with a different root. Be ready to share your web with the class and to talk about the meanings of the words you have organized on your web.

WORKSHOP 4: INCREASING YOUR AWARENESS OF WORD ELEMENTS

Here are some commonly used word parts, their meanings, and the definition of one word built from each part. In the blank column, write the word that fits the definition. Remember that *bio-* means "life" and that *tele-* means "sent over a distance." Work on this activity with a partner if your instructor suggests it.

	Word Part	Meaning of Part	Word	Meaning of the Word
1.	-scope	instrument for viewing	_____	instrument for viewing the heavens
2.	micro-	very small	_____	instrument for viewing small things
3.	-ology	the study of	_____	study of living things
4.	-ologist	one who studies	_____	one who studies small living things (Note: you must use both *bio* and *micro*)
5.	anthropo-	human person	_____	study of the development of humankind
6.	archaeo-	ancient times	_____	one who studies life in ancient times
7.	astro-	star	_____	study of heavens to predict human events
8.	chrono-	time	_____	study of time
9.	geo-	earth	_____	one who studies the earth and its forms
10.	hydro-	water	_____	study of water
11.	neuro-	nerves	_____	doctor who specializes in study of the nervous system
12.	patho-	disease	_____	person who studies tissues for evidence of disease
13.	psycho-	mind	_____	study of human behavior
14.	socio-	social	_____	person who studies human society
15.	theo-	god	_____	study of religion
16.	maxi-	greatest	_____	greatest amount possible
17.	mini-	smallest	_____	smallest amount possible
18.	frat-	brother	_____	organization for college men
19.	mat-	mother	_____	state of having mothered a child
20.	pat-	father	_____	state of having fathered a child
21.	ped- or pod-	foot	_____	one who walks, especially on city streets
22.	therm-	heat	_____	gadget for measuring temperature
23.	terr-	land, earth	_____	large piece of land
24.	mort-	death	_____	place for funerals
25.	ann(u)- or anni-	year	_____	happening once a year

Think
about . . .

How can we use word elements to crack the meaning of the word *dehydration?*

INDEPENDENT WORD STUDY: WORKING WITH WORD PARTS

Some word elements are clues to number meanings. For example,

mono-	means	one	*deca-*	means	ten
bi-	means	two	*cent-*	means	hundred
tri-	means	three	*mille-*	means	thousand
quadri-	means	four	*multi-*	means	many
quint-	means	five	*omni-*	means	all

Based on the word elements and meanings just given, pronounce each italicized word, and star the answer that gives its meaning.

1. In feudal times, the king was *omnipotent.*
   a. everywhere
   b. all powerful
   c. respected
   d. feared

2. In 1876 the United States celebrated the nation's *centennial.*
   a. ten-year anniversary
   b. hundred-year anniversary
   c. two-hundred-year anniversary
   d. thousand-year anniversary

3. In 1976 the United States celebrated the nation's *bicentennial.*
   a. ten-year anniversary
   b. hundred-year anniversary
   c. two-hundred-year anniversary
   d. thousand-year anniversary

4. How many *centimeters* are there in a meter?
   a. one
   b. ten
   c. one hundred
   d. one thousand

5. How many *milliliters* are there in a liter?
   a. one
   b. ten
   c. one hundred
   d. one thousand

6. The decade ending in 1870 saw the end of the Civil War. How long is a *decade?*
   a. one year
   b. ten years
   c. twenty years
   d. forty years

7. Because my friend was *bilingual,* she got a job as a translator. *Bilingual* means
   a. able to speak two languages.
   b. able to travel
   c. very intelligent.
   d. born outside the country.

8. Great Britain, France, and the United States entered into a *trilateral* trade agreement. *Trilateral* means
   a. having to do with business.
   b. three way.
   c. having to do with war.
   d. having to do with a triumphant victory.

9. Mr. Fitzpatrick fainted when he heard his wife had given birth to *quintuplets.* How many children were born?
   a. three
   b. four
   c. five
   d. six

10. The *quadricentennial* of the United States will take place in
    a. 2076
    b. 2176
    c. 2276
    d. 2376

11. The popular leader had a *multitude* of friends.
    a. ten
    b. a hundred
    c. a thousand
    d. a great number

12. No one can live for a *millennium.* How long is a *millennium?*
    a. ten years
    b. a hundred years
    c. two hundred years
    d. a thousand years

COMMON PREFIXES

A prefix is a letter or group of letters added to the beginning of a word. An example of a common prefix is *re-*, which means "again." To *reconsider* is simply to consider again. What meanings do you assign to these words?

- readjust _____

  _____

- reappoint _____

  _____

- reattach _____

  _____

- reassure _____

Seeing the prefix at the beginning of each word and assigning the meaning of *again* to it helps you to unlock the meaning of the whole word. However, not all words that begin with *re-* are built from the prefix. Cases in point are *read, ready,* and *reason.*

WORKSHOP 5: SEEING PREFIXES IN WORDS

With a workshop partner, pronounce each word that contains an italicized prefix. Then figure out the meaning of the italicized prefix and star the appropriate option. In the margin, jot a brief definition of each word containing a highlighted prefix.

1. Astrology is often considered a *pseudo*science because astrologers try to predict human events based on the stars.
   a. before   b. after   c. against   d. false   e. not

2. The man joined the *anti*war movement because he opposed violence in any form.
   a. before   b. after   c. against   d. false   e. not

3. As part of his *pre*operative treatment, he had to take antibiotics so that he would be ready for surgery.
   a. before   b. after   c. against   d. false   e. not

4. During the *post*war period, many people joined in to clear away the rubble.
   a. before   b. after   c. against   d. false   e. not

5. Because of his illness, he was *un*able to come.
   a. before   b. after   c. against   d. false   e. not

6. Two-year-old children often are *hyper*active.
   a. between   b. within   c. over   d. not

7. Although I wanted to go, it became *im*possible; I had to stay home.
   a. between   b. within   c. over   d. not

8. Because she was so unfriendly, I began to *dis*like her.
   a. between   b. within   c. over   d. not

9. When I traveled from New Hampshire to Massachusetts, I took the *inter*state highway.
   a. between   b. within   c. over   d. not

10. Because he hauled products from Los Angeles to San Francisco, he was said to be involved in *intra*state commerce.
    a. between   b. within   c. over   d. not

11. Because the ship was completely *sub*merged, we could not see it.
    a. under   b. above   c. around   d. across   e. before

12. The *trans*continental railroad connected the West and East coasts.
   a. under   b. above   c. around   d. across   e. before

13. The Revolutionary War *ante*dates the Civil War.
   a. under   b. above   c. around   d. across   e. before

14. The *super*intendent was in charge of the entire operation.
   a. under   b. above   c. around   d. across   e. before

15. Magellan's ship was the first to *circum*navigate the globe.
   a. under   b. above   c. around   d. across   e. before

16. The senator was *pro*war, a hawk who was ready to fight for a cause.
   a. against   b. for   c. not   d. half   e. together

17. The teacher drew a *semi*circle on the board next to a complete circle.
   a. against   b. for   c. badly   d. half   e. together

18. The executive *mis*managed the business; as a result the business lost money.
   a. against   b. for   c. badly   d. half   e. together

19. When nations *co*operate, peace is more likely.
   a. against   b. for   c. badly   d. half   e. together

20. Do not use a sharp tone of voice to *contra*dict someone.
   a. against   b. for   c. badly   d. half   e. together

WORKSHOP 6: MAKING A TABLE OF PREFIXES

Use the answers to the previous exercise to complete this summary chart of prefixes. Make your sample word one not used in the previous sentences.

Prefix	Prefix Meaning	Sample Word	Word Meaning
1. pseudo-			
2. anti-			
3. pre-			
4. post-			
5. un-			
6. hyper-			
7. im- or in-			
8. dis-			
9. inter-			
10. intra-			
11. sub-			
12. trans-			
13. ante-			
14. super-			
15. circum-			
16. pro-			
17. semi-			
18. mis-			
19. co- or com- or col-			
20. contra- or counter-			

COMMON SUFFIXES

A suffix is a letter or a group of letters that is added to the end of a word and may change the part of speech of that word. An example of a common suffix is *-ness*. It means "the state of." You have seen it on nouns formed from adjectives, such as *loveliness* (the state of being lovely), *thoughtfulness* (the state of being thoughtful), and *softness* (the state of being soft).

A second suffix you probably know is *-ical* or *-al*, which simply turns a noun into a word that can serve as an adjective. You have seen it on adjectives such as *practical* (adapted for actual use), *societal* (pertaining to society), and *theoretical* (based on theory).

Another common suffix is *-ize*, which means "to make." You have seen it on verbs such as *civilize* (to make civil), *personalize* (to make personal), and *categorize* (to put into categories).

Still another very common suffix is *-ion,* which means "state of" or "process of." You have seen it on nouns such as *invention* (the process of inventing), *limitation* (the state of being limited), and *innovation* (the process of innovating, or creatively changing).

Think
about . . .
What other examples do you know? Write some here.

WORKSHOP 7: SEEING SUFFIXES IN WORDS

Here are other suffixes. For each one, give the meaning of the sample word, reasoning from the meaning of the suffix. Then give an example of another word that contains the suffix.

Suffix	Meaning	Word	Meaning	Another Word
-able	able to be	likable	_____	_____
-ous or -ious	full of	joyous	_____	_____
-ful	full of	peaceful	_____	_____
-y	state of being	rainy	_____	_____
-ify	to make	simplify	_____	_____
-er or -or	a person who	banker	_____	_____
-ist	one who does, is concerned with, or holds certain beliefs	communist	_____	_____

Circle the suffixes in the italicized words. Then pronounce each word and write its definition using word elements and context clues.

1. It was a *memorable* occasion. I will always remember it.

2. Without *innovation* the world would stand still. Progress depends on *innovation.* (Reminder: You already know the meaning of *novice.*)

3. There must be some way of joining the work of the two committees. Good *articulation* is necessary.

Think
about . . .
With a partner, brainstorm a list of *-able* and *-tion* words. Be able to use the meaning of the suffix to tell the meaning of each word.

4. The oval arch was a *radical* departure from the way it was done before. In that respect it was an innovation.

5. Surface changes are not enough. Deep *structural* changes are required.

6. Scientists are concerned with *theoretical* ideas as well as practical applications.

7. Do not confuse him. Try to *clarify* the situation instead.

COMPOUND WORDS

A compound word is built from two other words. The resulting word has some of the meaning of the two building blocks. For example, *househusband* is a new word made from *house* and *husband*. A househusband is a husband who stays home and looks after house and family.

WORKSHOP 8: SEEING WORDS WITHIN WORDS

Can you brainstorm other compound words? Working with a classmate, come up with at least three such words and be ready to explain the meaning of each based on the combining parts. Then, using word elements and context clues, figure out the meaning of each italicized compound word.

1. One-parent *households* are becoming more common today.

2. As more married women enter the *workforce*, there is greater need for *daycare* for children.

3. If you don't balance your *checkbook* each month, you risk the possibility of an *overdraft*.

4. The work of *housekeepers* is *undervalued*; we do not seem to respect the work of those who keep our families running.

SYLLABLE SEGMENTS

So far, in this chapter we have been suggesting that when you see a new word, you should not look at it as one unit or as a series of individual letters. Rather, you should see the word in terms of its parts, pronouncing it based on its parts and using the meanings of the parts to crack the meaning of the new word. Sometimes just pronouncing the individual parts of a word helps you with the meaning, because in pronouncing the word segment by segment, you may recognize it as a word you use in talking.

As you probably know, the segments of a word are called syllables. Here are a few guidelines for pronouncing the syllable segments of a word:

1. Each syllable of a word contains one vowel sound. For example, pronounce the word *segment.* How many syllables are in the word? *Vowel* sounds? Pronounce the word *vowel.* How many syllables are in the word? *vowel* sounds?

2. Some words have a vowel followed by two consonants. Typically you break such words between the two consonants. Pronounce these words: *segment, syllable, suggest.* Where did you make the syllable break in each case? In the margin jot down some examples of words that divide in the same way.

3. Some consonants generally stick together and are pronounced as a whole; *br, gr, tr, st, str, cr, ph, ch,* and *sh* are examples. Pronounce these words: *machine, degrade, abrasive.* Where do these words divide into syllables? Why? In the margin jot down some examples of words that divide in the same way.

4. When words end with a consonant followed by *le,* pronounce this combination as one unaccented syllable. The word *syllable* is an example; so is the word *example.* Can you think of some others that work in the same way? List a few in the margin.

5. Some syllables are accented. You stress, or emphasize, them more than other syllables. The syllable you stress most carries the primary accent. A syllable you stress a little bit less carries the secondary accent. In contrast, some syllables are not accented.

The point here is not that you should memorize these five guidelines as rules. The point is to get in the habit of seeing words made up of syllable segments that you pronounce one by one in cracking the meaning of a new word. As you go on to study the selections in this book, you should try to see and pronounce the italicized new words in segments, focusing on the parts you have been learning about in this chapter: prefixes, suffixes, roots, and syllables.

SELECTION 1

Cohabitation (SOCIOLOGY)

A WORD STUDY WORKSHOP

Learning New Words

Study the elements in the chart. Predict the meaning of the sample words.

Word Element	Meaning	Word Element	Meaning
un- (as in *unmarried*)	not	equi- (as in *equality*)	equal
pre- (as in *premaritally*)	before	mari- (as in *marital*)	related to marriage
per- (as in *percent*)	for each	cent- (as in *century*)	one hundred
co-, com-, con-(as in *cohabit*)	together	habi- (as in *cohabit*)	to have or hold
deca- (as in *decade*)	ten	bene- (as in *benefit*)	good
signi- (as in *signify*)	sign	-fy (as in *signify*)	make
hetero- (as in *heterosexual*)	other		

Getting Ready to Read

Read the title, the two subheadings, the first sentence of the first paragraph, and the last sentence of the last paragraph of the selection.

- What is this selection about? _____

- What do you know about this topic? _____

_____

- How difficult do you gauge this selection to be? _____

_____

Reading with Meaning

Read the selection, using word elements to help you figure out important words.

Cohabitation
Kathryn Kelley and Donn Byrne

Did You KNOW?

Co- (com-, con-) is a prefix meaning "together." Other words with the prefix are *community* and *conflict*.

It may seem strange in the 1990s, but only a relatively few years ago, an unmarried couple who shared the same house or apartment were described as "living in sin" or "shacking up." **Cohabitation** was a daring act—and it was a violation of the law in many parts of the United States. Today, about 80 percent of the college couples who live together are married while 20 percent are not. The percentage of unmarried couples who engage in cohabitation (unmarried, heterosexual couples living together and engaging in sex) has risen dramatically—a figure about ten times greater now than in the 1950s.

One of the less serious problems is what to call the person with whom you are living—significant other, lover, roommate, housemate, cohabitor? The U.S. Census Bureau uses POSSLQ (Persons of Opposite Sex Sharing Living Quarters), but no one else seems to. Another possible term that is growing in popularity is *spousal equivalent* (Keeney, 1990). What are the implications of this increasingly familiar lifestyle for the institution of marriage?

Effects of Cohabitation

Those who cohabit are very likely to marry eventually, either the partner with whom they live or someone else. Does the experience of cohabitation affect a subsequent marriage? If marriages are enhanced by previous cohabitation, the effect is extremely small. Several studies comparing couples who did and did not live together prior to marriage showed no differences between them in emotional closeness, satisfaction, number of conflicts, or equality of sharing (Watson, 1983). There was slightly less marital satisfaction among those who had lived together before marrying, but this may simply reflect the typical decrease in satisfaction found during the first decade of intimate relationships. Perhaps for the same reasons, those who cohabit and then marry later on are found to have a divorce rate 80 percent higher than those who did not live together premaritally, according to a Swedish study of over 4,000 adults between the ages of 20 and 44.

Social and Legal Aspects of Cohabitation

Among the reasons for the increased popularity of cohabitation are the appeal of a seemingly uncomplicated alternative to marriage and the current acceptance of such living arrangements.

For example, college housing regulations have become less restrictive about cohabitation on most campuses. This change may represent a delayed effect of the politically active climate of the 1960s, including an emphasis by the women's movement supporting greater responsibility for women. Also, the availability of effective birth control methods makes it easier for those who are not married to engage in intercourse with relative safety.

A couple planning to cohabit could benefit, however, by considering some of the legal and practical issues involved. Couples who live together and then break up do not have the same legal rights as do married couples seeking a divorce. When there is joint property to be divided or the question of a monetary settlement, for example, the law is much less clear about cohabitors than about spouses. Other issues include such matters

FIGURE 3.3 Cohabitation

as insurance and health benefits, discriminatory tax laws, and inheritance in the absence of a will. For the loving couple embarking on a new life of romance and sexuality, these issues are seldom discussed or even thought about, but they can eventually arise as matters of extreme importance.   [548 words]

Monitoring Comprehension and Writing in Response

A. Using the information in the chart at the beginning of the selection, circle the word element or elements in each word that are clues to meaning. Then using that clue and the context of the word in the selection, propose a meaning for each word. Do this with a workshop partner.

1. cohabit

2. marital

3. premarital

4. equality

5. heterosexual

Think
about . . .

Study the diacritical marks that show you how to pronounce this word: măr´ ə təl. Pronounce *marital* in syllable units. The mark ə is a schwa. It indicates an unstressed vowel sound. Another example is found in běn´ ə fĭt. Pronounce all ten words with a partner, watching for syllable breaks.

6. significant

7. percent

8. benefit

9. unmarried

10. lifestyle (compound word)

B. What reasons do you see for not cohabiting before marriage? In your notebook write a paragraph in which you set forth those reasons as well as reasons for cohabitation, as you see them.

SELECTION 2

The Internet in Postindustrial Society (TECHNOLOGY)

A Word Study Workshop

Learning New Words

Your knowledge of prefixes can help you crack the meaning of a multisyllabic (many-syllable) word, especially when you already know the root at the base of it. Here is a chart of prefixes, some of which you have already studied, that will help you better understand the words and ideas in the selection. Predict the meaning of each sample word based on the meaning of the prefix.

Word Part	Meaning	Word Part	Meaning
re- (as in *review*)	again	de- (as in *depersonalize*)	do or make the opposite of
post- (as in *postwar*)	after	trans- (as in *transatlantic*)	across
inter- (as in *intercity*)	between	non- (as in *nonproductive*)	not
super- (as in *superfund*)	above, over	un- (as in *unattainable*)	not
fore- (as in *foresight*)	before, earlier	e- or ex- (as in *expectations*)	out of

Getting Ready to Read

Read the title and first paragraph. Then answer these questions before proceeding.

- What is this article going to be about? _____

- Based on the meaning of the prefix *post-*, predict the meaning of the term *postindustrial.* _____

- What comes to your mind when you think of the Internet? _____

  _____

- Evaluate the reading load for you of this article: light, average, heavy.

Reading with Meaning

Read the article. Think about the words in boldface type as you go along.

The Internet in Postindustrial Society

David Popenoe

In 1973, Daniel Bell described his expectations for the future of society in his book, *The Coming of Post-Industrial Society*. In contrast to the manufacturing base of industrial society, postindustrial society would rely on knowledge and information as it **evolved** from an economy that produced goods to one that would provide services.

The **Internet,** the technology that would make this possible, was in its infancy when Bell's book was published. While many Americans today regard the Internet as technology's latest toy, it is actually the product of the Cold War. The tensions between communist and **noncommunist** nations fed constant fears of a nuclear war. As a result, the United States wanted to develop a communications network that could survive such an attack. Ideas for such a system began to develop in the mid-1960s. And in 1969, the U.S. Defense Department commissioned the Advanced Research project Agency to create ARPANET—a huge military computer network.

The system they created allowed data to move freely around this military network so that if any of its computers became damaged, the data could be moved via alternate routes. When the American military split away from ARPANET in the early 1980s, the system became known as the Internet. Shortly thereafter, both academic institutions and other government agencies (particularly the National Science Foundation) joined the Internet and connected their own computer networks to the system.

In 1997 over 30 million households were connected to the Internet. That number jumped to over 60 million worldwide by the year 2000, convincing many businesspeople that the Internet will become the "powerful engine of economic growth." Recent transformations in the American workplace indicate that this is already happening.

Consider, for example, the *virtual workplace*. This term, which sounds more like science fiction than reality, refers to any worksite located outside the traditional office setting where work is done (Bredin, 1996). This is typically a high-tech home office that connects workers to other members of this virtual organization or to their clients.

Many Fortune 500 companies are **decentralizing** their operations in this way and **recreating** themselves around their information networks. The Internet, along with fax machines, toll-free telephone lines, and overnight mail services, makes all this possible. Virtual workplaces turn out to be bargains for corporations that want to cut the high cost of office space, especially in pricey urban areas. For example, Citibank has relocated its credit operations to South Dakota (*Time,* Spring 1995). Dell Computer, which employees 25 corporate sales executives working out of their homes in the suburbs of Manhattan and Seattle, operates a retail store with no location. And Journal Graphics, the vendor of transcripts for television programs, lists Grant Street, Denver, as its address but actually operates out of its employees' homes.

While some sociologists have questioned Bell's predictions about postindustrial society, these examples illustrate many of the changes that he **foresaw.** It is clear, for example, that we are entering the information age and that we have the technology necessary to support an economy based on its exchange. As the **transmission** of credit information becomes more secure, businesses will increasingly use the Internet to market financial and travel services (*Newsweek,* January 27, 1997). And they have already recognized that the Web is particularly well-suited for business-to-business marketing.

Changes in the American workplace also illustrate how businesses are decentralizing their operations and abandoning bureaucratic organizational styles in favor of more flexible forms. The Internet has created a **superhighway** that allows workers to telecommute. But, as Bell predicted, this may have some drawbacks. While the Internet will increase relationships among people, these are likely to be temporary and **unstable.**

The Internet clearly provides the kind of technology necessary for postindustrial society. But will the kind of economy it promises be good for society? Social analysts take two opposite positions on this question. Some, like Bell, are optimistic and believe that technology will free people from alienating labor. The Internet will spare Americans

Did You KNOW?

The root *volve-* is from the Latin word *volvere,* which means "to roll"; you have seen the root in *revolve* and *revolution.*

Did You KNOW?

The root *mit-* is from the Latin word *mittere,* which means "to send"; you have seen the root in *mission* and *remit.*

from many stressful parts of work—long commutes, rigid bureaucracies, and the watchful eye of the boss. But others see an increasingly stratified society that has no place for poorly educated, unskilled workers. While the Internet is regarded as the most democratic of media—where people are judged not by their race, gender, or social class—it is out of reach for millions of those people who lack access to a computer and a high-speed telecommunications link. For these Americans, the Internet does not promise such a rosy portrait of postindustrial society.

Monitoring Your Comprehension and Writing in Response

A. Pronounce each of these words by focusing on the word elements and the syllables. Then, based on the clues supplied by the word elements and the context, hypothesize and jot down the meaning of the words. Do this with a partner.

1. evolved

2. Internet

3. noncommunist

4. decentralizing

5. re-creating

6. foresaw

7. transmission

8. superhighway

9. unstable

B. In the article are many compound words: *drawbacks, worldwide, tollfree, overnight, worksite, network, households*. Quickly, put a slash between the component parts of each of these words. Tell a partner the meaning of the component elements and each compound word.

C. On your own, write a definition of the term *virtual workplace* based on the ideas cited in the article and the component elements of the compound word *workplace*.

SELECTION 3

Food Chains (ECOLOGY)

A Word Study Workshop

Learning New Words

As you read the next selection, you will notice some words built from affixes and roots. An example is the word *biological*, which is built from *bio*, meaning "life," and *ology*, meaning "the study of." Another example is *photosynthesis*, built from *phot-*, meaning "light," and *synthesis*, meaning "the combining of parts." The prefix *syn-* means "together."

As you read, look out for technical words, especially those made up of affixes and roots. Circle and pronounce the technical terms as you read. Using both context and word structure, figure out their meaning. In the margin write the meanings of words you circle.

This selection is typical of college science texts, which are often heavy with technical vocabulary. In reading, you have to unlock the meanings of the technical terms.

Getting Ready to Read

Preview this selection, which is taken from an environmental science book, by reading the title and first sentence and by studying the illustrations on pages 57 and 58.

- What is this selection about? _____

- What, if anything, do you already know about that topic? _____

  _____

- How difficult is the reading load for you? _____

- What two questions do you expect to answer by the time you finish reading the selection? Use the title to help you write the questions. _____

  _____

Reading with Meaning

Now read the selection, keeping in mind your purpose: to figure out the meaning of technical terms through use of the word elements.

Food Chains
Daniel D. Chiras*

In the biological world you are one of two things, either a producer or a consumer. (Only rarely can you be both.) **Producers** are the organisms that support the entire living world through photosynthesis. Plants, algae, and cyanobacteria are the key producers of

*From *Environmental Science*, Third Edition, by Daniel Chiras (©) 1991 by the Benjamin/Cummings Publishing Company. Reprinted by permission of the author.

Did You
KNOW?

Hetero- means "other."
You find it also on the
word *heterosexual. Auto-*
means "self." You see it
on the word *automobile.*

energy-rich organic materials. They are also called **autotrophs** (from the Greek root "troph"—to feed, nourish), because they literally nourish themselves photosynthetically, that is, by using sunlight and atmospheric carbon dioxide to make the food materials they need to survive. **Consumers** feed on plants and other organisms and are called **heterotrophs,** because they are nourished by consuming other organisms.

Consumer organisms that feed exclusively on plants are called **herbivores.** Cattle, deer, elk, and tomato hornworms are examples. Those consumers that feed exclusively on other animals, such as the mountain lion, are **carnivores.** Those consumers that feed on both plants and animals, such as humans, bears, and raccoons, are **omnivores.**

The interconnections among producers and consumers are visible all around us. Mice living in and around our homes, for example, eat the seeds of domestic and wild plants and, in turn, are preyed on by cats and hawks.

A series of organisms, each feeding on the preceding one, forms a **food chain.** Two basic types of food chains exist in nature: grazer and decomposer. **Grazer food chains,** like the one discussed above, are so named because they start with plants and with grazers, organisms that feed on plants. . . . In the second type—the **decomposer,** or **detritus, food chain**—organic waste material is the major food source. **Detritus** is organic waste which comes from plants and animals. . . .

Food chains are conduits for the flow of energy and nutrients through ecosystems. The sun's energy is first captured by plants and stored in organic molecules, which then pass through the grazer and decomposer food chains. In addition, plants incorporate a variety of inorganic materials such as nitrogen, phosphorus, and magnesium from the soil. These **chemical nutrients** become part of the plant's living matter. When the green plant is consumed, these nutrients enter the food chain. They are eventually returned to the environment by the decomposer food chain.   [366 words]

FIGURE 3.4 The Autotrophs
Plants Such As These Are Autotrophs; They Make Their Own Food Through Photosynthesis.

FIGURE 3.5 The Heterotrophs
Animals Such As These Are Heterotrophs; They Get Their Energy by Consuming Organic Matter.

Monitoring Comprehension and Writing with New Words

A. Here is a list of elements from words in Selection 3. Next to each is the meaning of the element. In the third column, write a word from the selection that contains the element. In the fourth column, write the meaning of the word, using the context and the word structure. You may work collaboratively.

Element	Meaning of Element	Word with the Element	Meaning of the Word
1. auto-	self	autotroph	organism that nourishes itself by making food
2. hetero-	other		
3. herb-	grass		
4. vore-	eat, devour		
5. carn-	flesh, meat		
6. omni-	all		
7. syn-	together		
8. phot-	light		
9. bio-	life		
10. inter-	between		

B. Complete the following chart. Refer to the article to find the answers.

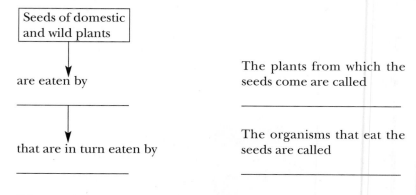

Seeds of domestic and wild plants	
↓	
are eaten by	The plants from which the seeds come are called
_____	_____
↓	
that are in turn eaten by	The organisms that eat the seeds are called
_____	_____

What kind of a food chain have you just diagrammed? _____

C. Mark the following either *T* (true) or *F* (false).

_____ 1. A human being is an omnivore.

_____ 2. A green plant is a carnivore.

_____ 3. A mountain lion is an herbivore.

_____ 4. Human beings are consumers.

_____ 5. Green plants are producers.

_____ 6. Photosynthesis is the process in which plants use sunlight and carbon dioxide to make food material.

D. Write two sentences in your notebook, one in which you tell about autotrophs and one in which you tell about heterotrophs. Writing after reading is an effective way to re-view what you have read and to firm up your understanding of new terms.

EXTENDING WHAT YOU HAVE LEARNED

Handling Unfamiliar Words in Reading

In Chapters 2 and 3, you have been learning how to handle unfamiliar words in reading. Figure 3.6 summarizes the steps in a comprehensive strategy for unlocking the meaning of new words. This word-unlocking strategy is particularly important as you read text-books that are heavy with technical terms. You need to know those terms to understand important ideas. This is especially true when you read science textbooks. In contrast, in doing recreational reading, you do not need to know the meaning of all the terms used; you often can get the main ideas without knowing the meaning of every word.

Applying the Strategy

Read two editorials in your local newspaper. Locate six words from the editorials that you can define based on your understanding of roots, prefixes, and affixes. Circle them. In the margin of the article, note the meanings of the circled words. Your instructor may ask you to share an editorial and the circled words with the class.

Building Your Vocabulary

Because a large vocabulary is important in reading, you should also develop a strategy for building your personal vocabulary. The strategy we introduced in this chapter is keeping a vocabulary notebook.

COMPREHENSIVE WORD-UNLOCKING STRATEGY:

1. Look at the unfamiliar word in relation to the sentence in which it appears. Ask: Does the sentence provide a clue to the meaning of the word?
   - Is there a definition built into the sentence? If so, what does it say?
   - Is there a synonym that provides a clue to the meaning? If so, what is it?
   - Are there explanations or descriptions that relate to the unfamiliar word? If so, do they suggest the meaning of the unfamiliar word?
   - Are there words nearby that express contrasting meanings? If so, do they hint at the meaning of the unfamiliar word?
   - Does the overall sense of the sentence supply a clue?

2. Look at the word in terms of its component parts: roots, prefixes, suffixes, other words, or syllables. Ask: Can I see word parts that I know? Can I use the parts to get at the meaning of the whole?

3. Ask: Can I use the parts and syllables to help me pronounce the word? Do I recognize the word by its sound?

4. Decide: Should I check the dictionary? Try out the various meanings that the dictionary gives to see which fits in the context of the sentence. If necessary, reread the sentence and even the surrounding paragraph to be sure of the meaning.

FIGURE 3.6 A Comprehensive Strategy for Unlocking Word Meaning

As you read a new word that has general usefulness, record it in a personal vocabulary notebook. Record the meaning of the word and a sample sentence using that word. For example, you could begin your vocabulary notebook with the words *clarify* and *innovation*. As you add words to your notebook, you may find it helpful to section it alphabetically. Keep a page for words that begin with the letter *a*, another page for *b* words, and so forth.

This strategy will work only if you think about the words you record after you have written them down in your notebook. For example, today as you walk around, consider where you might apply the word *innovation*. Where do you see examples of innovation? When have you been innovative?

If you record and keep thinking about two new words each day, your vocabulary will grow. Research shows that one or two encounters with a word are not enough for you to learn a word. To "own" a word—to make it yours—you must encounter that word many times. Therefore, from time to time, thumb through your personal vocabulary notebook and think about your entries. Make an effort to use those words in speaking and writing.

Going Online

Check these sites on the World Wide Web to find out more about words:

- <www.word-detective.com> *The Word Detective* is an online version of Evan Morris's syndicated column. Morris traces the origins of English words and solves etymological problems.

- <www.wilton.net/etyma.htm> *Wilton's Etymology Page* explains how popular expressions came into the English language.

- <www.pw1.netcome.com/~rlederer/index.htm> *Richard Lederer's Verbivore* is an online version of Lederer's newspaper column; it gives tips for researching words.

- <www.wordwizard.com> *The Word Wizard* supplies a variety of resources dealing with language.

PART THREE
COMPREHENSION

CHAPTER 4 Grasping the Main Idea of a Paragraph

CHAPTER 5 Grasping the Thesis, or Main Idea, of an Entire Selection

CHAPTER 6 Relating Main Ideas and Details

CHAPTER 7 Using Clue Words to Anticipate an Author's Thoughts

CHAPTER 8 Critical Thinking: Applying, Comparing, Inferring, Concluding, and Judging

 4

Grasping the Main Idea of a Paragraph

OBJECTIVE

In this chapter, you will develop a strategy for grasping the main idea of paragraphs and selections. Specifically, you will learn to

1. Identify the topic of a paragraph;
2. Distinguish between a general idea and specific details that support it;
3. Find the topic sentence when the main idea is stated explicitly;
4. Infer, or figure out, the main idea when it is implied; and
5. Distinguish among paragraph structures—inductive, deductive, and linear—and use the structure of a paragraph in determining the main idea.

At the same time, you will learn how to monitor, or check on, your own comprehension and use fix-up strategies when you know you do not understand.

GRASPING THE MAIN IDEA

When authors write, they have an idea in mind that they are trying to get across. This is especially true as authors compose paragraphs. They organize each paragraph around one topic—the topic that the paragraph is about. They make one major point about the topic. That major point of the paragraph is the *main idea*.

Sometimes writers state their main idea explicitly somewhere in the paragraph—at the beginning, in the middle, or at the end. The sentence in which they state the main idea is the *topic sentence*. At other times, writers include a sentence in which they almost state the main idea: They give a clear clue about it. At still other times, though, writers may leave the main idea unstated. In this case, understanding is more difficult for you; you must infer, or figure out, the main idea for yourself.

IDENTIFYING THE TOPIC

The first thing you must be able to do to get at the main idea of a paragraph is to identify the topic—the subject of the paragraph. Think of the paragraph as a wheel with the topic being the hub, the central core around which the whole wheel (or paragraph) spins. Your strategy for topic identification is to ask yourself, "What is this about?" You keep asking yourself that question as you read a paragraph. Sometimes you can spot the topic by looking for a word or two that are repeated. Usually you can state the topic in a few words.

Let's practice this topic-finding strategy. Reread the first paragraph in the section titled "Grasping the Main Idea." Ask, "What is it about?" To answer, you say to yourself in your mind, "The author keeps talking about paragraphs and the way they are designed. This must be the topic: paragraph organization." Reread the second paragraph in the section. Ask, "What is it about?" Did you say to yourself, "This is about different ways to organize a paragraph"? That is the topic.

WORKSHOP 1: TOPIC-FINDING

Return to Chapter 1, Selection 1—"A Nation on the Move: America Moves West." Collaborate with a workshop partner to identify the topic of each paragraph. In the margin, jot down your topics as you find them. For example, working with the first paragraph of "A Nation on the Move," you have three clues to the topic: the phrase "migrating into the region," the phrase "moving westward," and the title "A Nation on the Move" because this is the first paragraph of the selection. What is the topic? Write it in the margin next to the paragraph in Chapter 1. Then try the other paragraphs in that selection.

WORKSHOP 2: MORE TOPIC-FINDING

If you need more practice identifying the topic of a paragraph, reread Selection 2 of Chapter 1, jotting down the topic of each paragraph in the margin. Remember to ask the topic-finding question, "What is this paragraph about?" Remember to visualize the paragraph as a wheel that is spinning around a topic hub.

DISTINGUISHING BETWEEN GENERAL AND SPECIFIC POINTS

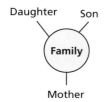

A second thing you must be able to do to get at the main idea is to distinguish between general and specific points. Which of these words expresses the most general concept: *family, daughter, son, mother?* The word *family* is the most general. A family is made up of specific people: daughter, son, mother, and others. The web in the margin highlights the relationship between the general word and the more specific terms.

WORKSHOP 3: DISTINGUISHING GENERAL AND SPECIFIC WORDS

Other general words are *furniture, fuel, transportation, foods,* and *countries.* Working in three-person teams, brainstorm and web specific items that are part of each of these general ones. Then think of a general word of your own and web specific components of it. Be ready to share your webs.

Just as some words express more general ideas than other words, some sentences express more general ideas than other sentences. For example, this is a general statement: *Teenage parents face numerous problems.* What are some specific sentences that support this general one by naming some of the problems teenage parents face? Here are some examples:

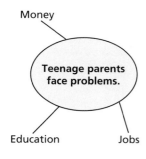

- Teenage parents often have little money to take care of their children.
- Teenage parents have trouble staying in school.
- Teenage parents often have to take lower-level jobs.

See the web in the margin that highlights the relationship between the general idea and the specific ones that are related to it.

WORKSHOP 4: DISTINGUISHING BETWEEN GENERAL AND SPECIFIC STATEMENTS

Some other general statements are listed next. Working alone or collaborating in teams, brainstorm and web specific points, or details that expand on each general statement. Remember that your specific points in each instance must support the general one: They should give examples, supply added detail, or clarify the general statement.

- *General Statement 1:* During their first year in college, students encounter problems they may not have had before.
- *General Statement 2:* All colleges have certain basic course requirements.
- *General Statement 3:* College students join sororities and fraternities for many different reasons.

IDENTIFYING TOPICS AND GENERAL STATEMENTS: MARRIAGE CUSTOMS

In a paragraph, the general point that the author is making about a topic is the main idea. The specific points are the details that support the main idea. Here is an example. The four sentences listed next are all about one topic. One of the four sentences expresses a general idea about that topic; you could use it as the topic sentence of a paragraph. The other three sentences expand the main idea by providing details, or specific points. You could use them as supporting sentences in a paragraph.

1. In days past, people married primarily for economic, social, and political reasons rather than for love.
2. Men who had a title but whose estates had dwindled to nothing married heiresses to restore the family fortune.
3. Marriage often was a way to strengthen existing social ties.
4. Political alliances between countries and regions were cemented through the marriage of sons and daughters of ruling monarchs.

What is the topic of these sentences? What are they all about? If you say, "Reasons for marriage in the past," you are getting at the hub of this wheel. Each sentence is talking about a reason or reasons for marriage. Note the repeated use of the word *marriage*. Note the word *reasons* in the first sentence.

Which is the most general statement? Sentence 1 is because it talks about general reasons for marriage: economic, social, and political. Sentences 2, 3, and 4 are details that elaborate on the economic, social, and political reasons. They support the general idea that people married for reasons other than love. Figure 4.1 maps the relationship between the main idea statement and the supporting details. Tell your workshop partner how the arrows in Figure 4.1 clarify the relationship.

WORKSHOP 5: DISTINGUISHING BETWEEN MAIN IDEA AND SUPPORTING DETAILS

The sentences in this activity describe marriage yesterday and today. In each group of sentences, one sentence states a more general idea; actually, it could stand as the topic sentence of a paragraph. The other sentences in each group give details related to that general idea. They could follow the topic sentence in the paragraph.

Working with a partner, identify the topic of the four sentences in each grouping by asking, "What are they all about?" Jot down the topic in the margin. Then star the most general sentence in the group. In doing this, keep asking, "Which statement expresses the most general idea about the topic?" When you have completed the ten items, select one group. In your notebook, draw a structure diagram that clarifies the relationship

Topic: Past reasons
for marriage

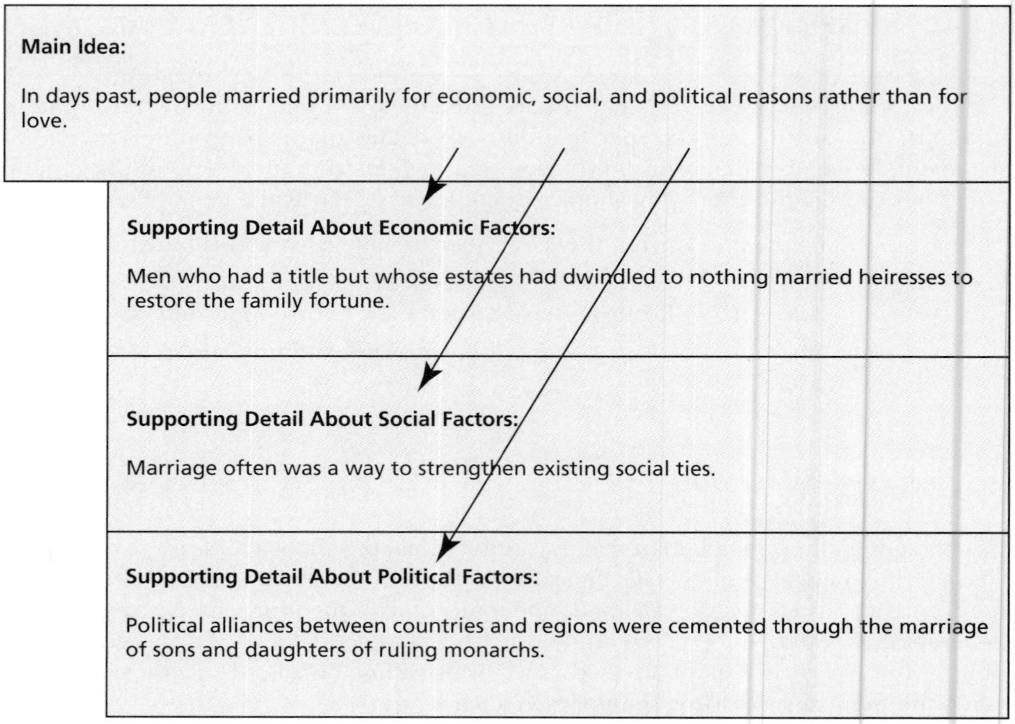

> **Main Idea:**
>
> In days past, people married primarily for economic, social, and political reasons rather than for love.
>
> ---
>
> **Supporting Detail About Economic Factors:**
>
> Men who had a title but whose estates had dwindled to nothing married heiresses to restore the family fortune.
>
> ---
>
> **Supporting Detail About Social Factors:**
>
> Marriage often was a way to strengthen existing social ties.
>
> ---
>
> **Supporting Detail About Political Factors:**
>
> Political alliances between countries and regions were cemented through the marriage of sons and daughters of ruling monarchs.

FIGURE 4.1   A Diagram, or Relational Map, Showing the Main Idea and Supporting Details
Note that the details support the main idea by elaborating on the economic, social, and political reasons for marriage.

between the general idea and the related details in that group of sentences. Use a design like that in Figure 4.1, or—better yet—create a design of your own to show the relationship. (Note: Because this activity requires higher-level thinking, a "think along" is given for Group one to demonstrate how to think through the relationships.)

Topic:

1. Group one
   a. In some cases, a marriage contract was arranged when the prospective bride and groom were children.
   b. Sometimes the contract for the arranged marriage was signed before the birth of the prospective bride and groom.
   c. In the past, marriages often were arranged by the young people's families; the bride and groom had little or no choice in the matter.
   d. Many times in an arranged marriage, the bride and groom had never seen each other before the ceremony.

   *[**A think along:** Sentence a talks about the contract in an arranged marriage, sentence b about signing the contract, sentence c about the lack of choice in an arranged marriage, and sentence d about the bride and groom in the arranged marriage. I say to myself, "They are all about arranged marriages. That's the topic. That is the common thread here—what the sentences are about. I will jot down the topic in the margin."*

   Which is the most general sentence? Sentence c gives the definition of arranged marriage: The bride and groom have no choice, which is the general idea of an arranged marriage. The first two sentences (a and b) support that idea with a detail about when marriages are arranged—in childhood or even at birth. The last (d) gives another fact about arranged marriages—that the couple may have never seen each other before the ceremony. The most general idea here is stated in sentence c.]

Topic:

2. Group two
   a. For their services in bringing a couple together, matchmakers received a fee.
   b. The matchmaker was an important player in the marriage game.

   c. Matchmakers knew many families in a region and could recommend a prospective mate.

   d. Matchmakers negotiated the contract between the families of the prospective bride and groom.

3. Group three   **Topic:**

   a. A woman without a dowry had few chances for marriage, despite how personable or attractive she might be.

   b. In some societies when a couple married, property passed from the family of the wife to the family of the husband.

   c. The property in question was called a dowry.

   d. A woman with a large dowry was considered highly marriageable, and she would have many suitors.

4. Group four   **Topic:**

   a. In this case, the property in question was called the bride's price.

   b. When a bride's price was the custom, women were viewed as valuable assets.

   c. The family losing a daughter had to be compensated for its loss.

   d. In some marriages, property passed from the husband's family to the wife's.

5. Group five   **Topic:**

   a. The woman's wealth was put under the control of her husband even though she might have been more capable than he to manage it.

   b. The man could beat his wife without fear of punishment.

   c. In taking her marriage vows, the wife promised to obey her husband.

   d. The woman's position in the marriage was inferior to her husband's.

6. Group six   **Topic:**

   a. Under a system of polyandry, a woman can take more than one husband at any one time.

   b. Monogamy, the most common marital arrangement, is the union of one man and one woman.

   c. Polygyny is the practice of having more than one wife at any one time.

   d. Marriage can take many forms, although not all are equally common.

7. Group seven   **Topic:**

   a. Today most couples choose their own mates and make their choices based on a variety of factors.

   b. Men and women look for compatibility in a marriage partner.

   c. Young people search for partners who "turn them on."

   d. Similar education level and interests are factors in the choice of a partner.

8. Group eight   **Topic:**

   a. Young adults place ads in the personal section of newspapers describing the kind of person they would like to meet.

   b. Some people go to singles bars to mingle and meet members of the opposite sex.

   c. In today's mobile society, people in search of a marriage partner may have trouble finding their ideal mate.

   d. Marriage brokers now use videos and computers to assist people in their pursuit of a mate.

9. Group nine   **Topic:**

   a. Today in some families, marriage is looked upon as an equal partnership between a man and a woman.

   b. Husbands and wives cooperate in doing the household chores.

   c. Both men and women contribute to the family assets by working outside the home.

   d. Husbands and wives share responsibility for the care of the children.

Topic: _____

10. Group ten
    a. In a recent study, more than 90 percent of teenagers indicated that they expect to marry at some point in their lives.
    b. Most people want to marry and have been married at least once by the time they reach age fifty-five.
    c. Research shows that more than 92 percent of men fifty-five years old or older have been married at least once.
    d. Studies indicate that more than 95 percent of women fifty-five years old or older have been married at least once.

GRASPING THE MAIN IDEA: DEDUCTIVE, INDUCTIVE, AND LINEAR PARAGRAPHS

In reading, it is important to identify the main idea of a paragraph or any other block of text. A strategy for sifting through information to grasp the main idea has these steps:

MAIN IDEA
STRATEGY

→ Identify the topic—what the paragraph or the block of text is about. Mentally visualize the topic as the hub about which the paragraph or text spins.

→ Ask as you read each detail, "How does this detail relate to the one before it? What are these details telling me about the topic? What point about the topic is the author making?"

→ Ask as you read a paragraph, "Is there a sentence that states—or almost states—the main idea?" State the main idea to yourself in your head.

→ If you cannot state the main idea to yourself, use a fix-up strategy: Reread while asking, "What point is the author trying to make?"

Keep asking these questions as you sift through informational paragraphs. Do not wait until you reach the end of the paragraph, section, or selection.

Finding the Main Idea in Deductive Paragraphs

Paragraphs have a structure that can help you identify the main idea. In this section, you will learn about different ways that authors structure, or design, their paragraphs.

Read the following paragraph and identify the topic. As you do, keep sifting through the data to see how each fact relates to others. Look for repeating words. Also look for a topic sentence that states the main idea. As soon as you identify the main idea, jot it in the margin.

> In the early days of our country, Virginia served as the breeding ground of presidents; of the first five presidents, four were Virginians. The father of our country and the first president was George Washington. He was born in Westmoreland County, Virginia, and spent his later years at his estate in Virginia, Mt. Vernon. The third president, Thomas Jefferson, was also a native Virginian. Raised in what is now Albermarle County, Virginia, he founded the University of Virginia, and his home in later years was Monticello, near the university. James Madison, the fourth president, was born in Port Conway, Virginia, and helped draft the Constitution for the state of Virginia. Like Washington, James Monroe, the fifth president, was born, in Westmoreland County; he was educated at the College of William and Mary in Williamsburg and studied law under Thomas Jefferson.

The topic is early presidents of the United States. The main idea is that Virginia was the birthplace of four of the first five presidents. This idea is stated in the first sentence.

Think
about . . .

What should you do to monitor, or check on, your comprehension as you read?

Topic sentence A sentence that states the main idea

Underline that sentence in the paragraph. It is the topic sentence because it develops the topic of the paragraph; it states the main idea.

Each sentence that follows the topic sentence supports the main idea. Each sentence tells something about a president that relates to his origins in Virginia. Notice that other facts about these presidents that do not relate to their beginnings in Virginia (for example, the names of their wives) are not included in the paragraph. That is the case because a well-written paragraph focuses on one main idea.

The structure of the paragraph about the Virginia presidents can be diagrammed, or mapped, like this:

> **Main idea (or topic sentence)**
>
> Supporting detail sentence
> Supporting detail sentence
> Supporting detail sentence
> Supporting detail sentence
> Supporting detail sentence
> Supporting detail sentence

A paragraph constructed in this way is a *deductive paragraph*. Deductive paragraphs begin with a topic sentence and then supply specific facts to support it. The deductive structure is a tidy design for paragraph writing. It makes reading easier because the main idea is stated at the beginning to guide your reading of the paragraph.

WORKSHOP 6: WEBBING A PARAGRAPH WITH MAIN IDEA/SUPPORTING DETAILS

Web the paragraph you just read about early presidents of the United States. Set the main idea (topic sentence) in the center of your web. Place the supporting points branching outward from the center of the web. How many branches logically should you have? Why?

Finding the Main Idea in Inductive Paragraphs

Read this revised paragraph about the early presidents. The topic is the same as in the first version. The main idea is the same. When you find a topic sentence, underline it. Think also as you read, "How does the paragraph differ from the first version?"

> George Washington, the father of our country and the first president, was born in Westmoreland County, Virginia, and spent his later years at his estate in Virginia, Mt. Vernon. Thomas Jefferson, the third president, was also a native Virginian. Raised in what is now Albermarle County, Virginia, he founded the University of Virginia, and his home in later years was Monticello, near the university. James Madison, the fourth president, was born in Port Conway, Virginia, and helped draft the Constitution for the state of Virginia. Like Washington, James Monroe, the fifth president, was born in Westmoreland County; he was educated at the College of William and Mary in Williamsburg and studied law under Thomas Jefferson. Clearly, Virginia supplied more than its share of presidents in the early days of our nation.

Did you underline the last sentence as the topic sentence of the paragraph? The last sentence expresses the idea that Virginia was the home of many of our early presidents.

The design of the paragraph is shown here:

Supporting detail sentence
Supporting detail sentence
Supporting detail sentence
Supporting detail sentence
Supporting detail sentence
Main idea (or topic sentence)

This design is an inductive one. An *inductive paragraph* provides a series of details and gives the main idea at the end.

When you read a paragraph in which the main idea is not stated in the first sentence, your job is more difficult. You must keep relating each new piece of information to those already given. Sifting through each new sentence, you must ask yourself, "In what way is this new piece of data like the ones that have gone before it? What are the sentences saying about the topic?" A repeating term (in this case, the word *Virginia*) may hint at the main idea as you read through the paragraph. The last sentence—the topic sentence—confirms the main idea.

Inferring the Main Idea When It Is Not Stated

Often in college texts, the author does not state the main idea. He or she leaves it to the reader to infer, or figure out.

Study this chart. As you look at it, ask yourself two questions. What is the topic of the chart? (Clue: The topic is stated directly.) What point is it making about the early presidents of the United States? (Clue: The point is not stated directly. You must infer it.)

Think
about . . .

Why is it important to talk to yourself in your head as you read? Do you do this?

Early Presidents of the United States			
Name	Number of President	Birthplace	Other Data
George Washington	1	Westmoreland Co., Virginia, 1732	Called the "father of our country"; lived at Mt. Vernon in Virginia
Thomas Jefferson	3	"Shadwell" in Goochland (now Albermarle) Co., Virginia, 1743	Founded the University of Virginia at Charlottesville, Virginia; lived at Monticello in Virginia
James Madison	4	Port Conway, Virginia, 1751, member of the Virginia planter class	Helped to draft the Constitution for the state of Virginia
James Monroe	5	Westmoreland Co., Virginia, 1758	Educated at the College of William and Mary in Williamsburg, Virginia; studied law under Jefferson

What is the topic of the chart? Write the topic in the margin here before continuing to read. Clue: The title gives the topic of the chart.

What is the chart saying about those early presidents? In answering that question, you will have inferred the main, unstated idea of the chart. Write the main idea in the margin before continuing.

Sifting through the data in the chart, did you see a way in which most of the data are related? How were these early presidents similar? What feature of their background was the same?

One clue to noting relationships within a body of data like this (or within a paragraph, which is like a body of data) is to identify words that repeat. In the data chart on the early presidents, the word *Virginia* repeats. The main idea is that these early presidents were Virginians.

Some paragraphs are like this chart; they have no topic sentence. The paragraph is simply a string of interrelated sentences. You must figure out what the main idea is. You must reason from the specific details to understand the general point the paragraph is making. This is what you actually did when you interpreted the chart about the early presidents on page 68. You had to infer the main idea because it was not stated explicitly.

Here is the same paragraph about early presidents of the United States, written without a topic sentence.

> George Washington, the father of our country and the first president, was born in Westmoreland County, Virginia, and spent his later years at his estate in Virginia, Mt. Vernon. Thomas Jefferson, the third president, was also a native Virginian. Raised in what is now Albermarle County, Virginia, he founded the University of Virginia, and his home in later years was Monticello, near the university. James Madison, the fourth president, was born in Port Conway, Virginia, and helped draft the Constitution for the State of Virginia. Like Washington, James Monroe, the fifth president, was born in Westmoreland County; he was educated at the College of William and Mary in Williamsburg and studied law under Thomas Jefferson.

To get the main idea of this paragraph, you must sift through the data and ask, "How does this sentence relate to the ones before it? What point is this sentence making about the topic?"

The linear design of the paragraph is simply this:

> Supporting detail sentence
> Supporting detail sentence
> Supporting detail sentence
> Supporting detail sentence
> Supporting detail sentence

Topic:

Main Idea:

WORKSHOP 7: IDENTIFYING AND INFERRING MAIN IDEAS

Return to the opening two paragraphs of this chapter (on page 61) under the heading "Grasping the Main Idea." Reread the paragraphs and review the topics you identified earlier. The first paragraph has a topic sentence. Underline it and tell yourself in your own words the point the author is making about the topic. The second paragraph does not have a topic sentence. Infer it. In the margin write the main idea, or the point the author is trying to make about the topic. Check what you have done with a workshop partner, explaining to one another how you got the main idea of each paragraph. Together, web the second paragraph in your notebook. For practice, try finding the main idea of each paragraph in the first selection of Chapter 1, for which you have already identified the topics.

Self-Monitoring and Fixing Up

As you read an assigned section of a chapter in a college textbook, you should monitor your comprehension, telling yourself the topic and the author's main idea—or point—paragraph by paragraph. Suppose that you are reading a selection that has a heavy reading load for you: It is very technical, filled with many unfamiliar terms. When you finish a paragraph, stop to tell yourself the main idea, using your main-idea-making strategy. (Strategy: Ask, "What is the author telling me about the topic? What word or words repeat? How are all the sentences related? Is there a sentence that states or almost states the main idea? Can I state the main idea for myself?")

If you have trouble telling yourself the main idea, apply this fix-up strategy:

MAIN IDEA FIX-UP
STRATEGY

→ Reread the paragraph.

→ Keep thinking as you reread, "Are any words or ideas most important? What point is being stressed? What is the author trying to tell me?"

→ Recite—or tell yourself in your head—the big point being made.

If you still do not understand, back up a paragraph or two, reread those paragraphs, and tell yourself the main idea of each one. With that as background, again reread the difficult paragraph, applying the fix-up strategy by talking to yourself in your head.

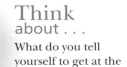

Think
about . . .

What do you tell yourself to get at the main idea?

WORKSHOP 8: MAKING AND FIXING UP MAIN IDEAS

Read the following six paragraphs that are part of the autobiographical account of one student's first days in college. As you read each paragraph, underline the topic sentence if there is one, or write the main idea in the margin. Having done this for each paragraph, collaborate with a partner and compare your answers. Talking together, use a fix-up strategy: Revise the main ideas you wrote earlier. Then talk briefly, comparing your feelings on entering college with the writer's feelings.

College: A Transition Point in My Life

When I first entered college as a freshman, I was afraid that I was not "up to it." I was afraid of being off by myself, away from my family for the first time. Here I was surrounded by people I did not know and who did not know me. I would have to make friends with them and perhaps also compete with them for grades in courses I would take. Were they smarter than I was? Could I keep up with them? Would they accept me?

I soon learned that my life was now up to me. I had to set a study program if I were to succeed in my courses. I had to regulate the time I spent in study and the time I spent in socializing. I had to decide when to go to bed, when and what to eat, when and what to drink, and with whom to be friendly. These questions I had to answer for myself.

At first, life was rough. I made mistakes in how I used my time. I made mistakes in overdoing the time I put into making friends. I also made mistakes in how I chose my first friends in college.

Shortly, however, I had my life under control. I managed to get myself to class on time, do my first assignments and hand them in, and pass my first exams with grades that satisfied me. In addition, I developed a small circle of friends with whom I felt comfortable and with whom I could share my fears. I set up a routine that was really my own—a routine that met my needs and that I established for myself.

As a result, I began to look upon myself from a different perspective. I began to see myself as an individual responsible for my own welfare and responsible for the welfare of my friends and family. It felt good to make my own decisions and see those decisions turn out to be wise ones. I guess that this is all part of what people call "growing up."

What did life have in store for me? At that stage in my life, I really was uncertain where I would ultimately go in life and what I would do with the years ahead of me. But I knew that I would be able to handle what was ahead because I had successfully jumped this important hurdle in my life: I had made the transition from a person dependent on my family for emotional support to a person who was responsible for myself.

WORKSHOP 9: WRITING PARAGRAPHS WITH MAIN IDEAS

Study this data chart (and its title) to determine the topic and to infer the unstated main idea. Record both in the margin before continuing.

The Second and Sixth Presidents of the United States			
Name	**Number of President**	**Birthplace**	**Other Data**
John Adams	2	Born in Braintree, Massachusetts, 1735	Graduated from Harvard in Cambridge, Massachusetts; on the drafting committee of the Declaration of Independence
John Quincy Adams	6	Born in Braintree, Massachusetts, 1767	Son of John and Abigail Adams

Topic:

Main Idea:

Having inferred the main idea, write it as the topic sentence of a paragraph in your notebook. Model your sentence after the topic sentence in the first paragraph about the early presidents from Virginia. Follow your topic sentence with sentences giving details about John Adams. Follow those sentences with ones telling details about John Quincy Adams. You will be writing a deductive paragraph. Revise your paragraph so that it is structured inductively. To do this, put your topic sentence at the end. Record both paragraphs in your notebook. Share your paragraphs with a workshop partner to see whether he or she can identify your topic sentence and the structure of your paragraphs.

SELECTION 1

Three States of the United States: Florida, Nevada, and Illinois (GEOGRAPHY)

A Main-Idea-Making Workshop

Expanding Your Vocabulary for Reading

Pronounce the italicized words in these sentences and think about their meanings before reading. Check the glossary if you are unsure. Record definitions in the space provided.

Did You KNOW?

The root *terra-* means "land." You see this Latin root in the words *territory, terrestrial,* and *Mediterranean.*

Did You KNOW?

The root *migra-* means "to move." You see this Latin root in the words *migrate* and *immigrate.* The prefix *ex-* or *e-* means "out of."

1. Because the *terrain* was rocky, I had to watch my footing to make sure I did not fall. (Use the root to help you unlock the meaning of *terrain.*) _____

   _____

   _____

2. Baja California in Mexico is a *peninsula,* a long, fingerlike projection of land that is bounded by water on three sides. (Use the definition given in the sentence.)

   _____

   _____

3. The state university is a *mecca* for researchers; it attracts many young scientists who want to learn more about genetic structure. (Use a synonym clue.) _____

   _____

4. During the French revolution, many *emigrés* fled their country to settle in England; they were searching for a safe haven at a time when their lives were at risk in their own country for political reasons. (Use the prefix, root, and context to help you determine the meaning.) _____

   _____

5. In an *arid* environment, there is little rainfall. (Use context.) _____

   _____

6. The *cascading* waters created a roar that could be heard a mile away. (Use context. If you are still in doubt, check the glossary.)

   _____

7. The town is *bisected* by a major interstate highway. As a result, the two parts of the town are entirely different in character. (Use context and word elements.) _____

   _____

8. Her *designation* as Chief Justice of the state supreme court was received with great enthusiasm. (Use context and substitution of a synonym.) _____

   _____

Getting Ready to Read

Preview the selection by reading the title and first paragraph.

- What is the topic? _____
- What do you already know about these states? _____

   _____

   _____

- How do you rate the reading difficulty for you: light, average, heavy?

Reading with Meaning: Making Main Ideas

Read the selection. As you read each paragraph, ask, "What is the topic of the paragraph? What is its main idea?" When you have trouble, reread and do a fix-up. Jot down the topic and the main idea of each paragraph in the margin. The first paragraph has been done for you.

Three States of the United States: Florida, Nevada, and Illinois

Fifty states make up the United States of America. Although the states are part of one unified nation that shares a common government, constitution, and heritage, the states are diverse. Each has unique characteristics that are often determined by its location, its terrain, and the peoples who have settled and continue to settle the land. In this article we look at three states that vary in major respects: Florida, Nevada, and Illinois.

1. **Topic:** The states of the United States
   Main Idea: The states, although similar, vary.

Florida

Florida is a low-lying peninsula bounded on three sides by water: on the east by the Atlantic Ocean, on the west by the Gulf of Mexico, and on the south by the Straits of Florida. Because it is a long, stretched-out peninsula, the state has more than 8500 miles of shoreline. Along its coasts are miles of white sand beaches, each more exquisite than the one before. East Coast beaches that you may have heard of because students head there for spring break are Miami Beach, Daytona Beach, and Fort Lauderdale. Well-known Gulf Coast beaches are located near the cities of Sarasota, Clearwater, and St. Petersburg.

2. **Topic:** _____

   Main Idea: _____
   _____
   _____
   _____
   _____

Florida is the southernmost mainland state of the United States and home of the southernmost mainland city, Key West. The state extends from 31° north latitude to 24.5° north latitude; only Hawaii is located at a more southern latitude. An outcome of its location is that Florida is blessed with a warm climate and lots of sunshine year-round. This explains the state's nickname—The Sunshine State.

3. **Topic:** _____
   Main Idea: _____
   _____
   _____

As a result of its beaches and its latitude, Florida has become a tourist mecca. More than 40 million tourists vacation in Florida each year. Visitors head to the beaches but also tour the space research center at Cape Kennedy, the Disney parks in Orlando, and the Everglades, the national park in south Florida. In addition, visitors have the opportunity to tour St. Augustine, founded in 1565 by the Spanish, to fish in coastal waters, and to enjoy water sports.

4. **Topic:** _____
   Main Idea: _____
   _____

Florida is also known for its citrus industry. Orange, grapefruit, lemon, and tangerine groves crisscross the northern and central parts of the state because citrus trees need sunshine. Florida leads the country in citrus production. In fact, 90 percent of the orange juice consumed in the United States comes from Florida oranges.

5. **Topic:** _____
   Main Idea: _____
   _____
   _____

Today Florida has a large and growing Cuban-American population. Location plays a major role in this development; Havana, the capital of Cuba, is located less than 100 miles across the Straits of Florida from Key West. Those emigrating from Cuba find in Florida cities a climate much like that which they enjoyed in Cuba and are welcomed by many Cuban emigrés who have already settled in South Florida.

6. **Topic:** _____

   Main Idea: _____
   _____
   _____

Nevada

Whereas Florida is a southern state surrounded by water, Nevada is an arid western state. Most of the rivers of the state stay right in the state. Rivers that cascade out of the mountain ranges flow into lakes or shallow areas, where they simply dry up. The state gets only 9 inches of rain each year on average, and farmers must depend on wells and irrigation to grow their crops.

7. **Topic:** _____

   Main Idea: _____
   _____
   _____

Much of the early development of Nevada came as a result of great and valuable deposits of gold and silver. Early settlers were prospectors, and mining was an important activity during the nineteenth century. For example, Carson City, the capital of Nevada, was founded in 1858 on the site of a trading post established in 1851 as a stop on the westward migration trail from Salt Lake City to California. Later Carson City served as a supply center for miners in the valley, especially after the discovery of the Comstock Lode

8. **Topic:** _____
   Main Idea: _____
   _____
   _____

in nearby Virginia City. The Comstock Lode is one of the richest silver deposits in the United States. As a matter of fact, Nevada is known as the Silver State.

After World War I, when mining became a less important contributor to the state's economy, Nevada developed as a gaming center. As legalized gambling thrived and gamblers came to Nevada from across the country, large hotels and resorts grew up in Las Vegas in the southern part of the state and in Reno and Lake Tahoe in the western part. As a result, today tourism is a major industry in Nevada.

Today Nevada is one of the fastest-growing areas of the country. Between 1980 and 1990 the population of the state grew by 50 percent. Between 1990 and 1998, the population went from 1,201,833 to 1,746,898. As air conditioning improves the quality of life, more and more Americans are finding that life in the hot, dry areas of Nevada has much to offer.

Illinois

Illinois, a midwestern state, is located in what is known as the heartland of America and is part of the great central plains farming area nestled between the Rockies on the west and the Appalachians on the east. Bounded by the Mississippi, Ohio, and Wabash Rivers and bisected by the Illinois River, Illinois is characterized by flat, level lands that once were covered with prairie sod. Because rainfall is substantial and the soil deep and rich, agriculture thrives in the state. Illinois is one of the major corn-growing areas of the United States. It is also important as a producer of dairy products.

Because of its location on Lake Michigan, its system of rivers, and its central location in America, Illinois also has developed as an industrial state. Its industries include the manufacture of industrial machinery, chemicals, and motor vehicles; steel making is an important industry as well. The city of Chicago is an important midwestern industrial hub. It is the state's largest city and the third largest metropolitan area in the United States.

One of the worst disasters of the nineteenth century was the great Chicago fire. In 1871 Chicago was a city of wood buildings. As legend explains, Mrs. O'Leary's cow knocked over a lantern and started a blaze that killed hundreds of people, destroyed millions of dollars of property, and left thousands of people without homes. After the fire, Chicagoans rebuilt their city using steel structures. They built their first skyscraper in 1875, the ten-story Home Insurance Building. Today Chicago is a city of skyscrapers that line the shore of Lake Michigan. It is home to the Sears Tower, the tallest building in the Americas.

Illinois is called the Land of Lincoln. This designation came about because Abraham Lincoln, the sixteenth president of the United States, was a resident of Illinois for much of his life. He is buried in the capital city of Illinois, Springfield. If you visit there, you can see the monument that was built in his honor.

Margin notes:

9. Topic: _____
_____
Main Idea: _____
_____

10. Topic: _____
_____
Main Idea: _____
_____
_____
_____

11. Topic: _____
_____
Main Idea: _____
_____

12. Topic: _____
Main Idea: _____
_____

13. Topic: _____
_____
Main Idea: _____
_____
_____
_____
_____

14. Topic: _____
_____
Main Idea: _____
_____

Monitoring Comprehension

Place a *T* (true) or *F* (false) on the line before each statement based on the main idea notes you jotted down in the margin during reading. You may look at your notes as you answer the questions.

_____ 1. The states of the United States are very similar in terrain.

_____ 2. Because Florida is a peninsula, it is a land of endless beaches.

_____ 3. Florida has lots of sunshine because of its latitude.

_____ 4. Because of its location and beaches, Florida has become a tourist mecca.

_____ 5. Florida is known as an industrial state.

_____ 6. Florida has a large and growing Cuban-American population.

_____ 7. Nevada is a midwestern state that enjoys ample rainfall.

_____ 8. Much of the early development of Nevada came about as a result of its valuable mineral deposits.

_____ 9. After World War I, Nevada developed as a summer beach resort area.

_____ 10. Today Nevada is a slow-growing area.

_____ 11. Illinois is a farming state located on the great plains and is part of the heartland of America.

_____ 12. Illinois has only minimal industry.

_____ 13. One of the worst disasters of the nineteenth century was the great Chicago fire.

_____ 14. Illinois has strong ties with Lincoln.

Reviewing Vocabulary

Star the word or words that are closest in meaning to the italicized one. Start by crossing out the options you know to be wrong.

1. The *terrain* was nothing like what I had expected; I expected that the land would be flat, but it actually was very hilly.
   a. the land as considered in terms of its natural features
   b. a vessel for holding soup
   c. the amount of rainfall in an area
   d. the size of an area in square miles

2. The millionaire built his home at the tip of a *peninsula* and thus could see water in almost every direction.
   a. a kind of drug useful in curing bacterial infections
   b. a spit of land surrounded on three sides by water
   c. a three-sided geometic figure
   d. a kind of pencil especially useful in drawing architectural plans

3. The restaurant became a *mecca* for the liberal thinkers in the area; they tended to gather there to talk about their ideas.
   a. a marketplace
   b. a place to access the Internet
   c. a goal or center of attraction for numbers of people
   d. a city

4. During the war, many *emigrés* left their homeland fearful that they would be killed if they remained; they found sanctuary in a neighboring country.
   a. people who leave their homeland fearing political persecution
   b. people who give up all hope
   c. people who rely on others for help and sanctuary
   d. people who have become nomads

5. Because of the *arid* climate, people could not make a living by farming.
   a. unpleasant
   b. extreme
   c. very wet
   d. dry

6. For a time, we stood and watched the water *cascading* over the falls.
   a. falling in a dashing manner
   b. barely flowing
   c. limping
   d. carrying

7. In geometry, we learned how to *bisect* an angle.
   a. break apart
   b. cut into three parts
   c. cut into two parts
   d. analyze

8. Our town's *designation* as the center of the New Year's Eve festivities for the county brought a lot of traffic into our area.
   a. clarification
   b. nomination or naming
   c. development of a plan
   d. picture

SELECTION 2

The Color of Money: Being Rich in Black and White (SOCIOLOGY)

A Main-Idea-Making Workshop

Expanding Your Vocabulary for Reading

Collaborating with a partner, read each sentence aloud, pronouncing the italicized words by looking at the word elements and syllable units. Use context and word elements to unlock the meanings of the italicized words. If you have trouble, check the glossary. Record the meaning of each word in the space provided. Select one word to add to your vocabulary notebook.

1. *Affluent* families have more opportunity to enjoy the finer things of life: up-to-date cars, nice homes, and exciting vacations. _____

   _____

2. Although my salary went up last year, there was a sharp increase in the cost of living. The resulting *inflation* meant that I was not better off. _____

   _____

3. The U.S. president's *counterpart* in England is the prime minister. _____

   _____

Getting Ready to Read

This selection comes from a college sociology textbook. In the book, the author puts a box around the selection and sets it off from the ongoing text. This is a very common technique used in textbooks. The boxed material may be a related story, or vignette; it may be an essay from another source, a summary of related research, or comments by other authors. Often you read the boxed material after reading the material to which it relates.

   Preview the title and the first and last paragraphs. With your workshop partner, answer these questions:

   • What do you predict the selection is about (the topic)? _____

   • What do you already know on this topic? _____

   • How heavy is the reading load for you? _____

Reading with Meaning

With your workshop partner, read the following essay, asking these questions as you read each paragraph: What is the topic? What is the main idea? For each paragraph, first write the topic in the margin. Then underline the topic sentence if there is one; if not, write your inferred main idea in the margin.

Did You KNOW?

Flu- (*fluv-, flux-, fluor*) is a Latin base that means "to flow." You see it also in these words: *fluent, fluently, fluid, flux, affluence,* and *influence.* Check your dictionary for other examples. Make a word tower of examples to highlight the shared element.

Did You KNOW?

Counter- (*contra-*) is a prefix that means "against." You see it in *counteract* ("to act in opposition to") and *contradict* ("to speak in a way that says the opposite"). Note the root *dict-* in *contradict* and the root *act-* in *counteract.* The root *act-* comes from the Latin verb *agere,* meaning "to do."

The Color of Money: Being Rich in Black and White

John Macionis

African-American families earn 55 cents to the white family's dollar, a fact that underlies the greater risk of poverty among people of color. But there is another side to black America—an affluent side—that has expanded dramatically in recent decades. The number of affluent families—those with annual incomes over $50,000—is increasing faster among African Americans than among whites. In 1990, more than 1 million African-American families were financially privileged; adjusted for inflation, this represents a fivefold increase over two decades before. Today, 15 percent of African-American families—more than 2 million adults and their children—are affluent. About 15 percent of Latino families rank as well off, too, while 30 percent of non-Hispanic white families and 35 percent of Asian families have that much income.

Topic:

The color of money is the same for everyone, but black and white affluence differs in several key respects. First, well-off people of African descent are not as rich as their white counterparts. About 45 percent of affluent white families (17 percent of all white families) earn more than $75,000 a year, a standard reached by only 38 percent of affluent African-American families (7 percent of all black families).

Topic:

Second, African Americans are more likely than white people to achieve affluence through multiple incomes. Families at this level typically have two employed spouses, perhaps with working children.

Third, affluent African Americans are more likely to derive their income from salaries rather than investments. Three-fourths of affluent white families have investment income, compared to just half of affluent African-American families.

Beyond differences in income, affluent people of color contend with social barriers that do not restrict whites. Even African Americans with the money to purchase a home, for example, may find they are unwelcome as neighbors. This is one reason that a smaller proportion of affluent African-American families (40 percent) live in the suburbs (the richest areas of the country) than do affluent white families (61 percent).

Topic:

Affluent Americans come in all colors. Yet race has a powerful effect on the lives of affluent people, just as it does on the lives of us all.   [375 words]

Topic:

Sources: O'Hare (1989), U.S. Bureau of the Census (1995), Welcher (1995).

Monitoring Comprehension and Writing in Response

A. Collaborating with your workshop partner, compare the topics and the topic sentences or inferred main ideas that you wrote or underlined. Explain your reasoning. Revise, or fix up, if you need to.

B. What are some signs that a person is affluent? In your reading notebook, write a paragraph in which you start with a topic sentence, such as "I tend to think of affluence in terms of . . . ." Then write several supporting sentences that elaborate by indicating specific signs of affluence. Do this by yourself.

C. Find each of the following words in the selection. With your workshop partner, take turns reading the sentences containing the words. Then write a sentence with each word, modeling your sentences after the ones in the selection. Also select one additional word from the selection that interests you. Create a sentence with it. Be ready to share with the workshop group.

1. affluent _____

2. inflation _____

3. counterpart _____

4. your word _____

SELECTION 3
Thomas Jefferson and His Presidency (HISTORY)

Independent Study

Expanding Your Vocabulary for Reading

The italicized words in the following sentences are from the selection. Pronounce them. Then use context and word element clues to crack the meaning of each. Write your hypothesized definition in the space provided.

1. Placing one's hand above one's heart as the flag goes by is *symbolic* of the respect a person feels for one's country. _____

   _____

2. Some people dislike it when the president of the United States enters to the sounds of trumpets. They believe that this *quasi-monarchical* entrance is more appropriate for kings and queens, not for presidents of a republic. _____

   _____

3. The king acted in an *autocratic* way, not taking into account the desires and needs of the people. _____

   _____

4. I am not one who can stand a great deal of *pretension*. I think that showing off is phony.

   _____

5. The signing of the Declaration of Independence was a *momentous* occasion for the new country. It was probably the most significant happening in the country's history.

   _____

6. The man thought that his wife *embodied* everything that was good and wonderful.

   _____

7. Many Americans *deplored* the events that happened at Kent State University that day. They expressed strong disapproval and wished that the events had never happened. _____

   _____

8. I was overwhelmed by the *squalor* I saw on the island. People lived under the most unfortunate conditions of dirt and misery and had none of the modern conveniences

that I was used to. _____

_____

_____

9. The optimist *envisaged* a world without poverty or want.

_____

_____

10. I was *devastated* to learn that my friend had died in the crash. _____

_____

11. In an *agrarian* economy, people farm; there is little or no industry.

_____

_____

12. I cannot resist the *lure* of faraway places; whenever I can I take to the road.

_____

_____

Getting Ready to Read

Preview by reading the title and the first paragraph. Then answer these questions.

• What is the topic of the selection? How do you know? _____

_____

• What do you already know about this topic? _____

• Write one question you think you might be able to answer based on your reading.

_____

• Judge the difficulty of the selection: easy, average, hard.

Reading with Meaning

Read the selection. Then reread to determine the main idea of each paragraph. Record the main ideas in the margin. The first paragraph has been done as a model.

Thomas Jefferson and His Presidency
John Mack Faragher

Thomas Jefferson began his presidency with a symbolic action worthy of a twentieth-century media-wise politician. At noon on March 4, 1801, he walked from his modest boardinghouse through the swampy streets of the new federal city of Washington to the unfinished Capitol. George Washington and John Adams had ridden in elaborate carriages to their inaugurals. Jefferson, although accepting a military honor guard, demonstrated by his actions that he rejected the elaborate, quasi-monarchical style of the two Federalist presidents, and their (to his mind) autocratic style of government as well.

For all its lack of pretension, Jefferson's inauguration as the third president of the United States was a momentous occasion in American history, for it marked the

1. **Main Idea:** Jefferson began his presidency with a symbolic act—a simple inauguration.

2. Main Idea: _____
_____
_____
_____
_____

peaceful transition from one political party, the Federalists, to their hated rivals, the Democratic Republicans. Beginning in an atmosphere of exceptional political bitterness, Jefferson's presidency was to demonstrate that a strongly led party system could shape national policy without leading either to dictatorship or to revolt. It was a great achievement.

Republican Agrarianism

3. Main Idea: _____
_____
_____

Jefferson brought to the presidency a clearly defined political philosophy. Behind all the events of his administration (1801–09) and those of his successors in what became known as the Virginia Dynasty (James Madison, 1809–17; James Monroe, 1817–25) was a clear set of beliefs that embodied Jefferson's interpretation of the meaning of republicanism for Americans.

4. Main Idea: _____
_____
_____

Jefferson's years as ambassador to France in the 1780s were particularly important in shaping his political thinking. Recoiling from the extremes of wealth and poverty he saw there, he came to believe that it was impossible for Europe to achieve a just society that could guarantee to most of its members the "life, liberty and . . . pursuit of happiness" of which he had written in the Declaration of Independence.

5. Main Idea: _____
_____
_____

The growth of the factory system in England horrified Jefferson, who deplored the squalor of teeming new factory towns such as Manchester in the north of England. He opposed industrialization in America: in the 1790s, when Alexander Hamilton and the Federalists had proposed fostering manufacturing in the United States, Jefferson had responded with outrage. He was convinced that the Federalist program would create precisely the same extremes of wealth and the same sort of unjust government that prevailed in Europe.

6. Main Idea: _____
_____
_____
_____
_____

Jefferson believed that only America provided fertile earth for the true citizenship necessary to a republican form of government. What America had, and Europe lacked, was room to grow. Jefferson envisaged a nation of small family farms clustered together in rural communities—an agrarian republic. He believed that only a nation of roughly equal yeoman farmers, each secure in his own possessions and not dependent on someone else for his livelihood, would exhibit the concern for the community good that was essential in a republic. More romantically, Jefferson also believed that rural contact with the cycles and rhythms of nature was essential to the republican character. Indeed, Jefferson said that "those who labor in the earth are the chosen people of God," and so he viewed himself, though his "farm" was the large slave-owning plantation of Monticello.

7. Main Idea: _____
_____
_____
_____
_____
_____

Jefferson's vision of an expanding agrarian republic remains to this day one of our most compelling ideas about America's uniqueness and special destiny. But expansionism contained some negative aspects. The lure of the western lands fostered constant mobility and dissatisfaction rather than the stable, settled communities of yeoman farmers that Jefferson envisaged. Expansionism caused environmental damage, in particular soil exhaustion—a consequence of abandoning old lands, rather than conserving them, and moving on to new ones. Finally, expansionism bred a ruthlessness toward Indian peoples, who were pushed out of the way for white settlement or who, like the Mandans, were devastated by the diseases that accompanied European trade and contact. Jefferson's agrarianism thus bred some of the best and some of the worst traits of the developing nation.

Monitoring Comprehension

Place a *T* (true) or *F* (false) on the line before each statement. Think in terms of the main ideas you have written in the margin.

_____ 1. Jefferson's inaugural was elaborate.

_____ 2. The peaceful transition from the administration of one political party to another was a great achievement.

_____ 3. Jefferson had a clear philosophy of how a country should be governed.

_____ 4. Jefferson never traveled abroad.

_____ 5. Jefferson feared industrialization and the squalor it had brought to England.

_____ 6. Jefferson envisaged an America in which people worked in factories.

_____ 7. Jefferson's vision of an agrarian America brought only positive results.

Reviewing Vocabulary

Star the option that best defines each italicized word. Start by crossing out the options you know to be wrong.

1. The president's first act was a *symbolic* one.
   a. positive
   b. standing for something
   c. personalized
   d. meaning nothing

2. The president entered the ball in *quasi-monarchical* style.
   a. almost like that of a king or queen
   b. not at all like that of a king or queen
   c. exactly like that of a king or queen

3. I could not live under an *autocratic* form of government.
   a. self-serving
   b. all-powerful and controlling
   c. pretentious
   d. bureaucratic

4. The *pretensions* of our friends who are far wealthier than we are disturbed us.
   a. showy displays
   b. wealth
   c. inconsiderateness
   d. thoughtlessness

5. The occasion was so *momentous* that I felt overcome with emotion.
   a. unimportant
   b. happy
   c. sad
   d. significant

6. The president's platform *embodied* all the major concerns of the day.
   a. contained in a definite form
   b. carried high in the air
   c. put into the human body
   d. clarified

7. I *deplored* what my friend had done.
   a. expressed great happiness about
   b. expressed alarm about
   c. expressed great sorrow about
   d. raised questions about

8. The young woman cried when she saw the *squalor* of the country she was visiting.
   a. large size
   b. misery and dirt
   c. small size
   d. unhappiness

9. The mayor *envisaged* a town in which there was no poverty or squalor.
   a. pictured in his mind
   b. worked for
   c. wished for
   d. governed

10. As we traveled through the country, we saw farmlands *devastated* by flooding.
    a. inundated
    b. covered
    c. destroyed
    d. turned about

11. The United States is no longer primarily an *agrarian* country.
    a. agricultural
    b. industrial
    c. monarchical
    d. autocratic

12. People moved west, *lured* by the idea of free or inexpensive lands.
    a. excited
    b. saddened
    c. attracted
    d. made happy

EXTENDING WHAT YOU HAVE LEARNED

Reading for Main Ideas

In this chapter you have been learning a strategy for identifying main ideas as you read paragraphs. List the steps you use to find the main idea of a paragraph.

1. _____

   _____

2. _____

   _____

3. _____

   _____

Applying the Strategy to Your Reading

Find an article in a newsmagazine such as *Newsweek* or *Time*. Preview the article to identify the topic. Then think about what you know about the topic. Read the article to identify the main idea of each paragraph. Jot the main ideas in the margin and bring the article to class to share with your peers.

5

Grasping the Thesis, or Main Idea, of an Entire Selection

OBJECTIVE

In this chapter, you will learn strategies for identifying the thesis, or major idea, of a selection.

GRASPING THE THESIS, OR MAIN IDEA, OF AN ENTIRE SELECTION

Have you ever read an article or essay, listened to a radio broadcast, or viewed a documentary and heard someone ask, "Can you tell me what the point of it is so I don't have to read it? What's the author trying to say?" In responding to the questioner, you had to consider the entire selection and come up with the main idea or ideas. We call the main idea of a selection the **thesis.** The thesis is the central, unifying idea or ideas that the author has in mind as he or she composes the article, broadcast, or documentary. To identify the author's thesis, apply this two-step strategy:

THESIS-MAKING STRATEGY

→ Think through the main ideas of the individual parts, or paragraphs, as you learned to do in Chapter 4.

→ Ask, "What big thought is the author trying to tell me in this selection? What overarching points is he or she trying to make about the topic?"

In some instances, an author states the major points explicitly. He or she can do this anywhere in the article, broadcast, or video, or even in a chapter or section of a textbook. Sometimes an author states the thesis in the title or at the beginning of the piece to guide your reading and help you get the point. Sometimes in extended selections, the thesis is stated twice: first in the introductory section and then in the concluding section. In still other instances, the author expresses the thesis somewhere in the middle.

Consider the selection about Florida, Nevada, and Illinois you read in Chapter 4. In the introduction, the author tells you that the states of the United States are diverse. She then uses facts about the three states to prove the diversity. Her thesis is simply that the states of the United States vary widely.

Macionis also sets forth his thesis explicitly in his essay "The Color of Money" in Chapter 4. Go back to that essay. Can you find the paragraph where he states his major thesis? If you have trouble, review the main ideas of the individual paragraphs. Ask yourself, "What are these ideas trying to tell me?" Underline the sentence that sums up Macionis's main point, or thesis.

WORKSHOP 1: IDENTIFYING THE STATED THESIS OF A SELECTION

Read the following column that appeared in a local newspaper, written by a woman who works in corporate communications. The author gives many clues as to the big idea she is communicating through her article. As soon as you get her point, underline some phrases and sentences where she emphasizes her main idea. The words *du jour* are French and mean "of the day." The word *civility* means "courtesy or polite behavior." The word *nascent* means "just coming into existence or developing." You may want to look up the word *anonymous* if you cannot get its meaning from context.

Give Them a Rude Awakening: Be Polite to Pushy People

Elizabeth Romanaux

We are living in a world where anonymous interactions are viewed as opportunities to act any way we choose and the choice du jour is complete rudeness. Behavior and language that might once have left listeners in an agony of embarrassment are tossed off so frequently and so carelessly that they've all but lost their value. If bad behavior is no longer shocking, what's next when we want to get people's attention and sock it to them? I vote for glacial politeness.

A few months ago I tapped the bumper of a car in front of me at an intersection with a yield sign. Where I might once have given a sheepish wave of apology before we went our separate ways, I was instead forced to deal with a slavering, shouting, cursing woman. She leapt from her car, jolting me with her unpleasant anger like static electricity on a doorknob.

Listening to her threaten me with the police, her insurance company, and everything else she could think of, I was aware of two things: My anger was rising and my teenage children were watching me. I might have liked to slap her across the face or run her down with my car, but I wanted the upper hand. I wanted to win the confrontation.

My rising anger brought with it a cold frigidity. I stood straight and still as a pole and said nothing as she ranted, waiting for her to wind down. After a few moments, she paused and looked at me uncertainly. I still did not respond, maintaining the facial expression of a person waiting at a bus stop—neutral but alert.

Meanwhile, other cars were honking at us to move. She began shouting at them. I finally spoke. "Madam. There is nothing wrong with your car. I will give you my phone number. If you have a problem later, you may call me." I walked to the car, wrote out my number, and handed it to her slowly and calmly. She could think of nothing else to say so we got in our cars and drove off.

"Wow, Mom, that lady was really mad," my 13-year-old said.

"That's true, but did you see how she acted when I refused to argue with her? She didn't know what to do next. I conquered her with civility."

My kids nodded thoughtfully. Getting the upper hand over someone through politeness was a new concept, but interesting. After a couple of minutes my 16-year-old said, "Sweet," and put his headphones back on.

Wherever I go, I make it a point to be completely and totally polite to others. Sometimes this has surprising results. Waiting for coffee amid a morning rush-hour squeeze in Manhattan, a street person cut in line in front of me. "I beg your pardon, sir," I said firmly. "The line forms at the rear." He looked at me with shock and amazement. "Lady, thank you for calling me 'sir,'" He moved quietly to the end of the line.

Not long ago, I was working as hard as a salmon returning upstream to its nascent waters, seeking something called Game Boy Yellow at our local mall. I wasn't sure what it is, but it was on my son's Christmas list. A teenage clerk first ignored me in favor of a phone call from a friend and when I asked her to please ring up my order, gave me the sort of look one usually reserves for a dead mouse found on one's doorstep—unmitigated disgust. I stopped writing my check and stood straight up, looking her right in the eye. "My dear madam," I said. "There's no need whatsoever for you to behave so impolitely to me."

Her jaw dropped and she looked embarrassed as a small smattering of applause came from others around me. A quiet remark worked better than all the counter-rudeness and vile language I might have been able to muster.

When you're out in public and you see a person prevailing through overwhelming politeness, it might be me. Or, it might be another person who is among the first to figure out that the power of rudeness has seen better days. If you really want to triumph in life's ordinary confrontations, try politeness. It works shockingly well.

1. Working with a partner, compose a sentence or two in which you sum up the main point of Romanaux's article. Then write a sentence or two in which you state your reaction to that point. Do you agree with Romanaux or do you disagree? Write your sentences in your notebook.

2. For further practice in summing up an author's stated thesis, reread "For Heaven's Sakes, Choose a Job you Enjoy!" on pages 12–13 of Chapter 1. The author states her thesis in the first and last paragraphs. Underline the thesis wherever she states it. Then write a sentence in your notebook in which you sum up the author's point. Also write a sentence or two in which you express your own opinion about her thesis.

Often authors do not state their main point explicitly; they suggest it only indirectly. You, the reader, must figure out the thesis from the paragraphs of the selection and from what you already know about the subject. In these cases, you must keep asking the main idea question as you go along: What big idea is this author trying to get across to me?

In the selections that follow, you will have the opportunity to identify the main ideas of paragraphs as you practice the main-idea making strategy you learned in Chapter 4 and to determine the thesis of an entire selection.

SELECTION 1
Doing Something About Osteoporosis While You Are Young (HEALTH AND FITNESS)

A Thesis-Building Workshop

Expanding Your Vocabulary for Reading

The italicized words in the following sentences are from the selection. A few are short words (such as *modest* and *blanket*) that you have met before but are used in an interesting way in the selection. Rely on word elements and the context to figure out the meanings. Record the meanings in the space provided.

1. If you get a flu shot in the fall, you will be less *susceptible* to flu and can look forward to a winter without it. _____

_____

2. Today, it is possible to make *synthetic* emeralds, diamonds, and rubies; if you buy one of these, look out because you may be getting an artificial stone, not a genuine

Did You KNOW?

The base *os-* or *osteo-* means "bone." Thus we have the words *ossify,* meaning "to become bony or to become rigid," and *ossification,* meaning "the process of becoming bony or rigid."

article. _____

_____

3. Because the man had trouble moving his legs, the doctor ordered physical *therapy* to help him recover ability to move his limbs. _____

_____

4. I failed to recognize the *complexities* of the case, for I had not understood that so many factors were involved. _____

_____

5. The scientist could not give a *blanket* recommendation that would apply to every case. She could only make suggestions that applied to individual cases based on the evidence at hand. _____

_____

6. There is a *dynamic* relationship between the blood and the cells; the blood brings nutrients to the cells to nourish them. _____

_____

7. The doctors found a spongy *mass* of cells in the patient's abdominal area. The mass was large and had fingers that extended in many directions. _____

_____

8. The man reached the *peak* of his influence at the age of 35. After that, his career went downhill. _____

_____

9. *Modest* amounts of that vitamin taken each day can make a difference in a person's overall health and fitness. _____

_____

Did You KNOW?

The base *dyna-* is from a Greek word meaning "power." Why do you think dynamite is called by that name?

Getting Ready to Read

Read the title and the first and last sentences of the article. Then think about and answer these questions.

- What is the topic of the article? _____
- Predict the thesis based on the title and the two sentences you just read. _____

_____

- Gauge the reading load for you. Is this a more difficult or less difficult article for you as compared to the one on politeness that you just read? _____

Reading with Meaning

Read the selection, which is from a biology textbook. Keep asking yourself, "What is David Krogh trying to tell me about osteoporosis?"

Doing Something About Osteoporosis While You Are Young
David Krogh

Osteoporosis is a thinning of bones that leaves its victims susceptible to bone fractures—breaks or cracks in bones, especially bones of the hips, spine, and wrist. It is generally thought of as a condition that affects women, and indeed 80 percent of the Americans who suffer from it are female. It is further thought of as a condition related to age, and this too is true in a sense, in that it is menopause—with its related hormonal changes—that generally brings about the onset of osteoporosis.

Most of the attention paid to osteoporosis has to do with prevention of it *in middle age,* which is to say prevention therapies that are undertaken beginning with menopause. Activities that generally keep us healthy—exercise, proper diet, not smoking—can play a part in this therapy. But the most well-known means of treating osteoporosis is one that involves replacing the hormones whose levels drop off with menopause. In hormone replacement therapy, women generally take pills or use skin patches that contain estrogen and a synthetic form of the hormone progesterone.

There is no doubt that hormone replacement therapy significantly reduces the risk of developing osteoporosis, and it seems to have a wealth of other benefits as well, most notably a reduction in the risk of heart disease. Against this, hormone replacement therapy appears to *raise* the risk of developing breast cancer. Given these complexities, there is no blanket recommendation about hormone replacement therapy. Instead, decisions need to be made on the basis of individual risk factors. (Is there a history of heart disease or breast cancer in the family, for example?)

There is another side to the prevention of osteoporosis, however—one that can involve *young* women, rather than middle-aged women. Bone is a dynamic tissue; at any given moment, the bone cells called *osteoclasts* are removing bone while the cells called *osteoblasts* are adding to it. It is the *balance* in this activity that changes through life. In a 15-year-old, there is much more bone being added than removed; in a 30-year-old these two activities are roughly balanced out; in a post-menopausal woman there is much more bone being removed than being added.

Human females attain almost all their growth in height by late adolescence, but they are still gaining in bone density up until about the age of 30. The critical thing is that the entire period until age 30 represents a *window of opportunity* to develop bone mass. And the more bone mass a woman has by 30, the less risk she will have of osteoporosis after menopause. Once the window of opportunity has closed, however, there is no possibility of raising *peak* bone density, meaning the highest bone density a woman will ever have. Whatever a woman achieves in this regard, she will achieve by age 30.

Most bone is deposited by late adolescence. But medical researcher Robert Recker and his colleagues at Creighton University found in the early 1990s that a group of women they tracked over several years added almost 13 percent to their bone mass during their 20s. Looking for lifestyle factors that might make a difference in adding bone, the researchers found three: physical exercise, intake of calcium and protein, and use of oral contraceptives. None of the women studied were heavy exercisers or had particularly high calcium intake. Thus, the research suggested that simple, modest increases in exercise and calcium during a woman's 20s might yield benefits decades later, when menopause begins and bones begin to thin.

Monitoring Comprehension and Writing in Response

Complete these activities collaboratively or independently as your instructor directs.

1. Sum up the main idea of Paragraph 1. _____
_____

2. Sum up the main idea of Paragraph 2. _____

   _____

   _____

3. Sum up the main idea of Paragraph 4. _____

   _____

   _____

4. Sum up the main idea of Paragraph 5. _____

   _____

   _____

5. Review the title and the main ideas of the paragraphs you have just written down. What big point is David Krogh trying to get across to you? Underline two or three sentences or groups of words that help you understand Krogh's thesis and write a sentence here that sums up his big point. _____

   _____

   _____

6. In your reading-response notebook, write a paragraph in which you explain the kinds of things you are doing to maintain a healthful lifestyle and to ensure that you have and long and happy life.

Reviewing Vocabulary

Star the option that provides the best definition for each italicized word as used in the sentences.

1. When the speaker knew that he had raised the crowd to a *peak* of excitement, he gradually lowered the tone and force of his remarks.
   a. high point   b. mountaintop   c. fast look   d. even level

2. Don't leap to make *blanket* judgments. You may get yourself into trouble.
   a. a wrap that is used to keep warm
   b. warm and smothering
   c. broad, all-inclusive
   d. modest

3. A *mass* of dandelions covered a large portion of the lawn.
   a. religious rite   b. large quantity together
   c. the common people   d. by the people

4. Under his leadership, the country made *modest* gains.
   a. shy   b. thoughtful   c. large   d. not too great

5. The *complexities* of the case really confused me.
   a. apartment complexes
   b. involved and interrelated component parts
   c. basic ideas
   d. beginning steps

6. Some people are highly *susceptible* to every suggestion their friends make.
   a. suspicious of
   b. next in line for

c. able to recognize
d. likely to be affected by

7. I realized that the product was *synthetic* because it did not have the characteristics of the original.

    a. not open   b. not sincere
    c. not able to be put together   d. not genuine

8. The man needed *therapy* to restore him to full functioning.

    a. treatment for illness or disability
    b. use of heat to raise temperature
    c. important and basic steps in a process
    d. consideration and thoughtfulness

9. The executive was a *dynamic* person.

    a. thoughtful and considerate
    b. filled with energy and on the move
    c. evil
    d. slow in taking action

SELECTION 2

Time Management: A Guide for Personal Planning (MANAGEMENT SCIENCE)

A Thesis-Building Workshop

Expanding Your Vocabulary for Reading

The italicized words are from the selection. Use word elements and the context to figure out their meanings. Record the meanings in the space provided. If you have trouble, check the glossary or a dictionary. Add one or two of the words to your personal vocabulary list.

1. The *interval* between the beginning of the college year and midterms is a frightening time for some new students. _____

   _____

2. During that time, you have to get your *priorities* straight. You must decide what is most important to you—doing well in your courses, going out and having a good time, or meeting a lot of people. _____

   _____

3. I have a major *objective*. My goal is to achieve at least a B average in college.

   _____

   _____

4. When you are a college student, you cannot *delegate* your responsibilities to someone else. You have to take care of them yourself. _____

   _____

5. I found it *cumbersome* to travel with two suitcases, a tote bag, and a briefcase.

   _____

   _____

Did You **KNOW?**

Ject- (or *jac-*) means "to throw." You find it on these words: *reject, interject, subjective,* and *ejaculate.*

Getting Ready to Read

Preview the selection.

1. Read the title of the next selection, the introductory paragraphs, the margin notes, and the subheadings. Based on your preview, predict what the article is about.

   _____

2. What do you already know about managing your time? What can you do to use your time wisely? Discuss these questions with a partner. Then jot down a few words or phrases that come to mind. _____

   _____

   _____

3. Set a purpose for reading. Read to find out the main idea, or thesis, this author is trying to communicate.

4. Gauge the reading load for you: light, average, or heavy.

Reading with Meaning

Read the selection, which is from a college textbook on management. If you take courses in management science, this is the kind of material you will read. As you read, note in the margin the main idea of each paragraph. If you have trouble, reread and ask, "What is Robbins trying to tell me?" Notice the helpful way in which this text provides definitions of terms in the margin.

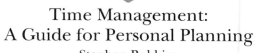

Time Management:
A Guide for Personal Planning
Stephen Robbins

Do any of the following describe you?

> You do interesting things before the uninteresting things?
> You do things that are easy before things that are difficult?
> You do things that are urgent before things that are important?
> You work on things in the order of their arrival?
> You wait until a deadline approaches before really moving on a project?

Time management
A personal form of scheduling time effectively

If you answered yes to one or more of these questions, you could benefit from time management. In this section, we'll present some suggestions to help you manage your time better. We'll show you that **time management** is actually a personal form of scheduling. Managers who use their time effectively know what activities they want to accomplish, the best order to take the activities in, and when they want to complete those activities.

Time as a Scarce Resource

Time is a unique resource in that, if it's wasted it can *never* be replaced. While people talk about *saving time,* the fact is that time can never actually be saved. It can't be stockpiled for use in some future period. If wasted, it can't be retrieved. When a minute is gone, it is gone forever.

The positive side of this resource is that all managers have it in equal abundance. While money, labor, and other resources are distributed unequally in this world, thus putting some managers at a disadvantage, every manager is allotted twenty-four hours every day and seven days every week. Some just use their allotments better than others.

Focusing on Discretionary Time

Managers can't control all of their time. They are routinely interrupted and have to respond to unexpected crises. It's necessary, therefore, to differentiate between response time and discretionary time.

The majority of a manager's time is spent responding to requests, demands, and problems initiated by others. We call this **response time** and treat it as uncontrollable. The portion that *is* under a manager's control is called **discretionary time.** Most of the suggestions offered to improve time management apply to its discretionary component. Why? Because only this part is manageable!

Unfortunately, for most managers, particularly those in the lower and middle ranks of the organization, discretionary time tends to become available in small pieces—five minutes here, five minutes there. Thus it is very difficult to use effectively. The challenge, then, is to know what time is discretionary and then to organize activities so as to accumulate discretionary time in blocks large enough to be useful. Those who are good at identifying and organizing their discretionary time get significantly more accomplished, and the things they accomplish are more likely to be high-priority activities.

Response time

Uncontrollable time spent responding to requests, demands, and problems initiated by others

Discretionary time

The part of a manager's time that is controllable

How Do You Use Your Time?

How do managers, or anyone for that matter, determine how well they use their time? The answer is that they should keep a log of daily activities for a short period of time, then evaluate the data they gather.

The best log is a daily diary or calendar broken into fifteen-minute intervals. To get enough information from which to generalize, you need about two weeks' worth of entries. During this two-week period, you enter everything you do in the diary in fifteen-minute segments. To minimize memory loss, post the entries as you do them. Keep in mind that honesty is important. You want to record how you actually spend your time, not how you *wished* you had spent your time!

When the diary is complete, you have a detailed time and activity log. Now you're ready to analyze how effectively you use your time. Rate each activity in terms of its importance and urgency (see Table 5.1). If you find that many activities received C's or D's, you'll find the next sections valuable. They provide detailed guidelines for better time management.

Five Steps to Better Time Management

The essence of time management is to use your time effectively. This requires that you know the objectives you want to accomplish, the activities that will lead to the accomplishment of those objectives, and the importance and urgency of each activity. We've translated this into a five-step process.

TABLE 5.1 *Analyzing Activities for Importance and Urgency*

Rate Each Activity for

Importance

A. Very important: must be done

B. Important: should be done

C. Not so important: may be useful, but is not necessary

D. Unimportant: doesn't accomplish anything

Urgency

A. Very urgent: must be done now

B. Urgent: should be done now

C. Not urgent: can be done sometime later

D. Time not a factor

1. *Make a list of your objectives.* What specific objectives have you set for yourself and the unit you manage?

2. *Rank the objectives according to their importance.* Not all objectives are of equal importance. Given the limitations on your time, you want to make sure you give highest priority to the most important objectives.

3. *List the activities necessary to achieve your objectives.* What specific actions do you need to take to achieve your objectives?

4. *For each objective, assign priorities to the various activities required to reach the objective.* This step imposes a second set of priorities. Here, you need to emphasize both importance and urgency. If the activity is not important, you should consider delegating it to someone below you. If it's not urgent, it can usually wait. This step will identify activities that you *must* do, those you *should* do, those you'll get to *when you can,* and those that can be *delegated to others.*

5. *Schedule your activities according to the priorities you've set.* The final step is to prepare a daily plan. Every morning, or at the end of the previous work day, make a list of the five or so most important things you want to do for the day. If the list grows to ten or more activities, it becomes cumbersome and ineffective. Then set priorities for the activities listed on the basis of importance and urgency.   [920 words]

Monitoring Comprehension and Writing in Response

Complete these activities collaboratively.

1. Think about the main idea of each paragraph in the selection. Do this by telling each main idea to yourself or a partner or two. Using a pencil, revise the main ideas you wrote down in the margin as you read.

2. What is Stephen Robbins trying to say about time management? To guide your thinking, answer these questions:

   • What does Robbins mean by "time management"? _____

   _____

   • On a scale of 1 to 5, with 1 very negative and 5 very positive, how does Robbins feel

   about time management? _____

   _____

   • What is the thesis of the selection? What is the major point Robbins is trying to

   communicate about time management? _____

   _____

   _____

3. Once you have written your answers to question 2, discuss them with a workshop partner or two. Having discussed your answers, you may want to revise them. Record here what you now think is the main thesis of the article.

   _____

   _____

4. Continue to collaborate with a partner or two. In your notebook, write a paragraph that states the thesis and some main ideas from the selection that support it. Start with a topic sentence that gives the thesis. Then add sentences that support it. Your paragraph will have a deductive design as shown on page 67.

Reviewing New Vocabulary

Insert each of these words in the sentence where it fits best. Use the process of elimination.

a. delegate   c. interval   e. priorities
b. cumbersome   d. objective

1. You must learn to _____ responsibility to those who work for you. You can't do everything yourself.

2. What is your primary _____ in taking a course in time management?

3. You must let a decent _____ elapse before you get married again.

4. What are your _____? What is most important to you? What is least important?

5. If a box is overly large, you may find it _____ to carry.

SELECTION 3

The Meaning of Democracy (POLITICAL SCIENCE)

A Thesis-Building Workshop

Expanding Your Vocabulary for Reading

The italicized words in the following sentences are from the selection. Use the context and word elements to help you figure out their meanings. Write down your hypothesized meanings in the space provided. You may check them in the glossary.

1. People who come from different cultures have different *traditions*—customs, beliefs, ways of doing things—that have been handed down from one generation to the next.

_____

_____

2. His *ideology* differed greatly from mine. He held a set of beliefs totally at odds with my beliefs in a democratic form of government. _____

_____

_____

3. Some governments *pervert* the meaning of democratic government, using the term "democracy" in ways that are antidemocratic. _____

_____

4. and 5. In some countries, the government *suppresses*, or puts down, any form of *dissent*. Even people who take peaceful action against their government are considered rebels and may be put in prison. _____

_____

_____

6. Often during political campaigns, candidates have *slogans* that sum up the direction in which they would lead the government if elected. One such slogan might be, "Put honesty back into government." _____

_____

Did You KNOW?

Suppresses is formed from two elements: the prefix *sup-*, meaning "under," and the base *press-*, meaning "to press." You see *press-* in such words as *impression* and *depress*.

7. Americans believe that each individual has certain *inalienable* rights—rights that cannot be taken away by the government. _____

_____

8. Each child or youth in the country is *entitled* to a free public education through age eighteen. _____

_____

9. I had not meant to *minimize* my friend's contribution, but I guess I had not complimented him sufficiently because he took offense. _____

_____

10. Unfortunately, *discrimination* continues in America; because of their race, gender, or religion, some people do not receive the respect and opportunities they are entitled to under the Constitution. _____

_____

11. To *ensure* that discrimination disappears across this nation, each person must study his or her own views and actions. _____

_____

12. The king was a *benevolent* monarch, looking out for the welfare of his subjects.

_____

_____

13. Ideologically, Stanley is a true *democrat*. He believes in such democratic traditions as individual dignity, equality under the law, participation by the people in decision making, and majority rule. _____

_____

Did You KNOW?

The element *mini-* means "small"; its opposite is *maxi-*, which means "large." You have seen these elements on such words as *minimum* and *maximum*.

Did You KNOW?

The suffixlike ending *-cracy* means "rule by"; the base *demo-* is from a Greek word that means "people."

Getting Ready to Read

Read the title, the four subheadings, and the margin notes. Then think about and answer these questions.

- What is the topic of the article? _____

- Predict the thesis based on the title, the notes, and headings you just read.

_____

- Gauge the reading load for you. Is this a more difficult or less difficult article for you as compared to the one on time management that you just read?

_____

Reading with Meaning

Read the selection, which is from a political science textbook. Keep asking yourself, "What is Thomas Dye trying to tell me about democratic government?"

The Meaning of Democracy
Thomas R. Dye

Throughout the centuries, thinkers in many different cultures contributed to the development of democratic government. Early Greek philosophers contributed the word **democracy,** which means "rule by the many." But there is no single definition of *democracy,* nor is there a tightly organized system of democratic thought. It is better, perhaps, to speak of democratic traditions than of a single democratic ideology.

Unfortunately, the looseness of the term *democracy* allows it to be perverted by *anti*democratic governments. Hardly a nation in the world exists that does not *claim* to be "democratic." Governments that outlaw political opposition, suppress dissent, discourage religion, and deny fundamental freedoms of speech and press still claim to be "democracies," "democratic republics," or "people's republics" (for example, the Democratic People's Republic of Korea is the official name of Communist North Korea). These governments defend their use of the term *democracy* by claiming that their policies reflect the true interests of their people. But they are unwilling to allow political freedoms or to hold free elections in order to find out whether their people really agree with their policies. In effect, they use the term as a political slogan rather than a true description of their government.

The actual existence of **democratic ideals** varies considerably from country to country, regardless of their names. A meaningful definition of democracy must include the following ideals: recognition of the dignity of every individual; equal protection under the law for every individual; opportunity for everyone to participate in public decisions; and decision making by majority rule, with one person having one vote.

Individual Dignity

The underlying value of democracy is the dignity of the individual. Human beings are entitled to life and liberty, personal property, and equal protection under the law. These liberties are *not* granted by governments; they belong to every person born into the world. The English political philosopher John Locke (1632–1704) argued that a higher "natural law" guaranteed liberty to every person and that this natural law was morally superior to all human laws and governments. Each individual possesses "certain inalienable Rights, among these are Life, Liberty, and Property."

Individual dignity requires personal freedom. People who are directed by governments in every aspect of their lives, people who are "collectivized" and made into workers for the state, people who are enslaved—all are denied the personal dignity to which all human beings are entitled. Democratic governments try to minimize the role of government in the lives of citizens.

Equality

True democracy requires equal protection of the law for every individual. Democratic governments cannot discriminate between blacks and whites, or men and women, or rich and poor, or any groups of people in applying the law. Not only must a democratic government refrain from discrimination itself, but it must also work to prevent discrimination in society generally. Today our notion of equality extends to equality of opportunity—the obligation of government to ensure that all Americans have an opportunity to develop their full potential.

Participation in Decision Making

Democracy means individual participation in the decisions that affect individuals' lives. People should be free to choose for themselves how they want to live. Individual participation in government is necessary for individual dignity. People in a democracy should not have decisions made *for* them but *by* them. Even if they make mistakes, it is better that

democracy Governing system in which the people govern themselves; from the Greek term meaning "rule by the many."

democratic ideals Individual dignity, equality before the law, widespread participation in public decisions, and public decisions by majority rule, with one person having one vote.

they be permitted to do so than to take away their rights to make their own decisions. The true democrat would reject even a wise and benevolent dictatorship because it would threaten the individual's character, self-reliance, and dignity. The argument for democracy is not that the people will always choose wise policies for themselves but that people who cannot choose for themselves are not really free.

Majority Rule: One Person, One Vote

Collective decision making in democracies must be by majority rule with each person having one vote. That is, each person's vote must be equal to every other person's, regardless of status, money, or fame. Whenever any individual is denied political equality because of race, sex, or wealth, then the government is not truly democratic. Majorities are not always right. But majority *rule* means that all persons have an equal say in decisions affecting them. If people are truly equal, their votes must count equally, and a majority vote must decide the issue, even if the majority decides foolishly.

Monitoring Comprehension and Writing in Response

Complete these activities collaboratively or independently as your instructor directs.

1. Sum up the main idea of Paragraph 1. _____

   _____

2. Sum up the main idea of Paragraph 2. _____

   _____

   _____

3. Sum up the main idea of Paragraph 3. _____

   _____

   _____

4. Review the title and the main ideas of the paragraphs you have just written down. What big point is Thomas Dye trying to get across to you about democratic government? Underline two or three sentences or groups of words that are clues that help you understand Dye's thesis and write a sentence here that sums up his big point.

   _____

   _____

5. In your reading-response notebook, write a paragraph in which you tell about one important feature of life under a democratic government and why you are glad you live within this kind of system rather than within a dictatorship.

Reviewing Vocabulary

A. Select the words from the following list and write them on the lines where they fit best based on the context. Cross out options as you use them. Use each option only once.

benevolent	democratic	dissent	discrimination
ensure	entitled to	ideologies	inalienable
minimize	perverted	slogan	suppress
traditions			

Americans should not _____ the fact that they are fortunate

to live in a _____ country in which each person has certain

_____ rights: life, liberty, and property. Although the ideals of a democratic government have been _____ in some countries (especially in countries with governments where people are not allowed to _____ in any way), in America each person is _____ respect and equal treatment before the law. Democratic _____ are firmly in place in America. Unfortunately, _____ still exists; Americans look forward to a time when no one is mistreated because of his or her gender, race, or religion. It is the responsibility of each citizen to reject _____ that would strip away the right of all people to participate in decisions that affect their lives.

B. You did not use four of the words listed in section A. Write sentences in which you use those words.

EXTENDING WHAT YOU HAVE LEARNED

Reading for the Thesis of a Selection

How do you figure out an author's thesis? Write your strategy here.

Applying Your Strategy

1. Read a column from the editorial page of a local newspaper. Read to determine the thesis the author of the column is trying to get across. Record the title of the article, the author's name, and his or her thesis on an index card. Bring your card to class to share.

2. Read a segment from a college textbook. Read to find out the thesis the author of the textbook is trying to get across in that segment of text. Record the title of the segment, the author's name, and his or her thesis on an index card. Bring your card to class to share.

6
Relating Main Ideas and Details

OBJECTIVE

In this chapter, you will learn strategies for thinking about details as you read. Specifically, you will learn to

1. Sort details to identify the more significant ones, and
2. Rely on approximations when reading numerical details.

In addition, you will have the opportunity to refine your main idea and fix-up strategies.

THINKING ABOUT DETAILS

In developing the main idea of a paragraph, a writer generally includes supporting detail. Some details relate directly to the main idea; these help support the point the writer is making. Other details relate in some way to the main idea, but they are not essential to the point the writer is making. In a way, these details are icing on the cake; they add interest and flavor.

IDENTIFYING SIGNIFICANT DETAILS

In reading, it is important to identify the significant details that support the point a writer is making. A basic strategy for doing this is to ask yourself two questions:

SIGNIFICANT DETAILS
STRATEGY

→ How does this detail relate to the main idea?

→ Does this detail support the main point, or is it icing on the cake?

Ask these questions as you read a paragraph. Do not wait until the end. Sorting significant from less essential details is a continuous process; you do it all the time as you read.

Let's apply this strategy to the details in a paragraph about author James Michener.

Think
about . . .
What is a significant detail?

The lobby of the hotel just outside Washington, D.C., was teeming with purposeful, name-tagged men and women awaiting the beginning of the afternoon convention schedule. Outside, motorists locked horns on the busy street, and a taxi broke free and sprinted to the hotel entrance. A man in a rumpled blue suit emerged, fumbled for the fare, and stepped through the door. He was bespectacled and looked like a college professor, which he once was. He carried a small overnight bag and was not wearing a name tag. He walked with an almost imperceptible limp, to the registration desk and handed a piece of paper to the clerk, who advised him, "Your room is ready, Mr. 'Mikener.'" America's most popular serious novelist eschewed an offer to carry his bag and walked to the elevator alone. None of the crowd in the lobby had noticed him.

The point the paragraph is making is that Michener was a humble man. What details from the paragraph support this picture of Michener? Before reading on, write down three details that support this main idea.

1. _____

2. _____

3. _____

Essential details include the fact that Michener carried his own bag, wore a rumpled suit, did not wear a name tag, and did not correct the clerk who mispronounced his name. These details support the idea of the paragraph—Michener as a humble man.

What about the less significant details in the paragraph about Michener? Write down at least one detail that has little bearing on the main idea.

_____

One rather insignificant detail is that motorists were locking horns. Another is that the street was busy. Even the fact that the hotel lobby was filled with people has little bearing on Michener's natural humility.

What function do these details have in the paragraph? They are the icing! They make an interesting beginning and add style to the writing. They also provide a contrast. Here were all these purposeful, name-tagged men and women, probably dressed for success. In contrast was this rumpled and fumbling man, America's most popular serious novelist.

Is it important to remember the lesser details? In most cases, no. As readers we move our eyes over them, getting the flavor of the writing and going on to details that support the main idea.

APPROXIMATING NUMERICAL DETAIL

Some paragraphs are filled with numerical detail—lots of numbers given in support of the main idea. A strategy to use here is to

**NUMERICAL DETAIL
STRATEGY**

→ Look at the precise details and approximate a ballpark figure.

Let's apply this strategy to another paragraph about Michener. Read it, asking two questions: What is the main idea? How will I handle all those numbers that relate to the main idea?

> Michener was 40 years old before he settled on a literary career, but in the many years since then he wrote 33 books that have sold 21 million copies, been translated into 52 languages, inspired 12 films and one smash Broadway musical. All but a few of his books are still in print and readily available. The popularity of such novels as *The Bridges at Toko-Ri, Hawaii, The Source, Chesapeake* and *Centennial* have made him America's most popular serious novelist—a distinction he viewed with considerable humility.

The main idea is that Michener was a prolific author; in his lifetime, he wrote many books. But what do you do with the numbers that support the main point?

Unless you are required to know these details, you generalize, based on the numbers. You do not try to remember that Michener wrote 33 books but think in terms of *more than 30 books.* Notice that this is a ballpark figure—in other words, an approximation. Similarly, you generalize that the books have been translated into *lots of languages,* and *some films* have been based on the books.

Think
about . . .
What are some things you already do to monitor your control over details?

Think
about . . .
What do you do when you make an approximation? When do you naturally use approximations?

Read this paragraph from the same Michener article. As you read a detail, do not try to remember it. Try for a ballpark approximation:

> Michener was probably the most traveled writer in history. He estimated he had been to Singapore 50 times, Burma 20 times and Bora Bora eight times. He lived and worked for extended periods in Afghanistan, Australia, Fiji, Hawaii, India, Israel, Japan, Mexico, Portugal, Samoa, Spain, Tahiti, Thailand and Vienna.

The main point of the paragraph is that Michener was widely traveled. Write two details from the paragraph—in ballpark terms—to support the point.

1. _____

2. _____

From the data you may have generalized that Michener visited some locations from 8 to 50 times. You may have noted that he traveled all over the world, from Spain to Tahiti. It probably is not essential to remember all the places mentioned.

In the remainder of this chapter, you will have the opportunity to practice your strategy for identifying significant details.

SELECTION 1
Great Constructions of the Past: The Biggest and Greatest (HISTORY)

A Reading Strategies Workshop

Getting Ready to Read

To handle main ideas and details with any degree of proficiency, you must be able to identify whether details support a main idea. For example, read this statement of a main idea:

> **Main Idea:** The Great Pyramids of Gizeh are the most famous of the pyramids of Egypt.

Now read these statements of detail, asking yourself, "Which of the statements provides a detail that supports the main idea—the idea that the Gizeh Pyramids are the most famous? Which are about pyramids but do not relate directly to the fame of the Pyramids of Gizeh?"

Significant detail: supports the idea of fame

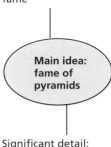

Main idea: fame of pyramids

Significant detail: supports the idea of fame

• The Step Pyramid is older than the Pyramids of Gizeh.
• The Great Pyramid at Gizeh is one of the Seven Wonders of the Ancient World.
• The Mayans also built pyramids.
• The Pyramids of Gizeh are located near the city of Cairo.

All the details are true, but only one supports the idea of the fame of the pyramids: The Great Pyramid at Gizeh is one of the Seven Wonders of the Ancient World. The Gizeh pyramid must have been outstanding and famous to be so named. The other facts—that the Step Pyramid is older, that the Mayans built pyramids, and that the Gizeh pyramids are located near Cairo—are true but do not relate directly to or support the main idea: the fame of the Pyramids of Gizeh.

Reading with Meaning

Working in teams, read the following main idea statements, decide on the topic of the main idea sentence in each group, and record the topic in the margin. Then decide on the detail that most strongly supports each main idea and star it. All the items deal with engineering accomplishments of the past. Someday you may visit these wonders of the world.

Great Constructions of the Past:
The Biggest and Greatest

1. **Main Idea:** The Great Sphinx is a colossal sculpture set like a guard near the Pyramid of Khafre in Egypt.
   a. The Great Sphinx has the head of a human and a body of a large lion.
   b. Thousands of sphinxes were built in ancient Egypt.
   c. The sphinx is part of Greek mythology.
   d. In Greek mythology, the sphinx was a winged monster with the head of a woman and the body of a lion.

2. **Main Idea:** The Colossus of Rhodes was a large bronze statue that once stood in the harbor of Rhodes, an island in the eastern Mediterranean Sea.
   a. Legend says that the Colossus stood across the harbor and ships passed between its legs.
   b. A famous American colossus is the Statue of Liberty.
   c. The human mind has always been intrigued by great statues.
   d. The Mediterranean Sea separates Europe from North Africa and has always been important in the trade of this area.

3. **Main Idea:** Some astronomers propose that the immense standing stones of Stonehenge in England were built by ancient people to measure solar and lunar movements.
   a. There are some similarities between Stonehenge and another ancient monument of stones near Avebury in England.
   b. So many visitors now come to Stonehenge that it is no longer possible to wander among the upright stones.
   c. Astronomer Gerald Hawkins used computers to test his belief, or hypothesis, that the stones related to astronomical movements.
   d. Stonehenge is a short day trip from London.

4. **Main Idea:** The term *romanesque* describes the style of architecture that was seen in western Europe between the end of the ninth and the twelfth centuries.
   a. Architects who worked during the ninth to the twelfth centuries had low social status.
   b. The church was a dominant force during the ninth to the twelfth centuries.
   c. The Durham Cathedral, begun in Durham, England, in 1093, is an outstanding example of romanesque architecture.
   d. Few romanesque cathedrals remain today exactly as they were originally constructed.

5. **Main Idea:** The gothic age (1150–1300) was a period of great cathedral building in France.
   a. The ribs on a gothic vault are there primarily for aesthetic purposes.
   b. People harnessed themselves to carts to pull the limestone building blocks from the quarry to the cathedral site.
   c. The people of the period felt that the cathedral belonged to them; they took pride in their gift to God.
   d. French cathedrals built during this period include Notre Dame de Paris, Rheims, Chartres, Amiens, Le Mans, Beauvais, and many other lesser-known ones.

6. **Main Idea:** The Suez Canal is an important transportational link that facilitates world trade.
   a. The Suez Canal connects the Mediterranean Sea with the Gulf of Suez and then with the Red Sea.
   b. The Suez Canal was constructed between 1859 and 1869.
   c. The modern-day canal was planned by a French engineer; the British underwrote much of the cost of the canal.

Think about . . .

As you read, do you wish you could travel to some of these far-away places? Which would you like to see the most?

d. The Suez Canal is a sea-level canal that is more than 100 miles long; it is longer than the Panama Canal.

7. **Main Idea:** Mount Rushmore is a national shrine that honors great American presidents.
   a. The same sculptor who worked on Stone Mountain in Georgia got the idea for Mount Rushmore.
   b. Mount Rushmore is located in the state of South Dakota in the Black Hills.
   c. It took fourteen years to carve the faces in the stone; the sculptor, Gutzon Borglum, died before the carving was completed.
   d. Carved in the rock of the mountain are the faces of four great presidents.

8. **Main Idea:** The Verrazano-Narrows Bridge is the longest suspension bridge in the United States.
   a. The Verrazano-Narrows Bridge was designed by O. H. Ammann.
   b. The Verrazano-Narrows Bridge is 4,260 feet long and spans the Narrows at the entrance to New York harbor.
   c. The Verrazano-Narrows Bridge was named for Giovanni da Verrazano, an Italian sailing in the service of France, who possibly was the first European to enter New York Bay.
   d. The Verrazano-Narrows Bridge has two levels; each holds six lanes of traffic.

SELECTION 2

He's My Son! (SOCIOLOGY)

A Story-Retelling Workshop

Expanding Your Vocabulary Through Reading

Here are five words from the selection you will read: *assumption, expectation, contradiction, situation, interaction.* These nouns have been formed from verbs to which the suffix *-tion* has been added. An assumption is something we assume, or take for granted. A contradiction is something that contradicts, or goes against another piece of evidence. An expectation is something that we expect, or anticipate. A situation is something that is situated somewhere. Interaction occurs when people interact with one another. Write two other words that have the suffix *-tion* in them. From what verb was each constructed?

_____   _____
word with *-tion*   verb   word with *-tion*   verb

When you read a noun with the suffix *-tion*, identify the verb from which it was constructed. You can use your understanding of the verb to figure out the meaning of the noun.

Getting Ready to Read

Read the title and the first sentence of the selection, which is from a college sociology text. Predict what you anticipate is going to happen next? Write your expectation here.

_____

_____

Reading with Meaning

Read to find out what happened, to identify the main idea (the thesis), and to retell the story, giving only details that relate to the main idea.

Think
about . . .

What do you say to yourself in your mind to figure this out?

Did You KNOW?

Other *-tion* words are *deletion, direction,* and *relation.*

He's My Son!
John Macionis

The automobile roared down the mountain road, tearing through sheets of windblown rain. Two people, a man and his young son, peered intently through the windshield, observing the edge of the road beyond which they could see only a black void. Suddenly, as the car rounded a bend, the headlights shone upon a large tree that had fallen across the roadway. The man swerved to the right and braked, but unable to stop, the car left the road, crashed through some brush, turned end upon end, and came to rest on its roof. Then a bit of good fortune: the noise of the crash had been heard at a nearby hunting lodge, and a telephone call from there soon brought police and a rescue crew. The driver, beyond help, was pronounced dead at the scene of the accident. Yet, the boy was still alive, although badly hurt and unconscious. Rushed by ambulance to the hospital in the town at the foot of the mountain, he was taken immediately into emergency surgery.

Alerted in advance, the medical team burst through the swinging doors ready to try to save the boy's life. Then, with a single look at his face, the surgeon abruptly exclaimed: "Oh, no! Get someone to take over for me—I can't operate on this boy. *He's my son!*"

How can the surgeon's reaction be explained?

This situation appears to contain a contradiction: If the boy's father died in the crash, how could the boy be the surgeon's son? The contradiction, however, exists only in the reader's *assumption* that the surgeon must be male. Inconsistency is resolved if we conclude that the surgeon is simply the boy's *mother.*

Social interaction is the process by which people act and react in relation to others. Through social interaction human beings create meaning in any situation. Every situation, however, is also shaped by assumptions and expectations rooted in the larger society of which we are a part.   [330 words]

Did You
KNOW?
Windshield, headlights, and *roadway* are compound words. Can you see the component words in them?

Monitoring Comprehension

1. What is the big idea, the thesis, that the sociologist is trying to get across through this

   story? _____

   _____

2. Turn to a workshop partner and tell him or her the story, leaving out the unessential facts and including only those necessary to get the tale across. Then together study the story and identify the details you left out. Why were those details not essential to

   the telling of the tale? _____

   _____

3. Mark the following as an essential (*E*) or unessential (*U*) detail.

   _____ a. The car came to rest on its roof.

   _____ b. There was a lodge nearby.

   _____ c. The father was killed.

   _____ d. The boy was injured.

   _____ e. The team burst through the swinging doors.

   _____ f. The surgeon said, "He's my son!"

   _____ g. The hospital was at the foot of the mountain.

   _____ h. The medical team was alerted in advance.

Reviewing Key Vocabulary

Place each word in the sentence where it best fits the context. Use each word only once. Use the process of elimination, and cross out options as you use them.

assumption   contradiction   expectation   interaction   situation

1. The _____ was resolved when the judge pointed out the inconsistency in the evidence.

2. He was operating under an unwarranted _____ that he later learned was untrue.

3. In that _____ there was only one thing that we could do—run for safety.

4. Professors try to encourage _____ among members of a class.

5. I bought the book with the _____ that it was a novel. I discovered immediately upon opening it that I was in error.

SELECTION 3
What Does McDonald's Pay? (ECONOMICS)

A Reading Workshop

Getting Ready to Read

Read the title and the first paragraph of this selection from a college economics text.

What do you think determines what McDonald's pays? _____

_____

Reading with Meaning

Read the selection to test your prediction and get at the main ideas. Read also to pick out the most essential details. Underline the topic sentences as you go along.

What Does McDonald's Pay?
Karl Case and Ray Fair

At two locations about 40 minutes apart in the Boston area, McDonald's hires workers at very different wage rates. At one franchise, a small sign on the counter reads "Help wanted, full or part time." If you ask about a job, however, you will find that they have only one part-time opening, and that the wage rate offered is the minimum wage, $3.35 per hour. At the other location, a large sign says "Full-time or part-time positions available, day or night shifts, excellent benefits and $7.00 per hour." The location has six openings.

Why would one restaurant pay wages nearly twice as high as an identical place with identical jobs in the same metropolitan area? The franchise owner simply finds that she has no applicants at lower wages, and even at the higher rates, she has a very difficult time keeping her available positions filled.

Clearly the two restaurants are buying labor in different labor markets. If people could move at no cost from one point to another, such wage differences would disappear. But there are costs. Neither of these restaurants is accessible by public transportation. Thus to take a job at one of them, you must live nearby or have a car. Restaurants such as McDonald's draw much of their labor from the supply of high-school students who want to work part time. Most of them don't have cars. The high-wage franchise is on a major highway at some distance from local high schools and residential areas; the low-wage franchise is in the center of a town.

Other facts as well probably affect the available labor supplies at the two locations. The median income of the four towns surrounding the high-wage franchise is 50 percent higher than the median income of the four towns surrounding the low-wage franchise. To the extent that the labor supply is made up of students, parents' income may well have an effect. Higher-income families may spend some of their money buying leisure for their children. Many lower-income families expect older children to contribute to the family income.

The data support this argument. In one of the lower-income towns, 82 percent of all high-school students held at least one part-time job during the school year. In one of the high-income towns, only 24 percent of high-school students held part-time jobs.

In the high-wage area, the demand for labor in general is also higher. A number of major employers relatively close by pay high wages and hire part-time workers. In addition, workers, whether or not they are students, are more likely to have cars in the high-wage area. Cars give them the ability to search for work over a wider geographical area.

This example illustrates at least three important points. First, labor supply depends on a number of factors including wage rates, nonlabor income, and wealth. Second, individual firms have very little control over the market wage; firms are forced to pay the wage that is determined by the market. Finally, because people cannot be moved free of charge, and because people do not reside at their workplaces, there is an important spatial dimension to labor markets. Different supply and demand conditions can and do prevail at different geographical locations. This is true across regions as well as within cities. Labor markets in different regions of the country—Northeast, South, and so forth—are very different.   [572 words]

Did You KNOW?

The base *medi-* means "middle." Related words are *intermediate* and *mediate.*

Monitoring Comprehension

In the last paragraph, the authors sum up their major points. For each point, give one or two details from the selection that support it. When working with numbers, use a ballpark figure. You may collaborate with a partner.

Think about . . .

Did you have to reread and fix up? At what point was fix-up most important for you?

1. **Main Idea:** Labor supply depends on a number of factors, including wage rates, nonlabor income, and wealth.

   Supporting Details: _____

   _____

2. **Main Idea:** Individual companies have little control over the wages they must pay.

   Supporting Details: _____

   _____

3. **Main Idea:** Because people cannot be moved free of charge, location influences what wages a company must pay.

   Supporting Details: _____

   _____

SELECTION 4

The Dream at Panama (GEOGRAPHY AND HISTORY)

A Reading Workshop

Expanding Your Vocabulary Through Reading

Pronounce the italicized words by breaking them into syllables. Then determine the meanings by using context clues and word elements. Record your definitions in the space provided.

Did You
KNOW?

Akin is from an old
Anglo-Saxon base, not
a Latin one. Related
words are *kin* and
kinship.

Think
about . . .

What sentence clues do
you use to figure out
the meaning of the
italicized words?

1. The *isthmus,* the narrow strip of land between the two islands, was visible only at low
   tide. _____
   _____

2. *Devastating* winds roared over the countryside, destroying everything in sight.
   _____
   _____

3. The situation that existed after World War II was *akin* to the situation after World
   War I. _____
   _____

4. All the energy he could *muster* was not enough for him to move the boulder.
   _____
   _____

5. For Washington, the Battle of Long Island was a *debacle.* He was forced to retreat with
   his troops. _____
   _____

6. The wagons became *mired* in the mud. We had no way to pull them out.
   _____
   _____

7. During the war, we had to endure *horrific* conditions: lack of food, medicine, adequate
   shelter, and even pure water.
   _____
   _____

8. The *incumbent* judge—the one currently in office—will try the case.
   _____
   _____

9. She was a *virtual* prisoner of the rebels for two months; there was a guard at her door,
   and she could not leave her home.
   _____
   _____

10. At the end of the month we were *inundated* with bills. There were so many we could
    not pay them. _____
    _____

11. The *continental divide* is a ridge of mountains that separates rivers flowing into one
    ocean from those flowing into the other. In North America, the continental divide
    is the ridge of the Rocky Mountains, which separates westward-flowing streams from
    eastward-flowing ones.
    _____
    _____

Getting Ready to Read

Preview the selection.

- Read the title and the first paragraph. Study the illustrations in Figure 6.1. What is the topic of the selection? Write the topic in the center of the following idea web.

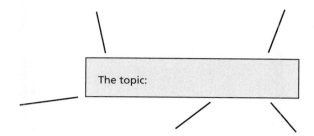

The topic:

- Talk with teammates about what you already know about the Panama Canal. Would you want to take a cruise ship through the Canal? Why? Then working together, add what you already know to the web. Include your opinions.
- What questions do you want to answer based on your preview of the selection?

  Write some questions here. _____

  _____

  _____

Reading with Meaning

Read the selection, keeping your purpose-setting questions in mind and visualizing what is being described. Then reread the article; for the numbered paragraphs, record significant details that support the main idea. If your instructor permits it, complete the activity with a partner. The first two paragraphs are done as models.

The Dream at Panama
George Cruys

Perhaps there is only the moon to compare with it. Of all the achievements of American engineering, only the landing on the moon and the planting there of a wrinkled flag can rival the construction of the Panama Canal as an epoch-making accomplishment. The Suez Canal, the trans-Siberian Railroad and the Taj Mahal all pale beside it. The canal's construction is more closely akin to the pyramids of Egypt in its scope and difficulty of execution, but in the modern era, there is only the moon.

    Like the landing on the moon, the construction of a canal across the narrow Isthmus of Panama was a dream long before it became reality. As early as 1534, Charles I of Spain proposed a canal at Panama, but it would take nearly 400 years for builders to catch up with his imagination.

    When the canal finally was proposed, it required all the creativity the twentieth century could muster. It was the largest public work ever attempted. Its engineers had to control a wild river, cut the continental divide, construct the largest dam and man-made lake known to that date and swing the largest locks ever constructed from the biggest cement structures ever poured. Along the way, two of the world's most devastating diseases had to be wiped out in one of their greatest strongholds. And all of this was to be done without the airplane or the automobile: Kitty Hawk rose into the headlines in 1903—the same year the U.S. signed a treaty with Panama—and there was no road across the isthmus until World War II.

    If Panama has had an unusual role in bygone dreams, it most certainly has a startling relationship to the hard facts of geography. The country is farther east than most people

1. **Main Idea:** The building of the Panama Canal is an epoch-making accomplishment. **Supporting Detail:** Building the canal is akin to building the pyramids.

2. **Main Idea:** The canal required great creativity. **Supporting Detail:** The engineers had to control a wild river.

FIGURE 6.1 Views of the Panama Canal Being Built
*(Panama Canal Company). For more views of and information about the
Panama Canal, log onto the Web and visit these sites:*
http://pharos.bu.edu/Egypt/Wonders/Modern/panama.html
http://www.greenarrow.com/panama/intro.htm.

imagine—the canal and about half of Panama actually lie east of Miami. Because of the country's shallow "S" shape and east-west orientation, it has places where the sun rises in the Pacific and sets in the Atlantic. More significantly, Panama is squeezed into the narrowest portion of Central America. At the canal, just 43 miles of land separate Atlantic and Pacific shores. Perhaps even more important, Panama offers the lowest point in the North American continental divide—originally 312 feet above sea level at the canal's Culebra Cut. By comparison, the lowest pass in the United States is nearly 5,000 feet.

3. Main Idea: Geographic relationships are important at the canal. **Supporting Detail:**

Spanish & French Era

The first path across the isthmus was Las Cruces Trail. A winding, difficult tunnel through the jungle from Panama City to Portobelo, it was built by slaves to transport riches to the Spanish Main. At the edge of the narrow trail a tangled mass of strange plants issues threatening noises even today. "It's O.K. in the daytime," said guide José Turner during a recent visit, "but imagine it at night."

California's gold rush sent thousands of prospectors to Panama in search of a quick crossing to the Pacific. By 1855, a small railroad operated between coasts and some prospectors paid $25 in gold just to walk along its tracks. Today the train costs $1.75 to ride and takes about an hour and a half to cross the continent. The new railroad encouraged engineers toward one of the greatest peacetime debacles in human experience: the ill-fated French attempt to build a sea level canal at Panama.

4. Main Idea: A railroad was built and encouraged the French to build a sea-level canal. **Supporting Detail:**

Crossing the canal today, it is hard to imagine the impossible challenge Panama presented just a century ago. Today's transit is so smooth and the surrounding grounds so parklike, the stories of horror in the jungle sound like tropical exaggerations. But in 1881, when the first party of French engineers arrived to dig the canal, the Isthmus of Panama was—as an American senator would later put it—"death's nursery."

Panama is inundated by seventy inches of annual rainfall on the Pacific side, and an improbable 144 inches on the Atlantic side. Up to six inches can fall in a single day. Fed by this rain, the Chagres River, which empties into the Atlantic just west of modern Cristobal, could rise more than forty-five feet. During one storm it rose ten feet in just twenty-four hours.

5. Main Idea: Excessive rainfall was a major problem. **Supporting Detail:**

The rain forest is a threatening wall of vegetation inhabited by all manner of equally threatening creatures. On Barro Colorado—a single island in modern Gatun Lake—there are twenty-two species of alligators, two species of crocodiles and thirty-seven species of serpents, while area mammals include the jaguar, puma and ocelot.

But the most formidable creature of Panama, when the French were deciding to build a canal there, was one of its smallest. The clean, soft skins of engineers and laborers were about to be welcomed by clouds of mosquitoes—and at the time that the French arrived, nobody knew that they carried disease.

6. Main Idea: The worst problem was the mosquito. **Supporting Detail:**

Malaria and yellow fever were the worst diseases, but others included nearly all of the bad ones: cholera, typhoid, dysentery, tuberculosis, smallpox, and—for a frightening interlude during the American era—black plague. In the twenty years that the French would labor to build their hopeless canal, roughly 20,000 people would perish—most of them from disease. Jules Dingler, the director of the French excavations in 1883, lost his entire family in Panama to disease—wife, son, daughter and prospective son-in-law. After two crushing years, he went home to France.

7. Main Idea: Many people lost their lives to diseases. **Supporting Detail:**

The French canal, spearheaded by Suez builder Ferdinand de Lesseps, became mired in mud, jungle, disease, rising costs, corruption and controversy. Leaders of the private undertaking were sentenced to prison; 25,000 Jamaican laborers were stranded when the company went bankrupt. In 1904 the French sold their interest in the canal to the United States for $40 million—a sum considerably short of the $287 million they had invested and vastly less than it had cost them in lives and broken dreams. . . .

8. Main Idea: French canal builders faced problems that made them give up the project. **Supporting Detail:**

The American Era

In 1906, when the bespectacled Theodore Roosevelt came to Panama to see the "Big Ditch" for himself, the occasion marked the first visit of an incumbent president to a foreign country in the history of the United States. It was a clear sign of the importance Roosevelt would place on the canal's construction.

9. **Main Idea:** U.S. signed a treaty with Panama in the early 1900s to establish a Canal Zone.
   Supporting Detail:

10. **Main Idea:** The key advantage was the virtual elimination of disease.
    Supporting Detail:

11. **Topic:** The Gatun Dam
    Main Idea:

    Supporting Detail:

12. **Topic:** Getting across the continental divide
    Main Idea:

    Supporting Detail:

13. **Topic:** The Culebra solution
    Main Idea:

    Supporting Detail:

At the turn of the century Panama was part of Colombia, ruled by Bogotá. When negotiations with Colombia for U.S. rights to build a canal came to a standstill, Panama proclaimed its independence in 1903 with key U.S. support. Less than a month later, a treaty with the Panamanian Republic established a Panama Canal Zone to be controlled by the U.S. "in perpetuity," extending five miles on either side of the proposed waterway.

The Americans arrived in 1904 equipped with several advantages over their French predecessors. Larger steam shovels, bigger train cars, a huge national effort supported by a closer home country and an astonishingly corruption-free administration all favored the American attempt. The new engineers, it was noted, were particularly adept at using the rails to transport excavated material.

The key initial accomplishment was the virtual elimination of disease by Dr. William Gorgas, a U.S. Army physician who had already survived a yellow fever attack in Texas and one of malaria in Panama. With exacting and lifesaving thoroughness, Dr. Gorgas wiped out the breeding grounds of mosquitoes in the construction area. In an immense effort which at times included as many as 4,000 sanitation laborers, Gorgas eliminated yellow fever by the end of 1905 and radically reduced malaria.

With disease on the wane, engineers set to work. By 1907 some 30,000 men had arrived, primarily from Barbados, Jamaica and the United States. Due to a shortage of available labor, Panama itself supplied just 357 workers for the canal.

The solution for the flooding Chagres River was to build an enormous dam that would create a lake over which ships could sail. Locks would raise ships to lake level, reducing the dig at Culebra on the continental divide to a conceivable scale. Ironically, both solutions had been previously suggested by Frenchmen.

The troublesome Chagres River was turned on itself. At the town of Gatun, engineers built what was, in its day, the largest earth dam ever constructed. One and a half miles long, half a mile wide at its base, Gatun Dam rose to 105 feet above sea level. Behind it gathered the waters of what was then the largest man-made lake in the world, 163-square-mile Gatun Lake. The massive waterway inundated several towns, rerouted the Panama Railroad, completely changed the geography of the canal area and furnished 23.5 navigable miles of the canal itself. The engineers had saved themselves a lot of digging, but there was still the question of the continental divide.

There are seventy hill formations along the canal route, but the cut across the continental divide at Culebra was the deepest and most difficult. The deeper the men dug, the more the mountains fell into the hole around them—sometimes burying steam shovels and railroad equipment. In 1912 alone, four and a half months were spent removing landslides from Culebra Cut. At one point, engineers discovered to their astonishment that the bottom of the excavation actually was rising under pressure from the surrounding mountains. In one place the ground rose six feet in five minutes.

The solution at Culebra was to keep removing dirt. Originally expected to require a 670-foot width, the final excavation grew to more than a quarter of a mile across and nine miles in length. Lt. Col. David Gaillard—the engineer in charge and the person who later would give his name to Culebra—would have been amused to note that the astronauts who returned from the moon brought with them just forty-seven pounds of lunar rocks.

The ditches at sea level and at eighty-five feet that crossed the continental divide were connected by the largest canal locks ever attempted. Radical in scale, they were reliable in operation. Seventy-two years after the opening of the canal, the same locks and seven-story, 700-ton lock gates are still in use, still activated by the same forty-horsepower motors. Nearly three quarters of a century after their construction, the tower control panels look almost exactly the same as the day they were built. It has proven to be a very workable design.

The Modern Era

The Panama Canal was completed under budget at $387 million. The *SS Ancon* made the first transit ahead of schedule on August 15, 1914, a landmark event overshadowed by the outbreak of World War I. . . .

The transit of the canal today holds a special fascination for anyone who enjoyed the amusement park water slide as a kid. The ship is raised and lowered eighty-five feet via six pairs of chambers. Each lock chamber is 1,000 feet long and 110 feet wide. When the chambers fill with water there is no sensation of movement but you are readily aware that something amazing is underway. The passage through the Gaillard Cut is a narrow, steep-walled slot. In the two-hour crossing of Gatun Lake you are sailing over what were once the most feared jungles of the American coast. Average transit time for the entire canal is about nine hours.

When you are sailing through the Panama Canal there is ample time to stand at the ship's rail and reflect. The deep green hills still look rugged, the thick clot of the jungle has not changed. Admittedly, there are no more pirate treasure mules, the French left long ago with their sad story, and the astronauts have been to the moon and back. But the canal—the realization of so many dreams—is there and it is working. It is probably the most fascinating place you can go to revel in the genius of first rate engineering until that day, far in the future, when you can stand by the flag on that distant lunar plain and stir up the dust with your boot.

Monitoring Comprehension and Writing in Response

Discuss the building of the Panama Canal with a partner or two. Talk about why the construction of the canal was important and yet so difficult to achieve. Talk also about what this achievement indicates about human beings' will to overcome obstacles.

Star the best response. Do not rely on your memory. Use your margin notes to check your answers. This is a self-assessment activity. Do it alone.

1. In scope and difficulty, the canal's construction was more closely akin to the
   a. Suez Canal.
   b. trans-Siberian Railroad.
   c. Taj Mahal.
   d. pyramids.

2. A canal in Panama was first proposed in the
   a. 1300s.
   b. 1500s.
   c. 1600s.
   d. 1700s.

3. The canal was built with the help of
   a. the airplane.
   b. the automobile.
   c. both the plane and the automobile.
   d. neither the plane nor the automobile.

4. Which of these statements is true?
   a. About half of Panama lies east of Miami.
   b. Panama is squeezed into the narrowest portion of Central America.
   c. Panama offers the lowest point in the North American continental divide.
   d. All are true.
   e. Both "b" and "c" are true.

5. A small railroad operated across the isthmus by
   a. the beginning of the 1700s.
   b. the middle of the 1700s.
   c. the beginning of the 1800s.
   d. the middle of the 1800s.

6. Today's transit of the canal is
   a. scary.
   b. challenging.
   c. smooth.
   d. horrific.

7. The annual rainfall on the Atlantic side is closest to
   a. 50 inches.
   b. 100 inches.
   c. 150 inches.
   d. 200 inches.

8. Which of these are found in Panama?
   a. crocodiles
   b. alligators
   c. serpents
   d. all of the above and then some

9. The worst diseases were
   a. malaria and yellow fever.
   b. cholera and typhoid.
   c. smallpox and black plague.
   d. smallpox and dysentery.

10. According to treaty, the Panama Canal Zone was to be controlled by
    a. Panama.
    b. Colombia.
    c. Bogotá.
    d. the United States.

14. **Topic:** Traveling the canal today
    Main idea:

    Supporting Detail:

15. **Topic:** The dream at Panama
    Main Idea:

    Supporting Detail:

Think about . . .
What is the meaning of *akin?*

Think about . . .
What is the meaning of the root *trans-?* How can you use it to figure out the meaning of *transit?*

11. Gorgas attacked malaria and yellow fever by
    a. changing the breeding patterns of mosquitoes in the area.
    b. wiping out the breeding grounds of mosquitoes there.
    c. interbreeding the mosquitoes to get a new breed.
    d. all of the above.

12. The large Gatun Lake was formed by
    a. building locks.
    b. building a dam.
    c. rerouting the railway.
    d. building a roadway.

13. The major construction problem at Culebra Cut was
    a. landslides.
    b. lack of money.
    c. the flooding river.
    d. weak concrete.

14. The locks used today are the
    a. same ones built initially.
    b. second set built.
    c. third set built.
    d. ones built by the French.

15. The first transit of the Panama Canal occurred at the time of the
    a. Spanish-American War.
    b. First World War.
    c. Second World War.
    d. Korean War.

16. The average transit time through the canal today is about
    a. 15 minutes.
    b. 2 hours.
    c. 9 hours.
    d. 2 days.

17. What impresses you most about the building of the canal? Write a sentence or two in your notebook explaining your choice.

18. When in your life have you overcome an obstacle? In your notebook, write a paragraph telling about your obstacle and how you conquered it.

Checking Your Word Power

Star the response that comes closest to the meaning of the italicized term. Use the process of elimination.

1. The *isthmus* of Panama is a
   a. canal.
   b. narrow strip of land.
   c. kind of crocodile.
   d. man who once ruled Panama.

2. A *devastating* storm is one that
   a. brings destruction.
   b. comes and goes quickly.
   c. is accompanied by thunder.
   d. occurs only at night.

3. I felt something *akin* to love.
   a. actual
   b. foreign
   c. similar, or related
   d. funny about

4. The building of the canal required all the creativity its builders could *muster*.
   a. play with
   b. carry
   c. pull
   d. call forth

5. The French *debacle* occurred because they tried to build a sea level canal.
   a. debate
   b. sudden departure
   c. complete breakdown
   d. happening

6. Their plan became *mired* in red tape.
   a. stuck
   b. mixed with
   c. married
   d. manufactured

7. They plodded on despite *horrific* problems: floods, landslides, and disease.
   a. causing honor
   b. causing pleasure
   c. causing sadness
   d. causing horror

Think
about . . .
What other words have
the same root as
horrific?

8. I will vote for the *incumbent* governor.
   a. one who is coming
   b. one holding office
   c. one who is running for
   d. one who is living in the state

9. The key accomplishment of the period was the *virtual* elimination of malaria.
   a. nearly complete
   b. absolute
   c. partial
   d. parallel

10. The waters of the overflowing river *inundated* the surrounding countryside.
    a. flooded
    b. watered
    c. irrigated
    d. washed

11. The *continental divide* is a
    a. railroad that divides the continent.
    b. mountain range that divides the continent.
    c. river that divides the continent.
    d. canal that cuts across the isthmus.

WORKSHOP: WRITING WITH MAIN IDEAS AND SIGNIFICANT DETAILS

According to the selection you just read, the construction of the pyramids of Egypt was an engineering feat akin to the construction of the Panama Canal. Read a brief selection in an encyclopedia about the pyramids, or get information off the Web at www.sis.gov.eg/sis-imgs/html/phara001.htm. Then decide on the main idea you want to express and some details you can use to support that idea. Map the main idea and the details on Figure 6.2. Using your idea map, write a paragraph about the pyramids. Start with a topic sentence that communicates the main point. Then write several sentences with details that support the main point you make in the topic sentence.

Main Idea:
Supporting Detail:
Supporting Detail:
Supporting Detail:
Supporting Detail:

FIGURE 6.2 A Guide for Plotting Main Idea and Supporting Details of a Paragraph Before Writing

Jot your thoughts directly on the guide before you begin to draft your paragraph.

EXTENDING WHAT YOU HAVE LEARNED

Building Your Knowledge Base

Circle or plot these locations on the map in Figure 6.3.

Central America	Pacific Ocean	North America
South America	Isthmus of Panama	Atlantic Ocean

Reviewing Your Strategy for Working with Details

1. What two questions should you ask yourself to determine whether a detail is significant?

   _____

   _____

2. How should you generally handle dates and numbers as you meet them in reading?

   _____

   _____

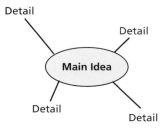

Practicing Your Strategy

Read an article that describes an event, person, or place. As you read, keep asking questions that help you get at the main idea and the details you need to support it. Web the main idea and some supporting details in your reading notebook. Be ready to share your web if your instructor requests it.

FIGURE 6.3 Central America and the Caribbean (Kăr′ə·bē′ən)

7

Using Clue Words to Anticipate an Author's Thoughts

OBJECTIVE

In this chapter, you will learn a strategy for using clue words to perceive relationships among ideas so that you can anticipate what is going to happen next in a sentence or paragraph. You will learn to use clue (or relation-stating) words such as these:

1. *One, two,* and *three,* which indicate the number of items to be enumerated (or named one by one) and discussed;

2. *For example* and *such as,* which indicate that an example is coming;

3. *Also* and *furthermore,* which indicate that more on the same idea is coming, and *but, however,* and *yet,* which indicate ideas in opposition;

4. *Similarly* and *on the other hand,* which indicate that a comparison or contrast is on the way;

5. *If/then, hence,* and *consequently,* which indicate a conditional relationship (a condition followed by an outcome);

6. *Because* and *for this reason,* which indicate that a reason is coming.

USING CLUE WORDS

In previous chapters, you learned that paragraphs have structure (see pages 66–70). For example, deductive paragraphs have a topic sentence followed by sentences that provide supporting details. Being able to perceive this kind of paragraph structure aids in comprehension; your perception gives you a framework for grasping the meaning.

Writers also rely on clue words to give structure to their writing and to help the reader predict, or anticipate, what the author will say next in a sentence or paragraph. If you know the way clue words function in writing, you can better understand important sentence relationships. In this chapter, you will learn to use clue (or relation-stating) words to anticipate what kinds of thoughts are coming next.

PARAGRAPHS OF ENUMERATION

A basic reading strategy is to use number words such as *first, second,* and *third* to guide your reading.

Preview this selection, which is typical of material in college science textbooks. Skim the title, the first sentence, and the italicized words. Then read the selection, keeping alert for number words that tell you how many items the writer is discussing. Circle the number words.

The Three Classes of Rocks
George Hennings

All the rocks in the earth's crust are grouped into three classes. When magma (the molten material beneath the earth's crust) and lava (the molten rock coming out on the earth's

Did You
KNOW?

Igni- means "fire." Other words with the base are *ignite* and *ignition*. *Meta-* means "change." *Morph-* means "form or shape." A related word is *morphology,* the study of forms and bodies, especially ones in the human body.

Think
about . . .

What do you think when you read number words such as *first, second,* and *third*? What do you tell yourself in your mind?

Did You
KNOW?

The prefix *ex-* or *e-* means "out of or away from." You see it here on the words *eruptions* and *explosions.* Other words with the prefix are *excavate* and *emigrate.* *Ex-* also means "former," as on the word *ex-president.*

surface) cool, they harden and become *igneous rocks,* the first class. The word *igneous* comes from the Latin word for fire.

As rocks are exposed to forces such as water and changes in temperature, the igneous rocks start to break apart chemically and physically. The broken rock particles may be transported downgrade by wind and water and come to rest as sediments. As time passes, sediments cover other sediments, layer on layer. Particles are pressed together; grains fit more tightly. Dissolved chemicals form cement, and particles turn into stone. Thus we have the formation of a second class of rock—*sedimentary rocks.*

Deeply buried sedimentary and igneous rocks are heated and squeezed together by enormous pressures. They change in form as grains rearrange themselves and minerals change their composition. The change in form is called metamorphism; the result is the third class of rock, the *metamorphic rocks.*

Did you circle the word *three* in the first paragraph? When you read that word, did you anticipate and say to yourself, "This is going to be about three classes of rock. The author will probably start by describing the first class, go on to the second, and finish with the third"? Did you circle the word *first* in the first paragraph, *second* in the second, and *third* in the third? Those words are clues to the way the author is developing his ideas: The author is enumerating, or naming, three items and discussing each in turn.

History and science writers often use this organizational pattern. In the first sentence of their first paragraph, they tell the number of items they are going to discuss. In this respect, that first sentence serves as the topic sentence for the paragraphs to follow. In the first paragraph and perhaps in others that follow, they name and discuss the first item—in this case igneous rocks. In the next paragraph or two, they name and talk about the second item. After discussing it, they introduce the third. At each transition, readers who are wise to the ways of writers monitor their comprehension by thinking, "Now the author is moving to the next point."

The writer of the geology paragraphs built a second organizing clue into the paragraphs. He italicized the names of the rock classes. A reader who realizes the importance of previewing before reading may pick up this clue during the preview. Learning in the first sentence that there are three classes of rocks, the reader scans the paragraphs to come, noting the three italicized rock types. The reader then knows that the first paragraph is about igneous, the second about sedimentary, and the third about metamorphic rock; he or she knows all that before reading the material. Here previewing pays dividends; it provides a framework for anticipating while reading.

Reread the selection on pages 115–116 and complete the idea map in Figure 7.1 that clarifies the structure of the selection. Also revisit the six objectives on the first page of this chapter. In this case, the objectives enumerate, or name in order, the items to be discussed. Many textbook authors use their introductory section to list the items they will discuss in the chapter or in a section of the chapter. If a list is available, give it some attention because you can use it to guide your reading.

WORKSHOP 1: ENUMERATION

Read the first sentence under each main heading of this chapter. How is Chapter 7 organized? How many strategies are discussed? What words are clues to the organization? Based on your preview and working with a partner, make a web that clarifies the structure of this chapter.

PARAGRAPHS WITH EXAMPLES

A second basic reading strategy is to look for relational words that hint that an example is coming. Read this short passage. As you read, circle any word or phrase that gives you a clue that the author is going to provide an example. An *eruption* is a forcing out of material, an outflow that is usually violent.

Thesis of the Entire Passage:

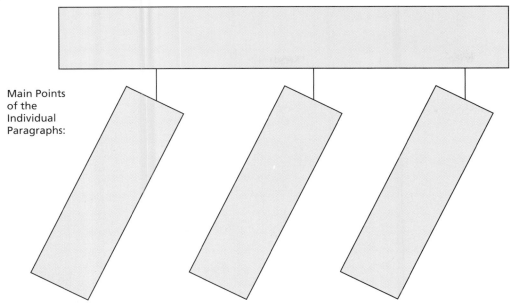

Main Points
of the
Individual
Paragraphs:

FIGURE 7.1   An Idea Map of a Passage
Map the passage by recording the thesis, or main point, of the entire passage about rocks in the top box. Record the main ideas of the individual paragraphs in the connecting boxes. Why are there three hanging boxes?

Cities have been completely destroyed by volcanic eruptions. A famous example is the destruction of the city of Pompeii in Italy by the eruption of Mt. Vesuvius. On the morning of August 24, A.D. 79, great explosions broke the stillness of the day. Columns of smoke, gases, and steam rose into the air. A rain of ash and glowing debris fell on Pompeii. Within several hours of the first volcanic rumblings, Pompeii was inundated under twenty feet of volcanic ash. Roofs collapsed, and people were suffocated by poisonous gases.

Did you circle the phrase *a famous example?* That phrase is a clue to the organization of the paragraph. The first sentence states the main idea. But then the writer shifts gears slightly: She supports the main idea with an example of one well-known volcanic eruption. Figure 7.2 helps you visualize the relationship among main and supporting ideas in the paragraph. Complete it by filling in the main idea and the supporting example.

Phrases like *a famous example* are clues you can use to anticipate what is coming. Reading it, you predict: "The author is going to give an example." Similar phrases that tell you that you can anticipate an example are *such as*, *for example*, and *for instance*. Sometimes a writer provides more than one example and introduces it with the phrase *another example* or *another instance*.

WORKSHOP 2: **EXAMPLE**

Read this paragraph, and compare it with the organization of the one about Vesuvius. Ask yourself, "How is it similar in design to the previous paragraph? How is it different?" The word *persists* used in the first (and topic) sentence means "keeps at it; does not give up."

The human race persists in living around volcanoes and even high up on their slopes. Vesuvius, "the pride and terror of Naples," is surrounded by Italian towns and villages and is covered with gardens, groves, and vineyards that extend far up toward its summit. Etna, a volcanic peak in Sicily, is cultivated up to an altitude of 4000 feet. On the slopes, there are orange and lemon groves and vineyards, all in sharp contrast to the black lava flows. Mount Rosso, the largest cinder cone on Etna, built in 1669 during

Did You
KNOW?

Vineyard is a compound word made from *vine* and *yard*. The sound of the *i* in *vineyard* is short, whereas the sound of the *i* in *vine* is long.

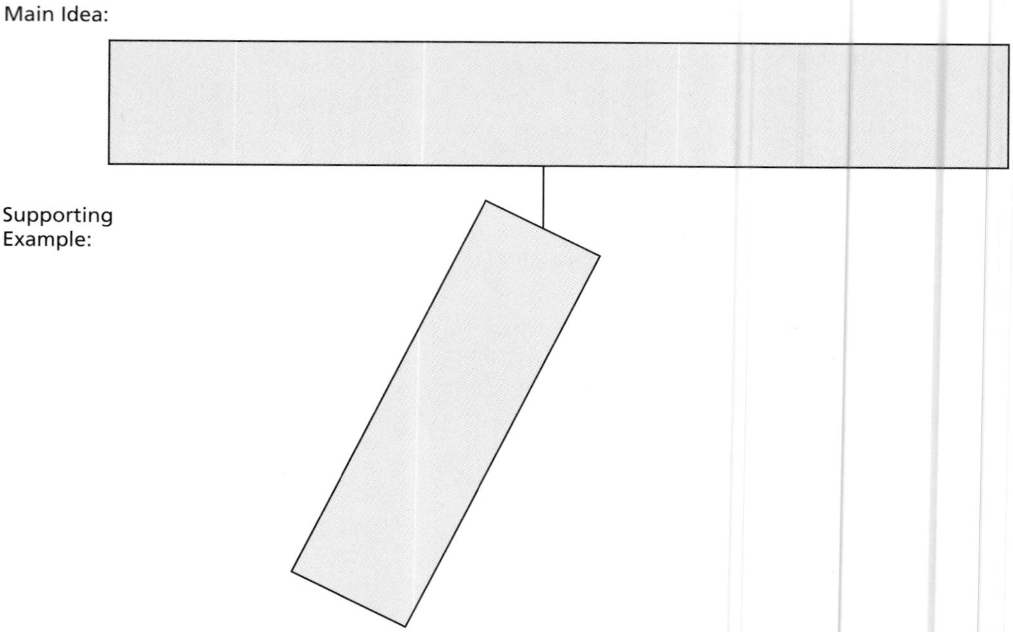

Main Idea:

Supporting
Example:

FIGURE 7.2   An Idea Map to Show Relationships in a Paragraph
Map the paragraph to show the relationship between the main idea and the supporting example. Record the main idea in the top box and the supporting example in the connecting box. Why is there only one hanging box?

the worst eruption in the history of Etna, is now green with vineyards halfway to its summit.

1. What is the main idea of the paragraph? _____
_____

2. How is the paragraph similar to the previous one about Vesuvius? _____
_____

3. How is it different? _____
_____

**Think
about . . .**

What goes through your mind when you read the words *for example?* What do you expect? Try making an idea map to show the organization of the Vesuvius and Etna paragraph.

If you said that both paragraphs start with a topic sentence, you recognized one aspect of their organization. If you said that the pattern was topic sentence supported by example, you recognized a second aspect. Both paragraphs rely on examples to support the main idea.

Now consider the differences. The first paragraph contains a single example: Vesuvius. The second paragraph contains two examples: Vesuvius and Etna. Also, the first paragraph provides a clue phrase (*a famous example*) that helps you anticipate a paragraph containing an example. The second paragraph does not. In the second case, you must figure out as you read about the towns and villages surrounding Vesuvius that this is an example. When you get to the sentence on Etna, you must figure out that it is a second example. In this case, what helps you predict during reading is your knowledge of the way authors organize their paragraphs.

PARAGRAPHS WITH ADDITIONAL INFORMATION: A CONTINUATION OF OR A CHANGE IN THE TOPIC

A third basic reading strategy is to look for words hinting that the author is getting ready to give more information in support of the topic or to supply information in opposition to the topic. Some words or phrases are clues about what the writer is going to do next.

Some words tell you that the author is going to say something more about the same idea. They are *and*-words; *and*-words include

and	also
too	additionally
in addition	furthermore
moreover	

Other words tell you that the author is going to change direction and provide details on the opposite side of the topic. They are the *but*-words; *but*-words include

but	yet
however	on the other hand
nevertheless	instead

Read this short paragraph:

Many people are familiar with the violent volcanic eruption that occurred at Mt. St. Helens in Washington State. In addition, people know about the

FIGURE 7.3 Mount St. Helens volcano in Washington State
(UPI/Bettman Newsphoto) Note: If you have access to the Internet, you can find information about volcanoes at these Web sites: www.aenet.org/canlaon/eruption.htm www.avo.alaska.edu/volcanoes.

1991 eruption at Mt. Pinatubo in the Philippines, which threatened the U.S. military installations at Clark Air Base and Subic Bay Naval Station. In the case of Mt. Pinatubo, more than 20,000 American military personnel and their families had to be evacuated on warships and cargo planes, and Clark Air Base had to be shut down. The Filipinos, however, had no way of escaping and were in a state of panic.

1. What do you anticipate when you read the words *in addition*? What do you know is going to happen next in the paragraph? _____

_____

2. What do you anticipate when you read the word *however*? What do you know is going to happen next in the paragraph? _____

_____

3. Make an idea map to clarify the organization of the paragraph.

 WORKSHOP 3: CONTINUATION OR CHANGE?

Read the following paragraphs aloud with a partner.

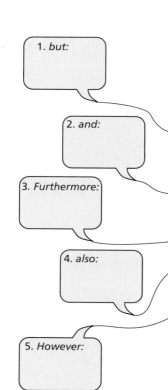

1. *but:*

2. *and:*

3. *Furthermore:*

4. *also:*

5. *However:*

Volcanic Action on Hawaii

Volcanoes formed the Hawaiian Islands in the Pacific Ocean 1 to 5 million years ago, *but* you can see signs of volcanic activity on the big island of Hawaii today. For example, if you visit Hawaii Volcanoes National Park, you can see the volcano called Kilauea (Kē lou āä). Kilauea has an immense crater that is $2\frac{1}{2}$ miles long, 2 miles wide, and 400 feet deep. Kilauea still smokes *and* from time to time it sends out fire and molten rock. You can actually walk on old Kilauea lava flows, from which unpleasant smelling gases are streaming into the air.

Furthermore, during recent eruptions Kilauea has been destructive. It has sent down lava flows that destroyed homes located just outside the national park. Some of the flows have *also* inundated roads and destroyed forested areas.

A second volcano on the island of Hawaii that has been active in recent times is Mauna Loa. Mauna Loa sent streams of molten lava flowing down its slopes in 1984. *However,* Mauna Loa is less active today than Kilauea.

Now reread the three paragraphs about Kilauea and Mauna Loa, emphasizing the italicized clue words. Think about how the author uses relation-stating words to maintain the same direction and add more details about the topic or to change direction and add details on the opposing side of the topic. In the balloons connected to the italicized clue words, write what the authors are doing at that point—giving an opposite idea or adding more information on the topic.

As a review, underline the topic (or main idea) sentence in each of the preceding paragraphs, if there is one. Then put a star by each example in the paragraphs.

Think about . . .

What goes through your mind when you read the words *however* and *but*?

PARAGRAPHS WITH COMPARISONS AND CONTRASTS

A fourth reading strategy is to look for words that hint that the author is getting ready to make a comparison or contrast. In comparing, writers tell how things or events are the same. In contrasting, writers tell how they differ. Here are some words and phrases that hint that an author is comparing or contrasting items:

Comparisons	Contrasts
similarly	on the other hand
as in the case of	on the contrary
like the	unlike the
the same as	in contrast to
in comparison with	whereas or whereas others

WORKSHOP 4: CONTRAST AND COMPARISON

Read these two paragraphs. As you read, put a star at the point where the authors begin to make a comparison or contrast. Ask yourself, "What are they comparing or contrasting? Are they giving similarities or differences?" The word *solidify* means "harden, or turn into a solid." *Viscous* means "sticky, or adhesive"; pancake syrup is viscous. *Fluid* means "liquidy, able to flow"; water is very fluid and can flow downhill rapidly.

When the lava first flows out of a volcano, it is red or white hot and very fluid. The lava soon cools on the surface, darkens, and crusts over. As it cools, it becomes more and more viscous. When the flow becomes very viscous, the under part may still be moving while the upper part crusts over and breaks up into jagged blocks, which are carried as a tumbling mass on the surface of the slowly moving flow. When eventually the flow comes to rest and solidifies, the resulting lava sheet is extremely rough. Its top is a mess of blocks and fragments, with many sharp points. Such lava flows are termed *block lava*. In Hawaii they are called *aa* (ă ă).

In marked contrast to the block lava, other flows harden with smooth surfaces, which have curious ropy, curved, and billowy forms. This is corded lava. The Hawaiians call it *pahoehoe* (pă-hō ā-hō ā).

1. In the two paragraphs, what two things are the authors describing?

   _____

   _____

2. Are they telling how the items differ or are the same? _____

   _____

3. What phrase do the authors use as a clue to tell you there is going to be a contrast?

   _____

   _____

4. How does the two-paragraph design help you make sense of the contrast? _____

   _____

Think
about . . .
What goes through your mind when you read *on the other hand*? What do you anticipate when you read *in the same way*?

The English language provides another clue that writers are developing a contrast in a paragraph: the use of the ending *-er* or the word *more*. For example, an author may begin one paragraph with the phrase *in older volcanoes* and may begin the follow-up paragraph with the phrase *in younger volcanoes*. The use of the comparative *-er* helps you figure out that the author is contrasting the two.

Think
about . . .

How did you figure out
the meaning of the
word *vesicle* in this
selection?

WORKSHOP 5: CONTRAST AND COMPARISON

Read these paragraphs. Circle the clue words that tell you that a comparison or contrast is being developed. Ask, "What is being compared or contrasted? Are similarities or differences being developed?" To help you understand these paragraphs, picture in your mind what the authors are describing.

Lavas, even after they have come out of a volcano, still contain dissolved gases. This is shown by the clouds of steam that escape from volcanoes for weeks and months. It is also shown by the bubble-like structures that result as the lava solidifies into rock. Viscous lava may become blown up by bubbles of expanding gas. Each bubble hole is a vesicle (like a sac). The vesicle is round if the lava was stationary while the hole was forming. In contrast, it is almond shaped if the lava was moving and drawing out the vesicle while the hole was forming. The upper portion of a flow, especially of a viscous lava, may contain so many holes that it has become a froth, like whipped cream. Rock froth is known as *pumice*.

In more fluid lava, the gas cavities, or vesicles, are much larger. In this case, the holes are very irregular in shape and size. They are so abundant that there is as much empty space as solid matter. The resulting rock is *scoriaceous*.

1. What is being compared or contrasted? _____

_____

2. Are similarities or differences being stressed? _____

_____

3. What clues do the authors use to let you know there is to be a contrast? _____

_____

4. How does the two-paragraph design help you to understand the contrast?

_____

PARAGRAPHS WITH CONDITIONAL RELATIONSHIPS ("WHAT-THEN?" PARAGRAPHS)

Think
about . . .

What goes through your
mind when you read *a
fifth reading strategy?*

A fifth reading strategy is to look for words that hint that a conditional relationship is being developed. Conditional relationships are common in scientific writing. When authors express conditional relationships, they state a condition and then tell what happens, or results, when that condition is met. A common language pattern for doing this is an *if* clause followed by a *then* clause, as in this sentence:

| If this condition exists, | then this results. |
| If the rocks are radioactive, → | then heat will build up. |

1. What happens if the rocks are radioactive? What then? What is the result?

_____

_____

Often the word *then* is left out; you must mentally add it as you read. You must think to yourself, "If this happens, what then?" Asking the "what-then" question is a simple strategy for interpreting a conditional relationship. Ask that question as you read this example:

If this condition exists,	then this results.
If magma reaches the earth's surface and is discharged from an opening, ⟶	it flows out on the surface, where it cools rapidly and solidifies.

2. What happens if the magma is discharged from the volcano? If this happens (if the condition is met), what is the outcome, or effect? _____

_____

 WORKSHOP 6: CONDITION

Read the following paragraph. Whenever you run into an *if*-clause, ask the "what-then" question to keep you on track. Ask, "If this happens, what then?"

The shape of the structure that builds up around the mouth of a volcano depends on the material that formed it. If the structure is made entirely of fragments, a steep cone is built. Slopes of 30 degrees or more are built up before the mass begins to slide. Volcanic structures of this kind are called *pyroclastic* (pī´rō klăs´ tǐk) *cones.* A pyroclastic cone built of huge blocks forms the summit of Etna. If a pyroclastic cone consists totally of cinders, it is called a *cinder cone.* Cinder cones are relatively small.

3. If the cone is made totally of fragments, what then? What is the effect, or result?

_____

_____

4. If a cone consists of cinders, what then? What is the effect, or outcome?

_____

_____

Other words that are clues to a conditional relationship include *consequently, therefore, thus,* and *hence.* Here are some examples:

If this condition exists,	then this results.
When the lava comes from the earth, it may be too thick to flow readily. ⟶	Consequently, a sluggish, pasty mass piles up over the mouth of the volcano as a great dome.

5. What happens if the lava is too thick, or viscous, to flow readily?

_____

_____

Think
about . . .
What is the topic sentence of this paragraph? Can you visualize the structure, or pattern, of the paragraph? Web the paragraph with the topic sentence at the center to clarify the pattern of the paragraph.

6. What word warns you that an effect may be coming? _____

_____

7. Rewrite the two sentences, substituting another clue word for *consequently* so that you get the feel for how this kind of conditional writing operates. Perhaps use *hence* or *thus* to express the conditional relationship.

_____

_____

If this condition exists,	then this results.
Sometimes the magma cools in the ground under a thick jacket of rocks; →	therefore, its dissolved gases cannot escape easily.

8. What happens when the magma cools under a thick jacket of rocks?

_____

9. What word is a clue that an effect is coming? _____

_____

10. Rewrite the sentence, substituting another clue word for *therefore* so that you better understand how this kind of conditional thinking operates.

_____

_____

_____

Sometimes the author states the outcome before the condition:

This results	if this condition exists.
Dissolved gases cannot escape easily →	if the magma cools in the ground under a thick jacket of rocks.

Reread the paragraph on page 122 that starts "Lavas, even after they have come out of a volcano. . . ." Underline two sentences that give the results before the condition.

CAUSE AND EFFECT PARAGRAPHS

A sixth reading strategy is to look for words that hint that the author is developing a cause and effect relationship. Writers of science textbooks or articles often give reasons why things happen or exist as they are. You can predict when writers are getting ready to provide causes and effects by looking out for these relational word clues:

because	for	as a result
for this reason	since	

Here is an example:

Reason, or cause	What happens, or the effect
Because rocks conduct, or carry, heat very poorly, ⟶	the magma loses heat slowly and solidifies slowly.

1. What clue word introduces the reason? _____

2. Why does the magma lose heat slowly? Complete this sentence in answering: The

   magma loses heat slowly and solidifies slowly because _____

   _____

Did you notice that in the model sentence, the reason ("Because rocks conduct, or carry, heat very poorly") comes before what happens? In the sentence you just wrote, the happening ("The magma loses heat slowly and solidifies slowly") comes before the reason. This indicates that reasons can come before or after the related event or happening, as shown in these two sentence maps:

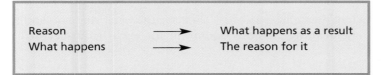

Reason	⟶	What happens as a result
What happens	⟶	The reason for it

WORKSHOP 7: CAUSE AND EFFECT

Read this paragraph and use the clue words that warn of "reason-giving" to figure out where the author is going to give reasons. Also ask, "Why does this happen?" The why question is a key one to ask when handling reasons.

> Because the Hawaiian volcano Mauna Loa is about sixty miles long and thirty miles wide and because it rises from a base 15,000 feet below sea level to 13,680 feet above sea level, it is known as the Monarch of Mountains. Because Mauna Loa is the world's largest active volcano, each year many tourists visit the island of Hawaii to view it.

3. Why is Mauna Loa known as the Monarch of Mountains? _____

   _____

   _____

4. What word introduces the reason? _____

   _____

5. Why do tourists visit Mauna Loa? _____

   _____

6. What word introduces the reason? _____

   _____

7. Rewrite the first sentence in the paragraph, placing the reasons after the happening they explain. Complete the sentence, "Mauna Loa is known as the Monarch of

Mountains _____

_____

Think
about . . .

As you read this paragraph and the next, ask yourself, "What clue word does the author use to help me see where she is going?"

Here is one caution before going on. Remember that when writers are giving reasons, they are telling you why something is as it is or why something happened as it did. The key question to ask as you interpret reasons is, "Why?" In contrast, when writers are expressing an if-then relationship, they are telling the conditions under which events occur. The key question to ask in handling if-then relationships is, "If that is true, then what?"

In the next sections of this chapter, you will read three selections, one from a text on human sexuality, one about astronomy, and one from a physical science text. Use the clue words to help you see the relationships the authors are developing and the organization of the paragraphs.

SELECTION 1
Forming a Friendship (HUMAN SEXUALITY)

A Reading Clues Workshop

Expanding Your Vocabulary for Reading

Pronounce each of the italicized words. Then use the word elements and the context to determine their meaning. Write a definition for each featured word in the space provided.

Did You
KNOW?

The Latin base *firm-* means "strong, firm"; the prefix *af-* is a form of *ad-*, which means "to or toward." Other words with the root are *infirm*, *confirm*, and *reaffirm*. Other words with the prefix are *admit* and *affix*.

1. The research *affirms* what I always knew—that success in college generally takes work.

   _____

   _____

2. Despite outside influences, she *consistently* held to the principles in which she believed.

   _____

   _____

3. When they didn't do well in the game, the children's *compensatory* behavior was to refuse to play. _____

   _____

4. John's personal *attributes* overcame his plain appearance. _____

   _____

5. The government was *stable* and not likely to be overturned by revolution.

   _____

   _____

6. The candidates' hostility toward each other was *overt;* they made no attempt to hide how angry they were.

   _____

   _____

7. The teams worked out a *reciprocity* whereby they took turns practicing on the small basketball court. _____

_____

8. The artist placed all the parts of her drawing in a *configuration* that was pleasing to the eye. _____

_____

Getting Ready to Read

Preview the next selection. Read the title, author, and introductory paragraph.

- What is the topic of the selection? _____

- Study the three headings that introduce the main sections of the article. For each, write a question that you expect that section to answer.

_____

_____

- Gauge for yourself the reading load of the selection.

Reading with Meaning

Read the selection, which is from a college text on human sexuality. Use the author's clue words such as *and, however, if . . . then,* and *because* to guide your reading.

Forming a Friendship
Kathryn Kelley and Donn Byrne

Once two people meet and begin to interact several factors come into play, influencing how the relationship develops. First, our initial impressions of others depend in large part on appearance. If our reactions are negative, the process stops. If we respond positively, the second factor comes into play: the extent to which we discover that we share similar beliefs and attitudes with the other person. Third, the final step in forming a close friendship occurs when we and the other person each feel and express a positive evaluation of the other. We will now examine these three factors in greater detail.

Physical Attractiveness: Life as a Beauty Contest

On first coming in contact with someone, we have a strong tendency to respond to **physical attractiveness**—that combination of facial features, body configuration, and general appearance that our culture defines as pleasing. We all have learned that "Beauty is only skin deep" and "You can't judge a book by its cover"; nevertheless, most people respond most positively to those they perceive as attractive. Even in childhood, attractive preschool girls are treated better than their less attractive peers by other children; the physically attractive children are helped more and hurt less. Also, attractiveness and unattractiveness remain as fairly stable characteristics throughout childhood and adolescence.

Other species also respond to overt physical characteristics—a peacock's tail, a deer's antlers, a swordtail fish's tail fin—suggesting an inherited tendency to attract mates on the basis of such clues.

Our culture also emphasizes the value of beauty. For example, advertisements instruct women to cover their embarrassing age spots, lose weight, change their hairstyle

Did You KNOW?

The prefix *re-* means "back or again." You see it here on the word *reciprocity*. The prefix *con-* or *com-* means "together." Notice the prefix on the words *consistently, compensatory,* and *configuration.*

1. How many factors about interaction will the author discuss? What are they?

2. If we respond positively, what then?

3. Nevertheless, what happens?

4. What is an example of our culture's emphasis on beauty?

5. What does the word *however* tell you that the author is going to do here?

and color, wear the right makeup, and so on. The mass media are found to stress slimness for women much more strongly than for men. Men, too, are told to take steps to avoid gray hair, dandruff, insufficiently white teeth, underdeveloped muscles, and a host of other "defects." One result is that both men and women focus on the attractiveness of the opposite sex in most of their interactions. Not surprisingly, then, attractive men and women receive more invitations for dates in a video-dating service than unattractive ones. Women are, however, able to overlook male unattractiveness if the men possess compensatory attributes such as status, money, power, or prestige.

6. If we learn to pay more attention to behavior, what then?

Physical attractiveness creates a halo around those who possess it. Both men and women assume that good-looking people also have a great many positive personal qualities. Our inflated view of attractive people can best be overcome if we learn to pay more attention to their behavior than to their appearance.

7. What important clue phrase is used?

Altogether, beauty has a number of benefits, however unfair this may be. Attractive men and women have more success with the opposite sex, including more dates, and they succeed in many other social situations as well. One explanation is that those who are attractive behave differently than those who are unattractive. For example, attractive males are relatively assertive and unafraid of rejection, and attractive women are relatively unassertive, and these are precisely the qualities each sex most prefers in the other in a dating situation. Beyond the dating age, the greater a person's physical attractiveness, the better off he or she is in educational level, income, status, and mental health.

8. Why do our perceptions of deficiencies lower self-esteem?

Because of the value we place on attractiveness, it follows that self-perceptions of deficiencies in appearance lower self-esteem and lead to efforts to improve how we look.

Similarity: Seeking Those Most Like Ourselves

Attraction toward a similar partner goes beyond physical appearance. Once we begin interacting with someone new, we try to discover as much as possible about his or her likes and dislikes. Throughout history it has been observed that people respond most positively to other individuals who are most similar to themselves, especially those who hold similar attitudes, beliefs, and values.

9. Do opposites really attract? What clue word tells you that is not true?

Research consistently finds that **attitude similarity** leads to attraction. You may hear that "opposites attract," but such mismatching works better in fiction than in real life. Attraction is a direct consequence of similar attitudes. Thus, friends, lovers, and spouses have similar views on most issues.

10. Give an example of matching between friends.

Matching occurs between friends whose daily habits are similar. We like friends who behave as we do and who make decisions similar to our own. High school friends resemble each other in drug use, for example. At least among women, patterns of smoking, drinking, and premarital sexual activity are more similar among groups of friends than among classmates in general. People who live together are more satisfied with the relationship if they have similar preferences about when to sleep and when to be active. For most characteristics that have been studied, similarity leads to attraction.

11. What word in this paragraph tells you that you are handling cause and effect?

Why is similarity so crucial in relationships? It appears that similarity has a positive effect because it helps confirm our judgments about the world. When another person agrees with us, he or she affirms or "validates" our view about politics, religion, and so on and also provides evidence that our judgments, tastes, and style of behavior are reasonable, normal, and wise. We find it rewarding when others provide this positive information.

Reciprocity of Positive Evaluations: If You Like Me, Let Me Know

12. Under what condition will a man be attracted to a woman? What word clues you in to the conditional relationship?

If someone is really your friend and if your interactions are positive, would you expect that person to evaluate you positively, help you whenever possible, and let you know you are liked? Many studies indicate that the communication of such positive evaluations between partners is the most crucial characteristic of a successful relationship.

Even when two people are dissimilar in their attitudes, a man will be attracted to a woman if she shows interest in him by maintaining eye contact, talking to him, and leaning toward him. When reciprocity of positive reactions occurs, either verbally or nonverbally, the relationship is strengthened for both individuals. Flattery, a desire to be together and to communicate, and any sign of affection indicate clearly that positive affect is operating in the friendship. In contrast, hostility, negative evaluations, or refusal to be helpful to one another creates negative affect, which clearly endangers the relationship.

13. What contrasting point is made in this paragraph?

Monitoring Comprehension and Writing in Response

Complete the first activity collaboratively, the second on your own.

A. Answer the questions in the margin by referring to the text at that point. Be ready to tell how you used the author's clue words to help you answer.

B. In your reading notebook, write a paragraph in which you explain how a male/female relationship develops. Include what is important to you in a relationship.

Reviewing the Featured Vocabulary

Place each word in the sentence in which its meaning is most appropriate. Use your know-for-sure/process-of-elimination strategy.

affirmed	compensatory	consistently	reciprocity
attributes	configuration	overt	stable

1. The young man had a very _____ relationship with his girlfriend; he had been seeing her for more than two years.

2. I was attracted to him because of his social _____ and his physical characteristics.

3. The president _____ scored at the top of her class; she always got As.

4. The agreement of _____ between the two clubs made it possible for a member of one club to eat in the dining room of the other.

5. During halftime, the band lined up in a _____ that spelled out the name of the university.

6. There was nothing underhanded in what the team captain did; he was always _____ and aboveboard in his actions.

7. The captain of the team _____ that he had never taken drugs.

8. In _____ education, a person learns things to make up for his or her deficiencies.

SELECTION 2:

The Sun Disappears: A Solar Eclipse (ASTRONOMY)

A Reading Clues Workshop

Expanding Your Vocabulary for Reading

Use word elements and context to figure out the meanings of the italicized words, which come from the selection you will read next. Write the meaning of each italicized term in the space provided.

1. The fighting armies saw a raven flying over the battlefield and decided it was an *omen* of bad things to come. _____

_____

Think about . . .

Pronounce each of the italicized words in syllable segments.

2. The power of the Netherlands gradually was *eclipsed* by the growing influence of Great Britain. _____

_____

3. The Vikings *terrorized* the people living to the south by killing, raping, and stealing.

_____

_____

Did You KNOW?

The root *part-* means "part or piece." Other words with the base are *particular* and *particle*.

4. My grandmother has only *partial* dentures because some of her teeth are still in good condition. _____

_____

5. The sun, when viewed from afar, has the shape of a *disk*. It appears to be round with a flat surface. _____

_____

6. Because of the breeze, first the candle *flickered*. Then it went out. _____

_____

Did You KNOW?

The suffix *-some* is from old English. It means "characterized by." You see it here on *awesome*. Other words that carry it are *handsome, cumbersome,* and *bothersome.* Similarly, the suffix *-dom* is from old English. It means "state or condition of." Words ending with it are *boredom* and *wisdom.*

7. The view of Victoria Falls in Africa is *awesome*. It makes us feel the power and beauty of nature. _____

_____

Getting Ready to Read

Preview the following selection by reading the title and studying the diagram.

• Write the topic of the selection. _____

_____

• What do you already know about the cause of an eclipse? Jot down some ideas here.

_____

_____

• Write at least one question that you hope to be able to answer after reading.

_____

_____

• Gauge the difficulty of the selection for you.

Reading with Meaning

Read the selection to get a general idea of what it is about. Then, with a partner, reread it, emphasizing the meaning of the italicized words as you take turns reading the paragraphs aloud. Together, study the way the italicized words are used to show relationships among ideas within the sentences. Explain to each other what the italicized clue words tell you. In the balloon connected to each italicized word, write down what that clue word tells you. For example, the clue word may tell you that the author is going to do one of the following:

1. write about a specific number of items;

2. provide an example;

3. add more information on the same aspect of the topic;

4. add more information on a different aspect of the topic;

5. make a comparison or contrast;

6. state a condition and the effect of that condition (if . . . then);

7. give a reason.

The first word balloon is filled in for you.

🔱

The Sun Disappears: A Solar Eclipse
George Hennings

1. Suppose that you lived in a long ago time when few people could read or write and when people knew little or nothing about the sun and the planets. Suppose, *too,* that suddenly on a lovely sunny day the sun disappeared *and* the world turned dark. What would you think? Would you think that the world was coming to an end? Would you think that this was a sign from an angry god? Over the centuries, day turning to night has terrorized, or frightened, people who saw the sun suddenly disappear from the sky.

   > 1. *too:* More information on the topic is coming.

   > 2. *and:*

2. *For example,* on May 28 in 585 B.C. the Medes—who were from what is now northern Iran—were in battle with the Lydians who lived in what is now Turkey. To the horror of both sides, the sun disappeared. The war had been going on for five years, *but* the Medes and Lydians were so frightened at this ill omen that they made peace.

   > 3. *For example:*

   > 4. *but:*

3. Today, astronomers are able to explain such disappearances of the sun. On its trip around the earth, *if* the moon passes directly between the sun and the earth, then it prevents rays of the sun from reaching the earth and causes a temporary darkening. This is what is known as a solar eclipse. A solar eclipse can last as long as seven and a half minutes.

   > 5. *if:*

   > 6. *if:*

4. You can do a simple experiment to show how the sun with a diameter 400 times wider than that of the moon can be blocked out, or eclipsed, by the moon. Close one eye. Hold up one finger in front of a large object across the room or out the window. Your finger represents the moon. The blocked object is the sun. Your finger has "eclipsed" the larger object. However, *if* your finger is too far from your eye and closer to the object, you can see part of the object around your finger. In this case, you have made a partial eclipse. Part of the object is visible.

   > 7. *Because:*

   > 8. *two:*

5. *Because* a total eclipse of the sun by the moon requires that the disk of the moon exactly cover the disk of the sun, *two* conditions must be met for a total eclipse to occur. First, *since* the sun is 400 times wider than the moon, the sun must be 400 times farther away than the moon *if* the disk of the moon is to cover the disk of the sun. And it is! Second, the moon must be directly in the line of sight between the earth and the sun. This does happen, but not very often.

   > 9. *since:*

   > 10. *if:*

Total Eclipse of the Sun

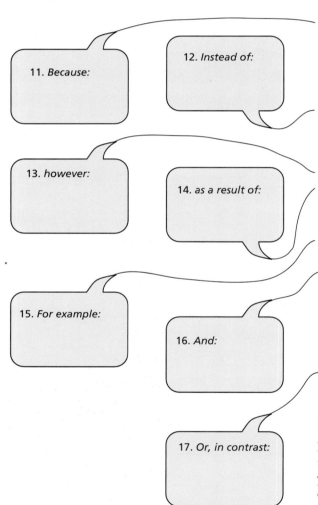

partial eclipse area

sun's rays

moon

earth

People in the path where the dark central shadow
hits the earth will see a total eclipse.

FIGURE 7.4 Diagram of an Eclipse

Note: For more information, illustrations, and diagrams, check these Web sites:
www.hao.ucar.edu/public/education/slides/slide9.html
www.jcc.uky.edu/faculty/vinced/classes/ast191/solar.htm.

11. *Because:*

12. *Instead of:*

13. *however:*

14. *as a result of:*

15. *For example:*

16. *And:*

17. *Or, in contrast:*

6. In 1991 there was a total eclipse of the sun. *Because* the moon passed directly in the line of sight between the sun and the earth, its shadow spread a path of darkness across the land. This path extended from Hawaii to South America in what astronomers called "the eclipse of the century."

7. *Instead of* being frightened by the eclipse as had ancient peoples, Americans flocked to Hawaii and Mexico to view the awesome sight. Scientists viewed the eclipse from an observatory on Hawaii's 13,796 foot Mauna Kea, a volcanic peak. In the continental United States, *however,* only a partial eclipse occurred. Unfortunately, *as a result of* a cloud cover, this partial eclipse was barely visible.

8. Interesting things happened during the 1991 eclipse. *For example,* animals in a zoo in Mexico City headed into their dens when the eclipse began. When the sun reappeared, roosters crowed as if it were morning. *And* light-sensitive lamps flickered on at the beginning of the eclipse and flickered off at the end.

9. The next total eclipse visible in the United States will occur in August 2017. How old will you be then? What will you think if you see it? Will you shake with fear, as did the peoples of the past? *Or, in contrast,* will you be able to explain to your children what causes a solar eclipse?

Monitoring Comprehension

Explain to a partner what causes a solar eclipse. Take turns at this. Incidentally, when you study for other college courses, you may find it helpful to explain what you have read to someone else. In explaining ideas to someone, you clarify your own understanding. Then on your own, mark the following items either *T* (true) or *F* (false).

_____ 1. In Mexico City, animals headed into their dens at the end of the 1991 eclipse.

_____ 2. For there to be a total solar eclipse, the moon must be directly in the line of sight between the sun and the earth.

———— 3. A total solar eclipse happens at least once a year in the continental United States.

———— 4. People have always understood the cause of a solar eclipse.

———— 5. In the past, people have been frightened by solar eclipses.

———— 6. The moon never moves.

Answer these questions, which are like the questions on some reading tests you may have to take. In each case cross out choices you know for sure are wrong to narrow the field.

7. Which sentence in the first paragraph comes closest to stating the main idea?
   a. the first
   b. the second
   c. the next to last
   d. the last

8. The purpose of the second paragraph is to
   a. give an example of the idea stated in the first paragraph.
   b. explain the cause of an eclipse.
   c. provide a contrasting idea to that expressed in the first paragraph.
   d. give details about eclipses, in general.

9. The purpose of the third paragraph is to
   a. give an example of the idea stated in the first paragraph.
   b. explain the cause of an eclipse.
   c. develop in more detail the idea expressed in the second paragraph.
   d. describe a specific eclipse.

10. In the third paragraph, the words *if the moon passes directly between the sun and the earth* tell
    a. the reason for an eclipse.
    b. an example of an eclipse.
    c. a condition under which an eclipse will occur.
    d. a contrasting idea.

11. The general purpose of the fourth paragraph is to
    a. provide an opposite idea to that stated in the third paragraph.
    b. expand on the ideas given in the third paragraph.
    c. take off in a direction that is totally different from that of the third paragraph.

12. In the fifth paragraph, the words *since the sun is 400 times wider than the moon* give
    a. the reason that the sun must be 400 times farther away than the moon if there is to be a total eclipse.
    b. an example of an eclipse.
    c. a contrasting idea.
    d. the conditions under which an eclipse will occur.

13. In the sixth paragraph, the word *because* tells you to expect
    a. an example.
    b. a reason.
    c. an effect.
    d. a contrasting idea.

14. In the seventh paragraph, the words *instead of* tell you to expect
    a. an example.
    b. a reason.
    c. an effect.
    d. a contrasting idea.
    e. the main idea.

15. The first sentence in the eighth paragraph (*Interesting things happened during the 1991 eclipse*) gives
    a. an example.
    b. a reason.
    c. a condition.
    d. a contrasting idea.
    e. the main idea.

16. In the eighth paragraph, the second sentence (*For example, animals in a zoo in Mexico City headed into their dens when the eclipse began*) gives
    a. an example.
    b. a reason.
    c. a condition.
    d. a contrasting idea.
    e. the main idea.

17. In the last paragraph, the words *Or, in contrast,* introduce
    a. the main idea.
    b. an opposite idea from that just expressed.
    c. an example.
    d. a reason.
    e. a condition.

Reviewing New Vocabulary

Select the word that best fits the meaning of each sentence. Use each word only once. Do the easy items first. Cross out options as you use them.

awe	flickered	partial
disk	omen	terrorized
eclipse		

1. As a result of the storm, the lights _____; however, they did not go off.

2. Some people look upon a rainbow as a good sign for the future. On the other hand, some people think of a rainbow as a bad _____ .

3. If you shine a light through a transparent red _____ that is placed on a transparent yellow one, then you will see orange.

4. In contrast to a solar _____ , a lunar eclipse occurs when the earth passes directly between the moon and the sun.

5. She had only _____ vision. Consequently, she needed glasses.

6. The vandals _____ the community. As a result, the community rose up and formed a citizens' watch force.

7. If you stand and look up at the great vaulting roof of the cathedral of Notre Dame in Paris, you will be filled with _____.

   Now reread the sentences in this exercise and circle the clue words you have learned in this chapter. In the margin, explain what each clue word tells you.

SELECTION 3

Elements Known to Ancient Civilizations (PHYSICAL SCIENCES)

An In-Text Review Test

Getting Ready to Read

In this section you will read four paragraphs titled "Elements Known to Ancient Civilizations." The title gives you the topic of the selection. An element is a substance, or material, such as gold, iron, oxygen, and hydrogen, that cannot be separated into simpler parts by chemical means.

- Before you read, name other elements that you know.

_____

Think about . . .

Some reading tests are constructed like this exercise, which is included to give you practice taking such tests. Your instructor may use it to test your ability to handle main ideas, supporting details, and clue words. Or your instructor may have you read and talk out the questions in workshop teams to review what you have been learning.

- Then predict: What elements were known to ancient people? Write your prediction here.

Reading with Meaning

Read to see whether your prediction is correct and whether you can recognize sentence relationships. You will have to answer multiple-choice questions about the main idea and sentence relationships very similar to questions that are asked on some standardized reading tests. In each case, cross out choices you know for sure are wrong to narrow the field. Star your answer.

Elements Known to Ancient Civilizations
Jay Pasachoff

Paragraph A

Not many of the elements occur in nature as pure substances, lying around waiting for someone to pick them up. A few do, and it is not surprising that these were known and collected for various uses in societies around the globe as far back as several thousand years B.C. *Sulfur* is one of those elements. It was known to burn with smelly results and have an odd appearance. Its use was probably confined to religious ceremonies. *Carbon* was also known since antiquity, because the charred bones of animals and portions of partially burned trees consist largely of carbon in the form of charcoal. Although we don't know all the uses primitive peoples made of charcoal, we do know that it was the key to releasing many other elements from their chemical combination in rocks. For example, if a copper-containing rock was heated in a hot fire with charcoal present, the carbon in the charcoal would combine with the other elements in the rock, leaving free metallic copper. In ways like this, people were able to discover the elements *copper, iron, lead, tin,* and *zinc,* although they didn't necessarily appreciate that these substances were elements. They just knew that they were useful.

> **Did You KNOW?**
>
> The root *prime-* means "first." You see it here on *primitive*. Other words with this Latin base are *primary* and *prime*.

1. What is the main idea of this paragraph?
   a. Not many elements occur in nature as pure substances, but ancient peoples made use of the few that do.
   b. Ancient peoples found copper, iron, lead, tin, and zinc very useful.
   c. If a copper-containing rock was heated in a hot fire with charcoal present, the carbon in the charcoal would combine with the other elements in the rock, leaving free metallic copper.
   d. Sulfur and carbon are two elements found free in nature.

2. The purpose of the sentence "Sulfur is one of those elements" is to
   a. state the main idea.
   b. support the main idea by providing a reason.
   c. support the main idea by providing an example.
   d. state an idea that is in contrast to the main idea.

3. The purpose of the sentence "Carbon was also known since antiquity" is to
   a. state the main idea.
   b. support the main idea by providing a reason.
   c. support the main idea by providing an example.
   d. state an idea that is in contrast to the main idea.

4. The purpose of the clause "if a copper-containing rock was heated in a hot fire with charcoal present" is to
   a. provide an example of carbon combining with other elements.
   b. state the condition under which carbon combines with other elements.

   c. contrast carbon with other elements found free in nature.
   d. state the main idea of the paragraph.

5. Which word or words in the paragraph introduce a reason?
   a. and   c. also
   b. because   d. for example

6. The word *although* is used twice in the paragraph. In both cases, the word introduces a/an
   a. reason.   c. opposite idea.
   b. example.   d. condition.

Paragraph B

Iron also arrived occasionally from the heavens in the form of iron-containing meteorites. Because of this, one might think that iron would have been thought of as a "heavenly" element, a gift from the gods. Instead, this honor has always fallen to the element *gold*. Gold doesn't fall from the skies, but it is found in its pure state in some places. It has the unusual property of never tarnishing like other metals do. Gold objects don't rust, as iron does, nor do they turn green or black on the surface, as do many other metals.

1. The main idea of the paragraph is that
   a. iron arrived from the heavens and for this reason ancient people considered it a heavenly gift.
   b. ancient people did not consider iron a gift from the gods.
   c. ancient people considered gold, not iron, as a gift from the gods because gold never tarnishes or rusts.
   d. gold objects are very valuable because they do not tarnish or rust.

2. The purpose of the sentence "Instead, this honor has always fallen to the element gold" is to
   a. state the main idea.
   b. provide an example of the idea stated in the previous statement.
   c. state a point that is opposite to that given in the previous statement.
   d. develop the idea stated in the previous statement.

3. The purpose of the sentence "It has the unusual property of never tarnishing like other metals do" is to
   a. state a contrast.
   b. provide an example of the idea stated in the previous statement.
   c. state a point that is opposite to that given in the previous statement.
   d. develop the idea stated in the previous statement.

4. What word or words set up a comparison in the paragraph?
   a. also   c. nor
   b. because   d. like

5. What relationship does the word *but* establish in this sentence: "Gold doesn't fall from the skies, but it is found in its pure state in some places"?
   a. It changes the direction of the thought.
   b. It introduces an example.
   c. It indicates that more on the same thought is coming.
   d. It indicates that the writer is going to list several points on the same topic.

6. What kind of relationship is established in the last sentence by the phrase "as do many other metals"?
   a. example   c. condition
   b. reason   d. comparison

Paragraph C

The ancient Egyptians used gold for jewelry and for coins. Gold is still used for jewelry, although pure gold is too soft for this purpose. Coins and jewelry, instead, are made of *alloys*. These are metals made by melting two or more metals in a pot together in such a way that they dissolve in one another. Gold coins are usually 90% gold and 10% copper. An alloy of gold and silver is called *white gold*.

1. The main idea of the paragraph is that
   a. coins and jewelry are and have been made from alloys of gold.
   b. an alloy of gold and silver is white gold.
   c. an alloy is made by melting two or more metals in a pot together so that they dissolve in one another.
   d. the ancient Egyptians used gold for jewelry and for coins.

2. The word *instead* in the third sentence suggests a/an
   a. example.
   b. continuation of the thought.
   c. change in the direction of the thought.
   d. reason.

3. The purpose of the sentence "These are metals made by melting two or more metals in a pot together in such a way that they dissolve in one another" is to
   a. state the main idea.
   b. give a detail to support the idea in the previous sentence.
   c. provide an example in support of the idea in the previous sentence.
   d. list several points relative to the main idea.

Paragraph D

Silver was one of the first metals to be used by human beings; alloys of silver continue to be used today in a variety of products, including jewelry and coins. Unlike gold, silver tarnishes to become blackish in color. On the other hand, silver is like gold in that it is melted with other elements to form alloys. One alloy is coin silver, consisting of 90% silver and 10% copper. A second alloy is sterling silver, which contains 92.5% silver and 7.5% copper. Other silver alloys today are used in dental fillings and for electrical contacts.

1. What is the main idea of the paragraph?
   a. Silver tarnishes to become blackish, so that it is necessary to use silver alloys instead of pure silver.
   b. Alloys of silver continue to be used today in a variety of products.
   c. Silver alloys are formed by melting silver with other elements such as copper.
   d. Sterling silver has a larger percentage of silver than coin silver.

2. The purpose of the sentence "Unlike gold, silver tarnishes to become blackish in color" is to
   a. establish a contrast between gold and silver.
   b. give a reason for the tarnishing of silver.
   c. show that gold is better than silver.
   d. give the condition under which silver will tarnish.

3. The purpose of the sentence "On the other hand, silver is like gold in that it is melted with other elements to form alloys" is to
   a. compare gold and silver.
   b. give an example of how an alloy is formed.
   c. give a reason for making alloys of silver.
   d. give a weakness of silver.

Did You
KNOW?

Duct- means "to lead." You see the Latin root here on *products.* Other words with this base are *conduct, deduce,* and *induct.*

4. The purpose of the sentence "One alloy is coin silver, consisting of 90% silver and 10% copper" is to provide a/an
   a. comparison.   c. reason.
   b. example.   d. condition.

5. The purpose of the sentence "A second alloy is sterling silver, which contains 92.5% silver and 7.5% copper" is to provide a/an
   a. comparison.   c. reason.
   b. example.   d. condition.

WORKSHOP 8: APPLYING WHAT YOU KNOW IN WRITING

In the previous sections, you have seen how authors organize their writing to express relationships and how they choose words and phrases that provide clues to the relationships they are developing. Using those clue words in reading, you can predict where a particular author is going next in a selection. Figure 7.5 is a summary of clue words authors use.

To gain control over these words, write sentences and paragraphs in your notebook using them. Begin by studying the following chart of data:

The Three States of Matter

The State	Characteristics	Relation to Heat	Examples
Solid	retains its volume (how much space it occupies) and shape		ice below 0°C; gold and silver at room temperature
Liquid	retains its volume but takes the shape of its container	may be formed by heating the solid form	water above 0°C; mercury at room temperature
Gas	takes the shape and volume of its container	may be formed by heating the liquid form	water vapor above 100°C; oxygen and hydrogen at room temperature

Working from the data in the chart, write a three-paragraph article about the states of matter. Model your paragraph after the one about the three classes of rocks that opens this chapter. Use the idea map in Figure 7.1 as a guide.

1. Start with a topic sentence that tells that there are three states of matter. Then in the same paragraph, tell about solids and give some examples.

2. Shift to a new paragraph about liquids. Use the phrase *in contrast* to make the transition. Again, include examples.

3. Shift to a third paragraph about gases. Include examples.

4. Take data from the chart in constructing your paragraphs.

5. Remember to use clue words to show key relationships. In this case, number words may be useful in identifying the three kinds of matter. Phrases such as *for example* or *an example of* may be useful when presenting examples. Phrases such as *if . . . then* may be useful in talking about conditions under which matter exists as a solid, liquid, or gas.

Go back and circle the key words you used to clarify the relationships you are expressing in your paragraphs. Note in the margin the kind of relationship you are establishing in each case. Use Figure 7.5 as a guide in doing this. Share your paragraphs with a partner. Have him or her help you edit your paragraphs so they express your ideas as clearly as possible.

What Is Going to Happen	Clue Words	Strategy for Handling the Clues
Writer is going to enumerate or discuss a number of items.	*Three* kinds, *two* problems, *four* reasons, the *first*, the *second*, the *third*.	Ask, "How many items is the author going to enumerate (list) or talk about?"
Writer is going to enumerate or describe examples to support a point	*An example is, for example, such as, for instance.*	Ask, "Is this an example of the point?"
Writer is going to provide more on the topic or to change the direction.	More on the topic: *and, also, in addition, moreover, furthermore, additionally.*	Ask, "Does this relate to what came before it?"
	Change of direction: *but, yet, however, on the other hand, nevertheless.*	Ask, "Does this present the other side of the point?"
Writer is going to compare or contrast.	Similarities are to be presented: *similarly, as in the case of, like the, the same as, like.*	Ask, "Is the author stating the way things are the same?"
	Differences are to be presented: *on the other hand, on the contrary, unlike the, in contrast to, whereas, while.*	Ask, "Is the author stating the way things differ?"
Writer is going to set up a conditional relationship.	*If . . . then, consequently, hence, thus.*	Ask, "If x, then what?"
Writer is going to give reasons.	*Because, for, as a result, since, for this reason.*	Ask, "Why?"
Writer is going to indicate *in spite of the fact that.*	*Although, even, though.*	Ask, "In spite of what?"

FIGURE 7.5 Clue Words That Show Relationships

EXTENDING WHAT YOU HAVE LEARNED

Applying the Strategies as You Read

Review the word clues contained in Figure 7.5. Then read an article from a science magazine such as *Scientific American* or a section from a biology or earth science text. As you read, write on a card several sentences with clue words that help you grasp what is happening in the article. On the card next to each clue word, write what you learned from that clue word: The author is going to enumerate the items to be considered, change the direction of the thought, continue with the thought, present an example, compare or contrast, give an if-then relationship, or give a reason. Be ready to share your findings with classmates.

Extending Your Vocabulary

Select several words from those emphasized in the chapter to use in writing and speaking. Record these in your personal vocabulary list. Include a model sentence for each.

Building Your Knowledge Base

Locate the Hawaiian Islands on a globe. Would you like to go there? What would you expect to see? Add the names of the following places to the map in Figure 14.1 on page 258: Mt. Etna in Sicily and Mt. Vesuvius in Italy.

8

Critical Thinking: Applying, Comparing, Inferring, Concluding, and Judging

OBJECTIVE

In this chapter, you will refine your strategies for thinking critically as you read. You will refine your ability to

1. Apply ideas to your life;
2. Compare items;
3. Infer, or read between the lines;
4. Conclude; and
5. Judge, or form opinions.

Think
about . . .

What topics will this
chapter cover? How do
the chapter subhead-
ings relate to this
numbered list?

APPLYING, COMPARING, INFERRING, CONCLUDING, JUDGING

As you learned in Chapter 1, reading is an active process in which you think about and expand ideas from a selection. Of course, to get involved while reading, you must be able to

- Find main ideas and sort significant from less significant details;
- Follow the author's train of thought and figure out sentence relationships.

But to read with full understanding, you must leap beyond the text, analyze relationships, and come up with your own ideas.

APPLYING

One way to leap beyond a text is to apply the author's ideas, points, and examples to your life. Your strategy for *applying* has three steps:

**APPLYING
STRATEGY**

→ Identify the main ideas, as in Chapter 4.

→ Identify the significant details and supporting examples, as in Chapters 6 and 7.

→ Ask, "How do the ideas and examples apply to me?"

WORKSHOP 1: APPLYING

Read the following paragraphs from a college marketing text. As you read, think first in terms of the main idea: What are the authors saying? Think in terms of the examples: What examples do they use to support the idea? Ask, "How do the examples relate to me? What products do I use because of the way they have been marketed?"

Marketing in a Changing World
P. Kotler and G. Armstrong

Did You KNOW?

Fac(e)- is from the Latin verb *facere* and means "to make." *Manu-* is from the Latin noun *manus* and means "hand." Other words with these roots are *surface* and *deface; manuscript* and *emancipate.*

Marketing touches all of us every day of our lives. We wake up to a Sears radio alarm clock playing an American Airlines commercial advertising a Bahamas vacation. Then we brush our teeth with Crest, shave with a Gillette Sensor razor, gargle with Scope, and use other toiletries and appliances produced by manufacturers around the world. We put on our Levi's jeans and Nike shoes and head for the kitchen, where we drink Minute Maid orange juice and pour Borden milk over a bowl of Kellogg's Cracklin' Oat Bran. Later, we drink a cup of Maxwell House coffee with a teaspoon of Domino sugar while munching on a slice of Sara Lee coffee cake.

The marketing system has made all this possible with little effort on our part. It has given us a standard of living that our ancestors could not have imagined.

Based on your reading and collaborating with two partners, complete the chart in Figure 8.1. Write the authors' main point or points in the main idea box, the authors' supporting examples in the box so labeled, and supporting examples from your life in the third box. In making connections between a reading selection and your life, you may want to visualize a series of boxes such as those in Figure 8.1 and mentally slot in the main idea and examples in the same way.

COMPARING

A second way to leap beyond a text and get involved while reading is to make comparisons. In *comparing,* you consider two or more items and determine how those items are similar and how they are different. The items can be people, events, ideas—almost anything, for that matter. Your strategy for comparing is to take these three steps:

COMPARING STRATEGY

→ Identify the significant features of each item you are comparing.

→ Ask, "What features do the items share, or have in common?"

→ Ask, "How do the items differ?"

Sometimes in reading a selection, you find a description or explanation of only one item. You still can and should make comparisons. You compare the item described or explained in a passage to ones with which you are already familiar.

• Ask, "What does this remind me of? How is it like what I already know? How does it differ?"

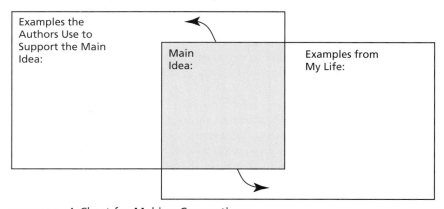

FIGURE 8.1 A Chart for Making Connections

	Gua	Viki
When was the experiment done?		
Who did the experiment?		
What procedure did the investigator use?		
What was the outcome?		
What did the investigation seem to prove?		

FIGURE 8.2 A Chart for Identifying Significant Features

WORKSHOP 2: COMPARING

Read the following two paragraphs. Your reading purpose is to compare the two experiments. How are they the same? How are they different? To this end, complete the data chart in Figure 8.2 after you read.

Can Chimpanzees Learn to Speak?
Jean Berko Gleason

In 1931 Professor and Mrs. W. N. Kellogg became the first American family to raise a chimpanzee and a child together. The Kelloggs brought into their home Gua, a seven-month-old chimpanzee, who stayed with them and their infant son Donald for nine months. No special effort was made to teach Gua to talk; like the human baby she was simply exposed to a speaking household. During this period, Gua came to use some of her natural chimpanzee cries rather consistently; for instance, she used her food bark not just for food but for anything else she wanted. Although Gua was rather better than Donald in most physical accomplishments, unlike Donald she did not babble and did not learn to say any English words.

In the 1940s psychologists Catherine and Keith Hayes set out to improve upon the Kelloggs' experiment by raising a chimpanzee named Viki as if she were their own child. They took her home when she was six weeks old, and she remained with them for several years. The Hayeses made every effort to teach Viki to talk; they had assumed that chimpanzees were rather like retarded institutionalized children and that love and patient instruction would afford Viki the opportunity for optimal language development. After six years of training, Viki was able to say four words: "mama," "papa," "cup," and "up." She was never able to say more, and the words she did say were very difficult to understand: in order to pronounce a *p*, she had to hold her lips together with her fingers.   [266 words]

Did You KNOW?

Optima- is from Latin and means "best." You find it in such words as *optimum, optimize,* and *optimist.*

Review the data you organized in Figure 8.2. In what ways were the two experiments similar? In what ways were they different?

One way to compare items is with a Venn diagram (see Figure 8.3). A Venn diagram is made up of two overlapping ovals. In the area of overlap, you list the characteristics shared by the two items. In the separate areas, you list the unique characteristics of the items you are comparing. Try it for a moment. Compare two of your friends. In your notebook, make a Venn diagram for them by putting the qualities they share in the

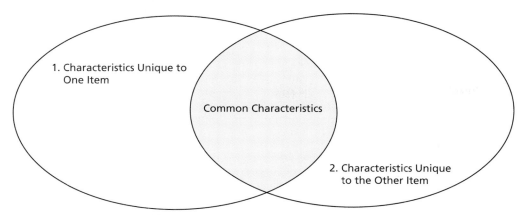

FIGURE 8.3 A Diagram for Making Comparisons
Write the characteristics of one item in the oval marked "1." Write the characteristics of the other item in the oval marked "2." In the "Common Characteristics" oval, list the characteristics shared by both items. This kind of diagram is called a Venn diagram. It is helpful in comparing two items.

central, overlapping area and their unique qualities on each side. In the same way, make a Venn diagram in which you compare two professors or two events in your life, or compare college life with life in high school.

Now apply comparison thinking to paragraphs you have read. Review the paragraphs about Gua and Viki. How were the experiments the same? How did they differ? Answer in your notebook by completing a Venn diagram as in Figure 8.3.

INFERRING

A third way to get involved actively while reading is to read between the lines and infer relationships not stated directly by the author. In *inferring*, you pick up hints or clues from the passage. You relate those clues to things you already know and come up with an idea that the author has only alluded to, or suggested indirectly.

The key strategy question in this case is this one:

INFERRING STRATEGY

→ What is the author suggesting (or hinting at) through the facts he or she is giving? What can I read into what he or she is saying? What connections can I make based on what I know?

Here is an example. What inference do you make as you read the sentence "When she saw him, her lips tightened"? Having seen people tighten their lips when they are angry (or when they are uptight about something), you may infer that the person was not pleased at all; she was angry. That is an inference, because the writer does not come right out and state, "She was angry." You must figure that out from the clues given.

To practice the inferring strategy, try the activities that follow.

 ### WORKSHOP 3: INFERRING

Complete the chart in Figure 8.4 by making an inference based on each statement and the related questions. Then indicate the clue in the statement that led you to your inference. Having completed the chart, you can draw a conclusion about the kinds of inferences you can make. You can infer the age of a person, the kind of person he or she is, the kind of relationship that exists between people, a person's feelings,

Think
about . . .
With what kind of material should you ask, "How are they different? How are they the same?"

Statement	Question	Inference	Clue in the Statement That Helps You Infer
His face was lined with wrinkles.	How old was he? What else might you infer?		
He had a scowl on his face as he passed me without speaking.	How did he feel about me? What else might you infer?		
The boy and girl were holding hands as they strolled through the mall.	What can you infer about their relation-ship?		
It was snowing heavily, and the light had almost disap-peared from the heavens.	What season of the year was it? What else can you infer?		
The car was swerv-ing from one side of the road to the other.	What can you infer was wrong here?		
A man remarks, "I do not believe a woman should serve on the Supreme Court."	What kind of man is he?		
He was dressed in a three-piece black suit, a white shirt, and a striped tie.	Where was the man going?		
There were tears running down his face.	What can you infer?		
I gave the grocer a quarter for the quart of milk.	What can you infer?		

FIGURE 8.4   A Chart for Practicing Inference-Making

the season of the year, the time of day, the place where the action takes place, or the rea-sons for actions.

WORKSHOP 4: INFERRING

Review the paragraph about marketing on page 141 and make some inferences about the authors of it. Are the authors male or female? in their thirties, forties, or fifties? affluent or needy? Decide with a partner. Then in your reading notebook, write down your inferences, supporting them with details from the paragraph.

WORKSHOP 5: INFERRING

Read and enjoy the following autobiographical selection by Judith Cofer.

A Partial Remembrance of a Puerto Rican Childhood: Primary Lessons

Judith Ortiz Cofer

My mother walked me to my first day at school at La Escuela Segundo Ruiz Belvis, named after the Puerto Rican patriot born in our town. I remember yellow cement with green trim. All the classrooms had been painted these colors to identify them as government property. This was true all over the Island. Everything was color-coded, including the children, who wore uniforms from first through twelfth grade. We were a midget army in white and brown, led by the hand to our battleground. From practically every house in our barrio emerged a crisply ironed uniform inhabited by the savage creatures we had become over a summer of running wild in the sun.

At my grandmother's house where we were staying until my father returned to Brooklyn Yard in New York and sent for us, it had been complete chaos, with several children to get ready for school. My mother had pulled my hair harder than usual while braiding it, and I had dissolved into a pool of total self-pity. I wanted to stay home with her and Mamá, to continue listening to stories in the later afternoon, to drink *café con leche* with them, and to play rough games with my many cousins. I wanted to continue living the dream of summer afternoons in Puerto Rico, and if I could not have it, then I wanted to go back to Paterson, New Jersey, back to where I imagined our apartment waited, peaceful and cool, for the three of us to return to our former lives. Our gypsy lifestyle had convinced me, at age six, that one part of life stops and waits for you while you live another for a while—if you don't like the present, you can always return to the past. Buttoning me into my stiff blouse while I tried to squirm away from her, my mother attempted to explain to me that I was a big girl now and should try to understand that, like all the other children my age, I had to go to school.

"What about him?" I yelled pointing at my brother who was lounging on the tile floor of our bedroom in pajamas, playing quietly with a toy car.

"He's too young to go to school, you know that. Now stay still." My mother pinned me between her thighs to button my skirt, as she had learned to do from Mamá, from whose grip it was impossible to escape.

"It's not fair, it's not fair. I can't go to school here. I don't speak Spanish." It was my final argument, and it failed miserably because I was shouting my defiance in the language I claimed not to speak. Only I knew what I meant by saying in Spanish that I did not speak Spanish. I had spent my early childhood in the United States where I lived in a bubble created by my Puerto Rican parents in a home where two cultures and languages became one. I learned to listen to the English from the television with one ear while I heard my mother and father speaking in Spanish with the other. I thought I was an ordinary American kid—like the children on the shows I watched—and that everyone's parents spoke a secret second language at home. When we came to Puerto Rico right before I started first grade, I switched easily to Spanish. It was the language of fun, of summertime games. But school—that was a different matter.

I made one last desperate effort to make my mother see reason: "Father will be very angry. You know that he wants us to speak good English." My mother, of course, ignored me as she dressed my little brother in his playclothes. I could not believe her indifference to my father's wishes. She was usually so careful about our safety and the many other areas that he was forever reminding her about in his letters. But I was right, and she knew it. Our father spoke to us in English as much as possible, and he corrected my pronunciation constantly—not "jes" but "y-es." Y-es, sir. How could she send me to school to learn Spanish when we would be returning to Paterson in just a few months?

But, of course, what I feared was not language, but loss of freedom. At school there would be no playing, no stories, only lessons. It would not matter if I did not understand a word, and I would not be allowed to make up my own definitions. I would have to learn silence. I would have to keep my wild imagination in check. Feeling locked into my stiffly starched uniform, I only sensed all this. I guess most children can intuit their loss of

Did You KNOW?

Hab- is a Latin base that means "have or hold as customary." Related words are *cohabit*, *habitation*, and *habituate*. Remember that the prefix *in-* or *im-* means "in or into." You have seen it on *inject*, *ingest*, and *immigrant*.

childhood's freedom on that first day of school. It is separation anxiety, too, but mother is just the guardian of the "playground" of our early childhood.

Now answer these questions, each of which calls for an inference. Support your inferences with evidence from the selection.

1. What time of year was it? _____
   _____

2. What kind of person was Judith's mother? How did she feel about Judith?
   _____
   _____

3. Who was Mamá? _____
   _____

4. What kind of person was Judith's father? _____
   _____

5. Why did Judith's father speak to her in English as much as possible? _____
   _____

6. Why was Judith concerned about not understanding a word in school? _____
   _____

7. What kind of relationship did Judith's parents have with one another? _____
   _____

8. What kind of person was Judith at this point in her life? _____
   _____

9. How did Judith feel about going to school? _____
   _____

10. What did Judith learn from this episode in her life? _____
    _____

CONCLUDING

A fourth kind of thinking that you should do as you read is *concluding*: developing conclusions based on the information given. A conclusion is a generalization about a topic. It is a big idea that you put together based on the facts. Very often you base your conclusions on the comparisons you have made and the inferences you have already drawn.

In formulating conclusions, the main question to ask yourself is this:

CONCLUDING STRATEGY

→ What big idea or ideas can I put together based on the facts give in the selection?

Review the paragraphs about Gua and Viki. What conclusions can you draw about whether chimpanzees are capable of humanlike speech? Write your conclusion here.

_____

Did you conclude that chimpanzees cannot learn to speak as humans do, even when given explicit instruction? That would be an acceptable conclusion based on the facts given. What details from the selection support that conclusion? Write some supporting facts here. _____

_____

     In drawing conclusions, you are getting at the ultimate meaning of things—what is important, why it is important, how one event influences another, and how one happening leads to another. Simply to get the facts is not enough. You must think about what those facts mean to you.

Think
about . . .

At what point in your reading do you ask, "What big idea can I make out of this? What can I conclude on the basis of it?"

JUDGING

A fifth way to leap beyond a text is to judge: to develop opinions of your own about the material you are reading and about how that material is written. To render a judgment about the material in a selection, ask questions like these:

**JUDGING
STRATEGY**

→ What is the point of view expressed in the selection?

→ What are the arguments for this point of view? What are the arguments against it?

→ Based on the arguments for and against, what do I believe is right? What do I believe is wrong?

Figure 8.5 shows a diagram that may help you to render a judgment about ideas you are reading. To render a judgment about how material is written, ask yourself these kinds of questions:

   • Is the selection clearly written? Is it awkwardly phrased or poorly organized?

     Review the section about Gua and Viki. What arguments support this kind of experimentation with animals? What are some arguments against experimenting with animals? Do you believe experimentation with animals is right? Try filling in Figure 8.5 with arguments for and against experimentation and then form a judgment based on the arguments.

Arguments For: Arguments Against:

_____ | Value Question: Is it right to | _____

_____   experiment with animals as   _____

_____   scientists did with Gua and   _____

_____   Viki?   _____

                                   ↓

                 My opinion:

                 _____

FIGURE 8.5   A Way to Put Together a Judgment: A Values Scale

THINKING AND READING

The main idea of this chapter so far is that you should be thinking about ideas continuously as you read. Generally you do this by asking and answering questions as you go along. These questions include the strategies at the top of page 148.

CRITICAL THINKING
STRATEGIES

→ *Applying:* How do the main ideas and examples relate to me and my life?

→ *Comparing:* Of what does this (person, place, event) remind me? How are these things similar? Different? How does this person, place, or event relate to other circumstances?

→ *Inferring:* What does this clue—hidden between the lines—tell me? What does it hint about the feelings involved, the age of the person, the kind of person he or she is, the kind of relationship that exists between people, the season of the year, the time of day, the place where the story is set, the date when the event took place?

→ *Concluding:* Why is this important or significant? Why did this happen? What is the ultimate meaning of these events?

→ *Judging:* Do I agree or disagree? Why? Is this accurate? Is this good or bad? Why?

In the selections you will read next, you will have the opportunity to apply, compare, infer, conclude, and judge.

SELECTION 1

Eat, Drink but the Dietary Doom-Sayers Won't Let You Be Merry (NEWSPAPER EDITORIAL)

A Critical Reading Workshop

Expanding Your Vocabulary for Reading

Use context and word elements to figure out the meanings of the italicized terms. Write the meanings in the spaces provided.

1. On his *binge*, the freshman really pigged out, eating and drinking everything in sight.

   _____

   _____

2. Most college students *frequent* the college center, the place where the action is.

   _____

   _____

3. It is dangerous to *imbibe* too much beer at any one time. _____

   _____

4. We are all *mortal*, human beings who live but who will die at some point.

   _____

   _____

5. Do everything in *moderation*. Don't overdo any one thing. _____

   _____

6. After living a life of moderation all week, on weekends some college students *indulge*

   and begin to live the high life. _____

   _____

Did You KNOW?

Mort- is a Latin root meaning "death." Words built from this root are *mortician, mortuary,* and *immortal.*

7. She was *conditioned* at home to sleeping nine hours at night. When she came to college, she had to recondition herself to less sleep. _____

_____

8. I give much *credence* to his opinion because he has researched the question thoroughly. _____

Did You
KNOW?
The base *cred-* means "to believe." Other words from this Latin root are *credible* and *incredible*.

Getting Ready to Read

Preview the selection by reading the title, the first couple of sentences, and the last couple of sentences.

- What is the topic of the selection? _____

- What do you predict Hall is going to say? _____

_____

Reading with Meaning

Read to test your prediction, to relate what the author says to your life, and to develop your own opinion on the topic.

Eat, Drink but the Dietary Doom-Sayers Won't Let You Be Merry
Lawrence Hall

I confess. I went on a crazy eating and drinking binge, and it was swell. For breakfast yesterday morning I had two cups of black coffee with sugar and the most buttery croissant ever made on this planet. As a mid-morning snack, I ate a two-egg, ham and Swiss cheese omelet and polished it off with some orange juice while watching CNN. At dinner, I had a piece of broiled beef and a salad and, later that evening, some strawberry ice cream. Also, lest I forget, I drank a bottle of beer and sipped some iced tea and birch beer soda during the course of the day.

Normally I don't eat and drink this way. But it was fun and fulfilling—if only to satisfy my stomach for a change and thumb my nose at those self-righteous food police who are forever dictating what we should eat, how much, and when. Not a week goes by without these police of the palate bad-mouthing something we enjoy, whether it's margarine, tomatoes, fish, fast foods, and all those starchy, sugary, and flavor-enhanced foodstuffs crammed on supermarket shelves or in cold cases.

Recently, they made a big deal about the dietary horrors of movie popcorn. Anyone who frequents the movies knows that those kernels popping around in that machine aren't haute cuisine. But it's buttery and salty and goes down well with soda water, and is the ideal movie refreshment—just like peanuts and Crackerjacks at a ballgame.

Without a doubt, America is hooked on junk food after being weaned for decades on Twinkies, Cheese-Doodles, chips of all kinds, hamburgers, french fries, and practically any other sort of "hurry up, I'm hungry" snacks and takeouts.

But that's not a crime for which consumers should be hanged in the supermarket parking lot or ridiculed or guilt laden for indulging. After all, many of them pay their taxes and rent, work like the dickens and pray to their Ultimate Maker. Why, I sometimes wonder, do so many folks get really bent out of shape over what's politically or medically correct to eat or drink? Why, for instance, should anyone feel guilty about craving a corned beef and cole slaw on rye?

With so many medical scientists and others proclaiming that "this is bad for you," and "eating this will give you cancer"—well I've just decided I'm not going to give any credence to whatever the food police say. I tried, desperately so, to heed much of what these medical Moses have handed down. But, over a period of years, I've grown a bit weary of their commandments of "Thou shall not" imbibe or ingest a constellation of things because they contain carcinogens, cholesterol, and chemical contaminants.

The margarine scare ticked me off. For years, the food police commanded that we forsake butter and lather and lace our foods with margarine. And, most of us—including myself—did that, too. The food police now contend there are too many fatty acids in margarine, and the stuff may contribute to 30,000 heart attacks a year.

But I say, "bah, humbug" to this scare, and the same to others that maintain my arteries may harden, my memory cells may short-circuit, and all sorts of things may injure my bodily system—all because I engage in mere mortal pleasures. . . . I'm going to eat and drink, in moderation, whatever I darn well please and I advise you to do the same. Yes, eat, drink and be merry. After all, tomorrow you could be a victim of a carjacking, a street mugging, an earthquake, or even a nuclear disaster.

Monitoring Comprehension and Writing in Response

Answer these questions, talking with a reading partner. Then collaborate to write out your answers.

1. What is the main idea Hall is making in the article? Do you agree or disagree with his point? Why? _____

    _____

    _____

2. When have you done what Hall did and gone on a binge? Describe a similar event in your life. _____

    _____

    _____

3. Why do people binge like this? Explain based on your own experiences.

    _____

    _____

    _____

4. Why do you think Hall is annoyed about the popcorn "big deal"? Infer a reason.

    _____

    _____

5. Why do you think Hall is so annoyed about the margarine scare? Infer a reason.

    _____

    _____

6. What can you infer about the kind of person Hall is? _____

    _____

7. What word in the last paragraph shows that Hall may not be as extreme as he previously suggested? _____

    _____

8. In your opinion, is this essay well written? Writing in your notebook, draft a paragraph in which you state your opinion in a topic sentence, and give specific points to support it. _____

_____

9. Write a paragraph in which you express a pet peeve or gripe. State frankly what bothers you, and then give an example or two from your own experiences.

Reviewing Key Vocabulary

Select the word from the list that best fits the context of each sentence. Check the glossary if you need to review the meaning of a word.

binge	credence	imbibe	moderation
conditioned	frequent	indulge	mortal

1. After dieting for more than a month, I went on a _____ and ate a hamburger and cheesecake.

2. Usually I eat in _____, but sometimes I let loose and binge.

3. We are all _____; we must all die in the end.

4. Most of us are _____ to expect instant rewards for our efforts, but that does not always happen.

5. Sometimes I just have to _____. I allow myself a reward for my good behavior.

6. If you _____ a great amount of alcohol, you should not drive.

7. College students _____ the college pub. They go there to socialize and relax.

8. Melissa gives much _____ to the opinions of her friends.

SELECTION 2

Moral Power or Gun Power (SOCIOLOGY)

A Critical Thinking Workshop

Expanding Your Vocabulary for Reading

Use word elements and the context to unlock the meanings of the italicized words. Write the definition of the italicized words in the space provided. Remember to use your knowledge of word syllables and word elements to help you pronounce the multisyllabic words.

1. The weather that winter was *unprecedented;* we had far colder weather than ever before.

_____

_____

2. The *reformers* wanted change. _____

_____

3. There were many *hard-liners* who strongly advocated keeping things as they were.

_____

_____

Did You KNOW?

The prefix *un-* means "not." You have seen it on such words as *unhappy, unsuccessful,* and *unrelenting.* Remember that the prefix *re-* means "back, again." You see it here on *reformers* and *repression.*

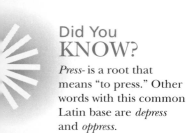

Did You
KNOW?

Press- is a root that means "to press." Other words with this common Latin base are *depress* and *oppress*.

4. *Repression* was severe. If anyone stepped out of line, he or she was immediately jailed.

_____

_____

5. We heard *ominous* rumblings of thunder in the distance and knew we were in for a terrible storm. _____

_____

6. *Turmoil* resulted when the alarm sounded and the electricity went out.

_____

_____

7. The two knights *dueled* over a minor disagreement that had turned into a major confrontation. _____

_____

8. The wealthy woman spent her money *indiscriminately* until she had very little left for important purposes. _____

_____

9. Students from all over the United States *converged* on Florida during spring break.

_____

_____

Getting Ready to Read

Read the title and the first sentence or two of the following selection, which comes from a college sociology textbook.

- What is this selection about? _____

- What do you already know about Tiananmen Square? Share what you know with a partner. Collaborate by writing down a few phrases that come to mind.

_____

Reading with Meaning

Read this selection to find out the major idea, or thesis, the author is trying to communicate and to think critically about the ideas presented.

Moral Power or Gun Power
John Macionis

Not since the revolution that brought the communists to power in 1949 has the People's Republic of China experienced anything like the events of the spring of 1989. Tiananmen Square—the central landmark of the capital city of Beijing—was the scene of an unprecedented five-week demonstration in support of greater political democracy. The demonstrators, numbering in the thousands, were initially mostly students encouraged by recent economic reforms to demand a greater voice in government. Clustered together in the shadow of the Great Hall of the People, some began a hunger strike; others resolutely displayed banners and headbands that proclaimed their goals. As the days passed, their numbers steadily increased, until more than 1 million of the city's people mixed uneasily with a growing number of soldiers around the square.

Reformers among the country's leaders supported the demonstration. Hard-liners strongly opposed it, urging the use of force to crush the protest. The balance of power slowly shifted toward a policy of repression. Ominous signs appeared: troops from other regions of China (denied news of how popular the protest had become) were trucked to the outskirts of the city. Waves of soldiers periodically tried to clear sections of the square; each time, the demonstrators held their ground. Premier Li Peng then announced that the "turmoil" was to be swiftly ended. Anxiety rose as the government ordered satellite dishes and other communication links operated by foreign news agencies shut down.

About 2 A.M. on the morning of Sunday, June 4, the political dueling ended in convulsions of violence and horror. From three sides, a fifty-truck convoy of ten thousand troops converged on the square. Soldiers leveled AK-47 assault rifles and began firing indiscriminately at the crowds. Tanks rolled over makeshift barriers, crushing the people behind them. Some demonstrators bravely fought back, but their fate had already been sealed. Within three hours, the prodemocracy movement had ended, and Tiananmen Square was awash with the blood of thousands of people.

Events such as those in Tiananmen Square make clear a lesson often lost in the concerns of daily life: the operation of every society is shaped by those who have the power to control events. Power, of course, takes many forms, but all are not necessarily equal. As they occupied the center of their nation's capital city, the Chinese people claimed the moral power to direct their own lives. The response of their government, in words once used by Chinese leader Mao Zedong, was: "Political power grows out of the barrel of a gun."

Monitoring Comprehension and Writing in Response

Collaborate with a partner to complete these activities.

1. In each paragraph, underline the sentence that states or almost states the main idea.

2. What is the main idea, or thesis, of the entire selection? _____
_____

3. Why do you think the students were at the forefront of the demonstrations?
_____
_____

4. Why do you think that troops from outside the city were trucked in to control the
demonstrators? _____
_____

5. Who won the political duel: the hard-liners or the reformers? _____
_____

What evidence in the selection supports your answer? _____
_____

6. Of what other events from the past or present do the events in Tiananmen Square
remind you? In what ways are the events the same? Different? _____
_____
_____

7. Do you agree with the Chinese people's claim that they had the moral power to direct
their own lives? Talk about reasons to support your opinion. _____
_____
_____

8. What is the meaning of the statement "Political power grows out of the barrel of a gun"? _____

_____

9. Do you agree or disagree with the statement in question 8? Explain your answer.

_____

_____

_____

10. If this kind of situation existed in your country, would you be willing to risk your life to bring change? Why? Why not? Write a paragraph in your notebook responding to these queries.

Reviewing Vocabulary

Place each of these words into the sentence where it best fits the context. Use the Know-for-sure/Process-of-elimination strategy.

converged	indiscriminately	repression
dueled	ominous	turmoil
hard-liners	reformers	unprecedented

1. The veterans _____ on the White House to bring their demands directly to the president.

2. _____ was everywhere at that time; no one was allowed to speak out on an issue in a way that differed from the government.

3. There were _____ shouts from the crowd indicating that turmoil could break out at any moment.

4. The situation was _____. Nothing like it had ever happened before.

5. The soldiers fired _____ into the crowds, striking anyone who happened to be there.

6. Alexander Hamilton _____ with Aaron Burr in a gunfight that stands out in American history.

7. The _____ wanted to keep things just as they were. The _____ wanted change. The result was an unsettled situation with lots of _____ that lasted many years.

SELECTION 3:

Native American Myths and Legends: The White River Sioux and the Cheyenne (LITERATURE—LEGEND)

A Critical Thinking Workshop

Expanding Your Vocabulary for Reading

Determine the meanings of the italicized words by using word elements and the context. Write the meanings in the spaces provided.

1. His achievements became *legendary;* they have been celebrated and described over and over again. _____

Think
about . . .
Pronounce the italicized words by saying them aloud with a partner. Ask, Where are the syllable breaks?

2. The general *rallied* the army after the defeat and later led the army to victory.

   _____

3. The *keening* of the women for the dead general filled the air; their wailing could be

   heard through the village. _____

   _____

4. The workers erected a *scaffold* to display the golden ornaments so that all could see

   them. _____

   _____

5. His first name is Grant, and his last name is Evans, or *vice versa*. _____

   _____

6. In the United States a ring on the third finger of the left hand *signifies* that the wearer

   is married. _____

   _____

7. She *aspires* to be a lawyer. She aims at this vocation because her mother is a lawyer.

   _____

   _____

8. My *coup* for the year is getting the contract to build the shopping center. I count it

   as one of my greatest accomplishments. _____

   _____

9. A peace-loving person, my grandmother *abhorred* war. She regarded it with extreme

   loathing. _____

   _____

10. No one knows the real reason for the *extinction* of the dinosaur; we know only that di-

    nosaurs ceased to be. _____

    _____

Did You KNOW?

Spir- is a root that means "to breathe." You have seen it in *conspire, respire,* and *inspire* as well as in the word *spire*.

Getting Ready to Read

Survey the selection by reading the title, author, headings, and introductory section.

- What is the selection about? _____
- What kind of selection is it? _____
- What do you already know about the topic and this kind of story? _____

  _____

  _____

Reading with Meaning

Read the following Native American legends. As you read, keep in mind the following questions:

1. How do the stories relate to you and your life? (***application***)

2. How are the two stories similar? How are they different? (*comparison*)

3. What do the legends tell you about the White River Sioux and the Cheyenne? (*inference*)

4. What conclusions can you develop about the Sioux and the Cheyenne and the way they view courage? (*conclusion*)

5. Do you view courage in the same way? If not, why not? (*judgment*)

Native American Myths and Legends: The White River Sioux and the Cheyenne
Richard Erdoes, as Told by Jenny Leading Cloud at White River, Rosebud Indian Reservation, South Dakota, 1967

War for many Indians was an exciting but dangerous sport. In a way it resembled a medieval tournament, governed by strict rules of conduct. The battlefield became an arena for an intensely personal competition of honor in which a young man might make a name for himself and earn the eagle feathers which signified adulthood. One could be killed in this game, but killing enemies was not the reason why men went to war. Total war resulting in the extinction of a tribe was almost unknown and generally abhorred.

The conduct of war was a ceremonial affair, full of magic and ritual. Men rode to war with protective medicine bundles, miracle-working pebbles, or medicine shields, their horses covered with sacred gopher dust or painted with lightning designs—all intended to make the wearer arrow- or bulletproof, and to give his horse supernatural speed.

The main object in any battle—and the only way to gain honors—was to "count coup," to reckon one's brave deeds. Killing a man from an ambush with a gun was no coup because it was easy—even a coward could do it. But riding up on an unwounded and fully armed enemy and touching him with the hand, or with one's coupstick, was a great feat. Stealing horses right under the enemy's nose was also a fine coup. Coups were proudly boasted of around campfires, their stories and details told and retold. In some tribes a young man could not aspire to marry unless he had counted coup.

Here are two stories that show how the Sioux and Cheyenne viewed war.

Chief Roman Nose Loses His Medicine

The Lakota and the Shahiyela—the Sioux and the Cheyenne—have been good friends for a long time. Often they have fought shoulder to shoulder. They fought the white soldiers on the Bozeman Road, which we Indians called the Thieves' Road because it was built to steal our land. They fought together on the Rosebud River, and the two tribes united to defeat Custer in the big battle of the Little Bighorn. Even now in a barroom brawl, a Sioux will always come to the aid of a Cheyenne and vice versa. We Sioux will never forget what brave fighters the Cheyenne used to be.

Over a hundred years ago the Cheyenne had a famous war chief whom the whites called Roman Nose. He had the fierce, proud face of a hawk, and his deeds were legendary. He always rode into battle with a long warbonnet trailing behind him. It was thick with eagle feathers, and each stood for a brave deed, a coup counted on the enemy.

Roman Nose had a powerful war medicine, a magic stone he carried tied to his hair on the back of his head. Before a fight he sprinkled his war shirt with sacred gopher dust and painted his horse with hailstone patterns. All these things, especially the magic stone, made him bulletproof. Of course, he could be slain by a lance, a knife, or a tomahawk, but not with a gun. And nobody ever got the better of Roman Nose in hand-to-hand combat.

There was one thing about Roman Nose's medicine: he was not allowed to touch anything made of metal when eating. He had to use horn or wooden spoons and eat from wooden or earthenware bowls. His meat had to be cooked in a buffalo's pouch or in a clay pot, not in a white man's iron kettle.

One day Roman Nose received word of a battle going on between white soldiers and Cheyenne warriors. The fight had been swaying back and forth for over a day. "Come and help us; we need you" was the message. Roman Nose called his warriors together. They had a hasty meal, and Roman Nose forgot about the laws of his medicine. Using a metal spoon and a white man's steel knife, he ate buffalo meat cooked in an iron kettle.

The white soldiers had made a fort on a sandspit island in the middle of a river. They were shooting from behind and they had a new type of rifle which was better and could shoot faster and farther than the Indian's arrows and old muzzle-loaders.

The Cheyenne were hurling themselves against the soldiers in attack after attack, but the water in some spots came up to the saddles of their horses and the river bottom was slippery. They could not ride up quickly on the enemy, and they faced murderous fire. Their attacks were repulsed, their losses heavy.

Roman Nose prepared for the fight by putting on his finest clothes, war shirt, and leggings. He painted his best horse, with hailstone designs, and he tied the pebble which made him bulletproof into his hair at the back of his head. But an old warrior stepped up to him and said: "You have eaten from an iron kettle with a metal spoon and a steel knife. Your medicine is powerless; you must not fight today. Purify yourself for four days so that your medicine will be good again."

"But the fight is today, not in four days," said Roman Nose. "I must lead my warriors. I will die, but only the mountains and the rocks are forever." He put on his great warbonnet, sang his death song, and then charged. As he rode up to the white's cottonwood breastwork, a bullet hit him in the chest. He fell from his horse; his body was immediately lifted by his warriors, and the Cheyenne retreated with their dead chief. To honor him in death, to give him a fitting burial, was more important than to continue the battle.

All night the soldiers in their fort could hear the Cheyennes' mourning songs, the keening of the women. They too knew that the great chief Roman Nose was dead. He had died as he had lived. He had shown that sometimes it is more important to act like a chief than to live to a great old age.

Activity A. Working with a partner who has also read the story about Chief Roman Nose, together complete the column labeled "Chief Roman Nose" in the data chart in Figure 8.6. When you have filled in that column, read the next legend.

Brave Woman Counts Coup

Over a hundred years ago, when many Sioux were still living in what now is Minnesota, there was a band of Hunkpapa Sioux at Spirit Lake under a chief called Tawa Makoce, meaning His Country. It was his country, too—Indian country, until the white soldiers with their cannon finally drove the Lakota tribes across the Mni Shoshay: The Big Muddy, the Missouri.

In his youth the chief had been one of the greatest warriors. Later when his fighting days were over, he was known as a wise leader, invaluable in council, and as a great giver of feasts, a provider for the poor. The chief had three sons and one daughter. The sons tried to be warriors as mighty as their father, but that was a hard thing to do. Again and again they battled the Crow Indians with reckless bravery, exposing themselves in the front rank, fighting hand to hand, until one by one they were all killed. Now only his daughter was left to the sad old chief. Some say her name was Makhta. Others call her Winyan Ohitika, Brave Woman.

The girl was beautiful and proud. Many young men sent their fathers to the old chief with gifts of fine horses that were preliminary to marriage proposals. Among those who desired her for a wife was a young warrior named Red Horn, himself the son of a chief, who sent his father again and again to ask for her hand. But Brave Woman would not marry. "I will not take a husband," she said, "until I have counted coup on the Crows to avenge my dead brothers." Another young man who loved Brave Woman was Wanblee

Cikala, or Little Eagle. He was too shy to declare his love, because he was a poor boy who had never been able to distinguish himself.

At this time the Kangi Oyate, the Crow nation, made a great effort to establish themselves along the banks of the upper Missouri in country which the Sioux considered their own. The Sioux decided to send out a strong war party to chase them back, and among the young men riding out were Red Horn and Little Eagle. "I shall ride with you," Brave Woman said. She put on her best dress of white buckskin richly decorated with beads and porcupine quills, and around her neck she wore a choker of dentalium shells. She went to the old chief. "Father," she said, "I must go to the place where my brothers died. I must count coup for them. Tell me that I can go."

The old chief wept with pride and sorrow. "You are my last child," he said, "and I fear for you and for a lonely old age without children to comfort me. But your mind has long been made up. I see that you must go; do it quickly. Wear my warbonnet into battle. Go and do not look back."

And so his daughter, taking her brothers' weapons and her father's warbonnet and best war pony, rode out with the warriors. They found an enemy village so huge that it seemed to contain the whole Crow nation—hundreds of men and thousands of horses. There were many more Crows than Sioux, but the Sioux attacked nevertheless. Brave Woman was a sight to stir the warriors to great deeds. To Red Horn she gave her oldest brother's lance and shield. "Count coup for my dead brother," she said. To Little Eagle she gave her second brother's bow and arrows. "Count coup for him who owned these," she told him. To another young warrior she gave her youngest brother's war club. She herself carried only her father's old, curved coupstick wrapped in otter fur.

At first Brave Woman held back from the fight. She supported the Sioux by singing brave-heart songs and by making the shrill, trembling war cry with which Indian women encourage their men. But when the Sioux, including her own warriors from the Hunkpapa band, were driven back by overwhelming numbers, she rode into the midst of the battle. She did not try to kill her enemies, but counted coup left and right, touching them with her coupstick. With a woman fighting so bravely among them, what Sioux warrior could think of retreat?

Still, the press of the Crows and their horses drove the Sioux back a second time. Brave Woman's horse was hit by a musket bullet and went down. She was on foot, defenseless, when Red Horn passed her on his speckled pony. She was too proud to call out for help, and he pretended not to see her. Then Little Eagle came riding toward her out of the dust of battle. He dismounted and told her to get on his horse. She did, expecting him to climb up behind her, but he would not. "This horse is wounded and too weak to carry us both," he said.

"I won't leave you to be killed," she told him. He took her brother's bow and struck the horse sharply with it across the rump. The horse bolted, as he intended, and Little Eagle went back into battle on foot. Brave Woman herself rallied the warriors for a final charge, which they made with such fury that the Crows had to give way at last.

This was the battle in which the Crow nation was driven away from the Missouri for good. It was a great victory, but many brave young men died. Among them was Little Eagle, struck down with his face to the enemy. The Sioux warriors broke Red Horn's bow, took his eagle feathers from him, and sent him home. But they placed the body of Little Eagle on a high scaffold on the spot where the enemy camp had been. They killed his horse to serve him in the land of many lodges. "Go willingly," they told the horse. "Your master has need of you in the spirit world."

Brave Woman gashed her arms and legs with a sharp knife. She cut her hair short and tore her white buckskin dress. Thus she mourned for Little Eagle. They had not been man and wife; in fact he had hardly dared speak to her or look at her, but now she asked everybody to treat her as if she were the young warrior's widow. Brave Woman never took a husband, and she never ceased to mourn for Little Eagle. "I am his widow," she told everyone. She died of old age. She had done a great thing, and her fame endures.

Activity B. Working with the same partner, fill in the column of the data chart in Figure 8.6 labeled "Brave Woman." Then do the "Think About" activities on the chart.

Monitoring Comprehension and Writing in Response

Still talking with your partner, answer these questions. Use the chart in Figure 8.6 to help you.

1. What was the most significant difference between Little Eagle and Red Horn?

_____

_____

2. Why did Brave Woman give her oldest brother's lance to Red Horn and her second

brother's bow to Little Eagle, and not vice versa? _____

_____

A. **Read about:** As you read, record data in the blocks of the data chart. Use the design of this chart to make similar grids for recording while reading and comparing stories.

	Main Characters	
	Chief Roman Nose	**Brave Woman**
Setting: time/place		
Tribe to which he/she belonged		
Personal qualities of the character		
The problem: the core of the legend		
Beginning event of the legend		
Central event in the legend		
Concluding event in the legend		
Meaning of the legend		

B. **Think about:**

1. In what ways are the two legends different? similar? Using your chart to make comparisons, in your notebook create a Venn diagram for the legends.

2. Which legend appeals to you more? Give reasons to support your judgment.

_____

FIGURE 8.6 Data-Gathering Chart: Comparing Stories and Making Judgments

3. Why did Red Horn pretend not to see Brave Woman? _____

_____

_____

4. Why did Little Eagle give his horse to Brave Woman? _____

_____

_____

5. Do you think Little Eagle realized that by giving away his horse, he was also giving away his life? Explain. _____

_____

6. Why did the Sioux warriors break Red Horn's bow and take his feathers away?

_____

_____

7. Today the deeds of Brave Woman are legendary. Do you believe she did the right thing when she went into battle with the warriors? Why? Why not? Would you have done what she did? Explain. _____

_____

_____

8. Do you believe the Sioux were right in killing Little Eagle's horse? Explain.

_____

_____

9. In what ways were Little Eagle and Roman Nose similar? _____

_____

_____

10. Why do you think Roman Nose forgot about the laws of medicine and ate with metal tools? _____

_____

11. Why did Roman Nose sing his death song before going into battle? What does this say about the kind of man he was? _____

_____

_____

12. What does honor mean to a Cheyenne or a Sioux? Write a paragraph in your notebook in which you explain and give a supporting example.

13. What does friendship mean to the Sioux? Write a paragraph of explanation in your notebook.

14. What is the most honorable or brave deed that you have read about or seen someone perform? In your notebook, write a paragraph in which you tell about that deed, much in the manner that Jenny Leading Cloud recounted the stories of Brave Woman and Roman Nose to her interviewer.

Reviewing Vocabulary

Select the word from this list that best fits the context of the sentence. Rely on the process of elimination.

abhorred	extinction	legendary	repulsed	signifies
aspires	keening	rallied	scaffold	vice versa

1. After her death, she became a _____ figure. People told and retold stories of what she had done.

2. They fought until the _____ of their enemies; by the end of the battle, none of the enemy was left alive.

3. That woman _____ cigarette smoking. It was something she hated more than anything else.

4. The Indians _____ the attackers who were trying to take their land; the attackers withdrew in disorder.

5. I will always help my brother, or _____.

6. They erected a _____ to hold all their equipment.

7. His signature on the contract _____ his acceptance of it.

8. During the battle, the troops _____ around their leader and continued to fight.

9. We heard the _____ of the women as they mourned their dead. The noise of it filled the air.

10. She _____ to become a Supreme Court justice. This is her greatest ambition.

EXTENDING WHAT YOU HAVE LEARNED

Reviewing Your Reading Strategies

List some questions you should keep in mind to leap beyond the facts as you read a selection.

_____

_____

_____

_____

_____

Think
about . . .
What kinds of things do
you ask yourself as you
read?

Applying the Strategies to Your Reading

Locate a book of short stories, Greek myths, fables, or legends in the library. Read two stories from the book and create a data chart for compiling information while reading. Then write a short paragraph in which you compare the two stories and draw a conclusion about them or create a Venn diagram based on the chart.

Gaining Ownership over Words

Select several of the words featured in this chapter. Record them in your personal vocabulary list. Try to use them in speaking and writing.

Building a Knowledge Base for Reading

Locate Minnesota, the Missouri River, and the Bighorn Mountains on the map in Figure 8.7.

FIGURE 8.7 The Little Big Horn Region

PART FOUR
STUDY READING

CHAPTER 9 Understanding and Studying for College Tests

CHAPTER 10 Adjusting Your Concentration Level and Reading Rate

CHAPTER 11 Interpreting Tables, Graphs, and Diagrams

 9

Understanding and Studying for College Tests: SQ3R, Highlighting, Charting, Webbing, Outlining, Summarizing, and Remembering

OBJECTIVE

In this chapter, you will become testwise: You will learn about objective (or short-answer) and subjective (or essay) examinations. You will also learn to use systematic study strategies that can help you read and review material on which you will be tested. Specifically, you will learn to

1. Use SQ3R;
2. Highlight and record notes directly in a textbook;
3. Organize content in data charts, webs, and outlines;
4. Summarize ideas; and
5. Remember.

UNDERSTANDING AND STUDYING FOR COLLEGE TESTS

In college, you generally have little choice about what you read: The instructor assigns blocks of texts, and you study them knowing that you will be tested on what you have read. In some respects, therefore, the fact that you will be tested determines the way you read the assignments. In this chapter, you will learn test-taking and study strategies that will help you become testwise.

UNDERSTANDING OBJECTIVE AND SUBJECTIVE TESTS

The kind of test you must take is a factor that can guide your pretest study. Some tests are objective, or short-answer. In this type of test, there is only one correct answer, and you may have to answer by recognizing or recalling facts and details. Objective tests may be multiple-choice, true-false, matching, or fill-in-the-blank.

Some tests are subjective. With subjective tests, you have to write out answers in which you express relationships, there are different ways to express an answer, and your instructor uses his or her judgment in assessing the depth and organization of your responses. Sometimes the test comprises only two or three questions, in contrast to a test in which you must write responses to ten or twelve questions. In both instances, the tests are called essay tests, but typically a test with few questions focuses on broader generalizations, whereas one with more questions gets at more specific points.

Because the kind of test you must take determines to some extent the type of information you must supply, early in the semester you should ask your instructor about the kinds of tests to be given in the course. Ask such questions as the following:

- What kinds of questions do you generally include on the tests: multiple-choice questions, essay questions requiring lengthy responses, or essay questions requiring shorter answers?
- Do the tests focus on class notes or the textbook? If both, in what proportion?
- Are students responsible for details, such as names and dates? Are students responsible for definitions of all the technical terms?

Ask the same questions again before the first test.

Objective Tests

So far in this book, you have relied on the know-for-sure/process-of-elimination test-taking strategy to complete fill-in-the-blank items with options that were supplied. You did the ones you knew for sure first and crossed out options as you used them. This gave you fewer options from which to choose when doing items you were less certain of. You have used a similar strategy with multiple-choice questions, crossing out choices you knew for sure were wrong to narrow the field. Here are some other specific techniques for taking objective, or short-answer, tests:

TEST-TAKING STRATEGIES:
OBJECTIVE TESTS

→ Wear a watch. Know the total time you have for the test. Check the halfway point in terms of the time and the number of questions.

→ Place your answer sheet near the hand you write with so that you do not waste time crossing that hand over the examination paper.

→ Put your name on your paper immediately.

→ Read the directions carefully. Think, "How am I to respond: by circling, underlining, or what?"

→ Rapidly preview the whole test to get a sense of what is being asked and how long the examination is.

→ Read each question thoughtfully. Think, "What is the question asking?" Restate the question in your own words. If permitted, circle key words in the stem of multiple-choice questions and in the true-false items.

→ When you hit an easy question, one you are positive you know, answer it quickly. Put a check next to it in the margin after answering so that you do not waste time on it again.

→ If you hit a difficult question, one you are very unsure of, skip it, continue with the next question, and come back to the difficult question when you have answered the others. You may get leads to the answer from other questions on the exam.

→ Do not leave a question unanswered if there is no penalty for guessing. Eliminate options that you know are wrong, then make a reasonable guess among remaining options.

→ Do not assume that the professor is out to trick you. Do not look for hidden traps.

→ Concentrate on the task. Do not watch what the professor or the other students are doing. Also, select a seat where you are away from distractions. Bad seats are located by the door and are crowded close to other students. Good seats allow you to spread out.

→ Use the full time allowed. If you get done early, check your answers, especially checking that you have marked the answers you intended. Do not waste time rethinking the questions you earlier marked as easy.

→ Change an answer if you have a logical reason to change. Research indicates that three out of four changes you make during fix-up time will be correct.

Practice with Multiple-Choice Questions

Now respond to these three items to pick up ideas for more specific things to consider when deciding on an answer, especially to multiple-choice items. In each case, first cross out choices you know for sure are wrong to narrow the field. Then star the correct choice.

1. A characteristic of an objective test is that
   a. you must write out the answers.
   b. there are different ways to express an answer.
   c. the instructor uses his or her judgment in assessing your answer.
   d. there is only one correct answer.
   e. none of the above.

2. Which is not an example of an objective-type test?
   a. multiple-choice
   b. true-false
   c. fill-in-the-blanks
   d. essay

3. Which of the following is (are) recommended for taking a short-answer test?
   a. Wear a watch.
   b. Glance over the entire test before beginning.
   c. Skip the hard questions on your first run-through.
   d. Answer the easy questions quickly.
   e. All of the above.

Let's talk about things you may have considered in answering. First, look at item 1. It is not stated as a question. When this is the case, restating the stem (the beginning part) as a question and circling the key words in it (e.g., *characteristic, objective*) can help you clarify what is being asked. Second, the last option is "None of the above." When "None of the above" is an option, you are handling what amounts to a true-false situation, which can make the question more difficult. You must go through the list of options, asking of each, "Is this true?"

Third, notice how item 1 is composed by identifying the place in the text around which the test maker built the item. Do you see that the first three options actually state the characteristics of subjective tests? The test maker used those characteristics as incorrect options when asking about objective tests. Instructors often use this approach when composing multiple-choice questions; they build questions around places in the textbook where the author compares two things and gives points about both. Instructors use points about one thing as incorrect options when asking about the other thing. As you study for multiple-choice tests, look out for places like that in the textbook.

Revisit item 2. The difficulty here is with the word *not* in the stem. As soon as you read a question with the word *not* in it, circle that word to emphasize to yourself that you are working with a negative. In answering, you must keep thinking, "Not an objective test." If the option gives you something that is an example of an objective test, eliminate it. Going through the first three options, you cross out each in turn. By using the process of elimination, you know that "essay" is the correct answer.

Reconsider item 3. Here the last option is "All of the above." If you are absolutely positive that two options are correct but are not so positive about one of the others, your answer still has to be "All of the above." That is the only possibility because you are certain that two options are correct. Also note that the question is built around a list included in the text. Where there are lists like this, your instructor may very well compose a multiple-choice question around the points in the list because the textbook author is supplying lots of options to include in the question.

In this section, you have been thinking about the design of multiple-choice questions as a means of helping you to answer them. Turn now to pages 135–138 of Chapter 7. You probably have taken the tests that follow the paragraphs in that section of the chapter. Working with a partner, restate each stem in your own words and circle key words in it. Think about how the questions are designed. Do the same with the test on pages 132–134. Notice in the true-false section of the test the words *never* and *always*. These words can be clues that an option is false; it is rare that something is never true or always true.

Subjective, or Essay, Examinations

Here are some kinds of questions that instructors use on essay tests with strategies for answering them:

TEST-TAKING STRATEGIES: ESSAY TESTS

→ *Definition questions,* which ask you to give the precise meaning of a term. (Example: "Define the word *theory*.") To answer this kind of question, start with the term and state, "A theory is. . . ."

→ *Give-an-example questions,* which ask you to provide an example, or a specific instance. (Example: "Give an example of a theory that made a radical difference in the way scientists viewed the earth.") To answer this kind of question, begin, "An example of a theory that made a radical difference in the way scientists viewed the earth is. . . ."

→ *Enumeration or listing questions,* which ask you to give a series of items. (Example: "List the names of four scientists who contributed to that discovery.") To answer this kind of question, do not give an extended explanation. Make a numbered list of the names, or whatever the question asks for.

→ *Explanation questions,* which ask you to explain *why* or *how*. (Example: "Explain why the Puritans left England to come to America.") To answer an explain-why question, start, "The Puritans left England to come to America because. . . ." If you want to give more than one reason, continue, "A second reason the Puritans came to America. . . ." The word *because* is useful in writing an answer to an explain-why question. To answer an explain-how question ("Explain how iron ore is made into steel"), give the steps in the process. Start, "There are four steps in the process in which iron ore is transformed into steel. The first is. . . . The second is. . . ." It helps to use number words—*four steps, the first, the second*—to answer explain-how questions.

→ *Evaluation questions,* which ask you to judge something. (Example: "Give your opinion of the word-processing capabilities of a computer.") To answer this kind of question, state what you think. Then give some facts to support your opinion.

→ *Discussion questions,* which ask you to talk about a particular topic. (Example: "Discuss the causes of the Civil War.") These are generally the most difficult questions to answer because they are vague. Do not answer by simply listing. You must include an analysis in your answer, suggesting why and how events happened as they did.

→ *Description questions,* which ask you to tell about the main characteristics of an event or item. (Example: "Describe a plant cell.") To answer this kind of question, talk about the key aspects of the plant cell. Sometimes you can use a diagram to clarify your written description.

→ *Comparison or contrast questions,* which ask you to tell how two things are the same or different. (Example: "Compare a plant cell with an animal cell.") In this case, first describe the animal cell, and then talk about the plant cell, telling how it is the same as and different from the animal cell.

→ *Summary questions,* which ask you to give the main points. (Example: "Summarize important points about use of the Internet.") This is another vague kind of question. To answer a summary question, think in terms of main ideas, or big points.

Practice with Essay Examinations

The following are examples of essay questions that require a short written answer. Circle the word that tells you the task you must do. Then write your answer in your notebook.

1. List three techniques important when you take an objective test that relate to how you handle specific questions.

2. Contrast an objective test to a subjective test.

3. Explain what you should do when you get to a multiple-choice item that has the word *not* in the stem.

4. Write a brief essay in which you summarize key points to keep in mind when taking a multiple-choice examination.

In the next section, you will work with several strategies that you may find helpful in studying assigned textbook selections on which you will be tested. As you encounter each strategy, think about which one works best for you.

STUDYING TEXTS: SQ3R

SQ3R is a popular strategy for systematically studying a textbook or a textbooklike article that has subheadings. Try the strategy as you do a first reading of a chapter on which you will be tested.

Step 1 in SQ3R is to survey, or preview, a chapter to be read and studied. The *S* stands for *survey.* When you survey, you

- Glance over the title and any introductory and summary paragraphs including focusing questions, statements of objectives, and review questions. You (1) identify the topic, (2) tell yourself what you already know about that topic, and (3) set your purpose for reading the chapter.

- Check the introduction to see whether it provides clues to the main point of the chapter and the organization of it (for example, does it say, "In this section, you will read about two ways . . ." or "In this section, we will consider four events . . ."?).

- Survey the subheadings, using them to predict what each subsection is about and to spark in your mind the things you already know about the topic. As you do this, scan related illustrations, boldface terms, and margin notes (if there are any) and *keep telling yourself what you already know.*

Step 2—another before-reading strategy—is to turn the major subheadings of a chapter into questions to answer while reading. The *Q* in SQ3R stands for *question.* For example, the heading that introduces this section of text is "Studying Texts: SQ3R." If you were to compose questions based on that heading, you might think, "What is SQ3R? What do I do when I use SQ3R to study a chapter? What do all the letters and the number mean?"

Step 3 is to read the chapter, keeping your questions in mind. That is the first *R* in SQ3R; the *R* means to *read* to find answers to your own questions. As you read, also keep sifting through details to get the main idea of the section, and keep alert for clues to tell you where the author is going. Clues, as you remember, include relation-stating words such as *first, second,* and *finally.*

Step 4 is to *recite*—the second *R* in SQ3R. After reading each major subdivision of a chapter, you stop to tell yourself the answers to the questions you made up earlier. Also tell yourself

- The main idea of that part of the text,
- The important points the author made to support the main idea,
- The points explained in the graphs, charts, or other visuals that accompany that part of the text, and
- The meanings of key terms defined in that subsection.

If you have trouble talking to yourself about what you have just read, reread it.

Step 5 is to *review*—the third *R* in SQ3R. You review when you finish reading a chapter. You review by again telling yourself the answers to the questions you made up before reading, at times by writing down the answers, and sometimes by rereading when you know you do not understand.

In sum, SQ3R is a five-step study plan that includes these components:

**SQ3R STUDY
STRATEGY**

Survey ⟶ Question ⟶ Read ⟶ Recite ⟶ Review

Reading the following selection, taken from a college text on child development, you will practice the steps in SQ3R.

SELECTION 1
The Child's Experience of Divorce (PSYCHOLOGY)

Independent Study

Expanding Your Vocabulary Through Reading

As you read, circle the unfamiliar words. Pronounce them by focusing on the syllables. Use word elements and context clues to figure out the meanings. Write definitions of any new words in the margin.

Getting Ready to Read

Survey   Preview by glancing over the title, authors' names, first paragraph, headings, and italicized words.

- What is the selection about? _____

- What do you already know on this topic? What experiences have you had with divorce? What phrases come to mind when you think about the effects of divorce on children? _____

  _____

- Do you recognize the names of the authors from Chapter 1? What do you think is their area of specialization? _____

**Think
about . . .**

When might you use SQ3R? What would you do before reading when you use SQ3R?

Question In the margin of the selection next to each of the two subheadings, write a question that you will answer as you read. Answering these questions will be your purpose for reading.

Reading with Meaning

Read As you read, try to answer the questions you have already written in the margin.

The Child's Experience of Divorce
Fergus Hughes, Lloyd Noppe, and Illene Noppe

Just as marital disruption cannot be regarded as an isolated phenomenon today, no complete discussion of children's development within the American family can exclude reference to the experience of divorce. Let us now examine that experience, describing the characteristics typically observed in children whose parents divorce and the individual variations in children's behavior.

Negative Outcomes

There have been nearly 200 studies to date of the typical behaviors of children undergoing the experience of parental divorce, and the findings are fairly consistent. For most children, parental divorce is associated with a number of negative outcomes. These include both "internalizing" problems, such as anger, resentment, anxiety, depression, guilt, and low self-esteem; and "externalizing" problems, such as antisocial behaviors, drug abuse, and social and academic difficulties (Amato, 1993, 1994; Amato & Keith, 1991a, 1991b; Doherty & Needle, 1991; Guidibaldi & Perry, 1985; Hetherington, Cox, & Cox, 1985; Kalter, 1984, 1987; Peterson & Zill, 1983). Some children become aggressive and noncompliant, and their homes are characterized by frequent parent-child conflict (Tessman, 1978; Hetherington, 1979). In fact, in two of every three cases studied, there appears to be a general overall deterioration in the mother-child relationship within the first year after divorce (Wallerstein & Kelly, 1975).

Individual Differences

Despite the general negative findings, it is important to remember that all children who live through a divorce do not behave in the same way. The specific behavior depends on the child's individual personality characteristics, age at the time of divorce, and gender. In terms of *personality*, when compared to those rated as relaxed and easygoing, children described as temperamental and irritable have more difficulty coping with parental divorce, as indeed they have more difficulty adapting to life change in general. Stress, such as that found in disrupted families, seems to impair the ability of temperamental children to adapt to their surroundings; the greater the amount of stress, the less well they adapt. In contrast, a moderate amount of stress may actually help an easygoing, relaxed child learn to cope with adversity (Hetherington, 1989).

There is some relationship between *age* and children's characteristic reaction to divorce. As the child grows older, the greater is the likelihood of a free expression of a variety of complex feelings, an understanding of those feelings, and a realization that the decision to divorce cannot be attributed to any one simple cause. Self-blame virtually disappears after the age of 6, fear of abandonment diminishes after the age of 8, and the confusion and fear of the young child is replaced in the older child by shame, anger, and self-reflection.

Gender of the child is also a factor that predicts the nature of reaction to divorce. The impact of divorce is initially greater on boys than on girls (Hetherington, Cox, & Cox, 1978; Hetherington, 1979). Compared to daughters, the sons of divorced parents tend to have a greater number of what might be called "social adjustment" difficulties: They are more aggressive, less compliant, have greater difficulties in interpersonal relationships,

Did You
KNOW?

The prefix *anti-* means "against." You see it here on the word *antisocial.* Other words that carry the prefix are *antipoverty, antiseptic,* and *antiperspirant.* The prefix *non-* means "not." You see it here on the word *noncompliant.* Other words with the perfix are *nonfunctional* and *nonverbal.*

and exhibit problem behaviors both at home and at school (Amato, 1994). Furthermore, the adjustment problems of boys are still noticeable even two years after the divorce. Girls' adjustment problems are usually internalized rather than acted out, and are often resolved by the second year after the divorce. However, as we shall point out in a later section, new problems may surface for girls as they enter adolescence and adulthood.

How can the relatively greater impact of divorce on boys than on girls be explained? The greater male aggression and noncompliance may reflect the fact that such behaviors are tolerated and even encouraged in males in our culture more than they are in females; even in the two-parent family males exceed females in the prevalence of aggressive, noncompliant behaviors (Hetherington & Cox, 1978). Furthermore, boys may have a particular need for a strong male model of self-control, as well as for a strong disciplinarian parent. Finally, boys are more likely to be exposed to their parents' fights than girls are, and after the breakup, boys are less likely than girls to receive sympathy and support from mothers, teachers, or peers (Hetherington, 1979).

Monitoring Comprehension

Recite   Talk to yourself in your head. Tell yourself the answers to the questions you wrote in the margin before you read.

Review for the Test   Review the selection with a partner. Tell one another the answers to your questions.

Because you are going to take an objective test on the selection, you should work on the details of the paragraphs, reviewing them in your head. Are there any questions you need to ask your instructor about the test before beginning your review?

STUDYING TEXTS: HIGHLIGHTING AND NOTE-TAKING IN A TEXTBOOK

Many college students make marks and notes in their textbooks as they read in anticipation of a test. For example, as they survey and read a chapter or section of text, they build an outline right in the book. They put a Roman numeral *I* before the first major heading, a capital *A* before the first second-level heading, and Arabic numbers *1, 2,* and *3* next to main points beneath the second-level heading. For example, if you were to do this with the selection "The Child's Experience of Divorce," which you read earlier in this chapter, you might have put a Roman numeral next to the title because it actually is a main heading in the chapter, a capital *A* before "Negative Outcomes," and a capital *B* before "Individual Differences." You might have inserted an Arabic number *1* at the point where the author talks about internalizing and a number *2* where the author talks about externalizing. Where would you have put numbers in the section under the heading "Individual Differences"?

You may also find it helpful to make other notes in your textbooks after reading a paragraph. Use these strategies:

HIGHLIGHTING-A-TEXTBOOK STRATEGY

1. If there is a main idea or topic sentence, underline it with a pen. Do the same with definitions you must remember. In the margin (or in a vocabulary section of your notebook) write the definition of a key term in abbreviated form to use in future study of the text. Using a pen for making in-text notes generally takes less time than using a highlighting marker.

2. If the author makes a series of related points within a paragraph, insert numbers in front of the points to keep track of them. Doing this helps if the author talks about "first," "second," and so on. Insert directly into the text a *1,* a *2,* and so forth, at such sites. Or list main points in the margin, listing a key word for each point to remind

---

Think
ABOUT . . .

What strategies do you use when you study a chapter of a textbook? How do surveying and questioning help you to study?

you of it. That is another advantage of using a pen rather than a highlighting marker: You can write clearer notes with a pen.

Generally it pays to underline points and make notes *after* rather than while reading a paragraph. By then, you know what is important in the paragraph and avoid marking sentence after sentence. There is no sense in marking almost every line of text, as many students do while reading. Marking too many lines wastes time.

WORKSHOP 1: HIGHLIGHTING

Activity A. Here is a paragraph from a college sociology text, with in-text notes made by a student. Study the notes to determine why that reader underlined and made notes in the margin as she did.

Cultural Change

The Greek philosopher Aristotle stated "there is nothing permanent except change." Caught up in day-to-day concerns, we may not notice changes because we are busy living our lives, not observing them. Cultural change is continuous, however, even if it is sometimes evident over a period of years. Consider, for example, changes in the American family over the past half century. Government records show that the [1]divorce rate is now more than twice as high as it was in 1940, when a family composed of a bread-winning father, a home-making mother, and their children was the norm. Between 1970 and 1990, the number of [2]single-parent households more than doubled, so that now a majority of children in the United States [at some point] live with only one parent before they reach the age of eighteen. Moreover, as women have become a much larger proportion of the labor force, more of them are [3]delaying marriage and children, or remaining single but perhaps having children all the same.

1. divorce rate

2. single-parent house-holds

3. delayed marriage and children

Why did the student underline the words she did? Why did she circle the phrase she did?

Why did she make the numbered list in the margin? _____

_____

Activity B. Read the next three paragraphs from the same textbook. Beside the first you will find a student's in-text notes. Use them as a model for making in-text notes on the remaining two paragraphs.

It is worth asking how such cultural changes are set in motion in the first place. Cultural change is caused in three general ways. The first is *invention*, the process of creating new cultural elements—video games, political parties, or polio vaccines, for example. The telephone (1876), the airplane (1903), and the aerosol spray can (1941) are inventions that have had a tremendous impact on our culture. The process of invention is going on constantly, as indicated by the thousands of applications received by the United States Patent Office each year.

Causes of change
1. invention example = airplane

Discovery, a second, closely related cause of cultural change, involves recognizing and understanding something already in existence—from a distant star, to the foods of a foreign culture, to the muscle power of American women. Discovery is often the result of scientific research; many medical breakthroughs happen this way. Yet discovery can also occur quite by accident, as when Marie Curie unintentionally left a "rock" on a piece of photographic paper in 1898 and discovered radium.

The third cause of cultural change is *diffusion*, the spread of both material and nonmaterial elements from one cultural system to another. Missionaries and anthropologists like Napoleon Chagnon have introduced many cultural elements to the Yanomamo. Elements of American culture have spread throughout the world through diffusion: jazz, with its roots deep in the culture of black Americans; computers, first built in the mid 1940s in a Philadelphia laboratory; and even the United States Constitution, on which several other countries have modeled their own political systems. On the other hand, much of what we assume is "American" is actually borrowed from other cultures. Ralph Linton (1937) has pointed out that commonplace elements of our way of life—most of our clothing and furniture, clocks, newspapers, money, and, of course, the English language—are all derived from other cultures. Obviously, as the technology of travel and communication makes the world smaller, the rate of cultural diffusion is likely to increase.

STUDYING TEXTS: CHARTING, WEBBING, AND OUTLINING

Think about . . .

When do you predict as part of reading? Why is it important to predict?

Data charting is another systematic study strategy that can help you read a college textbook. As with using SQ3R and highlighting the text, step 1 in using data charting is to survey the selection you are going to read. You look at the same things as you did with SQ3R—the introductory and concluding paragraphs, the headings, and so forth—predict what the section is about, and think about what you already know on the topic. (If you own the textbook, you may also highlight at this stage by building an outline into the text by numbering the main headings.)

Step 2 is to use the subheadings to create a data chart for taking notes while reading. You do this before reading the selection. For example, surveying the section on cultural change, you might see the three italicized terms and use them to sketch a chart like this one, to which you would add definitions and examples as you read.

Cause of Change	Definition	Examples
Invention		
Discovery		
Diffusion		

Or you could make a web for taking notes. In that case, you would put the topic in the center of the web, in this instance "Causes of Cultural Change." You would connect the causes to the central hub with lines and then add the definition of each term and examples as offshoots of the individual terms, as shown here:

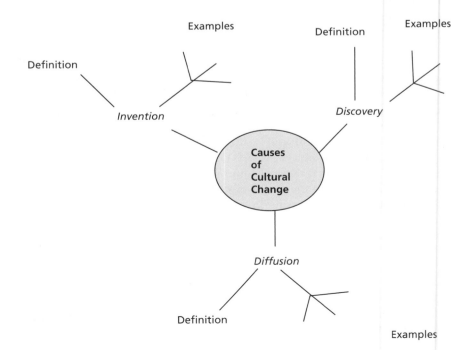

Or you could begin a formal outline by listing the italicized terms like this:

Causes of Cultural Change

I. Invention
   A. Definition
   B. Examples

II. Discovery
   A. Definition
   B. Examples

III. Diffusion
   A. Definition
   B. Examples

Step 3 is to read the selection. As you finish the segment of text under a subheading, you stop and write down the main idea and important details of that section in the appropriate area of your data chart or web, using key words and phrases. You do this for the material under each subheading. In the case of a formal outline, you would use capital letters, numbers, and lowercase letters to list subpoints under the headings you previously listed.

Step 4 is to reread the material on your data chart, your web, or your outline and then recite it to yourself in your mind until you can do this without looking at your notes.

Step 5 is to review the material several times by reciting it to yourself.

The data charting, webbing, or outlining strategy is particularly useful when you are reading in a library textbook and you cannot make notes in it. Working with two partners, go back and fill in the data chart, the data web, and the formal outline based on cultural change. Each one of you should use a different technique. Compare your results. Decide which technique is most useful for you.

Here is a selection from a college music textbook. Try using the data-charting strategy to study it.

SELECTION 2
African-American Folk Music, the Blues, and African-American Spirituals (MUSIC)

Independent Study or Reading Workshop

Expanding Your Vocabulary Through Reading

As you read, circle unfamiliar words. Use word elements and context clues to figure out their meaning. Write a definition of new words in the margin.

Getting Ready to Read

Survey Preview the selection by reading the title, author, first paragraph, and headings.

- What is the topic of the selection? _____

- What do you already know about this topic? Write some phrases that come to your mind about African-American music. _____

  _____

- Now build an outline directly into the text by putting a number (1, 2, 3, etc.) before each major subheading.

Data Chart   Make the outline of a data chart based on the major subheadings from the selection. You will read this selection to identify important ideas and supporting details.

Reading with Meaning

Read   As you read each subsection, stop and write down main ideas and supporting details on your data chart under the appropriate subheading label.

Recite   After reading each subsection of text, stop and tell yourself the material you have recorded on the chart. Also review in your mind the meaning of any italicized terms. You may prefer to work with a partner, reading each subsection to yourself and then deciding together what to record on your chart.

African-American Folk Music, the Blues, and African-American Spirituals
Daniel Politoske

African-American Folk Music

Of all the ethnic influences that have gone into the creation of popular music in America, probably the most important has been that of black Africa. West African music, though very different from European music, shared with it certain basic characteristics of harmony. Thus, when the two traditions were brought together in America by slavery, it was possible for them to blend. African-American folk music was just the first of many important and widely influential results.

Generally pressed into slavery by European adventurers on the west coast of Africa, the hundreds of thousands of African-Americans who began arriving in America in 1619 brought with them a highly developed musical tradition and a habit of incorporating music into every activity of life. Religion, dance, and work were some of the main functions it served. Much of their music came to America intact. Once here it was gradually altered to meet new needs. The banjo, unique to America, is thought to have African roots. The use of drums, the most important instrument of West Africa, was continued in the New World.

Field Holler

African-Americans developed a wide repertory of songs, both secular and religious. One early type of secular song, perhaps the closest of all to African prototypes, was the *field holler* that slaves often sang while working. A field holler was the yearning cry of a slave working alone, a sound midway between a yell and a song, whose words determined the tone. It began with a high, long-drawn-out shout and then glided down to the lowest note the singer could reach. Such songs were characterized by falsetto tones, swoops and slides from note to note, complicated and unexpected changes of rhythm, and an occasional line of melody from Anglo-American ballads or hymns. They were heard not only in the fields but wherever an African-American worked at hard, lonely tasks. When slavery ended, the songs were taken onto the docks, into the railroad camps, and onto the Mississippi River.

Group Work Song

Related to the field holler was the *group work song*. This, too, was close to African sources, for whenever Africans worked together at a task they found it natural to pace their labor with a song. Field hands sang as they hoed or picked the cotton. Rowing songs were used to time the strokes on the flat-bottomed boats of the south. Later on, work songs were chanted by chain gangs and by railroad workers, whose backbreaking, dangerous labor was regulated by the rhythmic chanting of the song leader. The leader played a very important part in the group work song, choosing the song to be sung, setting the pace, adjusting it to the feel of the work being done, and improvising catchy lyrics and musical byplay to fire the energies of the other workers. A good song made the work go faster and better and relieved the weary monotony of it.

Although there was great variety in their lyrics and uses, the earliest work songs were almost entirely African in sound and structure. They made use of the African call-and-response pattern, expressive African vocal techniques such as those used in the field holler, and occasional syncopated African rhythms built around a steady meter. Most work songs were sung with the leader and chorus responding to each other, but some were performed almost in unison, with incidental improvised variants.

Ring Shout

Another musical style that closely resembled its African counterparts was the *ring shout,* a shuffling dance with chanting and handclapping. To an African, dancing was a natural part of worship, but as the Bible was thought to prohibit dancing in church, slaves had to be content with a short shuffling step executed counterclockwise in a ring. This circular movement was accompanied by excited clapping and a kind of *shout song* that provided more rhythm than melody. Biblical stories supplied the words for the shout songs, which were chanted in the customary leader-chorus fashion. Starting slowly, the music gathered speed and intensity with the hypnotic repetition of body movements and musical phrases.

Song Sermons

In many African-American religious services, the sermon also took on some of the qualities of song, generally with a driving, hypnotic rhythm. Delivering such a *song sermon,* the preacher would at different times speak, chant, or sing, steadily increasing speed and passion as the song proceeded. The congregation, caught up in the pulse of the rhythm, would interject rhythmic cries or abbreviated lines of melody, using words such as "Amen!" or "Yes, my Lord!"

Lining Out

Lining out was a technique borrowed from white colonial churches. In many of these churches hymn books were in short supply; in others many of the people of the congregation were illiterate. Thus, it was common practice for the preacher to sing each line of a hymn or psalm and then wait for the congregation to repeat it. This technique adapted itself perfectly to the African call-and-response pattern.

The Blues

The invention of the *blues* represents a major contribution of African-American folk music. Its influence on popular music has been notable, even since 1960. The blues style is characterized by distinctive *blue notes* produced by slightly bending the pitch of certain tones of the major scale. The style was somehow right for plaintive songs of sadness. A whole repertory of such songs grew up, created by unrequited lovers, prisoners, lonely people far from home, and thousands of others who needed to ease their pain by expressing it.

African-American Spirituals

In many respects, the religious counterpart of the blues was the *spiritual.* Developed largely in rural areas in the mid-nineteenth century, spirituals did not receive much public attention until they were made popular after the Civil War by groups who performed harmonized arrangements such as the Fisk University Jubilee Singers. *Nobody Knows the Trouble I've Seen* and *Steal Away* are among the most familiar examples. The African-American spiritual was superficially similar to spirituals written early in the nineteenth century. However, it is the African-American spiritual that has remained important to the present day. The music of the African-American spiritual was in effect an extremely

Did You
KNOW ?
The prefix *super-* means "above or over." You see it here on the word *superficially.* Other words with the prefix are *supervise,* and *superior.*

successful mixture of church melodies and harmonies and West African rhythms and styles of performance. [1,046 words]

Monitoring Comprehension

Review for the Test When you have read the selection, go back and tell yourself or a partner the ideas, facts, and definitions you wrote on your chart. Get ready to take a test on what you have read. Before studying for and taking that test, read the section of this chapter (pp. 178–179) that deals with remembering strategies.

STUDYING TEXTS: WRITING SUMMARIES

Research shows that writing summaries of content you have read is one of the best ways to learn it. In writing a summary, you generally start by writing a sentence that states the thesis, or main point, of a section of text you have just read. Chapter 5 explains how to identify the thesis. Then using the subheadings as a guide, you write sentences, providing details that support the main point. Here is a summary based on the selection "The Child's Experience of Divorce." Notice that the first sentence of the summary states the main point and that in some cases, successive sentences provide supporting details based on the topic sentence of the related paragraph.

> For most children, parental divorce has negative outcomes, although individual children respond differently to divorce depending on their personality, age, and gender. Negative outcomes include internalizing problems, such as anger and resentment, and externalizing problems, such as social and academic difficulties. Temperamental children have more difficulty coping with parental divorce than do easygoing youngsters. Younger children are likely to experience self-blame, fear of abandonment, and confusion, whereas older children are likely to experience shame, anger, and self-reflection. Interestingly, the impact of divorce initially is greater on boys than on girls.

WORKSHOP 2: SUMMARIZING

Study the notes you made on your data chart as you read the selection about African-American folk music. Then in your notebook write a summary paragraph. Start by composing a topic sentence based on the two introductory paragraphs about the importance of black folk music in America. Then compose a sentence based on each subsection to provide supporting detail. In other words, write a sentence about the field holler, the group work song, and so on. Your summary will have about eight sentences.

STUDYING MATERIAL WITHOUT HEADINGS

In some college courses, especially in the humanities when you are studying literature, you will be assigned selections in which there are no subheadings and no illustrative charts or pictures. In such cases, the strategies discussed so far in this chapter are difficult to use, and you must modify them. Of course, you should start by previewing the material: looking over the title, the author's name, and any introductory paragraphs. Before reading, you need to predict what the selection is about and think about what you already know on the topic. Then compose several general questions you hope to answer by reading the selection.

As you read, keep your questions in mind. As with SQ3R, do not try to read the entire selection nonstop. Stop periodically to tell yourself the answers to your questions and to tell yourself the important ideas and supporting details. When you finish the selection, review by telling yourself the main points. Review also by writing a summary of the article as described in the previous section.

Think about . . .

Write a summary of the four paragraphs about cultural change given earlier in this chapter, using your in-text notes to remind you of main ideas. What steps should you take in writing a summary? Why might it be helpful in this case to write a summary with about four sentences?

SELECTION 3

The Achievement of Desire (LITERATURE—AUTOBIOGRAPHY)

A Study Skills Workshop

Expanding Your Vocabulary Through Reading

As you read, circle a couple of unfamiliar words. Using word elements and context clues, figure out the meanings of your circled words. Write their definitions in the margins.

Getting Ready to Read

Survey   Preview the selection by glancing over the title, author's name, and footnote. Skim the first paragraph as part of your prereading survey.

- What is the topic of the selection? _____

- What thoughts come to your mind as you begin to read? _____
_____

Question   Write two or three general questions you hope to answer through reading. This selection, as you will see, is not from a textbook. It is from an autobiography of a type you will have to read in college humanities courses. There are no subheadings.

_____

_____

_____

Reading with Meaning

Read and Recite   As you read this section, stop at the end of each paragraph. Ask yourself, "What is the main idea Rodriguez is trying to get across? What points does he use to support that idea?" Recite the answers to yourself at the end of each paragraph.

The Achievement of Desire
Richard Rodriguez*

OPEN THE DOORS OF YOUR MIND WITH BOOKS, read the red and white poster over the nun's desk in early September. It soon was apparent to me that reading was the classroom's central activity. Each course had its own book. And the information gathered from a book was unquestioned. READ TO LEARN, the sign on the wall advised in December. I privately wondered: What was the connection between reading and learning? Did one learn something only by reading it? Was an idea only an idea if it could be written down? In June, CONSIDER BOOKS YOUR BEST FRIENDS. Friends? Reading was, at best, only a chore. I needed to look up whole paragraphs of words in a dictionary. Lines of type were dizzying, the eye having to move slowly across the page, then down, and across. . . . The sentences of the first books I read were coolly impersonal. Toned hard. What most bothered me, however, was the isolation reading required. To console myself for the loneliness I'd feel when I read, I tried reading in a very soft voice. Until: "Who is doing all that talking

---

*Richard Rodriguez is the son of working-class Mexican immigrant parents. He spoke Spanish as a child. He graduated from Stanford and Columbia Universities, did graduate work at the Warburg Institute in London and the University of California at Berkeley, and today works as a writer and lecturer. You may have seen him on public television.

to his neighbor?" Shortly after, remedial reading classes were arranged for me with a very old nun.

At the end of each school day, for nearly six months, I would meet with her in the tiny room that served as the school's library but was actually only a storeroom for used textbooks and a vast collection of *National Geographics*. Everything about our sessions pleased me: the smallness of the room; the noise of the janitor's broom hitting the edge of the long hallway outside the door; the green of the sun, lighting the wall; and the old woman's face blurred white with a beard. Most of the time we took turns. I began with my elementary text. Sentences of astonishing simplicity seemed to me lifeless and drab: "The boys ran from the rain. . . . She wanted to sing. . . . The kite rose in the blue." Then the old nun would read from her favorite books, usually biographies of early American presidents. Playfully she ran through complex sentences, calling the words alive with her voice, making it seem that the author somehow was speaking directly to me. I smiled just to listen to her. I sat there and sensed for the first time some possibility of fellowship between a reader and a writer, a communication, never *intimate* like that I heard spoken words at home convey, but one nonetheless *personal*.

One day the nun concluded a session by asking me why I was so reluctant to read by myself. I tried to explain; said something about the way written words made me feel all alone—almost, I wanted to add but didn't, as when I spoke to myself in a room just emptied of furniture. She studied my face as I spoke; she seemed to be watching more than listening. In an uneventful voice she replied that I had nothing to fear. Didn't I realize that reading would open up whole new worlds? A book could open doors for me. It could introduce me to people and show me places I never imagined existed. She gestured toward the bookshelves. (Bare-breasted African women danced, and the shiny hubcaps of automobiles on the back covers of the *Geographic* gleamed in my mind.) I listened with respect. But her words were not very influential. I was thinking then of another consequence of literacy, one I was too shy to admit but nonetheless trusted. Books were going to make me "educated." *That* confidence enabled me, several months later, to overcome my fear of silence.

In fourth grade I embarked upon a grandiose reading program. "Give me the names of important books," I would say to startled teachers. They soon found out that I had in mind "adult books." I ignored their suggestion of anything I suspected was written for children. (Not until I was in college, as a result, did I read *Huckleberry Finn* or *Alice's Adventures in Wonderland*.) Instead, I read *The Scarlet Letter* and Franklin's *Autobiography* and whatever I read I read for extra credit. Each time I finished a book, I reported the achievement to a teacher and basked in praise my effort earned. Despite my best efforts, however, there seemed to be more and more books I needed to read. At the library I would literally tremble as I came upon whole shelves of books I hadn't read. So I read and I read and I read. . . . Librarians who initially frowned when I checked out the maximum ten books at a time started saving books they thought I might like. Teachers would say to the rest of the class, "I only wish the rest of you took reading as seriously as Richard does." [851 words]

Monitoring Comprehension

Review   Review until you can tell yourself the main point, or thesis, and some supporting details from the selection. Share the thesis and details with a partner. Together write a summary, which includes the thesis and the supporting details. Your instructor will give you a short essay quiz later to check your understanding, just as an English instructor might quiz you on your reading. Before studying for and taking that quiz, read the next section of this chapter that deals with remembering strategies.

REMEMBERING FOR TESTS

To be a successful test taker, you must remember what you have read and studied. How do you remember so that you can do well on a test? First, as this chapter has suggested, you must understand that simply reading over the textbook and your class notes once

Did You KNOW?

The Latin root *grand-* means "great." You see it here on the word *grandiose*. Other words with the root are *grandfather* and *grandeur*.

or twice is not enough. Having applied the steps of SQ3R and even having gone back to highlight the key points, you must then organize the content for study and go over it several times in preparation for a test. For example, in preparing for a short-answer test in history where you may be asked to recall or recognize dates, events in a series, names, terms, and causes, you may benefit from making lists of facts for yourself. A good way to do this is to make an index card or a page in your notebook for each of the following:

Think
about . . .
How do you prepare for tests? Do you have a specific strategy? What works for you?

- A list of dates with a notation as to what happened on each date;
- A list of events in the order in which they occurred, with a notation as to why each event is significant;
- A list of names with a notation as to what is significant about each person or place named;
- A list of key terms with a definition for each;
- Diagrams that relate causes to important events.

As you review for a test, keep telling yourself in your mind the points in your test notes. Do this over and over until you "own" them—that is, you can repeat them to yourself without looking at your notes. Do this on several spaced-out occasions; research shows that distributed practice is better than a single long study period.

In preparing for essay tests in disciplines such as history, sociology, and psychology, you may find it helps to web important generalizations and supporting details such as facts and definitions. Using your webs as a basis for study, you recite the generalizations and supporting details until you can do this without looking at your "prep" notes. Some students predict questions, web relationships based on the questions, and write out answers to their hypothetical questions, realizing that if the instructor does not ask the particular questions they have predicted, the practice is still beneficial.

Studying for a ten- to twelve-question essay test in a science discipline such as biology, you may also find it helpful to create a set of review notes in which you

- List technical terms with definitions, especially noting relationships among terms;
- Chart differences and similarities between two related structures or processes (e.g., a plant cell versus an animal cell; digestion versus assimilation);
- List and describe the steps or levels in a sequence or process (e.g., the steps in cell division), especially noting how one step leads into the next; and
- Make labeled diagrams of structures (e.g., the parts of a flower) with an explanation of the functions of the components parts.

WORKSHOP 3: **REMEMBERING**

With a partner, study Selection 1 of Chapter 1, "A Nation on the Move," in preparation for taking a short multiple-choice test on it. Together make a set of review notes (perhaps expanding on the web you made when you first read the selection). Study your notes until you are sure you know the material. Practice telling one another the important points. You may be tested on what you have studied.

Think
about . . .
What kind of mind talk do you do in preparing for a test? Why is simply reading over your notes and rereading your textbook not a good way to study for a test?

WORKSHOP 4: **REMEMBERING**

With a partner, reread Selection 3 of Chapter 1, "The Signs of Life," and web the key points and supporting details. Assume that you will take an examination in which you must write paragraph answers in response to short essay questions. Use the chart you made originally and your web to recite the key ideas and supporting details. You may be asked to share your web with the class and write out an answer to a short essay question.

EXTENDING WHAT YOU HAVE LEARNED

Applying SQ3R, Highlighting, Data Charting, Webbing, Outlining, Summarizing, and Remembering to Your College Reading

Select a chapter from a textbook, perhaps one you are reading for another course you are taking. On a piece of paper, record the name of the text and its author. Then survey a section of a chapter, and on the paper write some questions to be answered through reading. Base your questions on the major headings. Read the section, stopping at the end of each subsection to make in-text notes and to recite the answers to the questions you wrote before reading. When you have read the entire section, review what you have read so that you can share what you have learned with classmates. Select a second section from the textbook. Use another strategy, such as outlining or summarizing, to study it. Be ready to give your opinion of the strategy that is best for you.

Making Vocabulary Your Own

Select several words from those you circled in the selections in this chapter and make them your own. Record them and a sample sentence in your personal vocabulary list.

# 10

Adjusting Your Concentration Level and Reading Rate

OBJECTIVE

In this chapter, you will practice a strategy for increasing your concentration level and varying your reading rate. Specifically, you will learn to

1. Block out unrelated thoughts;
2. Concentrate on getting the gist as you go along;
3. Read in chunks of meaning, moving your eye quickly across the lines and pausing only two or three times on each line to pick up a "mindful" at each pause; and
4. Vary your reading rate according to the kind of material you are reading.

You will also have the opportunity to respond to selections by answering objective questions similar to those on timed reading and achievement tests you may have to take. This will allow you to practice the test-taking strategies you learned in Chapter 9.

ADJUSTING YOUR CONCENTRATION AND READING RATE

Faced with extended reading assignments, do you complain that you cannot concentrate and that you read too slowly? Does your mind wander? Does it take you longer to complete reading assignments than it takes your friends? Here are some ideas for overcoming these problems.

Developing Your Powers of Concentration

You must concentrate on the task at hand if you are to read rapidly with a high level of comprehension. For rapid reading, you must block out external distractions: movements of other students in the room, the noise of people talking, the noise of cars in the distance. You must look for a quiet place to study, without loud music and radio talk in the background. You must block out thoughts that do not relate to the reading task: fears of not doing well, thoughts about other events, thoughts about how other people are doing. How do you do this?

The strategies you have already learned help you to concentrate. With longer selections, one of those strategies is previewing the selection by running your eyes quickly over it before beginning, noting the title, introduction, conclusion, headings, and italicized words, if there are any. Based on your preview, you make predictions of what is to come and raise questions you will answer through reading. As you learned in the first chapter of this book, having a purpose in mind helps you to understand what you are reading. It also helps you to concentrate.

With longer selections, it pays to stop after reading sections of text to recite main ideas and supporting details. At first you may think this slows you down. It does not. It helps you to monitor your comprehension and to apply fix-up strategies if necessary.

With some selections that are preceded or followed by questions, surveying those questions before reading the selection can be beneficial. Previews of this kind should be rapid, but research indicates that your ability to answer those questions increases if you know them ahead of time. That makes sense, doesn't it? So where it is allowed, before reading, quickly glance over the questions you must answer after reading.

Think
about . . .

What do you do to increase your concentration while studying? What are some of the things you now do that may cut down on your concentration?

Think
about . . .

To find out your reading rate, record the time when you start reading and the time when you finish reading a selection. Subtract your starting time from your ending time. Turn to Appendix B to get your reading rate. Record times in minutes and seconds.

Reading in Chunks of Meaning

It is important to read in chunks of meaning, or phrasal units, rather than focus on every word. Reading in chunks, or *chunking*, not only helps you understand what you read but also increases your reading speed.

 WORKSHOP 1: WHAT'S INVOLVED IN RAPID READING (LEARNING THEORY)

Independent Study

Preview the following selection by reading the title and predicting what you will learn by reading the selection. Based on the title, devise a purpose-setting question. Notice that the selection is set on the page in a narrow column to help you focus on chunks that have meaning.

Record your starting time. Read the selection. Be prepared to record your ending time as soon as you finish the selection and before you answer the follow-up questions.

What's Involved in Rapid Reading
Nila Smith and H. Alan Robinson

Investigations of eye movements have shown
that the rapid reader's eyes
move fleetingly across the lines,
pausing briefly two or three times on each line,
picking up an "eyeful" of words at each pause,
while the eyes of the poor reader
pause on every word
or on small word units.
  It is the mind, of course,
that controls the eye movements.
  The great value
of eye-movement investigations
is that they furnish us
a picture of the different ways
in which the mind works
in perceiving reading symbols.
  They tell us
that the mind of the poor reader loafs along,
picking up very small units at a time,
while the eyes of the excellent reader
race over the lines,
gathering an entire, meaningful idea at a glance.
  Cultivating the habit of reading for *ideas* not only increases speed
but also increases understanding.
  A person who reads one word at a time
thinks in terms of the meanings
of these separate words
and thus "can't see the woods for the trees."
  The first and most important instruction is,
"Read for Ideas!"
If you can cultivate the habit
of rapidly picking up one complete thought unit
after another,
the eye movements
will take care of themselves.

Based on your reading, star the best answer after eliminating the least likely choices and complete the critical thinking question. Items 1–5 are of the type found on timed reading tests.

1. Most important in rapid reading is
   a. keeping the eyes moving.
   b. reading for ideas.
   c. keeping the lips still.
   d. keeping the head still.

Think
about . . .

Can you restate items 1 and 5 as questions?

2. How do rapid readers move their eyes in reading?
   a. They pause two or three times per line.
   b. They never pause while reading.
   c. They look primarily at the first words on a line.
   d. They look primarily at the last words on a line.

3. What controls eye movements?
   a. the body
   b. the eyes themselves
   c. the hand
   d. the mind

4. What is the meaning of the phrase *can't see the woods for the trees* in this selection?
   a. There are many woods in a forest.
   b. The trees get in the way of seeing the forest.
   c. In reading, it is important to focus on the big ideas rather than on the individual words.
   d. In reading, it is important to focus on individual words rather than on the big ideas.

5. The authors of the selection believe that eye movement investigations are
   a. worthless because they tell us little about how expert readers function.
   b. worthless because eye movements have nothing to do with skillful reading.
   c. valuable because they provide a picture of the ways the mind works in perceiving word symbols.
   d. valuable because they tell us much about the way the eye is put together.

6. *Critical Thinking Question:* What does this article say to you about how you should function as you read? Write a sentence or two. _____

_____

Practicing Reading in Chunks of Meaning

Efficient reading requires that you not dwell on individual words. Pointing your finger at or focusing your eyes on each word slows down your reading. So does moving your lips to say each word as you read and moving your head from left to right as you read lines.

Here is a summary of "Do nots" to help you read more efficiently:

**EFFICIENT READING
STRATEGY**

→ Do not point at each word as you read.

→ Do not move your head or lips while reading. Reading is thinking, not mouthing individual words.

→ Do not focus on individual words; rather, keep your eyes moving across lines and down the page, and focus on meaningful phrases.

Varying How Fast You Read

Most people vary how fast they read depending on what they are reading. Most people slow down when they read technical articles or difficult textbooks. They read more quickly when faced with general articles in magazines and newspapers and light content, as in some novels.

Expert readers also vary their speed depending on their familiarity with the content they are reading. They read rapidly on topics with which they are familiar. They read more slowly when faced with new material. For example, if you are reading about AIDS and already have a lot of knowledge on that topic, you might just skim the article, focusing on the new points and skipping material you know. In contrast, if you are reading about the discovery of the microscope and you know nothing about that subject, you may have to slow down.

WORKSHOP 2: A FABLE: THE TORTOISE AND THE HARE (LITERATURE)

Independent Study

Think about . . .

You may want to time your reading of this story. Record starting and ending times. Turn to Appendix B for further directions.

Preview this story by thinking about the title and the author, telling yourself what you know about fables, and predicting what will happen when a tortoise and a hare get together in a fable. The selection is set on the page in phrasal units to help you read in chunks of meaning. The phrase *to no avail* means "of no use or value." If you already know this fable, you should be able to zip through it.

A Fable: The Tortoise and the Hare
Aesop

Hare was very proud of the way he could run.
One day he boasted to all the other animals in the forest,
"I am the fastest of all the animals.
No one can run faster than I can.
I challenge any one of you to a race."
From the back of the crowd of animals gathered around Hare
came a voice.
"I accept that challenge!" said the voice.
The animals turned to see who the voice was.
They discovered it was Tortoise.
Hare laughed when he saw
that his challenger was Tortoise.
He bragged,
"I could beat you with one leg tied behind my back."
Tortoise replied, "We will see.
Keep your boasts to yourself
until the end of the race."
The other animals charted out a lengthy race track,
and the race began.
At a signal from Owl, who was the starter,
Hare darted down the track
and was out of sight
before Tortoise had moved more than a foot.
When Hare looked back
and saw that he could not even see Tortoise,
he announced, "Such a race is almost beneath me.
I am a little sleepy from boredom.
I will take a nap."

With that,
he curled up on the side of the race track
and went to sleep.
  Meanwhile, Tortoise plodded slowly along,
step after step.
He, too, got a little sleepy,
but he persisted
until he saw the end of the track in sight.
"Only a little farther, now,"
Tortoise said to himself.
  Just then, Hare woke up.
He saw Tortoise nearing the finish line.
He hopped up
and sprinted forward.
But to no avail.
Tortoise crossed the finish line with time to spare.
  "The winner is Tortoise, by a hair," announced Owl.
Looking back, Tortoise said to Hare,
"Slow and steady wins the race."   [306 words]

Based on your reading of the passage, select the best answer. Mark items *T* (true) or *F* (false). Write your answers to the critical thinking questions.

_____ 1. The story about "The Tortoise and the Hare" is a fable.

_____ 2. "The Tortoise and the Hare" is by Aesop.

_____ 3. In the story, the Tortoise was the challenger.

_____ 4. The Hare was particularly proud of the way he looked.

_____ 5. At the beginning of the story it appeared as if Hare would be the winner.

_____ 6. The ultimate winner of the race was Tortoise.

_____ 7. The word *persistent* can be used to describe Hare.

_____ 8. The word *overconfident* can be used to describe Hare.

_____ 9. The stated moral of the story means that speed does not count for everything in a race.

_____ 10. In reading, as well as in racing, speed is the most important factor.

11. *Critical Thinking Question:* What is the main idea of this fable? _____

_____

12. *Critical Thinking Question:* When have you been in a situation in which the main idea

of this fable was important to you? Describe that situation here. _____

_____

_____

WORKSHOP 3: THE MICROSCOPE AND MICROORGANISMS (BIOLOGY)

Independent Study

Preview the following very short selection from a science textbook by glancing over the title and Figure 10.1, predicting what you will learn through the passage, and devising a purpose-setting question. The word *crude* in this selection means "rough, not fine." Before reading, recall that the prefix *micro-* means "small." A microorganism is an organism so

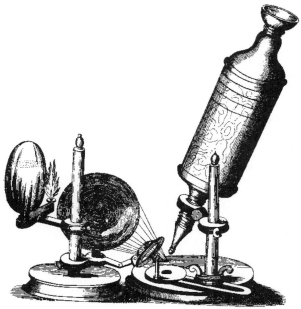

FIGURE 10.1   An Old Microscope from Hooke's
Micrographia
(Courtesy of the New York Academy of Medicine Library)

small that it can be seen only under a microscope. The selection has been set in phrasal units to help you read in chunks. Because it is more technical than the last selection, you will probably read more slowly.

The Microscope and Microorganisms
Thomas Brock, David Smith, and Michael Madigan

Although the existence of creatures too small to be seen with the eye
had long been suspected,
their discovery was linked to the discovery of the microscope.
Robert Hooke described the fruiting structures of molds in 1664,
but the first person to see microorganisms in any detail
was the Dutch amateur microscope builder Anton van Leeuwenhoek,
who used simple microscopes of his own construction.
Leeuwenhoek's microscopes
were extremely crude by today's standards,
but by careful manipulation and focusing
he was able to see organisms as small as bacteria.
He reported his observations in a series of letters
to the Royal Society of London,
which published them in English translation.
His observations were confirmed by other workers,
but progress in understanding the nature of these tiny organisms
came slowly.
Only in the nineteenth century
did improved microscopes become available
and widely distributed.   [152 words]

Based on your reading of the passage, select the best answer. Mark items either *T* (true) or *F* (false) and write a response to the critical thinking question.

_____ 1. Robert Hooke was the first person to see microorganisms in any detail.

_____ 2. By today's standards Leeuwenhoek's microscope was very fine.

_____ 3. Improved microscopes became available in the seventeenth century.

_____ 4. Leeuwenhoek was able to see organisms as small as bacteria.

_____ 5. The discovery of microorganisms was linked to the invention of the micro-scope.

_____ 6. The prefix *micro-* means "large."

7. *Critical Thinking Question:* How would your life be different if the microscope had never been invented? _____

_____

In the next section are four selections. One comes from an autobiography of a writer (Eudora Welty), the second from a computer magazine, the third from a professional booklet, and the fourth from a best-selling book. Concentrate as you read, focus on meaningful chunks and set your rate according to the difficulty of the material for you.

SELECTION 1

One Writer's Beginnings (LITERATURE—AUTOBIOGRAPHY)

Concentrated Reading

Getting Ready to Read

Before you begin, read the title. From it, predict what the selection will be about, given the fact that you know it is autobiographical. Ask yourself, "What will I learn by reading this selection?" You will answer multiple-choice questions after reading.

Reading with Meaning

One Writer's Beginnings
Eudora Welty

Jackson's Carnegie Library was on the same street where our house was, on the other side of the State Capitol. "Through the Capitol" was the way to go to the Library. You could glide through it on your bicycle or even coast through on roller skates, though without family permission.

I never knew anyone who'd grown up in Jackson without being afraid of Mrs. Calloway, our librarian. She ran the Library absolutely by herself, from the desk where she sat with her back to the books and facing the stairs, her dragon eye on the front door, where who knew what kind of person might come in from the public? SILENCE in big black letters was on signs tacked up everywhere. She herself spoke in her normally commanding voice; every word could be heard all over the Library above a steady seething sound coming from her electric fan; it was the only fan in the Library and stood on her desk, turned directly onto her streaming face.

As you came in from the bright outside, if you were a girl, she sent her strong eyes down the stairway to test you; if she could see through your skirt she sent you straight back home: you could just put on another petticoat if you wanted a book that badly from the public library. I was willing; I would do anything to read.

Think about . . .

You may want to record starting and ending times for your reading of these selections. Use the directions in Appendix B to find out your reading rate.

Did You **KNOW?**

The root *mit-* or *mis-* means "to send or let go." You see it here on the word *permission.* Verbs with the root are *permit, remit, omit, commit,* and *admit.*

My mother was not afraid of Mrs. Calloway. She wished me to have my own library card to check out books for myself. She took me in to introduce me and I saw I had met a witch. "Eudora is nine years old and has my permission to read any book she wants from the shelves, children or adult," Mother said. . . .

Mrs. Calloway made her own rules about books. You could not take back a book to the Library on the same day you'd taken it out; it made no difference to her that you'd read every word in it and needed another to start. You could take out two books at a time and two only; this applied as long as you were a child and also for the rest of your life, to my mother as severely as to me. So two by two, I read library books as fast as I could go, rushing them home in the basket of my bicycle. From the minute I reached our house, I started to read. Every book I seized on, from *Bunny Brown and His Sister Sue at Camp Rest-a-While* to *Twenty Thousand Leagues Under the Sea*, stood for the devouring wish to read being instantly granted. I knew this was bliss, knew it at the time. Taste isn't nearly so important; it comes in its own time. I wanted to read immediately. The only fear was that of books coming to an end.

My mother was very sharing of this feeling of insatiability. Now, I think of her as reading so much of the time while doing something else. In my mind's eye *The Origin of Species* is lying on the shelf in the pantry under a light dusting of flour—my mother was a bread maker; she'd pick it up, sit by the kitchen window and find her place, with one eye on the oven. I remember her picking up *The Man in Lower Ten,* while my hair got dry enough to unroll from a load of kid curlers trying to make me like my idol, Mary Pickford. A generation later, when my brother Walter was away in the Navy and his two little girls often spent the day in our house, I remember Mother reading the new issue of *Time* magazine while taking the part of the Wolf in a game of "Little Red Riding Hood" with the children. She'd just look up at the right time, long enough to answer—in character—"The better to eat you with, my dear," and go back to her place in the war news.   [671 words]

Think
about . . .

Were you able to focus on groups of words? Were you able to "chunk" as you read?

Monitoring Comprehension

Using the process of elimination, star the best answer without looking back at the selection. Write the answers to the critical thinking and vocabulary questions.

1. As a child, Eudora Welty felt that reading was
   a. a wonderful thing to do.
   b. a very difficult task, especially for her.
   c. something best left to librarians like Mrs. Calloway.
   d. a weekend pastime.

2. What phrase best describes Mrs. Calloway, as Eudora Welty perceived her?
   a. a warmhearted person   c. a mother substitute
   b. a dragon   d. a fellow reader

3. How did Mrs. Calloway test the girls coming into the library?
   a. She checked that they did not coast through the Capitol building on roller skates.
   b. She checked that they had their own library cards.
   c. She checked that they were over nine years of age.
   d. She checked that they wore enough petticoats so she could not see through their skirts.

4. Which statement best describes Eudora Welty as a reader?
   a. She read everything she could get her hands on.
   b. She had a high degree of literary taste even as a child.
   c. She followed the dictates of the librarian as to which books to read.
   d. She read very few books—only the best.

5. Which of the following was a rule in Mrs. Calloway's library?
   a. Children could check out only two books at a time, but adults could take four books.
   b. Children and adults could check out only four books at a time.

    c. Children and adults could check out only two books at a time.
    d. Children could check out books only when accompanied by an adult.

6. Eudora Welty remembered seeing *The Origin of Species* under a light dusting of flour. This came about because
    a. Eudora's mother was a poor housekeeper.
    b. Eudora's mother read as she baked bread.
    c. Eudora read the book as her mother baked bread.
    d. Eudora read the book as she herself baked bread.

7. How did Eudora get to the library?
    a. by walking
    b. by bus
    c. by bicycle
    d. by a car driven by her mother

8. Eudora Welty's attitude toward reading probably was influenced most strongly by the fact that
    a. her mother loved to read.
    b. her house was located near the library.
    c. she liked going to the library.
    d. she liked the librarian.

9. *Critical Thinking Question:* How does your view of reading compare with Eudora Welty's? Why do you think your feelings about reading differ from hers (if they do)?

_____

_____

_____

10. *Vocabulary Question:* What is a petticoat? What elements do you see in the word that

you recognize? _____

_____

SELECTION 2

Big Brother Is Watching You (PERSONAL FINANCE)

Concentrated Reading

Getting Ready to Read

This selection is from a computer magazine (*MacUser*). First read the title. Predict what the article is about. What do you hope to learn from the article?

Reading with Meaning

Big Brother Is Watching You
Robert Wiggins

In his book *1984*, George Orwell envisioned a future society where every aspect of a person's life was watched and controlled by the evil Big Brother. We are now . . . years past that infamous year, and have avoided the dismal fate Orwell had in store for us. Or have we?

    When you walk into a store and purchase a product with a credit card, most of the time the credit card company is immediately informed of the purchase (and makes the decision to accept or deny the charge) via telecommunications. As point-of-sale terminals become more sophisticated, you may not even know it is happening.

When you apply for a loan, a credit card or try to rent an apartment, a computerized credit check is usually run on you, and almost every aspect of your financial life is scrutinized. Thanks to federal legislation, there are now ways to see your credit report and offer rebuttals for inaccuracies that may have gotten into your report. Prior to these laws, there were many horror stories about false and even malicious information that had been carried in some credit reports and widely circulated. TRW, the largest credit reporting service, in a brilliant marketing move, is even selling a service to allow you to periodically review and update your credit history (something you can do for free if you are denied credit based on a TRW report).

When you have a brush with the law, no matter how minor, they can tap into the FBI's National Crime Information Center (NCIC) computer and instantly find out if you've ever been arrested or otherwise managed to get into any law enforcement files. The FBI Advisory Policy Board recently approved proposals to link NCIC to IRS, INS, Social Security, SEC and several other data bases and to create a system to track anyone *suspected* of a crime. More and more organizations, including private companies, are pushing to gain access to this system and, in the absence of legislation, the same excesses that used to be possible in credit reporting will be extended to law enforcement. Orwell may not have been so far off.   [363 words]

Monitoring Comprehension

Mark the items *T* (true) or *F* (false) based on the information in the article. Do not reread or look back. Write the answers to the critical thinking and vocabulary questions.

———— 1. George Orwell envisioned a world in which people's lives were watched by an evil power.

———— 2. The article suggests that some aspects of the world envisioned by Orwell have come to be.

———— 3. Federal legislation prevents your seeing your credit report if you have been denied credit.

———— 4. Usually when you try to rent an apartment, a credit check is run on you.

———— 5. You can see your credit report only by paying for the service.

———— 6. The National Crime Information Center is under the control of TRW.

———— 7. Today there are federal laws that determine who can tap into NCIC data banks.

———— 8. Private companies are pressing to gain access to the data in the National Crime Information Center.

———— 9. George Orwell's prediction was for the world in 2001.

———— 10. Every time you buy anything with a credit card, the credit card company is immediately informed before credit is granted.

11. *Critical Thinking Question:* How do you feel about having your credit rating so readily available? What dangers do you see in this? ————————————

————————————————

————————————————

12. *Vocabulary Question:* What elements do you recognize in the word *telecommunications?* What does the word mean? ————————————

————————————————

————————————————

SELECTION 3

Language and Communication (BIOLOGY)

Concentrated Reading

Getting Ready to Read

This selection comes from a booklet published by a professional organization. Before reading, read the title. Predict what the article is about. What do you hope to learn by reading the article?

Think about . . .
What have you been doing to increase your concentration while reading?

Reading with Meaning

Language and Communication
Alan Mandell

One of the characteristics that distinguishes human beings from the other animals is their highly developed ability to communicate—that is, to transfer ideas from one individual to another through abstract visual or oral symbols, and especially to record these symbols so that they can communicate with individuals far away in place or time. Many of the other animals also communicate with each other in a less complex but nevertheless interesting fashion. Some birds have a repertoire of calls, each of which appears to have a significant meaning to other birds. Worker bees have a sign system, by which they inform other bees in the hive of the direction and distance to a food supply. Some animals communicate by using a chemical language; the odors they produce may attract or repel other animals. Still others project messages by gestures, facial expressions, or body attitudes. Communication by use of a language composed of abstract symbols—particularly recorded symbols—appears, however, to be confined to the human animal.   [168 words]

Monitoring Comprehension and Writing in Response

Star the best answer. Write your answers to the critical thinking and vocabulary questions.

Think about . . .
Restate the stems of these items as questions.

1. The main idea of this selection is that
   a. although other animals can communicate, only humans have a language composed of abstract symbols that they can record.
   b. all animals have a system of communication.
   c. worker bees communicate with one another.
   d. to be abstract is to be better.

2. According to the selection, bird calls
   a. are simply pleasant sounds that enrich the environment.
   b. have a meaning to other birds.
   c. have no meaning.
   d. are part of the chemical language birds use to communicate.

3. Which is an example of chemical language?
   a. body attitudes
   b. gestures that animals use to communicate
   c. sympathetic facial expressions
   d. the odors animals produce that attract or repel other animals

4. When the article talks about recorded symbols, it is talking about
   a. speech.   c. writing.
   b. sounds.   d. computer activity.

5. Worker bees use their sign system to tell other bees of
   a. impending danger.
   b. the direction and distance to food.
   c. changes in the weather.
   d. ways to improve the structure and design of the hive.

6. *Critical Thinking Question:* Why do you think that ability to use language is so important? What things could you not do if you could not use language? _____

   _____

   _____

   _____

7. *Vocabulary Question:* Use the context to predict the meaning of *repertoire.* Write your prediction here. _____

   _____

SELECTION 4

Love Isn't Easy (LITERATURE—ESSAY)

Concentrated Reading

Getting Ready to Read

The next selection is an essay from the bestseller *All I Really Need to Know I Learned in Kindergarten: Uncommon Thoughts on Common Things,* by Robert Fulghum. In it, Fulghum uses humor to reflect on the meaning of life and to get across some basic truths about life. One reviewer (in *Washington* magazine) wrote about the author, "Fulghum is a natural-born storyteller who can pluck your heartstrings, tickle your funny bone and point up a moral all at the same time." Preview the essay by reading the title and thinking about what it means to you.

Reading with Meaning

Love Isn't Easy
Robert Fulghum

This is about a house I once lived in. An elderly lakeside cottage built at the end of the road at the end of the nineteenth century. A summer place for a family who traveled by horse and buggy out from Seattle through deep woods and over steep hills on logging trails. It was wild there, then, and it is wild there still.

The house was off the ground on bricks, surrounded by thickets of blackberry bushes and morning-glory vines bent on a struggle to the death. And even though it is only minutes, now, from downtown, squirrels, rabbits, feral pussycats, and "things" I never saw but only heard had long established squatters' rights on the property.

And raccoons. We had raccoons. Big ones. Several.

For reasons known only to God and the hormones of raccoons, they chose to mate underneath my house. Every spring. And for reasons known only to God and the hormones of raccoons, they chose to mate underneath my house at three A.M.

Until you have experienced raccoons mating underneath your bedroom at three in the morning, you have missed one of life's more sensational moments. It is an uncommon event, to say the least. If you've ever heard cats fighting in the night, you have a clue. Magnify the volume and the intensity by ten. It's not what you'd call a sensual and erotic sound. More like a three-alarm fire is what it is.

I remember the first time it happened. Since conditions were not conducive to sleep, I got up. When I say I got up, I mean *I GOT UP*. About three feet. Straight up. Covers and all.

When I had recovered my aplomb and adjusted to the new adrenaline level, I got a flashlight and went outside and peered up under the house. This lady raccoon and her suitor were squared off in a corner, fangs bared, covered with mud and blood, and not looking very sexy at all.

Neither my presence nor the beam of light could override what drove them on. With snarls and barks and screams, the passionate encounter raged on. While I watched, the matter was finally consummated and resolved. They had no shame. What had to be done was done. And they wandered off, in a kind of glazy-eyed stupor, to groom themselves for whatever might come next in the life of a raccoon.

I sat there in the rain, my light still shining into the trysting chamber. And I pondered. Why is it that love and life so often have to be carried forth with so much pain and strain and mess? I ask you, why is that?

I was thinking of my own sweet wife asleep in the bed right above me, and our own noises of conflict mixed with affection. I wondered what the raccoons must conclude from the sounds a husband and wife make at night—the ones that sound like "If-you-really-loved-me-you-would-not-keep-making-such-a-mess-in-the-bathroom," followed by "OH YEAH? WELL LET ME TELL YOU A FEW THINGS. . . ."

Why isn't love easy?

I don't know. And the raccoons don't say.   [534 words]

Monitoring Comprehension and Writing in Response

Answer the questions by placing *T* (true) or *F* (false) on the line. Write out your answers to the critical thinking and summary questions.

_____   1. The house that is the setting of this story is somewhere near Seattle.

_____   2. The raccoons that lived on the property were rather small.

_____   3. The raccoons chose to mate under Fulghum's house in mid-afternoon.

_____   4. Fulghum describes the experience of having raccoons mate under one's house as one of life's sensational moments.

_____   5. The first time raccoons mated under his house, it was raining.

_____   6. The mating raccoons wandered off when Fulghum flashed a light at them.

_____   7. When the raccoons had mated, they simply fell asleep on the spot.

_____   8. When the raccoons had mated, Fulghum sat there and thought about life.

_____   9. Fulghum compared the noises of the raccoons mating to the noises of conflict that occur between husbands and wives.

_____   10. Fulghum concluded by saying that love is easy.

11. *Critical Thinking Question:* How does Fulghum's conclusion about love relate to your own life? What examples from your life can you cite to support his conclusion? What examples from your life can you cite to disprove his conclusion?

_____

_____

_____

_____

_____

Did You
KNOW?

The root *clude-*, *clos-*, or *clus-* means "to close." You see it here on the word *conclude*. Lots of words carry this root: *disclose, exclude, foreclose, preclude, seclude, closet,* and *claustrophobia.*

12. *Collaborative Activity—Summary Writing:* With a partner write a brief summary of the Fulghum piece. Start with a sentence that gives Fulghum's main point. Then write three or four sentences that provide supporting detail. Record your summary in your

notebook. _____

EXTENDING WHAT YOU HAVE LEARNED

This chapter has proposed a number of strategies for building your concentration and varying your rate of reading. Perhaps the best single way of improving your reading efficiency is practice. You must spend time reading to become a better reader. Spending spare time reading rather than viewing television as a "couch potato" is essential. To this end, visit a library to select a book for personal reading. Make your selection a book on a topic that interests you. For example, if you enjoyed the humorous story by Robert Fulghum, you may select his book to read. Once you have chosen a book, carry it with you. Whenever you have a spare moment, read that book. Set a time limit for finishing it. Then go back to the library for another book. You should try to read at least one book for recreation during every three-week period. If you do that and vary the kinds of books you read, you will find your concentration and reading speed increasing.

Also buy a stenographer's notebook. As you read, write brief summaries and reactions to what you read in your notebook. Periodically reread what you have written. Writing summaries is one of the best ways to increase your reading comprehension.

11

Interpreting Tables, Graphs, and Diagrams

OBJECTIVE

In this chapter, you will learn strategies for

1. Accessing information from tables, graphs, and diagrams, and
2. Developing relationships based on the data contained in them.

TABLES, GRAPHS, AND DIAGRAMS

Many textbooks have accompanying figures, or illustrations. You should look over these visuals during your before-reading preview. In previewing, just read the captions to get a rough idea of the data available in the figures. Later as you read the text, you should study each figure at the point where it is referenced (for example, "See Figure 2.5" or "as shown in Figure 12.4"). Usually figures are indicated numerically; Figure 4.7 is the seventh figure in Chapter 4.

Did You
KNOW?

Vis- is from Latin and means "to see." Words with the root are *visuals*, *visor*, and *envision*.

TABLES

One way in which textbook authors present information or data is in a table with labeled rows and columns. An example is shown in Figure 11.1.

To interpret a table, do the following:

TABLE INTERPRETATION
STRATEGY

→ Read its title or caption.

→ Read the labels on the rows and columns, studying the labels indicating the units that apply to numerical data (for example, area in square miles, population in millions, numbers given as percentages).

→ Analyze the data for relationships: Which is biggest? Smallest? Which is first? Last? Which is fastest? Slowest? What feature is shared by the items? Is there a pattern, or trend, within the data? How do the data relate to the information in the running text?

→ Hypothesize reasons and cause and effect relationships: What can account for the data? Why is this true?

WORKSHOP 1: READING A TABLE

Activity A. After studying the table in Figure 11.1, answer these items with a partner. Remember to turn the stem of an item into a question to clarify what the problem is and use the process of elimination to narrow the field.

1. The table tells the reader
   a. population changes of selected states of the United States in relation to area.
   b. the relative importance of different states within the United States.

State	Area (square miles)	Population (millions), 1990 Census	Population (millions), 1998 Estimate	Increase in Population from 1990 to 1998 (millions)
Alaska	589,757	0.55	0.61	+0.06
California	158,693	29.79	32.67	+2.88
Florida	58,560	12.94	14.92	+1.98
Montana	147,138	0.80	0.88	+0.08
New York	49,576	18.00	18.18	+0.18
North Carolina	52,586	3.49	3.84	+0.35
Texas	269,338	16.99	19.76	+2.77

FIGURE 11.1 Table Showing Population Changes as Related to Area of Some States of the United States from 1990 to 1998

    c. the comparative wealth of different states within the United States.
    d. just the geographic size of selected states within the United States.

2. The area of Alaska is given as 589,757. This means that there are 589,757
    a. people living in Alaska.
    b. square miles of territory in Alaska.
    c. acres of territory in Alaska.
    d. people living in Alaska per each square mile of territory.
    e. people living in Alaska per each acre of territory.

3. The population of California in 1990 according to United States Census figures was
    a. 158,693.
    b. 29.79.
    c. 297,000.
    d. 2,979,000.
    e. 29,790,000.

4. The estimated population of Florida in 1998 was
    a. 12.94.
    b. 12,940,000.
    c. 14.92.
    d. 14,920,000.
    e. 58,560.

5. The population of Montana between 1990 and 1998 increased by
    a. 800,000.
    b. 880,000.
    c. 80,000.
    d. 8,000.

6. The maker of this table figured out the data in the column marked "Increase in Population" by
    a. subtracting the population in 1990 from the population in 1998.
    b. adding the population in 1990 to the population in 1998.
    c. multiplying the population in 1990 by the population in 1998.
    d. dividing the population in 1990 by the population in 1998.

7. Of the states listed in Figure 11.1, the state with the smallest number of people living on each square mile in 1998 (or the state with the smallest population density) is
    a. Alaska.   d. Montana.
    b. California.   e. Texas.
    c. Florida.

Activity B. Using the following explanations, check your answers to items 1–7.

1. The answer to the first item is "a." The table tells you the population of selected states of the United States in relation to area. You learn that from the title and from the labels at the heads of the columns. The table does not provide information about the relative importance or comparative wealth of the selected states. If you chose either option "b" or "c," you read too much into the table. If you chose option "d," you did not see all there is in the table. The table gives more than geographic size; it gives population data as well.

2. The answer is "b." The number 589,757 tells the number of square miles that make up the state of Alaska. You know that because the heading of the column is "Area (square miles)," not "Area (acres)."

3. The answer is "e." The population of California in 1990 was 29,790,000. You must look in the column labeled "Population (millions), 1990 Census." The number given for California is 29.79, but remember that this number is in millions of people. Therefore, you must multiply the given number (29.79) by 1 million. The result is 29,790,000. This shows how important it is to read the labels on both columns and rows of a data table.

4. The answer is "d." The estimated population of Florida in 1998 was 14,920,000. You get the information from the column labeled "Population (millions), 1998 Estimate." In the column so labeled and in the row for Florida is the number 14.92. Again you must remember that the number is in millions. You must multiply by 1 million to get 14,920,000.

5. The answer is "c." The population of Montana increased from 1990 to 1998 by 80,000. You get the information from the column labeled "Increase in Population." The number given there is 0.08. This means 0.08 million, so you must multiply 1 million by .08. The result is 80,000.

6. The answer is "a." The increase in population from 1990 to 1998 is calculated by subtracting the population in 1990 from the population in 1998. The difference between the two numbers is the increase in population.

7. The answer is "a." The least densely populated state of those given is Alaska. You could figure this out precisely by dividing the total population of the state (610,000 people in 1998) by the total area of the state (589,757 square miles) to get the number of people per each square mile. If you used a calculator to do the division, you would find out that there are only 1.03 persons living on each square mile of Alaskan territory. This is in contrast to a state such as New York, where there are 366.7 people per square mile. Of course, the people are not spread out evenly across the land; for example, in New York State the population density of the cities is much greater than 366.7 and the population density of the rural areas is much less. The number 366.7 is only an average. You do not have to do any arithmetic to see that Alaska is the least densely populated and New York is the most densely populated. The area of Alaska is the largest of all the states listed in the table. The population of Alaska is the smallest of all the states listed. Logically, then, the number of people occupying each square mile of Alaskan territory is the smallest among all the states listed in the table.

WORKSHOP 2: APPLYING THE BASIC STRATEGY

Apply the principles of table reading that you just learned to answer these items. Use data given in Figure 11.1.

8. The area of Texas is
   a. 269,338 square miles.
   b. 16,990,000 square miles.
   c. 19,760,000 square miles.
   d. 269,338 acres.

9. The population of North Carolina in 1998 (estimated) was
   a. 349,000.
   b. 3,490,000.
   c. 384,000.
   d. 3,840,000.
   e. 3,500,00.

10. The population of New York in 1990 was
    a. 18,000,000.
    b. 180,000.
    c. 18,180,000.
    d. 181,800.
    e. 18,000.

11. What happened to the population of New York between 1990 and 1998?
    a. It increased by 180,000 people.
    b. It increased by 18,000 people.
    c. It increased by 18,000,000 people.
    d. It decreased by 18,000 people.
    e. It decreased by 180,000 people.

12. The population of Alaska in 1990 was
    a. 589,757 people.
    b. 550,000 people.
    c. 610,000 people.
    d. 60,000 people.

13. The population of California in 1998 (estimated) was
    a. 158,693 people.
    b. 29,790,000 people.
    c. 32,670,000 people.
    d. 2,880,000 people.

14. What happened to the population of California between 1990 and 1998?
    a. It increased by 158,693 people.
    b. It increased by 32,670,000 people.
    c. It increased by 2,880,000 people.
    d. It decreased by 32,670,000 people.
    e. It decreased by 2,880,000 people.

WORKSHOP 3: REASONING FROM A TABLE

From a data table such as the one in Figure 11.1, you can make comparisons and hypothesize reasons. Use the data in Figure 11.1 to answer these questions.

15. Of the seven states listed in Figure 11.1, which is the largest in terms of geographic area?
    a. Texas.
    b. New York.
    c. Alaska.
    d. California.
    e. Montana.

16. Of the seven states listed in Figure 11.1, which had the largest population in 1990?
    a. Texas.
    b. New York.
    c. Alaska.
    d. California.
    e. Montana.

17. Of the seven states listed in Figure 11.1, which had the largest population in 1998?
    a. Texas.
    b. New York.
    c. Alaska.
    d. California.
    e. Montana.

18. Of the seven states listed in Figure 11.1, which one had the greatest numerical increase in population between 1990 and 1998?
    a. Texas.
    d. California.
    b. New York.
    e. Montana.
    c. Alaska.

19. Of the seven states listed in Figure 11.1, which one had the smallest numerical increase in population between 1990 and 1998?
    a. Texas.
    d. California.
    b. New York.
    e. Montana.
    c. Alaska.

20. Of the two, which was the more densely populated state in 1998? (To answer this, just relate the size of the population to the size of the territory.)
    a. Florida.
    b. New York.

21. Of the two, which was the more densely populated state in 1998?
    a. Montana.
    b. Florida.

22. Of the two, which was the more densely populated state in 1998?
    a. California.
    b. Alaska.

23. *Hypothesize reasons:* Why is the state of California increasing its population at such a fast rate? Make a couple of educated guesses. _____

    _____

    _____

24. *Hypothesize reasons:* Why does the table show changes in population of the selected states but not changes in area? _____

    _____

25. *Hypothesize effects:* What problems result from very rapid population growth? What problems result from high population density? _____

    _____

    _____

SELECTION 1

The Fifty States of the United States (GEOGRAPHY)

In-Text Test

Figure 11.2 contains data on the states within the United States according to a 1998 estimate. Use those data to answer the following items. Read the title and the labels on the rows and columns before answering. Restate each stem as a question. Circle key words in the stems.

1. The order of the largest five states in land area from largest to smallest is
   a. Alaska, Texas, California, Montana, New Mexico.
   b. California, Texas, New York, Florida, Illinois.
   c. Alaska, Montana, South Dakota, South Carolina, Rhode Island.
   d. Delaware, Pennsylvania, New Jersey, Florida, Connecticut.
   e. Rhode Island, Delaware, Connecticut, Hawaii, New Jersey.

State	Area in Sq. Miles	Rank in Area	Entered Union	Entry Order	Population 1998	Pop. Rank 1998	Pop. Per Sq. Mile 1998
Alabama	51,609	29	1819	22	4,351,999	23	84.3
Alaska	589,757	1	1959	49	614,010	48	1.0
Arizona	113,909	6	1912	48	4,668,631	21	41.0
Arkansas	53,104	27	1836	25	2,538,303	33	47.8
California	158,693	3	1850	31	32,666,550	1	205.8
Colorado	104,247	8	1876	38	3,970,971	24	38.1
Connecticut	5,009	48	1788	5	3,274,069	29	653.6
Delaware	2,057	49	1787	1	743,603	45	361.5
Florida	58,560	22	1845	27	14,915,980	4	254.7
Georgia	58,876	21	1788	4	7,642,207	10	129.8
Hawaii	6,450	47	1959	50	1,193,001	41	185.0
Idaho	83,557	13	1890	43	1,228,684	40	14.7
Illinois	56,400	24	1818	21	12,045,326	5	213.6
Indiana	36,291	38	1816	19	5,899,195	14	162.6
Iowa	56,290	25	1846	29	2,862,447	30	50.9
Kansas	82,264	14	1861	34	2,629,067	32	32.0
Kentucky	40,395	37	1792	15	3,936,499	25	97.5
Louisiana	48,523	31	1812	18	4,368,967	22	90.0
Maine	33,215	39	1820	23	1,244,250	39	37.5
Maryland	10,577	42	1788	7	5,134,808	19	485.5
Massachusetts	8,257	45	1788	6	6,147,132	13	744.5
Michigan	58,126	23	1837	26	9,817,242	8	168.9
Minnesota	84,068	12	1858	32	4,725,419	20	56.2
Mississippi	47,716	32	1817	20	2,752,092	31	57.7
Missouri	69,686	19	1821	24	5,438,559	16	78.0
Montana	147,138	4	1889	41	880,453	44	6.0
Nebraska	77,227	15	1867	37	1,662,719	38	21.5
Nevada	110,540	7	1864	36	1,746,898	36	15.8
New Hampshire	9,304	44	1788	9	1,185,048	42	127.4
New Jersey	7,836	46	1787	3	8,115,011	9	1,035.6
New Mexico	121,666	5	1912	47	1,736,931	37	14.3
New York	49,576	30	1788	11	18,175,301	3	366.6
North Carolina	52,586	28	1789	12	7,546,493	11	143.5
North Dakota	70,665	17	1889	39	638,244	47	9.0
Ohio	41,222	35	1803	17	11,209,493	7	271.9
Oklahoma	69,919	18	1907	46	3,346,713	27	47.9
Oregon	96,981	10	1859	33	3,281,974	28	33.8
Pennsylvania	45,333	33	1787	2	12,001,451	6	264.7
Rhode Island	1,214	50	1790	13	988,480	43	814.2
South Carolina	31,055	40	1788	8	3,835,962	26	123.5
South Dakota	77,047	16	1889	40	738,171	46	9.6
Tennessee	42,244	34	1796	16	5,430,621	17	128.6
Texas	267,338	2	1845	28	19,759,614	2	73.9
Utah	84,916	11	1896	45	2,099,758	34	24.7
Vermont	9,609	43	1791	14	590,883	49	61.5
Virginia	40,817	36	1788	10	6,791,345	12	166.4
Washington	68,192	20	1889	42	5,689,263	15	83.4
West Virginia	24,181	41	1863	35	1,811,156	35	74.9
Wisconsin	56,154	26	1848	30	5,223,500	18	93.0
Wyoming	97,914	9	1890	44	480,907	50	4.9

FIGURE 11.2 Data Chart for the States of the United States (1998 Estimate)

2. The smallest state in land area is
   a. Connecticut.
   b. Delaware.
   c. Hawaii.
   d. New Jersey.
   e. Rhode Island.

3. The first state to enter the Union was
   a. Delaware.
   b. Georgia.
   c. New York.
   d. South Carolina.
   e. Florida.

4. The first states to enter the Union were generally located
   a. along the Pacific Coast.
   b. along the Atlantic Coast.
   c. along the Gulf of Mexico.
   d. along the Mississippi River.
   e. outside the continental United States.

5. The last two states to enter the Union were located
   a. along the Pacific Coast.
   b. along the Atlantic Coast.
   c. along the Gulf of Mexico.
   d. along the Mississippi River.
   e. outside the continental United States.

6. The most densely populated state—the one with the greatest population per square mile—is
   a. Connecticut.
   b. New Jersey.
   c. New York.
   d. Massachusetts.
   e. Rhode Island.

7. The most densely populated states tend to be those admitted to the Union
   a. between 1787 and 1788.
   b. between 1800 and 1850.
   c. between 1851 and 1900.
   d. between 1901 and 1950.
   e. after 1950.

8. The least densely populated state is
   a. Rhode Island.
   b. Wyoming.
   c. Alaska.
   d. Montana.
   e. New Jersey.

9. The state with the smallest number of people is
   a. Alaska.
   b. Arizona.
   c. Hawaii.
   d. North Dakota.
   e. Wyoming.

10. *Hypothesize reasons:* Why do you think the first states to be admitted to the Union are located where they are? _____

    _____

    _____

    _____

11. *Hypothesize reasons:* Why do you think the most densely populated states are located where they are? _____

    _____

    _____

    _____

    _____

12. *Relate the data to yourself:* If you live in the United States, locate your home state in Figure 11.2. How does your home state compare with other states? Can it be

categorized as a large or small state in terms of population? In terms of area? Was it admitted early to the Union? Later? Hypothesize why. _____

_____

_____

_____

13. On the map in Figure 11.3, mark

- the first thirteen states to be admitted to the Union,
- the last two states to enter,
- the state with the smallest population,
- the state with the largest population,
- the state with the greatest population per square mile, and
- the state with the smallest population per square mile.

Create a key with a labeled symbol to indicate the states you have marked.

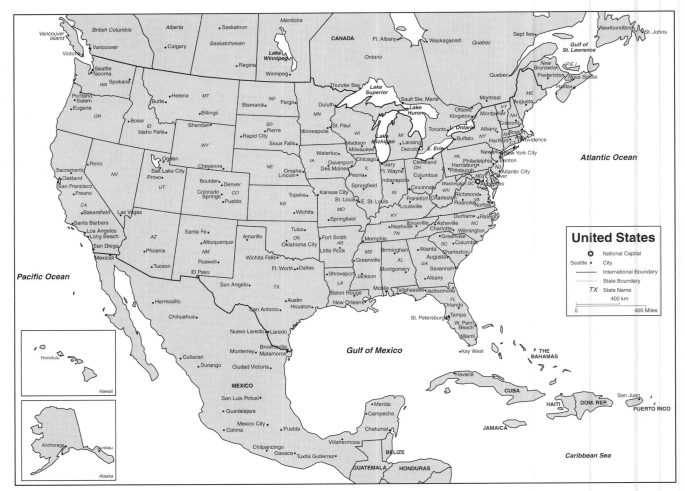

FIGURE 11.3 Map of the United States

14. Write a question that can be answered with information from the data chart in Figure 11.2 and the map in Figure 11.3. _____

_____

_____

_____

15. Write a second question based on Figure 11.3. _____

_____

_____

_____

16. Write a third question based on Figure 11.3. _____

_____

_____

_____

PICTOGRAPHS

A pictograph is a graph that uses picture symbols. Each picture symbol represents a fixed amount as given in a key. For example, study Figure 11.4. It is a pictograph that shows the population of the world from 1950 to 2050. The data for the years 2010, 2030, and 2050 are estimated. At the bottom is the key. It tells you that each person symbol on the pictograph stands for 500 million (500,000,000) people. Incomplete person symbols stand for a part of that number. A half a person symbol stands for 250 million, a quarter of one for 125 million, and so on.

An advantage of a pictograph is that you can make comparisons at a glance because the data are presented visually. A disadvantage is that when there are parts of a picture symbol, you must estimate the amounts for which they stand. Your answer is an approximation, not as exact as an answer based on a table.

Study the pictograph in Figure 11.4. What was the population of the world in 1950? Count the number of symbolic people. There are four symbols plus a part of a person symbol. That part appears to be a little bit more than half. Because each person symbol stands for 500 million people, you could estimate that the population of the world in 1950 was about 2.3 billion.

Did You KNOW?

Graph- (as well as *graphy-* and *gram-*) means "writing" and is a Greek combining form. Other words with the elements are *photograph, telegram,* and *geography.*

WORKSHOP 4: INTERPRETING A PICTOGRAPH

Collaborating with a partner or working independently, use the data in Figure 11.4 to estimate the following information.

1. The population of the world in 1970: _____

2. The population of the world in 1990: _____

3. The population of the world as estimated for 2010: _____

4. The population of the world as estimated for 2030: _____

5. The population of the world as estimated for 2050: _____

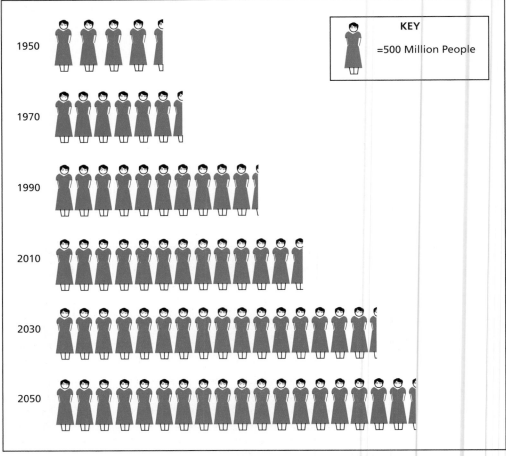

FIGURE 11.4 Pictograph Showing World Population from 1950 to 1990 and Population Projections from 2010 to 2050

6. *Describe the trend:* What happened to the population of the world between 1950 and 1990? _____

7. *Hypothesize reasons:* Why did the population of the world change as it did, and why will it continue to change in the way estimated in the pictograph? _____

_____

8. *Hypothesize the future:* What events could effect the estimates of world population as given in the pictograph? _____

9. *Hypothesize outcomes:* What problems do you see as the world moves from 2010 to 2050 and the population changes as estimated in the pictograph? _____

_____

CIRCLE (OR PIE) GRAPHS

A pie graph is a picture that shows percentages. It is based on a circle. The whole circle stands for 100 percent of the data. The individual wedges (or pieces of the pie) give information about the parts that make up the entire pie, or circle.

Study Figure 11.5, which is typical of what you find in college sociology textbooks. The title (which you should read first when studying a graph) tells you what the graph

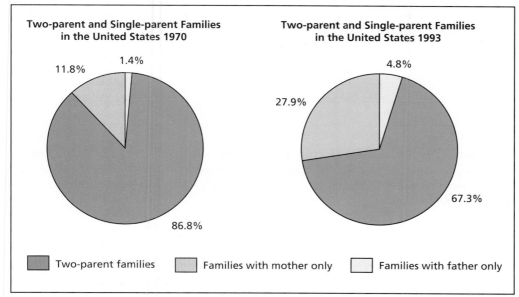

FIGURE 11.5 Circle (or Pie) Graphs Showing Two-Parent and Single-Parent Families in the United States, 1970 and 1993

is about—in this case, U.S. families with a single parent in the home and families with two parents in 1970 and 1993. The total circle represents 100 percent of the families in the United States. If you add the percentages shown around the pie, you get 100 percent. To work effectively with a circle graph, you must understand percentages and realize that each percentage gives you "parts of 100."

WORKSHOP 5: INTERPRETING CIRCLE GRAPHS

Think about Figure 11.5 and answer these questions.

1. The kind of family found most often in the United States in 1993 was a
   a. two-parent family.
   b. mother-only family.
   c. father-only family.

2. The kind of family found most often in the United States in 1970 was a
   a. two-parent family.
   b. mother-only family.
   c. father-only family.

3. The number of two-parent families in the United States between 1970 and 1993 went down by
   a. 19.5 percentage points.
   b. 67.3 percentage points.
   c. 86.8 percentage points.
   d. 11.8 percentage points.
   e. 27.9 percentage points.

4. How did the number of families led by a mother change between 1970 and 1993?
   a. The number went up 16.1 percentage points.
   b. The number went down 16.1 percentage points.
   c. The number stayed the same.
   d. The number went up 3.4 percentage points.
   e. The number went down 3.4 percentage points.

5. *Hypothesize:* What do you think caused the changes in the composition of families in the United States between 1970 and 1993? Make an educated guess based on all that you know. _____

_____

_____

_____

Note: The Bureau of the Census provides data such as that in Figure 11.5. You can access those data on the World Wide Web. The address for the Census Bureau is http://www.census.gov. You may want to visit that Web site, locate some interesting data, and make a pie graph.

BAR GRAPHS

Another way in which data are represented visually is the bar graph. Each bar on the graph presents a piece of information. Bars can be arranged vertically or horizontally.

 WORKSHOP 6: READING BAR GRAPHS

Activity A. Study Figure 11.6. Start by reading the title. What does the graph show? Give the topic of the graph here:

1. Topic: _____

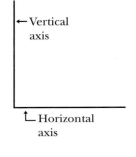
←Vertical axis

└ Horizontal axis

Now consider the data. Across the bottom on the horizontal axis are labels that identify the areas of the world for which data are given. Down the left-hand side of the graph on the vertical axis are the numbers (in this case, percentages) that guide you in interpreting each bar. For each area, there are two bars. The darker one gives data on energy production. The lighter one gives data on energy consumption.

Here is how you read the graph. Western Europe produces about 7 percent of the world's energy. It uses about 18 percent of the world's production of energy. A good hypothesis to make at this point is that Western Europe probably has to import sources of energy to make up the difference between its production and consumption.

Activity B. Answer these questions based on the graph. Work with a partner.

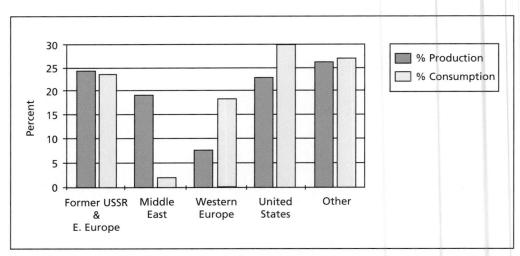

FIGURE 11.6 Bar Graph Showing World Energy Production and Consumption

2. What percentage of the world's energy production comes out of the Middle East? See page 269 for a map of the Middle East. _____

_____

3. What percentage of the world's energy is consumed in the Middle East? _____

_____

4. Is the Middle East more likely to be an energy importer or exporter? Explain.

_____

_____

5. Does the United States produce all the energy that it uses? _____

_____

6. Where does the United States probably get some of the energy that it uses? _____

_____

7. Are the former USSR and the Eastern European countries likely to be big exporters of energy? Explain. _____

_____

8. Hypothesize: What problems do you see when countries use more energy than they produce? _____

_____

SELECTION 2

Immigration to the United States (HISTORY)

In-Text Test

Study the graph in Figure 11.7 for the information needed to answer these questions. Use this activity to test your ability to interpret a graph.

1. What kind of information is given in the graph?
   a. world immigration patterns
   b. immigration to the United States, 1850–1899
   c. emigration from Europe to the United States, 1850–1899
   d. emigration from Europe and Asia, 1850–1899
   e. all of the above

2. How many people immigrated to the United States from 1890 to 1899?
   a. 2,000,000 people   d. 3,650,000 people
   b. 2,750,000 people   e. 5,250,000 people
   c. 3,200,000 people

3. During which decade did the greatest number of people immigrate to the United States?
   a. 1850–1859
   b. 1860–1869
   c. 1870–1879
   d. 1880–1889
   e. 1890–1899

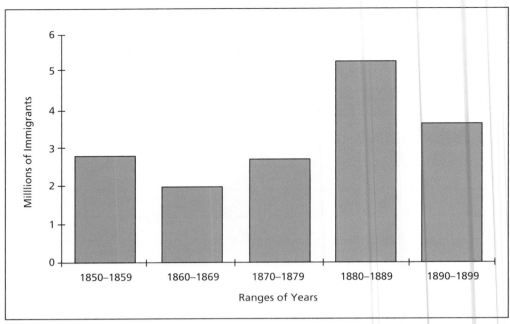

FIGURE 11.7 Bar Graph Showing Immigration to the United States, 1850–1899

4. During which decade did the smallest number of people come to the United States from other countries?
   a. 1850–1859
   b. 1860–1869
   c. 1870–1879
   d. 1880–1889
   e. 1890–1899

5. How did the number of people immigrating to the United States from 1890 to 1899 compare with the number immigrating from 1880 to 1889?
   a. The number from 1890 to 1899 was less than that from 1880 to 1889.
   b. The number from 1890 to 1899 was greater than that from 1880 to 1889.
   c. The number in both periods was approximately the same.

6. How did the number of people immigrating to the United States from 1850 to 1859 compare with the number immigrating from 1870 to 1879?
   a. The number from 1850 to 1859 was much less than that from 1870 to 1879.
   b. The number from 1850 to 1859 was much greater than that from 1870 to 1879.
   c. The number in both periods was approximately the same.

7. *Hypothesize reasons:* Think about the decade in which immigration to the United States was the lowest. Can you account for the low that occurred during that decade? If you can, write a sentence that explains why there was a drop in immigration during that period. _____

   _____

   _____

8. *Relate data to yourself:* During what years did members of your family or you come to the United States? Why did they or you immigrate? _____

   _____

   _____

LINE GRAPHS

A line graph is another way to represent numerical data visually. Like a bar graph, a line graph has two labeled axes: vertical and horizontal. In interpreting a line graph, you must take care to read the labels on the axes.

SELECTION 3

Age at First Marriage (SOCIOLOGY)

An Interpretive Workshop

Figure 11.8 is an example of a line graph. Preview it by reading the title. The topic of the graph is the median age at first marriage by sex in the United States between 1890 and 1990. A median is a midpoint. Look at the points on the vertical axis labeled "Age at First Marriage." The marked points start with age 18 and go up to age 28 in two-year increments, or jumps. In the same way, the years are given in five-year increments along the horizontal axis. Why are there two lines going across the graph?

Working with a partner, write down at least eight pieces of information you can get from this line graph. Include at least one hypothesis as to causes. The first item is done for you as a model.

1. In the 1950s women tended to marry for the first time at a younger age than today.

2. _____

   _____

3. _____

   _____

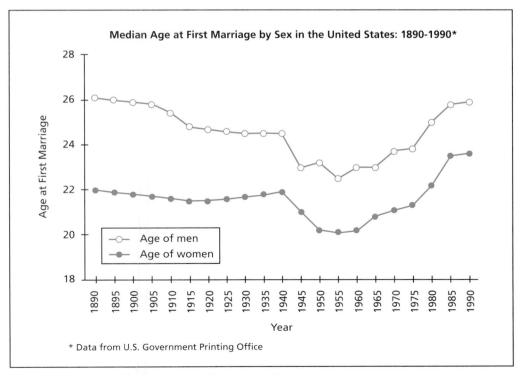

FIGURE 11.8 Line Graph Showing Median Age at Marriage

4. _____
   _____

5. _____
   _____

6. _____
   _____

7. _____
   _____

8. _____
   _____

SELECTION 4

Weather in New Delhi and Santiago (CLIMATOLOGY)

An In-Text Test

Preview the two line graphs in Figure 11.9. Read the titles and the labels on the vertical and horizontal axes. Note that each graph has two lines. The top solid line gives the average high temperature in that location. The bottom solid line gives the average low temperature there. Note again that the units on the vertical axis increase in equal increments, although the increments on the two graphs are different.

Now study the graphs and answer these questions.

1. During what month does the temperature reach its highest point in New Delhi?
   a. April   d. July
   b. May   e. August
   c. June

2. During what month does the temperature reach its lowest point in New Delhi?
   a. November   d. February
   b. December   e. March
   c. January

3. What is the average high temperature in New Delhi during October?
   a. 65° Fahrenheit   d. 97° Fahrenheit
   b. 93° Fahrenheit   e. 102° Fahrenheit
   c. 105° Fahrenheit

4. *Critical Thinking Question:* Is New Delhi in the Northern or Southern Hemisphere?
   a. Northern   b. Southern

5. During what month does the temperature reach its highest point in Santiago, Chile?
   a. January   d. April
   b. February   e. December
   c. March

6. During what month does the temperature reach its lowest point in Santiago?
   a. May   d. August
   b. June   e. September
   c. July

7. What is the average high temperature in Santiago during October?
   a. 45° Fahrenheit   b. 66° Fahrenheit

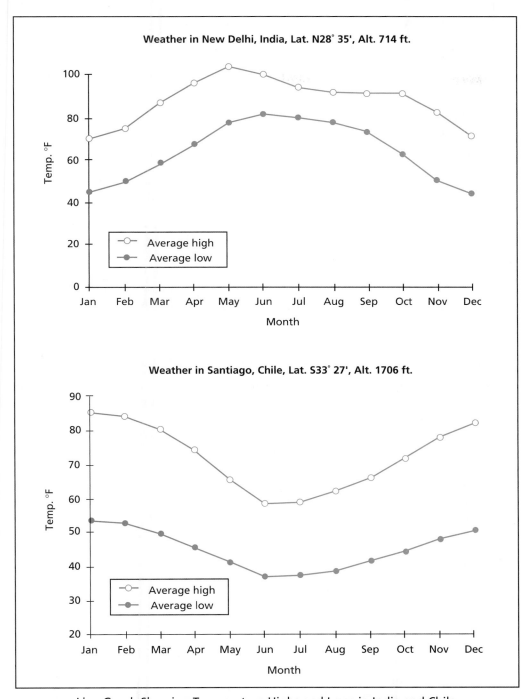

FIGURE 11.9 Line Graph Showing Temperature Highs and Lows in India and Chile

c. 72° Fahrenheit   e. 83° Fahrenheit
d. 75° Fahrenheit

8. *Critical Thinking Question:* Is Santiago in the Northern or Southern Hemisphere?
   a. Northern   b. Southern

LINE DRAWINGS

As you may have discovered when you tried to answer questions 4 and 8, some geographic understanding may be helpful in reading and comprehending graphs. To answer those questions correctly, you had to know that the hottest months are June, July, and August

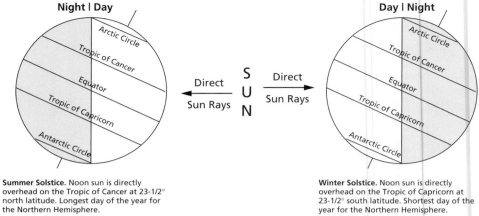

Night | Day

Day | Night

Direct Sun Rays ← S U N → Direct Sun Rays

Summer Solstice. Noon sun is directly overhead on the Tropic of Cancer at 23-1/2° north latitude. Longest day of the year for the Northern Hemisphere.

Winter Solstice. Noon sun is directly overhead on the Tropic of Capricorn at 23-1/2° south latitude. Shortest day of the year for the Northern Hemisphere.

FIGURE 11.10 Line Drawing Showing the Seasons in the Northern Hemisphere

in the Northern Hemisphere. The hottest months are December, January, and February in the Southern Hemisphere. In short, the Northern and Southern hemispheres experience summer at opposite times of the year.

WORKSHOP 7: INTERPRETING LINE DRAWINGS

Study Figure 11.10. It is a line drawing that shows why there are seasons. Answer the following questions on the basis of the line drawing.

1. At the summer solstice in the Northern Hemisphere, the direct rays of the sun strike the
   a. Arctic Circle.
   b. Tropic of Cancer.
   c. Equator.
   d. Tropic of Capricorn.
   e. Antarctic Circle.

2. At the winter solstice in the Northern Hemisphere, the direct rays of the sun strike the
   a. Arctic Circle.
   b. Tropic of Cancer.
   c. Equator.
   d. Tropic of Capricorn.
   e. Antarctic Circle.

3. Figure 11.10 indicates that
   a. the earth rotates on its axis.
   b. the earth revolves around the sun.
   c. the earth is tilted on its axis.
   d. all of the above are true.

There is no one strategy to use to understand line drawings. Each drawing has characteristics that make it unique. However, general steps to take include these:

LINE DRAWING INTERPRETATION STRATEGY

→ Read the title.

→ Carefully study all labels.

→ Explain the drawing to yourself in your own words.

SELECTION 5

Television Viewing, Reading, and School Achievement (POPULAR PSYCHOLOGY)

Independent Study

Expanding Your Vocabulary for Reading

You will find the phrase *average proficiency* in the figures that accompany this selection. The word *proficiency* means "ability" or "skill." If you are proficient in doing something, you are able to do it well; you are skilled. The average is a midpoint in a group of grades or scores. To find your average in a course, you add up all your grades (for example, 74 + 92 + 87 = 253) and divide by the number of grades (in this case, 3). The result (in this case, 84.3) is your average proficiency, or ability level, as you have demonstrated it through your performance in the course. Incidentally, some students find it useful to keep track of their average proficiency in courses as they progress through a semester.

Getting Ready to Read

Preview the selection by reading the title and looking over the two related graphs. Predict: What point do you think the article is going to make? How does it relate to you?

Reading with Meaning

Television Viewing, Reading, and School Achievement

How do you spend your free time? Do you head for the pub? Do you hit the malls with friends? Do you settle back to take in a TV show or two? Or do you pick up a book and relax by reading it?

The way you answer these questions may determine how much you know about important topics and ultimately how well you do in college. According to a recent study by Ravitch and Finn, students who spend considerable time viewing television know less history than students who watch TV for fewer hours each day. Students who spend many hours each day in front of a TV set had much lower average proficiency scores on a history achievement test than those who spend just a couple of hours. (See Figure 11.11.) Similarly, students who spend some free time each day reading on their own for pleasure have more knowledge of literature than those who never read. (See Figure 11.12.)

Research tells us that the knowledge readers bring to reading determines what they get out of a text—in other words, their comprehension. As Ravitch and Finn explain, "Some background knowledge is necessary to understand and interpret any text. . . . The more advanced the text, the more background knowledge is necessary to read it with understanding." Furthermore, those students who have a fund of knowledge on a topic are able to think critically about it, draw conclusions, and make judgments.

What do these data mean to you—a student who wants to succeed in college? Think about that question. Hopefully, you will spend more time reading and less time doing things that do not add to your knowledge base. Hopefully too, some of your independent reading will focus on subjects like history, science, and literature that you must take in college.

Monitoring Comprehension and Writing in Response

Activity A. Mark each item either *T* (true) or *F* (false).

_____ 1. In general, male students scored higher on the history proficiency test than female students did.

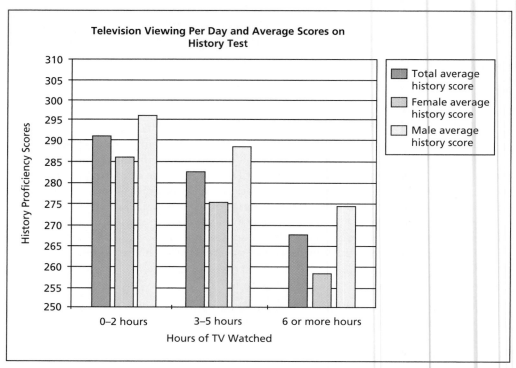

FIGURE 11.11 Bar Graph Showing the Relationship Between TV Watching and History Test Scores

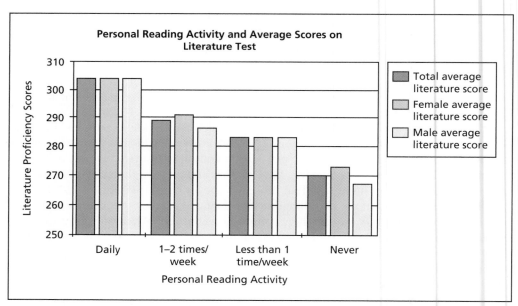

FIGURE 11.12 Bar Graph Showing the Relationship Between Reading Activity and Literature Test Scores

_____ 2. In general, students who spent six hours or more in TV viewing each day scored, on average, more than 20 points less on a history proficiency test than those who spent zero to two hours in TV viewing per day.

_____ 3. In general, female students who spent some time each day reading on their own scored the same on a literature proficiency test as male students who read each day.

———— 4. In general, the scores of male students on a literature proficiency test decreased as they spent less time reading on their own.

———— 5. In general, the scores of female students on a literature proficiency test increased as they spent more time reading on their own.

Activity B. Answer these questions in your notebook.

6. *Critical Thinking Question:* Write down two conclusions you can draw based on your interpretation of the graphs and your reading of the selection. ————————————

————————————————————————————————

————————————————————————————————

7. *Critical Application Question:* What can you do to increase your chances of success in college? ————————————————————————————

————————————————————————————————

EXTENDING WHAT YOU HAVE LEARNED

Going from Visuals to Words: Tables

Locate a table. Study it. Then write a paragraph in which you summarize what the table is saying. Be ready to share what you have written.

Going from Visuals to Words: Graphs

Locate a bar or line graph. Study it. Then write a paragraph in which you summarize what the graph is saying. Be ready to share what you have written.

Going from Visuals to Words: Line Drawings

Locate a line drawing. Study it. Then write a paragraph in which you summarize the data presented in the drawing. Be ready to share what you have written.

PART FIVE
SPECIALIZED READING

CHAPTER 12 Understanding Opinions and Persuasive Writing

CHAPTER 13 Understanding Definitions and Explanations

CHAPTER 14 Understanding Descriptions and Narratives

CHAPTER 15 Interpreting Style, Tone, and Mood

12

Understanding Opinions and Persuasive Writing

OBJECTIVE

In this chapter, you will develop strategies for understanding writing in which one of the author's purposes is to express his or her opinions.

UNDERSTANDING OPINIONS

At times, authors write to state their opinions or judgments and perhaps to persuade you to accept their point of view. Newspaper editorials, syndicated columns, political and social cartoons, and letters to the editor are forums for judgmental and persuasive writing. So are film and book reviews. Reading these pieces, you know you are dealing with opinion.

Opinions and judgments are found in a variety of other writing. Authors may have as their primary intent to explain or give an account. However, they color their explanation or account with their feelings. Those feelings give a point of view, or a *bias*, to their writing. Actually it is very difficult for writers to avoid bias and be completely impartial. Writers' personal experiences are sieves through which they filter information as they write.

DETECTING OPINION AND BIAS

What strategies can you use to detect that the author is presenting opinion rather than fact? What strategies can you use to detect an author's personal bias toward the subject? Here are four strategies.

A first strategy is to identify the kind of piece you are reading. Ask, "Is this an editorial? A column from the opinion page? A book or film review?" If the answer is yes, you are probably dealing with an opinion. A related strategy is to identify the publisher and writer. Ask, "Is the publisher an organization or group with a known point of view? Is the author known for supporting a particular view? Is he or she a well-known authority in that field?" For example, a selection published by an antiwar group and written by a leading pacifist is likely to contain opinion and reflect an antiwar point of view.

A second strategy is to notice words indicating that an author is giving opinion. Some words are obvious signals of opinion giving. An author states, "I believe," "I feel," or "I like," "I think." Other words that hint the author is advocating a particular course of action are "we should," "you ought to," "you should have," or "it would have been better to." Still other words send an evaluative message similar to the message carried by the grades A, B, C, D, and F assigned by professors:

unacceptable	acceptable	more acceptable	most acceptable
good	better	best	
invalid	least valid	valid	more valid
valuable	very valuable	invaluable	
worthless	worthy	worthwhile	
poorly done	well done		
unique	marvelous	terrible	outrageous

A third strategy is to think about an author's choice of words and what message he or she is sending through the specific words chosen. Words often communicate an implied, or associated, meaning that goes beyond a strict dictionary definition. The implied meaning that a word carries is called the *connotation*. The dictionary meaning (without the feelings and personal associations that people bring to a word) is the *denotation*. Some words communicate a positive connotation, others communicate a negative connotation, and others have no particular connotation.

For example, consider these three common words: *thin, slim,* and *skinny*. Of them, which communicates the most positive view, the most negative view, or a neutral view? On the lines provided, write the three words from the most negative to the most positive:

Most Negative Word	**Neutral Word**	**Most Positive Word**
1. _____	2. _____	3. _____

Consider these pairs of words. In each case, circle the one that carries the more positive message to you.

egghead	genius
Big and Tall Man's Shop	Fat-man's Shop
hard worker	grind
changed his mind	waffled on the issues

Consider these sets of words. In each case, circle the one that carries the most positive message to you. There is really no right answer.

beautiful	gorgeous	pretty
fat	obese	chubby
delicious	tasty	scrumptious
steaming	hot	scalding

As you read, you should be aware of words such as these that carry particularly positive or negative connotations. They are clues to an author's bias.

A fourth strategy is to ask, "Is there another side to the issue? How would someone with other beliefs have described the situation, place, or person in question? How would someone on the other side of an issue have explained it?"

CLARIFYING THE OPINION, ASSESSING THE PROOF, AND FORMULATING YOUR OWN OPINION: O/P/O

Once you have decided that a selection expresses an opinion, you must clarify what the author is saying—what his or her opinion is. To do this, you ask yourself, "What is this writer advocating?" In answering, state the author's opinion in your mind in your own words. This is the first "O" step: opinion clarification.

Generally a well-formulated judgment includes both the author's opinion and some support for that opinion—the proof. As you read opinion-stating paragraphs, therefore, an important task is to assess the validity of the judgment being expressed by considering the facts the author musters in support of it. To do this, ask, "What proof does the author offer in support of his or her opinion? Is the proof on target. Is it sufficient? Does the author prove his or her point?" Answering these questions in your mind, you are taking the "P" step.

In addition, you must ask, "How do I feel about this? Do I agree? Disagree? Why? Why not? Should I reserve judgment on this issue because the argument is insufficient to convince me either way?" In reading opinion and judgment, you should try to develop your own opinion. This is the final "O" step.

Reading the next selections, keep asking yourself the O/P/O questions identified in the previous section. Apply these strategies:

O/P/O
STRATEGY

→ Decide whether you are reading an opinion by
  - Considering the kind of piece you are reading,
  - Identifying words that indicate opinion,
  - Noting words that communicate positive or negative connotations, and
  - Asking yourself whether there is another way to view the facts.
→ Take the first "O" step: Clarify the author's opinion by restating it to yourself.
→ Take the "P" step: Assess the argument, or proof, that the author offers in support of his or her opinion. Ask, "Is it on target? Is it enough?"
→ Take the final "O" step: Generate your own opinion on the subject.

If you have trouble at any point, reread and fix up, using mind talk to state the author's opinion and his or her proof.

Figure 12.1 is a guide to help you as you clarify an author's opinion, assess the facts offered in support of it (the proof), and come up with your own opinion on the subject.

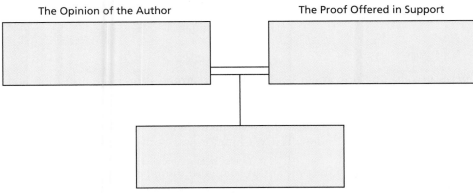

The Opinion of the Author   The Proof Offered in Support

Your Opinion Based on What You Have Read

FIGURE 12.1 A Chart for Interpreting Opinions: O/P/O

SELECTION 1

The Eight Best Presidents—and Why (LITERATURE—ESSAY)

A Reading Workshop

Expanding Your Vocabulary for Reading

Using the context and word elements, figure out the meaning of the italicized words. Check your ideas in the glossary. Record the meaning of the terms in your reading notebook.

1. By limiting himself to two terms, Washington set a *precedent* that other presidents followed for many years.

2. After years of peace and prosperity, people got *complacent* and began to believe that good times would last forever.

3. The rebels were *roundly* beaten by the well-trained troops. Few escaped injury or death.

4. The student took the job out of *economic* necessity; her financial condition required it.

5. That executive was known for his words of *deprecation.* He rarely, if ever, offered praise to his employees.

6. The business executives formed a *trust,* a combination of companies to control the production and price of goods. This is an illegal economic practice in this country.

7. The Greeks built a *pantheon* to honor their gods.

8. I do not want a *synthetic* diamond; I want a genuine one.

9. During the Middle Ages, the lord of the manor was the *sovereign* of the land. He had the power of life and death over all the people who lived on his estate.

Getting Ready to Read

Preview the selection by glancing over the title, author, and subheadings.

Reading with Meaning

Read each section of this selection. Keep asking yourself, "What is Truman's judgment of this president? What words tell me he is presenting his opinion? What facts support his opinion?" Working collaboratively, answer the questions in the margin after reading each subsection.

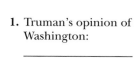

The Eight Best Presidents—and Why
Harry S. Truman

George Washington

There isn't any question about Washington's greatness. If his Administration had been a failure, there would have been no United States. He had all the background that caused him to know how to make it work, because he had worked under the Continental Congress. Some Presidents have limited their roles to being administrators of the laws without being leaders. But Washington was both a great administrator and a great leader.

   I guess, in fact, that the only anti-Washington thing I can say is that he made a mistake when he established the precedent of the two-term Presidency, and even there he had a good personal reason for wanting that, at least for himself. He was attacked viciously by the press of his day; he was called so many terrible things that he told friends

---

Did You KNOW?

Pan- means "all or every" and is a Greek root. *Theo-* is also from Greek and means "god." Related words are *panorama, panacea,* and *theology.*

Think about . . .

What questions do you ask yourself as part of your preview?

---

1. Truman's opinion of Washington:

_____

_____

_____

2. Circle words that indicate you are dealing with an opinion.

even during his first term that he wasn't going to run again. But Thomas Jefferson and James Madison and Alexander Hamilton persuaded him to go ahead and serve a second term and finally he did. After he'd gotten through his second term, though, he made up his mind that he just wouldn't take it anymore, and he quit. That established the precedent. . . .

Thomas Jefferson

Jefferson also had his share of press criticism and people who didn't like him, and I wonder how many people remember our history and realize how close Jefferson came to losing the election in 1800, and how close Aaron Burr came to being our third President. . . .

Jefferson was called a runaway President because he pushed through our purchase of Louisiana over a lot of opposition. I think Jefferson's purchase of Louisiana was one of the best decisions ever made because, if we hadn't taken over Louisiana, then either Britain, France, or Spain would have owned it and our country would have ended at the Mississippi River, whereas the greatest part of our development has been our ability to expand beyond the Mississippi. I don't like this talk about runaway Presidents, because the truth is that a President just does what he has to do.

Andrew Jackson

Jackson was elected after a period of what they called in James Monroe's time "the era of good feeling." Well, when the era of good feeling got to feeling too good, meaning that the people and the government became too complacent and too lazy, why, the country went to the dogs, as it has always done. You have got to have opposition if you're going to keep a republic going. Old Jackson remedied that, and he did it in a way that was perfectly satisfactory to all concerned. The economic royalists, the favored few, had control of the government by controlling the finances of the country. A man named Nicholas Biddle and his Bank of the United States had all the government's money, and Jackson took the money away from him and in effect put all the dollar bills back into the Treasury of the United States, where they ought to be, by spreading the funds into various state banks. And, of course, he was roundly abused for doing things of that sort.

James Knox Polk

This choice may surprise some people. Polk isn't much thought about these days. First, he exercised his powers of the Presidency as I think they should be exercised. He was President during the Mexican War, in an age when the terrible burden of making decisions in a war was entirely in the hands of the President. And when that came about, he decided that that was much more important than going to parties and shaking hands with people.

Second, he bought the Southwest part of the country for just about the same price that Jefferson paid for Louisiana; and third, he did something that most of the rest of us who were Presidents weren't able to do: He decided when he went in there that he would only serve one term, and that's what he did. He knew exactly what he wanted to do in a specified period of time and did it, and when he got through with it he went home. He said a moving thing on his retirement: "I now retire as a servant and regain my position as a sovereign." He was right, absolutely right. I've been through it, and I know.

Abraham Lincoln

Lincoln was a strong executive who saved the government, saved the United States. He was a President who understood people, and, when it came time to make decisions, he was willing to take the responsibility and make those decisions, no matter how difficult they were. He knew how to treat people and how to make a decision stick, and that's why his is regarded as such a great Administration.

Carl Sandburg and a lot of others have tried to make something out of Lincoln that he wasn't. He was a decent man, a good politician, and a great President, and they've tried to build up things that he never even thought about. I'll bet a dollar and a half that

3. Put checks by the reasons Truman gives to support his opinion.

1. Truman's opinion of the Louisiana Purchase:

    _____

    _____

    _____

2. Circle a word that indicates you are dealing with an opinion.

3. Put a check by the reason Truman gives to support his opinion.

1. Truman's opinion of Jackson: _____

    _____

    _____

2. Circle words that indicate you are dealing with an opinion.

3. Put a check by the reason Truman gives to support his opinion.

1. Truman's opinion of Polk: _____

    _____

    _____

2. Circle words that indicate you are dealing with an opinion.

3. Put checks by the reasons Truman gives to support his opinion.

1. Truman's opinion of Lincoln: _____

    _____

    _____

2. Circle words that indicate you are dealing with an opinion.

3. Put checks by the reasons Truman gives to support his opinion.

if you read Sandburg's biography of Lincoln, you'll find things put into Lincoln's mouth and mind that never even occurred to him. He was a good man who was in the place where he ought to have been at the time important events were taking place, but when they write about him as though he belongs in the pantheon of the gods, that's not the man he really was. He was the best kind of ordinary man, and when I say that he was an ordinary man, I mean that as high praise, not deprecation. That's the highest praise you can give a man, that he's one of the people and becomes distinguished in the service that he gives other people. He was one of the people, and he wanted to stay that way. And he was that way until the day he died. One of the reasons he was assassinated was because he didn't feel important enough to have the proper guards around him at Ford's Theatre.

Grover Cleveland

1. Truman's opinion of Cleveland: _____ _____ _____

2. Circle words that indicate you are dealing with an opinion.

3. Put checks by the reasons Truman gives to support his opinion.

At least Cleveland was a great President in his first term; in his second term, he wasn't the same Grover Cleveland he was to begin with. Cleveland reestablished the Presidency by being not only a Chief Executive but also a leader. Cleveland spent most of his time in his first term working on bills that came from the Congress, and he vetoed a tremendous pile of bills that were passed strictly for the purpose of helping out people who had voted for the Republican ticket. He also saw to it that a lot of laws passed, if he felt those laws were needed for the good of the general public, even if the laws weren't popular with some members of the Congress.

For the most part, however, Cleveland was a considerably less impressive man in his second term. He had a terrible time with strikes, and he called out the soldiers, and they fired on the strikers. It was also during Cleveland's second term that a number of smaller companies got together and formed great big companies for the suppression of competition. That's why I say Cleveland was a great President only in his first term.

Woodrow Wilson

1. Truman's opinion of Wilson: _____ _____ _____

2. Circle words that indicate you are dealing with an opinion.

3. Put checks by the reasons Truman gives to support his opinion.

I've been asked which Presidents served as models for me when I was President myself, and the answer is that there were three of them. Two were Jefferson and Jackson, and the third was Woodrow Wilson. In many ways Wilson was the greatest of the greats. He established the Federal Reserve Board. He established the Federal Trade Commission. He didn't make a great publicity stunt of being a trustbuster, the way Teddy Roosevelt did, but the trust situation was never really met until Wilson became President. Wilson also established the League of Nations, which didn't succeed but which served as a blueprint for the United Nations, which might succeed yet, despite its problems.

All a good President tries to do is accomplish things for the good of the people, and if you want to call that liberal, then I'm with you. I guess the best way to describe Wilson, if I've got to use a label, is to say that he was a commonsense liberal. He wasn't one of these synthetic liberals who aren't very liberal to people who think differently from the way they do. He was a genuine liberal who used his heart and his brain.

Franklin Delano Roosevelt

1. Truman's opinion of Roosevelt: _____ _____ _____

2. Circle words that indicate you are dealing with an opinion.

3. Put checks by the reasons Truman gives to support his opinion.

It goes without saying that I was highly impressed by him for a thousand reasons, but a main reason is that he inherited a situation that was almost as bad as the one Lincoln had, and he dealt with it. And he was always able to make decisions. Presidents have to make decisions if they're going to get anywhere, and those Presidents who couldn't make decisions are the ones who caused all the trouble.

It took a President who understood the United States and the world, like Roosevelt, to come along and start to get the country back on its feet again in the Depression, and also to make Americans remember that we're a world power and have to act like a world power.

We also, of course, got the United Nations as a result of Roosevelt's Administration and mine, which is exactly what the League of Nations was supposed to be in the first place. I'm not saying that the United Nations is a perfect organization, or ever will be. It's far from flawless, and it's weak in many ways. But at least it's a start.

Monitoring Comprehension and Writing in Response

Complete Parts A and B collaboratively, Parts C and D independently.

A. Place an *F* before statements of fact and an *O* before statements of opinion.

_____ 1. George Washington was the first president of the United States.

_____ 2. Thomas Jefferson was elected president in 1800.

_____ 3. Washington was both a great administrator and a great leader.

_____ 4. You need opposition if you're going to keep a republic going.

_____ 5. A good president is going to get criticized.

_____ 6. Jackson remedied the situation in a way that was satisfactory to everyone.

_____ 7. When Polk said, "I now retire as a servant and regain my position as a sovereign," he was absolutely right.

_____ 8. The Louisiana Purchase occurred during Jefferson's administration.

_____ 9. Lincoln was a strong executive.

_____ 10. Lincoln was an ordinary man.

_____ 11. Cleveland was a great president during his first term but a poor one in his second term.

_____ 12. Cleveland spent a great deal of time working on bills that came from Congress.

_____ 13. Wilson helped establish the League of Nations.

_____ 14. Wilson was a genuine liberal who used his heart and his brain.

_____ 15. Franklin Roosevelt was a great president because he was always able to make decisions.

_____ 16. The United Nations is far from flawless, and it is weak in many ways.

_____ 17. Truman believed that Woodrow Wilson was a great president.

_____ 18. Truman believed that big companies were not good for the country.

_____ 19. Big companies are not good for the country.

_____ 20. Wilson was the greatest of the greats.

B. With a partner or two, complete the O/P/O chart in Figure 12.1 to clarify the opinion that Truman states about one president. Each group should select a different president and be prepared to present its chart to the class.

C. Choose some words from the selection vocabulary to include in your personal vocabulary list. Then place the words from this list in the space provided. Use each word once. Cross out options as you use them.

complacent	pantheon	sovereign
deprecatory	precedent	synthetic
economic	roundly	trusts

1. Before the exam, the student was far from _____; he had not studied, and he feared he would fail.

2. The _____ situation in the country was questionable; interest rates and unemployment were high.

3. I buy only genuine articles. Do not try to sell me something that is _____.

4. The _____ had many servants to do her bidding.

5. That teacher is not known for praising his students. Rather, he has a reputation for making _____ remarks.

6. The tennis star was _____ beaten in the championship match. Right from the beginning, she didn't have a chance.

7. Going into the basilica in Florence, I felt as though I was entering the _____ of the gods.

8. During Cleveland's administration, smaller companies got together to form _____ to suppress competition.

9. That court case set the _____ for the cases to follow. Future judges referred to the case in making their decisions.

D. Of all the presidents, which do you believe was the greatest? Write a paragraph in which you state your opinion and support that opinion with facts. Or choose the president whom you believe was the poorest and write a paragraph in which you state the reasons for your opinion. If possible, check the Web at http://fos.net/users/collect/uspres.html for a few facts about each president and his signature.

SELECTION 2

The Genius of Mark Twain: Discovery of Huck Finn "Draft" Underlines Author's Greatness (NEWSPAPER COLUMN)

Independent Study

Expanding Your Vocabulary for Reading

Using context and word elements, figure out the meaning of each italicized word. Check your ideas in the glossary and record the meaning of the term in your notebook.

1. She spoke in a *dialect* of English that I had trouble understanding; it was different from the variety of English I speak.

2. Mark Twain is considered a *literary* giant; he wrote many great books and contributed to our reading pleasure.

3. The sovereign *mandated* that all young people serve in the military.

4. *Legions* of people flock to the seaside in the summertime to enjoy the sun and the surf; because of this, the beach was crowded.

5. Because he wanted only real, or genuine, articles, he bought an *authentic* eighteenth-century table.

6. That child was *incorrigible;* he would not do anything he was told to do. Regardless of how often he was punished, he kept misbehaving.

7. The woman was *obsessed* with the idea that she would win the lottery; as a result, she spent thousands of dollars buying chances.

8. She had the *foresight* to take out insurance in case of accident; as a result, she was prepared when misfortune struck.

9. The council *banned* the sale of the book in the city; they did not want people reading it.

10. The author spent many months writing the *manuscript* for his book. When his book was published, however, the church banned it.

11. He has an *irrepressible* sense of humor; nothing could stop him from telling a joke.

Getting Ready to Read

This article is from the "Viewpoint" page of a newspaper. Written by Lawrence Hall, a columnist who is African-American, it is similar to the articles you find on the editorial pages of a regional newspaper. You should make it a habit to read a regional newspaper, especially the editorial pages.

Preview the article by reading the title and the first, second, and last paragraphs.

Reading with Meaning

Read the selection. Keep asking, "What is Hall's judgment of Twain and Huck Finn? What words does he use that tell he is dealing with opinion? What facts does he cite to support his judgment?" Then answer the questions in the margin.

The Genius of Mark Twain: Discovery of Huck Finn "Draft" Underlines Author's Greatness

Lawrence Hall

Recently, I pulled from the bookshelf the *Illustrated Works of Mark Twain* and reread *Huckleberry Finn*. Needless to say, I was so transported back in time that the entire reading—which I accomplished in a day—was mindboggling. It was, truly, an incredible experience. There I was on a raft, on the Mississippi with such characters as the incorrigible, homeless Huck Finn who escaped from "civilization" with the slave Jim. And as they got caught up in funny and violent experiences, Huck and Jim spoke a strange kind of southern dialect which, at first, was difficult to comprehend until my eyes and brain became familiar with the language.

What prompted me to reexperience this book was the announcement by a well-known auction house of a literary find. The first half of the original text of *Huckleberry Finn*, written in longhand, was recently found in a trunk in a Hollywood attic. The second half of the original manuscript is in the custody of the Buffalo, N.Y., public library.

The startling thing about this discovery was the 665-page manuscript differed greatly from the published text which many of us may once have read and loved. For example, the manuscript features a dramatic scene in which Jim discusses his experiences with corpses and ghosts on a stormy night, and a 54-page fight scene aboard the raft.

Rereading this book reminded me of the sad state of humor in this country. There is so much bad, ugly and violent humor in these strange times—so much so that most folks haven't the slightest notion of what humor is all about.

The irrepressible Twain, "the Lincoln of our literature," was probably one of the few wits in this nation to employ humor successfully throughout his life. Twain, whose real name was Samuel Langhorne Clemens, held that humor "is only a fragrance, a decoration. Humor must not professedly teach and it must not professedly preach, but it must do both if it would live forever. By forever, I mean 30 years."

Much of Twain's literary work has stood the test of time—at least more than his mandated 30 years. H. L. Mencken hailed him as "the one authentic giant of our literature . . . the full equal of Cervantes and Molière, Swift, and Defoe." The proof of Mencken's contention can be seen clearly in *Huckleberry Finn*.

Now, I know there are legions of folks—including many black Americans—who look upon *Huckleberry Finn* as nothing more than a racist tract, with Jim stumbling and bumbling through the book, ridiculed and treated as if he were sub-human. But, it's very

Did You KNOW?

Script- or *scrib-* means "writing" and is from the Latin word *scribere*. Words with the root are *manuscript* (*manu-,* meaning "hand"), *scripture, scribble,* and *prescription.*

Think about . . .

What questions do you ask yourself as you preview?

1. Circle some words that suggest Hall is stating his opinion rather than facts.

2. What is Hall's opinion of *Huckleberry Finn?*

3. Underline a sentence from the paragraph that states a fact.

4. Underline a sentence that states a fact.

5. Circle a line from the paragraph that gives an opinion.

6. Circle the point at which Hall is expressing an opinion in this paragraph. Underline a fact.

7. Mencken wrote that Twain was an equal of Cervantes. Opinion or fact? Why?

8. Hall says that it's very easy to get hung up reading this book for racial slights. Opinion or fact? What makes you think so?

9. When Keough calls *Huckleberry Finn* a book that has no peer, is he expressing opinion or fact? How do you know?

10. When Hall writes that Twain took several years to complete a book, is he expressing opinion or fact?

11. Was the library committee's statement that the book was immoral fact or opinion?

12. The book went on to sell 500,000 copies. Is this fact or opinion?

13. When Hall concludes with the statement, "Ah, what riches Twain left for his readers," is he expressing opinion or fact?

easy to get hung up reading this book for possible racial slights and in the process miss the fine humor which flows from Twain's pen.

This is one of the main points of William Keough, an English professor at Fitchburg State College in Massachusetts in his new book, *Punchlines: The Violence of American Humor.* "*Huckleberry Finn* is a book all African-Americans should insist on; it is a book to make white America blush. Huckleberry Finn still shocks and dazzles. . . . *Huckleberry Finn* is certainly not a book without flaws; but as a portrait of frontier American society, warts and all, it has no peer."

Twain wrote this book in fits and starts, and tortured himself trying to find a way to end it. But that was the way he normally worked, taking several years to complete a book. When he completed the book, Twain sold it by subscription in advance of publication, and easily collected 40,000 people willing to buy a copy.

After it was finally published, the Concord, Mass., public library committee banned the book in 1887, claiming it was subversive, immoral and not wholesome literature for America's reading public.

Ironically, less than a century later, the Congress of Racial Equality (CORE) in the late 1950s successfully sued to have the book banned in Brooklyn because of what it perceived to be racial slurs throughout the book.

Nonetheless, Twain saw a bigger profit in his book being banned by the library. He declared, "That will sell 25,000 copies of our book for sure!" The book went on to sell 500,000 copies then, and today it's difficult to ascertain how many millions of copies have been sold.

One thing is certain, though. The profit from *Huckleberry Finn* helped to feed Twain's obsession with get-rich schemes. For instance, he toyed with investing in, among other things, a carpet-pattern machine and a mechanical organ. Alas, Twain lacked foresight in his investments. He foolishly decided not to invest in Alexander Graham Bell's telephone because he didn't see it as a sound risk. But he lost $300,000 on a new typesetting machine, and other ventures.

Thank goodness, Twain was a better writer than an investor in get-rich schemes. The newly discovered manuscript of *Huckleberry Finn* at least will pay off, with a new version of life on the Mississippi River aboard a raft. Ah, what riches Twain left for his readers.

Monitoring Comprehension

Complete the chart in Figure 12.2 based on the questions in item 1. Then answer the other questions in the space provided.

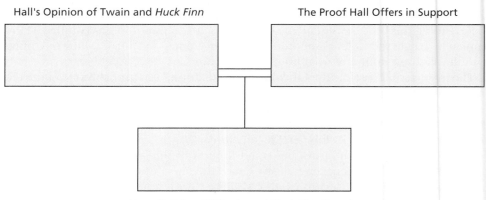

FIGURE 12.2   A Chart for Interpreting Hall's Opinion of Twain and *Huckleberry Finn:* O/P/O

1. What is Lawrence Hall's opinion of Mark Twain? or *Huckleberry Finn?* What proof does Hall offer in support of his opinion? What is your opinion? On the O/P/O chart in Figure 12.2, record the answers to these questions.

2. What words that carry a positive connotation does Hall use to help you see his point of view? List some here.

   _____

   _____

3. Hall quotes Professor Keough. What is Keough's opinion of *Huckleberry Finn?*

   _____

   _____

4. *Critical Thinking Question:* Do you agree with Hall and Keough? Explain why or why not.

   _____

   _____

   _____

   _____

Reviewing Highlighted Vocabulary

Fill in the blanks with words from this list. Use context clues to help you.

authentic	foresight	legions	manuscript
banned	incorrigible	literary	obsessed
dialects	irrepressible	mandates	

1. Shakespeare is considered one of the _____ giants of all times.

2. Twain worked several years completing the _____ for one of his books.

3. The college student was so _____ with keeping thin that he barely ate anything.

4. The writers of the Constitution had the _____ to mandate a government with a system of checks and balances.

5. There are numerous _____ in the English language; where you grow up determines which one you speak.

6. The youngster was _____; he would not obey his parents or his teachers.

7. The countryside was infested with _____ of grasshoppers. The grasshoppers were so numerous that there were no crops left after they arrived.

8. The restaurant _____ anyone from entering who was not dressed in formal attire.

9. I have an _____ first edition of that manuscript. I know it is genuine.

10. Mark Twain had an _____ sense of humor. It showed up in everything he wrote.

11. The law _____ that the police explain a prisoner's rights to him or her before questioning.

SELECTION 3

School Thoughts from *I Know Why the Caged Bird Sings* (LITERATURE—AUTOBIOGRAPHY)

In-Text Test

Expanding Vocabulary for Reading

Use the context and word elements to figure out the meaning of each italicized term. Check the glossary if you are unsure. Write the meaning in your notebook.

1. The prime minister had an *aura* of authority that made her stand out from the others in the room.

2. The people were so convinced of their *invincibility* that when they lost the war, they could hardly accept it.

3. Until his mother called a halt, the older boy *intimidated* his younger brother, making him fearful and timid.

4. The shopper was struck by the *rarefied*, or very refined, atmosphere in the elite store.

5. I experienced severe *trauma* each time I recalled the appalling accident.

6. His *florid* complexion indicated to me that the man had been drinking.

7. The teacher told me to *elaborate* on what I had said, but I could not think of anything more on the topic.

8. The student's interest *diminished* as time went on; soon she was asleep.

9. The dollar is the major unit of *currency* in the United States, whereas the pound is the major unit of currency in England.

10. Her behavior was often *frivolous;* as a result, she got a reputation for not being a serious person.

Getting Ready to Read

Preview the title, the name of the author, and the introductory matter before reading. If possible, check this Web site for poems by Angelou: www.pics.com/~spyder/bitrswet.htm.

Reading with Meaning

Read the selection to see how Maya Angelou felt about George Washington High School and her teacher there. As you read, think about similar experiences you had in high school.

Did You
KNOW?

Vinc- or *vict-* means "to conquer." Here it is in *invincibility*. Related words are *victim, victory,* and *convince*. Remember that the prefix *in-* has two possible meanings: "in or into" and "not." Which meaning does it carry in the word *invincibility?*

Think
about . . .

What questions and thoughts go through your mind as you preview?

School Thoughts from *I Know Why the Caged Bird Sings*
Maya Angelou

In this selection Maya Angelou describes her experiences, first in her local high school and then in George Washington High School in San Francisco.

Although my grades were very good (I had been put up two semesters on my arrival from Stamps), I found myself unable to settle down in high school. It was an institution for girls near my house, and the young ladies were faster, brasher, meaner and more prejudiced than any I had met at Lafayette County Training School. Many of the Negro girls were, like me, straight from the South, but they had known or claimed to have known the bright lights of Big D (Dallas) or T Town (Tulsa, Oklahoma), and their language bore up their claims. They strutted with an aura of invincibility, and along with some of the Mexican students who put knives in their tall pompadours they absolutely intimidated the white girls and those Black and Mexican students who had no shield of fearlessness. Fortunately I was transferred to George Washington High School.

The beautiful buildings [of George Washington High] sat on a moderate hill in the white residential district, some sixty blocks from the Negro neighborhood. For the first semester, I was one of three Blacks in the school, and in that rarefied atmosphere I came to love my people more. Mornings as the streetcar traversed my ghetto I experienced a mixture of dread and trauma. I knew that all too soon we would be out of my familiar setting, and Blacks who were on the streetcar when I got on would all be gone and I alone would face the forty blocks of neat streets, smooth lawns, white houses and rich children.

In the evenings on the way home the sensations were joy, anticipation and relief at the first sign which said BARBECUE or DO DROP INN or HOME COOKING or at the first brown faces on the streets. I recognized that I was again in my country.

In the school itself I was disappointed to find that I was not the most brilliant or even nearly the most brilliant student. The white kids had better vocabularies than I and, what was more appalling, less fear in the classrooms. They never hesitated to hold up their hands in response to a teacher's question; even when they were wrong they were wrong aggressively, while I had to be certain about all my facts before I dared to call attention to myself.

George Washington High School was the first real school I attended. My entire stay there might have been time lost if it hadn't been for the unique personality of a brilliant teacher. Miss Kirwin was that rare educator who was in love with information. I will always believe that her love of teaching came not so much from her liking for students but from her desire to make sure that some of the things she knew would find repositories so that they could be shared again.

She and her maiden sister worked in the San Francisco city school system for over twenty years. My Miss Kirwin, who was a tall, florid, buxom lady with battleship-gray hair, taught civics and current events. At the end of a term in her class our books were as clean and the pages as stiff as they had been when they were issued to us. Miss Kirwin's students were never or very rarely called upon to open textbooks.

She greeted each class with "Good day, ladies and gentlemen." I had never heard an adult speak with such respect to teenagers. (Adults usually believe that a show of honor diminishes their authority.) "In today's *Chronicle* there was an article on the mining industry in the Carolinas (or some such distant subject). I am certain that all of you have read the article. I would like someone to elaborate on the subject for me."

After the first two weeks in her class, I, along with all other excited students, read the San Francisco papers, *Time* magazine, *Life* and everything else available to me. Miss Kirwin proved Bailey right. He had told me once that "all knowledge is spendable currency, depending on the market."

There were no favorite students. No teacher's pets. If a student pleased her during a particular period, he could not count on special treatment in the next day's class, and that was as true the other way around. Each day she faced us with a clean slate and acted as if ours were clean as well. Reserved and firm in her opinions, she spent no time in indulging the frivolous.

She was stimulating instead of intimidating. Where some of the other teachers went out of their way to be nice to me—to be a "liberal" with me—and others ignored me completely, Miss Kirwin never seemed to notice that I was Black and therefore different. I was Miss Johnson and if I had the answer to a question she posed I was never given any more than the word "Correct," which was what she said to every other student with the correct answer.

Years later when I returned to San Francisco I made visits to her classroom. She always remembered that I was Miss Johnson, who had a good mind and should be doing something with it. I was never encouraged on those visits to loiter or linger about her desk.

Think
about . . .
What words tell you that Angelou is stating opinion? What proof does she supply to support her opinion?

She acted as if I must have had other visits to make. I often wondered if she knew she was the only teacher I remembered.

Monitoring Comprehension and Writing

Answer on your own. Be ready to talk about and support your answers.

1. What was Angelou's opinion of the "Negro girls straight from the South"?

_____

_____

_____

2. What proof does the author present to support her opinion?

_____

_____

_____

3. How did Angelou feel as she rode the streetcar to George Washington High School? Why do you think she felt that way?

_____

_____

_____

4. Describe when you have felt the same way.

_____

_____

_____

5. What was Maya Angelou's opinion of the "white kids" at George Washington High?

_____

_____

_____

6. What proof does the author present in support of her opinion?

_____

_____

_____

7. What was Angelou's opinion of her teacher, Miss Kirwin?

_____

_____

_____

8. What proof does she present to support her opinion?

_____

_____

_____

9. How were the students in Miss Kirwin's class able to learn if they never opened their books? How do you know this?

_____

_____

_____

10. Someone named Bailey had told Angelou that "all knowledge is spendable currency, depending on the market." What did he mean by that? Do you agree? Why? Why not? Support your opinion with reasons.

_____

_____

_____

_____

11. What is your opinion of Maya Angelou? Write a paragraph in your notebook in which you express your opinion, and support your opinion with reasons.

_____

_____

12. Do you remember a teacher from elementary or high school whom you admired? Following Maya Angelou's model, write a paragraph or two describing that teacher. In your paragraph, state your opinion of him or her, and include examples or points to support your opinion. To get started, jot down any words that come to mind to describe the teacher. Then build your paragraph with those words.

Reviewing Highlighted Words

Place the words from this list in the appropriate spaces in the sentences.

aura	elaborate	intimidate	rarefied
currency	florid	invincibility	trauma
diminished	frivolous		

1. The bully tried to _____ me, but I was not afraid of him.

2. There is a real _____ of strength and gentleness about Maya Angelou; her distinctive air makes her stand out among other writers.

3. If you cannot _____ on that topic, tell me what you know about any other related topic.

4. When the wind _____ and the rain stopped, I knew the storm was over.

5. When I traveled in France, I had to learn to use the French _____ because there are no dollars and cents in that country.

6. Her _____ behavior annoyed us. We wanted to be serious, but she acted in the opposite way.

7. She experienced extreme _____ at the death of her father.

8. In the _____ atmosphere of that elite college, I grew restless for the ordinary happenings I was accustomed to at home.

9. I was never convinced of the _____ of our army. As a result, I was not surprised by the defeat.

10. The speaker was so angry that his face became _____. I feared he would have a heart attack.

Select several of the new vocabulary words and enter them into your personal vocabulary list to use in writing and speaking.

EXTENDING WHAT YOU HAVE LEARNED

Applying Reading Strategies

Select an editorial or a syndicated column from a newspaper. Record the title, author, date, and newspaper on an index card. Read the column, applying the strategies for reading persuasive writing. On the card, record the main topic of the column, the point of view of the writer, and the evidence the writer cites in support of the point of view. Does the author make you agree with him or her?

Extending Your Vocabulary

Select several of the words featured in this chapter to record in your personal vocabulary list. Include a model sentence for each. Try to use your words in speaking and writing.

Writing an Opinion with Supporting Proof

1. Think about an issue of current interest. Phrase that issue as a question. For example, "Should smoking be banned in all public buildings? Should college tuition be raised? Should candidates for public office be judged on the way they handle their private lives?" Decide how you feel about the issue. In your notebook write a paragraph or two in which you state your opinion, and support that opinion with reasons.

2. Write a brief summary of a book you have read or a film you have seen. Then express your opinion of the book or film and support your opinion by describing things about the film or book that you liked. Do this in your reading notebook.

13

Understanding Definitions and Explanations

OBJECTIVE

In this chapter, you will develop strategies for reading different kinds of writing, specifically

1. Writing that is intended to define, and
2. Writing that is intended to explain.

These strategies are useful in reading college texts, especially scientific texts.

READING DEFINITIONS AND EXPLANATIONS

Not all writing communicates the same kinds of meanings. Some sentences in a selection are definitions. In these sentences, an author states the meaning of a word or phrase by giving qualities associated with it. In contrast, some sentences provide explanations, describe something, give an account of what happened, or express opinions. This chapter provides strategies for dealing with definitions and explanations. These strategies are important as you read technical content in college courses and study for exams.

DEFINITIONS

Some textbook authors use clue words that tell you they are introducing an important term and are going to define it; they connect a term and a definition using such words as *is, means, refers to, is called,* and *is termed.* Authors may print important words in boldface or italics. A basic strategy for recognizing a definition is to watch out for these clue words.

Study the following sentences from *Human Anatomy and Physiology,* by John W. Hole, Jr., and identify the clue words that indicate that a term is being defined.

1. "*Plasma* is the straw-colored, liquid portion of the blood in which the various solids are suspended."

   • What is the simple clue word that links the term *plasma* with its definition?

   _____

2. "The term *hemostasis* refers to the stoppage of bleeding, which is vitally important when blood vessels are damaged."

   • What is the clue phrase that links the term *hemostasis* with its definition?

   _____

3. "If a blood clot forms in a vessel abnormally, it is termed a *thrombus*. If the clot becomes dislodged or if a fragment of it breaks loose and is carried away by the blood flow, it is called an *embolus*."

   • What is the clue phrase that ties the term *thrombus* to its definition?

   _____

Did You
KNOW?
Hem- means "blood."
A related word is
hemoglobin.

• What is the clue phrase that ties the term *embolus* to its definition?

_____

Some textbooks place definitions of technical terms in the margin. When that happens, read the margin definition before reading the paragraph that contains the term.

Strategies for Reading Definitions

Because definitions, especially in the natural sciences, may be complex, a first strategy for understanding a definition is to reread the definition when you encounter one and to picture what is being defined in your mind's eye. This process of mental picturing is called *visualizing*. Visualizing is particularly helpful in grasping definitions when you are dealing with concrete objects. In cases where definitions are very complex, it helps to sketch your mental image on paper.

A second useful strategy is to paraphrase the definition. *Paraphrasing* means saying it to yourself in your own words. A related strategy is to devise an equation that puts together the term and its definition and write it in the margin of your text. A good check is to compare your equation to the definition in the glossary of the book.

How do these strategies work? Here is an example: Reading the definition of *plasma* just given, you might picture in your mind's eye the straw-colored liquid without its suspended solids. You might paraphrase by saying to yourself, "*Plasma* is the liquid part of the blood without the solids." You then might build an equation like this:

Plasma = Liquid part of blood without the suspended solids

If you are studying a textbook section on which you will be tested, you might record that equation in your notebook or in the margin of the text. Finally, you compare your equation to the glossary definition and repeat the definition in your head.

In sum, your strategy for working with a definition has these components:

DEFINITION COMPREHENSION STRATEGY

→ Be alert for words that indicate you are dealing with a definition.

→ Reread the definition and picture what is being defined in your mind's eye.

→ Paraphrase the definition in your own words.

→ Devise an equation that includes the term and its definition. Record the equation in a vocabulary section of your notebook or in the margin of the text. This strategy is useful if you are studying a textbook for a college course in which you must take a test.

→ Monitor your comprehension by comparing your equation to the definition in the glossary of the book and repeating the definition in your head.

Reread the other natural science definitions on page 233. In your mind, state them in your own words. Then write them as equations in the space provided.

1. Hemostasis = _____

2. Thrombus = _____

3. Embolus = _____

Practicing the Strategies

Preview each short section by noting the title and the words in italics. Your purpose in reading is to find out the meaning of the italicized terms.

Think
about . . .

Why is it important in science courses to know the vocabulary? How do you handle new terms when you meet them in college reading?

Think
about . . .

Do you have to take science as part of your college program? In such courses, you may have to read some material that does not interest you. What do you say to yourself in your mind as you read this material? How do you handle yourself?

WORKSHOP 1

Anatomy and Physiology
John W. Hole, Jr.

Anatomy is the branch of science that deals with the structure of body parts, their forms and arrangements. Anatomists observe body parts grossly and microscopically and describe them as accurately and in as much detail as possible. *Physiology,* on the other hand, is concerned with the functions of body parts—what they do and how they do it. Physiologists are interested in finding out how such parts carry on life processes. In addition to using the same observational techniques as the anatomists, physiologists are likely to conduct experiments and make use of complex laboratory equipment.   [101 words]

1. Reread the definition of *anatomy.* Tell it to yourself in your own words. Then write an equation with the term and the definition.

   Anatomy = _____

   _____

2. Reread the definition of *physiology,* paraphrase it, and then write an equation with the term and the definition.

   Physiology = _____

   _____

Did You KNOW?

Logy- and *-nomy* are Greek combining forms that work like suffixes and mean "science or study of." Other words that carry these forms are *psychology* and *geology, economy* and *astronomy.*

WORKSHOP 2

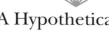

A Hypothetical Cell
John W. Hole, Jr.

Because cells vary so greatly in size, shape, and function, it is not possible to describe a "typical" cell. However, for purposes of discussion, it is convenient to imagine that one exists. Such a hypothetical cell would contain parts observed in many kinds of cells, even though some of these cells in fact lack parts included in the imagined structure.

 Commonly a cell consists of two major parts, one within the other and each surrounded by a thin membrane. The inner portion is called the *cell nucleus,* and it is enclosed by a *nuclear membrane.* A mass of fluid called cytoplasm surrounds the nucleus and is, in turn, encircled by a *cell membrane.*   [119 words]

1. Reread the sentence that begins "Such a hypothetical cell. . . ." What is a hypothetical cell? Now write an equation that defines one.

   Hypothetical cell = a cell that _____

2. Picture, or visualize, a hypothetical cell with its two parts and two membranes. Sketch your mental image here. Label the parts.

3. Reread the sentence that includes the term *cell nucleus*. Put together a definition and record it here in equation form:

Cell nucleus = _____

4. Reread the sentence that includes the term *cytoplasm*. Put together a definition and record it here in equation form:

Cytoplasm = _____

_____

Think
about . . .

What are two things you
can do after reading to
clarify definitions in
your mind?

5. Reread the sentence that includes the term *cell membrane*. Tell yourself a definition of the term and record it here in equation form:

Cell membrane = _____

6. Now reread the sentence that includes *nuclear membrane*. Tell yourself a definition of the term and record it here in equation form:

Nuclear membrane = _____

_____

7. Finally, referring to your equations, revisualize the cell, and make any changes in the sketch in item 2 that you believe to be necessary based on your definitions.

WORKSHOP 3 _____

The Cell Membrane
John W. Hole, Jr.

The *cell membrane* is the outermost limit of the living material within a cell. It is extremely thin—visible only with the aid of an electron microscope—but is flexible and somewhat elastic. Although this membrane can seal off minute breaks and heal itself, if it is damaged too greatly the cell contents are likely to escape and the cell will die.

In addition to its function of maintaining the wholeness of the cell, the membrane serves as a gateway through which chemicals enter and leave. However, this "gate" acts in a special way: it allows some substances to pass and excludes others. When a membrane functions in this way, it is said to be *selectively permeable*. A *permeable* membrane, on the other hand, is one that allows all materials to pass through freely.   [140 words]

1. Picture in your mind's eye a selectively permeable membrane. Then paraphrase the definition and write an equation:

Selectively permeable membrane = a membrane that _____

_____

2. Picture in your mind's eye a permeable membrane. Then paraphrase the definition and write an equation:

Permeable membrane = a membrane that _____

_____

SELECTION 1
Diffusion and Osmosis (BIOLOGY)

Independent Study

Expanding Your Vocabulary for Reading

The word *concentration* in the next selection applies to the amount of matter in a particular area. For example, where there is a high concentration of people, there would be many people in a particular area; where there is a low concentration of people, there would be few there. In the following diagrams each dot represents one person. Label the diagrams given here to show areas of high and low concentration. Label one *high concentration;* label the other *low concentration.*

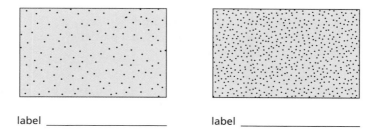

label _____   label _____

A *molecule* is a particle of matter. An *ion* is an electrically charged particle. See whether you can figure out the meaning of *haphazard* by using context clues as you read.

Getting Ready to Read

Preview the selection. What questions do you ask yourself as part of your preview? Your purpose in reading is to understand the definition of the italicized words.

Reading with Meaning

As you read, apply your reading-for-definition strategy: Record in the margin a sketch of your mental picture of what is going on, an equation that clarifies the definition given at that point in the text, or both. Do not do this after reading the entire passage. Do it as you go along. Read a definition. Stop to visualize, sketch, paraphrase, and write an equation.

Diffusion and Osmosis
John W. Hole, Jr.

Diffusion is the process by which molecules or ions scatter or spread from regions where they are in higher concentrations toward regions where they are in lower concentrations. As a rule, this phenomenon involves the movement of molecules or ions in gases or liquids.

Actually, molecules in gases and molecules and ions in body fluids are constantly moving at high speeds. Each of these particles travels in a separate path along a straight line until it collides and bounces off some other particle. Then it moves in another direction, only to collide again and change direction once more. Such motion is haphazard, but it accounts for the mixing of molecules that commonly occurs when different kinds of substances are put together.

For example, if you put some sugar into a glass of water, the sugar will seem to remain at the bottom for a while. Then slowly it disappears into the solution. As this happens, the moving water and sugar molecules are colliding haphazardly with one

In the margin, record equations for diffusion and osmosis. Draw a sketch to show haphazard motion. At home, add some sugar to a glass of water. Watch to see what happens, and tell yourself what is happening.

another, and in time the sugar and water molecules will be evenly mixed. This mixing occurs by diffusion—the sugar molecules spread where they are in higher concentration toward the regions where they are less concentrated. Eventually the sugar becomes uniformly distributed in the water. This condition is called *equilibrium*.

Osmosis is a special kind of diffusion. It occurs whenever water molecules diffuse from a region of higher concentration through a selectively permeable membrane, such as a cell membrane.   [259 words]

Monitoring Comprehension and Writing in Response

Select the best response. Remember to restate each stem as a question and circle key words to clarify what is being asked. Refer back to your margin notes to answer.

1. The concentration of a material in an area is the
   a. area in which a material is found.
   b. amount of that material found in a particular area.
   c. kind of material it is.
   d. name of the material.

2. The phrase *haphazard motion* as used in this selection means motion that is
   a. orderly.
   b. careful.
   c. without a pattern or design.
   d. continuous.

3. The process by which molecules or ions move from regions of higher concentrations to regions of lower concentrations is termed
   a. diffusion.   b. equilibrium.   c. osmosis.

4. The process by which water molecules move from regions of higher concentrations to regions of lower concentrations across a selectively permeable membrane is called
   a. diffusion.   b. equilibrium.   c. osmosis.

5. The state when a material that is dissolved in another substance becomes uniformly distributed in that substance is known as
   a. diffusion.   b. equilibrium.   c. osmosis.

6. In questions 1 through 5, five different clue words were used to let you know you were dealing with definitions. What are they? Write them here.

   a. _____

   b. _____

   c. _____

   d. _____

   e. _____

7. What is the purpose of the first sentence in the first paragraph?
   a. to define diffusion   c. to give an opinion of diffusion
   b. to explain diffusion   d. to provide an example of diffusion

8. What is the purpose of the second sentence in the first paragraph?
   a. to elaborate on, or extend,   c. to state the main idea
      the definition   d. to give a conclusion
   b. to give a specific example

9. *Critical Thinking Question:* Explain what happens when you spray perfume into the air. Tell a classmate. Use the words *concentration* and *haphazard* in your explanation. Decide whether this is an example of diffusion or osmosis. Then, collaborating with a classmate, write an explanation in your notebook.

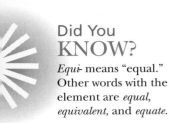

Did You
KNOW?

Equi- means "equal." Other words with the element are *equal, equivalent,* and *equate*.

Before leaving this section, go back and check your answers against the definitions given in the text. This is what you should do when you read difficult terms and definitions in a college text. Remember to make a mental picture for each definition.

SELECTION 2
Understanding Whole Numbers (MATHEMATICS)
A Reading Workshop

Getting Ready to Read
Preview the selection. What should you do as part of your preview?

Reading with Meaning
Read this selection to learn the meaning of the important mathematical terms used.

Understanding Whole Numbers
Jeffrey Slater

Often we learn a new concept in stages. First comes learning the new *terms* and basic assumptions. Then we have to master the *reasoning*, the logic, behind the new concept. This often goes hand in hand with learning a method for using the idea. Finally, we can move quickly with a *shortcut*.

For example, in the study of stock investments, you must learn the meaning of such terms as *stock, profit, loss,* and *commission* before tackling the question "What is my profit from this stock transaction?" After you learn how to answer this question, you can quickly answer many similar ones.

You can watch your understanding of mathematics grow through this same process. Consider whole numbers. The ideas associated with the whole numbers can be so familiar that you have already jumped to the "shortcut" stage. But with a little patience in looking at the terms, reasoning, and step-by-step methods, you'll find your understanding deepens, even with these very familiar numbers, the whole numbers.

To count a number of objects or to answer the question "How many?" we use a set of numbers called **whole numbers.** These whole numbers are as follows:

0, 1, 2, 3, 4, 5, 6, 7, 8, 9, 10, 11, 12, 13, 14, 15, . . .

There is no largest whole number. The three dots (. . .) indicate that the set of whole numbers goes on indefinitely. Our number system is based on tens and ones and is called the decimal system (or the base 10 system). The numbers 0, 1, 2, 3, 4, 5, 6, 7, 8, 9 are called **digits.** The position, or placement, of the digits in the number tells the value of the digits. For example, in the number 521, the "5" means 5 hundreds (500). In the number 54, the "5" means 5 tens, or fifty. For this reason, our number system is called a **place-value** system.

Consider the number 5643. The four digits are located in four places that are called, from right to left, the ones, tens, hundreds, and thousands places. By looking at the digits and their places, we see that in the number 5643

- the 5 means "5 thousands."
- the 6 means "6 hundreds."
- the 4 means "4 tens," or "forty."
- the 3 means "3 ones."

The *value* of the number is 5 thousand, 6 hundred, 4 tens, 3 ones.

To indicate the value of even greater numbers we can use the following diagram, which shows the names of even more places.

Hundred millions	Ten millions	Millions	Hundred thousands	Ten thousands	Thousands	Hundreds	Tens	Ones

Monitoring Comprehension

1. Write equations for each of the following terms. Check the selection as you write. Work with a partner in the workshop.

   • Reasoning = _____

   • Whole number = _____

   • Digit = _____

   • Place-value system = _____

   _____

Think
about . . .

You should make up your own review exercises like this after reading a block of text loaded with definitions. What things should you make yourself do after reading a hard definition?

2. *Critical Thinking Question:* Following the step-by-step method outlined in the article, indicate what the number 97,210 means.

   • The 9 means _____.

   • The 7 means _____.

   • The 2 means _____.

   • The 1 means _____.

   • The 0 means _____.

3. What is the value of 97,210? _____

EXPLANATIONS

As you may have discovered from the selections you just read, definitions and explanation go hand in hand; having defined a term, the author moves on to explain it. This happens in the selection on diffusion and osmosis when Hole defines *diffusion* and then explains what happens when the molecules and ions in body fluids travel, collide, and bounce off one another. As Hole explains, haphazard molecular motion of this kind "accounts for the mixing of molecules that commonly occurs when different kinds of substances are put together."

Strategies for Reading Explanations

In explaining, an author tells why or how, illustrates with an example, states the conditions under which something happens, clarifies relationships, compares, contrasts, and generalizes. Clues that help you figure out that an author is explaining are words such as the following:

   • *One, two,* and *three,* which indicate the number of items to be discussed or the steps in a sequence of events;
   • *For example* and *such as,* which indicate an example;
   • *Also* and *furthermore,* which indicate a continuation of the idea, and *but* and *however,* which indicate ideas in opposition;

- *Similarly* and *on the other hand*, which indicate a comparison or contrast;

- *If/then* and *consequently*, which indicate a condition or effect relationship; and

- *Because* and *for this reason*, which indicate a cause and effect relationship.

See Chapter 7 for a full discussion of how to use these clue words to anticipate the direction in which an author is taking you.

The first component of a strategy for reading to understand explanations is attending to these clue words. Take a moment to reread Selections 1 and 2. As you do, circle the clue words that help you follow the author's explanation and think about what those words are telling you.

A second component is visualizing, or picturing in your mind's eye, what the author is explaining. This is useful when the explanation is about something concrete. For example, if a passage is explaining how food is digested in the digestive tract, as you read, you might visualize that tract: mouth, esophagus, stomach, small and large intestines, rectum, and associated organs. You hold that picture in your mind, relating what the passage is saying at any one point to the appropriate part of your visual image. Or, if there is a diagram in the text, you refer to it, following the diagram as you read the text.

A third component of a strategy for reading explanations is talking to yourself in your mind or (when the passage presents tough ideas) talking to yourself out loud. We call this "thinking along" or "thinking aloud." Here is a difficult passage by John W. Hole, Jr., followed by a *think-along*. The think-along demonstrates the kinds of thoughts that might come to the mind of a student encountering the material for the first time.

> To illustrate how diffusion accounts for the movement of various molecules through a cell membrane, let us imagine a container of water that is separated into two compartments by a permeable membrane (Figure 13.1). This membrane has numerous pores that are large enough for water and sugar molecules to pass through. Sugar molecules are placed in one compartment (A) but not in the other (B). As a result of diffusion, we can predict that although the sugar molecules are moving in all directions, more will spread from compartment A (where they are in greater concentration) through the pores in the membrane and into compartment B (where they are in lesser concentration) than will move in the other direction. At the same time, water molecules will tend to diffuse from compartment B (where they are in greater concentration) through the pores into compartment A (where they are in lesser concentration). Eventually, equilibrium will be achieved when there are equal numbers of water and sugar molecules in each compartment.

The Think Along—What Might Go On
in Your Mind as You Read

"To illustrate" . . . oh, the author is going to give an example. . . . This example shows how different molecules move through a membrane. . . . There is this beaker divided into two parts . . . with a permeable membrane between. . . . I remember about permeable membranes. . . . They let anything through.

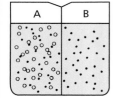
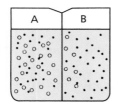
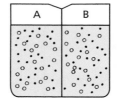

° = sugar molecules

• = water molecules

FIGURE 13.1 Diffusion of Molecules Through a Membrane

"This membrane has pores" . . . there are pores . . . tiny holes . . . like in the skin. These are big ones that let both water and sugar go through to the other side.

From the diagram I can see that they put water and sugar in compartment A but only water in compartment B. . . . "As a result of diffusion". . . What is going to happen? . . . Let's see. There are no sugar molecules in compartment B. . . . There are more water molecules in compartment B than in compartment A. What will happen? . . . I bet the sugar will move from A to B. . . . The water will go from B to A . . . through the pores . . . from areas of high concentration to areas of low concentration. . . . through diffusion.

I can see the sugar moving. . . . I'll add arrows to the picture in Figure 13.1 to show the sugar moving from left to right.

There is equilibrium at the end . . . eventually . . . takes time. . . . Equilibrium means the same number of water molecules in both compartments . . . and the same number of sugar molecules in both compartments. . . . I'll label the last diagram "in a state of equilibrium." This is an example of diffusion.

Think
about . . .

What are some things you should do in your mind as you read difficult explanations? What might you record on paper?

Reading a very complicated explanation such as this one, you do not just read the words. You must verbalize and visualize the ideas, expressing them in your own words and perhaps in a diagram of your own making. You must relate what is in the passage to what you already know on the topic. Especially helpful is to compare what is stated to something similar; say to yourself, "This is like . . ." (as in the reference to the skin in the think-along). You must also constantly predict based on what you already know about the topic and what you already have read. You say to yourself, "I bet. . . ."

When talking to yourself in your mind or out loud, you should avoid using vague phrases. Do not just use "this stuff" or "that part." Use, instead, the terms you are learning—in this case, *diffusion, concentration,* and *equilibrium.* Using the terms as you think about the selection reinforces your understanding of them. Thinking about a passage as you read, you should also raise questions. Examples from the think-along are the questions "What is going to happen?" and "What will happen?"

In sum, your strategy for monitoring your comprehension as you read explanations has these components:

EXPLANATION COMPREHENSION STRATEGY

→ Use clue words (such as *for example, if/then*) to predict where the writer is going and what he or she is going to do.

→ Visualize in your mind's eye what is being explained. Make a sketch if you believe that will clarify the explanation. Refer to the visuals in the text while reading a related explanation. Add words, lines, or arrows to the text illustrations.

→ Think along or think aloud in these ways:

Paraphrase the explanation, drawing on what you already know and using any technical vocabulary you know.

Make comparisons between things explained and similar things you know about.

Predict as you read, saying to yourself, "I bet. . . ." Try to keep ahead of the writer and anticipate what he or she is saying.

Ask yourself questions as you read.

Answer your own questions or ones that the author raises in the text. Do this as you read.

→ Reread to clarify points. Review the explanation in your mind, using key vocabulary.

SELECTION 3
Pavlov's Conditioning Experiments (EXPERIMENTAL PSYCHOLOGY)

A Reading Workshop

Expanding Your Vocabulary for Reading

Use the context and word elements to figure out the meaning of each italicized word. Write the meaning of each term in your notebook. Be ready to tell how you deciphered the meaning of the terms.

1. He always had a stomachache after eating because his *digestive* juices were not working as they should.

2. Whenever I see and smell a pizza, I begin to *salivate*. I simply drool in anticipation.

3. The scientist *devised* a way to overcome the effects of that hormone.

4. Receiving a low grade on the test was the *stimulus* that made me settle down and study for the course.

5. The president took a *neutral* position, neither positive nor negative.

6. The judge's entrance into the court was the *cue* for all those in the room to rise.

　　In the article, you will encounter the word *conditioning*. Conditioning is a scientific term that refers to a form of learning, acquiring specific patterns of behavior in the presence of well-defined stimuli. You might say, "I was conditioned at an early age to pick up my belongings before leaving the house. Each day my father made sure I did this before I was allowed to go out."

Getting Ready to Read

Glance over the title and the subheadings of this section from a college psychology text. Look at the diagram. Gauge the reading load. What questions do you ask and answer as part of your preview?

Reading with Meaning

As you read this selection, record your thoughts in the margin. Your think-along can include rephrasing ideas in your own words, relating a point to something you already know, asking and answering questions, predicting before the authors make a point, and visualizing by sketching. If you prefer, you may collaborate with a partner and tell him or her your thoughts as you read the selection paragraph by paragraph together. You may also want to underline words expressing the main idea of each paragraph.

　　The names and dates set within parentheses refer to the researchers who proposed the theories and the years they presented their ideas.

☼

Pavlov's Conditioning Experiments
Charles Morris

Classical conditioning was discovered almost by accident by Ivan Pavlov (1849–1936), a Russian physiologist who was studying the digestive processes. Since animals salivate when food is placed in their mouths, Pavlov inserted tubes into the salivary glands of dogs in order to measure how much saliva they produced when they were given food. He noticed, however, that the dogs salivated before the food was in their mouths: The mere sight of food made them drool. In fact, they even drooled at the sound of the experimenter's

Did You
KNOW?
Cue and *queue* are homophones, words that are pronounced the same but are spelled differently and carry different meanings. A queue is a line. People form a queue to wait for a bus.

Write your thoughts, especially your definitions of key terms, as you read each paragraph.

footsteps. This aroused Pavlov's curiosity. What was making the dogs salivate even before they had the food in their mouths? How had they learned to salivate in response to the sound of the experimenter's approach?

Pavlov's Experiment

In order to answer these questions, Pavlov set out to teach the dogs to salivate when food was not present. He devised an experiment in which he sounded a bell just before the food was brought into the room. A ringing bell does not usually make a dog's mouth water, but after hearing the bell many times just before getting fed, Pavlov's dogs began to salivate as soon as the bell rang. It was as if they had learned that the bell signaled the appearance of food, and their mouths watered on cue even if no food followed. The dogs had been conditioned to salivate in response to a new stimulus, the bell, which would not normally have caused that response (Pavlov, 1927).

The Elements of Classical Conditioning

Generally speaking, *classical conditioning* involves learning to transfer a natural response from one stimulus to another, previously neutral stimulus. Pavlov's experiment illustrates the four basic elements of classical conditioning. The first is an *unconditioned stimulus (US)*, like food, which invariably causes a certain reaction—salivation, in this case. That reaction—*the unconditioned response (UR)*—is the second element and always results from the unconditioned stimulus: Whenever the dog is given food (US), its mouth waters (UR). The third element is the neutral stimulus—in this case, the ringing of the bell—which is called the *conditioned stimulus (CS)*. At first, the conditioned stimulus does not bring about the desired response. Dogs do not normally salivate at the sound of a bell—unless they have been conditioned to react in this way. Such a reaction is the fourth element in the classical conditioning process: the *conditioned response (CR)*. The conditioned response is the behavior that the animal has learned to produce in response to the conditioned stimulus. Usually, the unconditioned response—salivation, in our example—and the conditioned response are basically the same. [See Figure 13.2.]

Without planning to do so, you may have conditioned your own pet in a way very similar to Pavlov's experiments. Many cats and dogs come running at the sound of a can opener or a certain cupboard door, rubbing around their owner's legs, looking in the dishes in which they are fed, or otherwise preparing for the food that they have learned to associate with particular sounds or activities.

Monitoring Comprehension

Answer the questions by writing in the space provided. Continue to work with your partner.

1. What did Pavlov observe about his dogs' salivation that aroused his curiosity?

   _____

   _____

   _____

2. What did Pavlov condition his dogs to do? _____

   _____

3. How did Pavlov go about conditioning his dogs? In other words, what were the steps in his experiment? _____

   _____

   _____

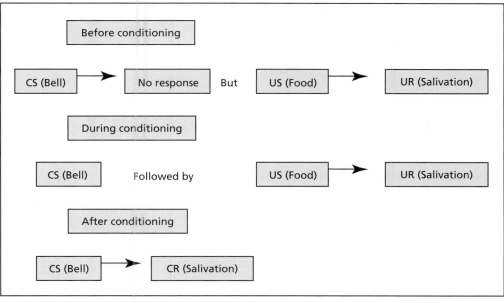

FIGURE 13.2 A Model of the Classical Conditioning Process
An arrow means "results in."

4. Interpreting definitions is important in understanding explanations. Write equations for the following scientific terms found in the selection:

   a. Unconditioned stimulus = _____

   b. Conditioned stimulus = _____

   c. Unconditioned response = _____

   d. Conditioned response = _____

5. *Critical Thinking Question:* Explain why cats and dogs come running when they hear the sound of a can opener. Use the terms *conditioned response* and *conditioned stimulus* in your answer. _____

   _____

   _____

Think
about . . .

Never leave a difficult block of text without telling yourself important definitions and points. Why is this a good rule?

Vocabulary Review

Select the word from the list that best completes each sentence.

devised	cue	salivate
digestive	neutral	stimulus

1. I have a very sensitive _____ tract. I get indigestion very easily.

2. Sometimes I _____ so much that I start to drool.

3. Crashing his car was the _____ that made him finally change his driving habits.

4. President Wilson _____ a plan for a world organization that would monitor relations between member states.

5. The stage manager gave the actor her _____ when it was time for her to say her lines.

6. Switzerland remained _____ during World War II. It did not join forces with either side in the combat.

SELECTION 4

Daydreaming (PSYCHOLOGY)

A Collaborative Mindtalk Workshop

Expanding Your Vocabulary for Reading

Use the context and word elements to figure out the meaning of each italicized word. Check the glossary to verify your hypothesis. Write the meaning in your notebook. Be ready to tell how you got the meaning.

1. The *protagonist* in a story or play is the leading character. Opposing him or her is the *antagonist,* the source of conflict in the story.

2. Long John Silver is the *arch* villain of *Treasure Island.* In the story he is cunning and shrewd.

3. As people grow older, they tend to *reminisce* about times gone by; in other words, they enjoy thoughts about what they did in earlier days.

4. He lived a *humdrum* existence, with little variation and almost no excitement to break his everyday, ordinary activity.

    In the article you will encounter the term *ASC.* These initials stand for "altered states of consciousness," or mental states in which people's thoughts and feelings differ noticeably from those that occur when they are fully awake and reasonably alert. Some altered states are sleeping, dreaming, and daydreaming.

Getting Ready to Read

Glance over the title, the source of the article, and the first paragraph.

1. What is the selection about? _____

2. Do you daydream? When do you daydream? What do you daydream about? Tell a partner about your daydreams. Then together make an idea web in which you record the ideas and words that come to mind when you think about your daydreams.

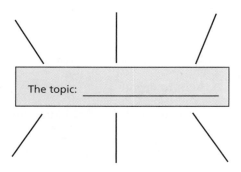

The topic: _____

Did You KNOW?

Pro- means "for"; *anta-* or *anti-* means "against." Other words with these prefixes are *proponent, proactive, antiwar,* and *antithesis.*

Think about . . .

Do you ever say to yourself as you read a college textbook, "This is really boring"? What do you do when you have to read material that bores you?

3. What do you think you might learn from reading the selection, given the fact that it is from a psychology textbook? _____

_____

_____

Reading with Meaning

As you read, record your thoughts in the margin. Your think-along can include rephrasing ideas in your own words, relating a point to something you already know, asking and answering questions, predicting before the author makes a point, and visualizing by sketching. If you prefer, work with a partner and tell him or her your thoughts as you read the selection together. You may also want to underline words that express the main idea of each numbered paragraph.

Daydreaming
Charles Morris

Write your thoughts here as you read each paragraph. ASC = altered state of consciousness.

1. In James Thurber's book *The Secret Life of Walter Mitty,* the protagonist mentally departs from his humdrum daily existence for a series of fantastic and heroic ventures. In the comic strip "Peanuts," Snoopy is well known for his imaginary adventures as the archrival of the Red Baron. A college student sitting in psychology class may actually be lost in thoughts of summer sun and fun on the beach. Although it requires deliberate effort to enter an ASC via hypnosis, drugs, or meditation, *daydreaming* is an ASC that occurs seemingly without effort.

2. Typically, daydreaming occurs when you would rather be somewhere else or be doing something else—escaping from the demands of the real world for a moment. You may reminisce pleasantly about last year's vacation or leave the daily college grind behind and fantasize about your future as a business tycoon. And sometimes, as in the case of Walter Mitty or Snoopy, you may project yourself into fantastic, unlikely adventures. Daydreams provide the opportunity to write, act in, and stage manage a private drama for which you are the only audience.

3. Although daydreaming may seem to be a random and effortless process, psychologists have discovered that people's daydreams tend to fall into a few distinct patterns and that different people tend to prefer different kinds of dreams (Singer, 1975). People who score high on measures of anxiety tend to have fleeting, loosely connected daydreams related to worrying. They take little pleasure in their daydreams. In contrast, people who are strongly achievement oriented tend to have daydreams that concern achievement, guilt, fear of failure, and hostility. These dreams often reflect the self-doubt and competitive envy that accompany great ambition. Still other people derive considerable enjoyment from their daydreams and use them to solve problems, think ahead, or distract themselves. These "happy daydreamers" tend to have pleasant fantasies uncomplicated by guilt or worry. And finally, some daydreamers display unusual curiosity about their environment and place great emphasis on objective thinking. These people tend to have daydreams whose contents are closely related to the objective world and are marked by controlled lines of thought.

4. Intelligence, as well as personality, also affects our daydreaming. One group of researchers discovered that intellectually gifted adolescents—those who have experienced considerable academic success—tend to have daydreams with less guilt and fear of failure than their less gifted peers.

5. If daydreaming is nearly universal, does it serve any useful function? Can Walter Mitty justify his fantasies on a practical basis? Some psychologists argue that daydreams have little or no positive or practical value. These psychologists hold that daydreams are essentially a retreat from the real world that occurs when inner needs cannot be expressed in actual behavior. We daydream, they claim, when the world outside does not meet our needs or when we want to do something but cannot; they suspect that the daydream may actually substitute for more direct and effective behavior.

6. By contrast, other psychologists have stressed the positive value of daydreaming and fantasy. Freudian theorists have traditionally held that daydreams allow us to express and deal with various desires, generally about sex or hostility, that would otherwise make us feel guilty or anxious (Gaimbra, 1974). And Pulaski (1974) suggests that daydreaming can build cognitive and creative skills and help people survive difficult situations. For example, it is difficult to imagine an artist or writer succeeding without an active fantasy life. Pulaski notes that daydreaming has also helped prisoners of war survive torture and deprivation. Her view suggests that daydreaming and fantasy can provide welcome relief from everyday—often unpleasant—reality and can reduce internal tension and external aggression.

7. Singer goes one step further in proposing that daydreams are not just a substitute for reality or a form of tension-relief, but an important part of our ability to process information. Singer suggests that during the daytime, as we process the vast, potentially overwhelming array of information received through our senses, we single out some of the material for later review and further processing during quieter moments when we have less to do. When the opportunity arises—perhaps during a dull moment—we rework some of this information and transform it into new and more useful forms. Daydreams and dreams provide a window through which we can watch this process of dealing with "unfinished business." In the long run, then, although daydreaming temporarily distracts us from the real world, Singer believes that it also allows us to take care of important unfinished business so that we are in fact *better* able to cope with our environment when the pace of real-world activity quickens again.   [772 words]

Monitoring Comprehension, Part I

Reread the selection. Jot down in the margin any more thoughts that come to your mind as you reread. Or listen to your reading partner do a think-along. As you listen to him or her read and verbalize aloud, write any new thoughts in the margin. Remember to keep paraphrasing as you read.

Now talk to your partner about the ideas in the selection. Answer these questions together as you refer back to your margin jottings. Then together write down your explanations.

1. Why do people daydream? _____
_____

2. Do all people have the same kinds of daydreams? Explain your answer.
_____
_____

3. What kinds of daydreams do you have? Use the categories of daydreams from paragraph 3 to categorize your own dreams. _____
_____

4. Explain the functions that daydreams serve, according to different researchers.
_____
_____

5. What is Freud's view of daydreams? _____

_____

6. What is Singer's view of daydreams? _____

_____

7. *Critical Thinking Question:* Is it good to daydream? Why? Why not? Decide and give a

reason. _____

_____

Monitoring Comprehension of Main and Supporting Ideas, Part II

Refer back to the selection as you answer on your own. These questions are more difficult than some you have been asked to do; they are similar to questions on some standardized reading tests. Your instructor may ask you to answer the questions as a way to
practice test-taking strategies. Remember to restate each stem as a question.

1. The main idea of the first paragraph is that
   a. the protagonist in the Thurber book departs from reality to have a series of
      imaginary ventures.
   b. *ASC* means "altered state of consciousness."
   c. daydreaming occurs seemingly without effort.
   d. it takes deliberate effort to enter ASC via hypnosis, drugs, or meditation.

2. An example that supports the main idea in paragraph 1 is
   a. the protagonist in the Thurber book departs from reality to have a series of
      imaginary ventures.
   b. *ASC* means "altered state of consciousness."
   c. daydreaming occurs seemingly without effort.
   d. it takes deliberate effort to enter ASC via hypnosis, drugs, or meditation.

3. Which of the following statements presents a contrast to the main idea?
   a. The protagonist in the Thurber book departs from reality to have a series of
      imaginary ventures.
   b. *ASC* means "altered state of consciousness."
   c. Daydreaming occurs seemingly without effort.
   d. It takes deliberate effort to enter ASC via hypnosis, drugs, or meditation.

4. Review paragraph 3. Which sentence states the main idea?
   a. the first sentence   c. the next to last sentence
   b. the second sentence   d. the last sentence

5. In the remaining sentences in paragraph 3, the author
   a. explains the patterns into which people's dreams fall.
   b. explains when daydreams occur.
   c. explains the function of daydreams.
   d. defines daydreaming.

6. In paragraph 3, the purpose of the third sentence is to
   a. state the main idea.
   b. elaborate on the idea stated in the previous sentence.
   c. give examples relative to the idea stated in the previous sentence.
   d. provide an opinion.

7. In paragraph 4, the phrase "those who have experienced considerable academic success" refers to
   a. daydreamers.
   b. a group of researchers.

    c. intellectually gifted adolescents.
    d. daydreamers who have less fear of failure.

  8. The main idea of paragraph 6 is stated in
     a. the first sentence.
     b. the last sentence.
     c. one of the middle sentences.
     d. none of the above—the main idea is unstated.

  9. The second sentence in paragraph 6 provides
     a. a definition important in the paragraph.
     b. an example in support of the idea in the first sentence of the paragraph.
     c. an unrelated detail.

 10. The main idea of the last paragraph is that daydreaming is
     a. a substitute for reality.
     b. a form of tension-relief.
     c. an important part of our ability to process information.

 11. What view of dreams is given in the last paragraph?
     a. Dreams serve little or no practical value.
     b. Dreams have a positive value.
     c. Dreams have a negative effect on our mental health.

 12. The word *us* is used throughout the selection. To whom does it refer?
     a. psychologists   c. the author of the selection
     b. scientific researchers   d. people in general

 13. In the space provided, write down four words or phrases from the selection that were
     key ones in helping you see relationships between ideas within it. Record what mean-
     ing you made with each word you select. One example is given as a model.

Word	Meaning
a. *And finally*	The author is dealing with the last kind of dream.

     b.

     c.

     d.

     e.

Summarizing to Increase Comprehension

Research suggests that writing a summary of a passage increases your understanding of
what you have read. In your notebook, write a short paragraph in which you sum up the
way people use daydreams. The best way to summarize is to start with a sentence that
gives the main idea of the complete passage. Then write several sentences that give key

Main Point, or Thesis:

Supporting Ideas:

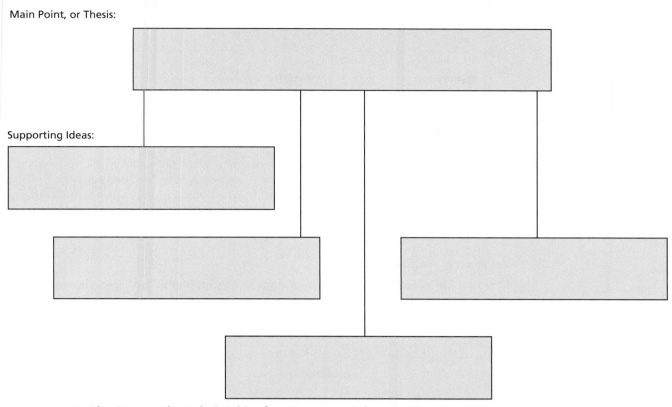

FIGURE 13.3 An Idea Map to Plot Relationships for a Summary Before Writing One
*First, identify the thesis of the selection. Next, identify the supporting ideas. Record the thesis in the
top box and the supporting ideas in the connecting boxes. Then use your idea map to write a
summary paragraph that includes those points.*

details. Collaborating with a partner, use the idea map in Figure 13.3 to plot the main idea
and supporting ideas before writing the summary on your own.

Vocabulary Review

Select the word from the list that best completes each sentence.

antagonist	humdrum	reminisce
arch	protagonist	

1. Although I knew I should root for the hero, I could not help but feel sorry for the

   _____.

2. The _____ in the story, the hero, succeeded only after many attempts.

3. By the end of the story, his _____ enemy had become his friend.

4. As part of our daydreams, we sometimes _____ about times gone by.

5. Life for him was _____ because he had nothing to break the dullness
   of his existence.

EXTENDING WHAT YOU HAVE LEARNED

Reviewing Strategies for Reading Explanations

List here at least four things you can do to increase your comprehension as you read
explanations.

1. _____

2. _____

3. _____

4. _____

Applying the Strategies for Reading Explanations

Read an explanation of some phenomenon in a natural science or social science textbook. As you read, apply the strategies for reading explanations as outlined on page 242. Jot down the name of the book and the pages you read on an index card. On the card, list some of the thoughts that came to your mind as you read. Be ready in class to explain the phenomenon you read about.

Reviewing Vocabulary

Reread these words and the brief definitions given with them. Then select the word from the list that best fits the context of each of the sentences. Add several of these words to your personal vocabulary list.

a.	anatomy	study of the structure of body parts
b.	concentration	amount of material in an area
c.	diffusion	movement of material from areas of high concentration to areas of low concentration
d.	haphazard	random, or by chance
e.	nucleus	inner portion of the cell, or the core of something
f.	physiology	study of the way the body functions
g.	plasma	liquid portion of the blood
h.	protagonist	the leading character in a play, the leader of a cause, the opposite of the antagonist
i.	reminisce	think about the past

1. There was such a high _____ of moths in that area that there was not enough food for them.

2. His activity was _____; it was without order or pattern.

3. Clark is interested in studying the structure of body parts, or what is known as _____. In contrast, Karin is interested in studying the functioning of the body, or _____.

4. The core part of the cell is the _____.

5. During the Renaissance, there was a general _____ of ideas—a movement of those ideas from where they originated across most of Europe.

6. As the ex-president got older, he would _____ about the important things that happened during his presidency.

7. Laurence Olivier played the role of the _____ in the play. He took the lead because of the strength of his past performances.

8. Medical research with the patient's _____ gave doctors a clue to the source of her blood disease.

 14

Understanding Descriptions and Narratives

OBJECTIVE

In this chapter, you will develop strategies for reading descriptions and narratives. Specifically, you will learn to

1. Visualize when reading descriptions and narratives;
2. Interpret metaphors and similes and create comparisons of your own;
3. Grasp sequences and chronology;
4. Identify causes of events and influential factors in narratives;
5. Compare events and lives with others that you know; and
6. Get at the ultimate meaning of events and lives.

READING DESCRIPTIONS AND NARRATIVES

Authors write with different purposes in mind. As discussed in Chapter 13, an author's purpose may be to define or explain. In any one paragraph, an author may include statements of definition and explanation, moving from one to the other as the topic demands. The author first may define his or her terms and then explain relationships.

At other times and sometimes within the same selection, authors write with the intent to describe or to give an account of something. The first kind of writing is *description;* the second is *narrative.* This chapter focuses on these two kinds of writing.

DESCRIPTION

In a description, a writer uses words to paint a picture of something: a person, a scene, or even a feeling. In describing, the writer tells the most significant features, or attributes, of the thing he or she is talking about.

Descriptions range from very precise to very creative. In science, descriptions tend to be exact, as when an author describes an apparatus or an organism. Descriptions in poetry are more imaginative. In general, descriptions do not occur alone; they blend with definitions and explanations.

A strategy for reading descriptions has two components:

DESCRIPTION COMPREHENSION
STRATEGY

➜ Visualize in your mind what the author is describing.

➜ Relate what the author is describing to something you know.

Reading Descriptions

Read the following description of Walden Pond, written by Henry David Thoreau in the 1800s. The word *exclusively,* as Thoreau uses it, means "not including anything else." The *circumference* is "the distance around." As you read, pretend your mind is a camera and take a picture of the pond with it. At the same time, in the margin write phrases that help you to snap a picture, or to visualize it, in your mind.

In the margin, jot down phrases that help you to visualize or draw a picture of the pond.

Walden Pond

Henry David Thoreau

Walden Pond is a clear and deep green well, half a mile long and a mile and three quarters in circumference, and contains about sixty-one acres; a perennial spring in the midst of pine and oak woods, without any visible inlet or outlet except by the clouds and evaporation. The surrounding hills rise abruptly from the water to the height of forty to eighty feet, though on the south-east and east they attain to about one hundred and one hundred and fifty feet respectively, within a quarter and a third of a mile. They are exclusively woodland.

The shore is composed of a belt of smooth rounded white stones like paving stones, excepting one or two short sand beaches, and is so steep that in many places a single leap will carry you into water over your head. . . . The stones extend a rod or two into the water, and then the bottom is pure sand.

Reading this, did you picture the green pond with a ring of stones and woodland surroundings? Did you visualize the pine and oak trees and the abrupt rise of the hills? Creating a picture in your mind's eye is the first component of a strategy for reading description.

A second component is relating what is being described to something you already know. Sometimes the author of a text helps you to do this by providing an analogy, or creative comparison. For example, Thoreau called the pond a well. Picture a well with its steep sides. Does visualizing a well help you picture how Walden Pond looks?

When Thoreau called Walden Pond a well, he was using a *metaphor*. A metaphor is an expressed comparison between two essentially different things. A metaphor differs from a *simile*, which is an expressed comparison of two different things that relies on the word *as* or *like* to make the comparison. Here is Thoreau's metaphor set in diagram form:

> Walden Pond with
> its steep banks is ┐
> └→ a well
> with its steep sides.

Think
about . . .

As you read the description, what thoughts went through your mind? Did you wish you were there swimming in the pond rather than reading about it? Could you picture yourself doing that? Picturing in the mind is a good strategy for reading descriptions.

At times, creating a metaphor or simile of your own when a writer does not supply one can help you to visualize. For example, visualizing a rice field on a windy day, you might think, "The rice field in the wind looked like an ocean with waves moving to and fro." In doing that, you would have created a simile that paints a clearer picture.

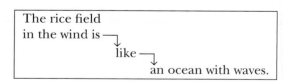

> The rice field
> in the wind is ┐
> └→ like ┐
> └→ an ocean with waves.

Now read this description of an eagle by nineteenth-century English poet Alfred Tennyson. As you read, apply these strategies: Visualize the scene and in the margin write phrases that help you picture it. Relate what is being described to something you know or identify the creative comparisons the author has used. The word *azure* means "blue." A *crag* is a projecting outcropping of rock.

The Eagle

Alfred Tennyson

He clasps the crag with crooked hands:
Close to the sun in lonely lands,
Ringed with the azure world, he stands.

The wrinkled sea beneath him crawls;
He watches from his mountain walls,
And like a thunderbolt he falls.

Write phrases that help you to visualize.

Close your eyes for a minute. Visualize the scene—an eagle on a projecting rock high above the sea, the big yellow sun in the background, the blue sky behind, the sea with its ripples below. Then the eagle "falls," diving from his craggy perch.

A key word that helps you to paint a picture of the action part of the poem in your mind's eye is *thunderbolt*. Did you think of a thunderbolt, coming loudly and sharply, as you visualized the eagle? The word *thunderbolt* in this context is a simile, for here the word *like* makes the connection between two different things—the diving downward movement of the eagle and the clap of a thunderbolt.

```
The eagle falls ┐
                ↓
             like ┐
                  ↓
                  a thunderbolt.
```

Go back now to Chapter 13. Reread the segment about the cell membrane on page 236. Do you recognize the very effective metaphor the author uses to clarify his science content? Hole uses the metaphor of a gate to help you picture a membrane. How are a gate and a membrane the same? Both are barriers between things. Extend the metaphor. Picture a gate with a latch. A man wants to get through. He can do it by lifting the latch. A horse wants to get through. She cannot pass through because she cannot operate the latch. Is this gate permeable or selectively permeable? This example shows that metaphors are as important in scientific writing as in poetry and stories.

Practicing Visualizing

Here are some descriptions that use metaphor. Reading them, picture in your mind's eye the object being described, using the metaphor to help you visualize. In the outer margin, jot down words that help you see the picture in your mind.

WORKSHOP 1: LAND VIEWS

The lands along the Missouri–Kansas border are a green patchwork of lush creek bottoms and rolling pastures, where eastern forests begin their retreat to western prairies. Farms, small towns, and cities pulse with the strength of the American heartland.

Spring here brings thunderstorms to soak the earth and renew the cycle of life. As dusk comes, cottonwoods stir in the warm breeze, robins pull worms from damp lawns, and lightning bugs flash their Morse messages against darkening skies. In overgrown hollows, deer and quail move through groves of hawthorn, oak, and walnut, and water moccasins hunt frogs in pristine lotus ponds. The meadows are fringed with daisies, clover, and wild rose.

Write phrases here that help you visualize.

1. What is a patchwork quilt? _____

2. What picture does the author paint by calling the lands here a green patchwork?

_____

_____

3. What things do you know that pulse? _____

_____

4. How do farms, towns, and cities pulse? _____

_____

5. What is the Morse code? How does it work? _____

_____

6. What picture does the author paint by saying that "lightning bugs flash their Morse messages against darkening skies"? _____

_____

WORKSHOP 2: MOON VIEWS

Write phrases here that help you visualize.

Moon

Emily Dickinson

The moon was but a chin of gold
  A night or two ago,
And now she turns her perfect face
  Upon the world below.

1. Draw a picture of the moon when it was "but a chin of gold."

2. What phase of the moon was Dickinson describing with her first metaphor? A metaphor is a creative comparison between two things. _____

_____

3. Draw a picture of the moon when it has a "perfect face."

4. What phase of the moon was Dickinson describing with her second metaphor?

_____

5. Why didn't Dickinson simply use the names of the phases of the moon that she was describing? Why did she use the creative comparison of a metaphor? _____

_____

SELECTION 1

Florence the Magnificent: The City of Dante and David, Michelangelo and Machiavelli, the Medicis, Guccis and Puccis (ART)

A Reading Workshop

Expanding Your Vocabulary for Reading

Using the context and word elements, figure out the meaning of each italicized word. Jot down the meaning in your notebook. Check your definition in the glossary. In the selection, you will meet the words *palazzi* and *basilicas*. A basilica is a great church. A palazzo is a large dwelling place on the order of a palace.

1. The crowd was so *unruly* that a dozen police officers were needed to keep order.

2. When the *cornerstone* of the skyscraper was laid, a ceremony was held to celebrate the event.

3. She was a *petulant* child, inclined to be irritable whenever she did not get her own way.

4. The faces of the *gargoyles* on the cathedral stared down like avenging demons.

5. After many unsuccessful *forays* into the country to raid, the bandits gave up their plundering.

6. Michelangelo painted the *frescoes* on the ceiling of the Sistine Chapel in Rome.

7. The books were stacked in such a *higgledy-piggledy* way that when I touched them, they came falling down like Humpty Dumpty.

8. The sidewalks were so crowded that I was *jostled* with each step I took, and I felt like a puppet on a string.

Getting Ready to Read

Preview the selection by reading the title and the headings and scanning the first paragraph.

If you have Internet access, see these Web sites for a 3-D view of Florence and a view of the Ponte Vecchio: www.dada.it/hotel.city/piantine.htm and www.vra.oberlin.edu/florence.html.

- Many students choose Italy as the country they would most like to visit, and they list cities such as Rome, Venice, and Florence as ones they would most like to see. Would you like to go to Italy? Write here the reasons why you would or would not like to go to Italy. Write down places you would like to see there. _____

_____

_____

_____

Reading with Meaning

Read the selection, visualizing what the author is describing. In the margin, write words from the selection that paint pictures for you. Also record equations for the metaphors and similes. The first two items are completed as models. You may do this with a partner. Read silently and stop at the end of each paragraph to complete the margin notes together. Remember that the Renaissance was the great period of learning in Europe during the fourteenth, fifteenth, and sixteenth centuries. It marked the transition from the medieval to the modern world.

Did You KNOW?

Cornerstone is a compound word formed from *corner* and *stone*. Other compound words that incorporate the word *stone* are *lodestone, milestone,* and *touchstone*. Check them in a dictionary.

Write phrases that help you visualize; write equations for metaphors and similes.

Florence the Magnificent: The City of Dante and David, Michelangelo and Machiavelli, the Medicis, Guccis and Puccis

Anne Zwack

1. Simile: *Ring of hills = palm of a giant hand*

2. Simile: *Orange roofs and domes = bunch of marigolds*

3. Good descriptive phrase:

4. Good descriptive phrase:

"The God who made the hills of Florence was an artist," wrote Anatole France as he looked down at the city, ringed by hills as though cupped in the palm of a giant hand, its orange roofs and domes jumbled like an unruly bunch of marigolds. Not just God, but centuries of Florentines have been artists. The Florentines invented the Renaissance, which is the same as saying they invented the modern world. For nearly three centuries, from Giotto's time to Michelangelo's, Florence was the hub of the universe, not only producing palazzi, basilicas and countless art treasures, but also generating ideas that form the cornerstone of twentieth century thought.

Five centuries after the Renaissance, despite neon lights in the storefronts and swarms of mopeds and Fiats honking petulantly where horses and carts once rumbled past, Florence remains a Renaissance city. The streets in the center are still paved with uneven flagstones, and away from the main thoroughfares they're so narrow that the jutting eaves on opposite sides almost touch, keeping you dry on a rainy day if you hug the ochre-yellow walls. As it is, there is a war of wills every time you meet someone coming toward you on a sidewalk no wider than a ledge, and your umbrellas tend to get into a clinch.

FIGURE 14.1 Map of Italy

On a sunny day, look up at the skyline, at the leafy terraces, the square towers, the odd gargoyle or coat of arms worn smooth by time. The forbidding palazzi, built of massive blocks of brown stone, still seem to bristle as though in expectation of forays by bands of Guelfs or Ghibellines, the two warring factions that divided Florence in the Middle Ages. And the faces of today's townspeople come straight out of the frescoes painted centuries ago, when their ancestors were busy building the biggest dome in Christendom.

The City's Pleasures

The most magical walk in Florence is down the Lungarno (literally, "along the Arno," as the streets skirting the river are called). Swallows wheel above the dome of the Church of San Frediano and over the higgledy-piggledy rooftops of houses. Some of the buildings, jostling each other in a hodgepodge of styles, have foundations in the water. The iron lampposts, whose lion's feet grip the parapets all along the river, look as though they were still lighted by gas. Rowers in kayaks occasionally skim over the surface of the fast-flowing yellow river, which gurgles beneath the arches of stone bridges.

Rebuilt after World War II, the bridges are not as ageless as they appear. Only one remains from early days: the Ponte Vecchio, or Old Bridge, which was so quaint, with its goldsmiths' shops elbowing for room on either side, that Hitler ordered his troops to leave it standing. The present structure dates from 1345, and the tiny jewelers' boutiques that seem stuck to the sides of the bridge like limpets to a rock were once butcher shops.

Art and Architecture

Whether you spend a lifetime seeing Florence or a few days, there are a number of things you must not miss. One, in the Accademia, is Michelangelo's *David* (of which there are two copies, one in the Piazza Signoria and one in the Piazzale Michelangelo). Frowning down from his pedestal, his sling over his shoulder and every vein and sinew bursting out of the white marble, David makes the rest of us feel very small. One wonders how Michelangelo would have portrayed Goliath. There's more marble and more Michelangelo in the Medici Chapel behind the Basilica of San Lorenzo: the 16th century genius was responsible for both the architecture and the sculpture of the reclining figures of *Night and Day* and of *Dawn and Dusk.* . . .

In the days when justice was rough, . . . the building that is now the Bargello Museum was Florence's courthouse, and condemned men were strung out of the windows of its tower. Today the museum houses Renaissance statues. . . . There is also another David, this one by Donatello, and it is said to be the first nude statue of the Renaissance.

The Pitti Palace crouches like an enormous yellow crab around Pitti Square, one of the few parking areas in Florence. The palace was built by a Renaissance nobleman, Luca Pitti, who wanted his mansion to be bigger and better than anyone else's. It is now divided into five museums. . . .

Like most Florentine basilicas, the Duomo, or cathedral, is striped in a geometric patchwork of different colored marble. It looks huge even by today's standards, let alone those of 1296, when the cornerstone was laid. No one had succeeded in hoisting aloft a massive dome since the building of the Pantheon in Rome. But Brunelleschi, the great Renaissance architect, solved the problem in the early 15th century by building two separate domes, one on top of the other, like two salad bowls of different sizes. If you can face the 463 steps that lead to the very top, you actually can walk between the two layers of the dome. Or you can climb Giotto's bell tower, which Longfellow called "the lily of Florence blossoming in stone." . . .

Perhaps my greatest Florentine pleasure is watching the sun set from Piazzale Michelangelo, with the entire city at my feet. The lights hover like fireflies over the slowly darkening town, and the arches of the bridges show black against the fierce red of a sun that sets twice, once in the waters of the Arno and once in the Tuscan heavens. At this time the light takes on the gossamer texture of a down powder puff, dusting the roofs and domes a hazy apricot, and I find myself sharing with D. H. Lawrence the "feeling of having arrived, of having reached the perfect centre of man's universe."

5. Good descriptive phrase:

6. Good descriptive phrase:

7. Good descriptive phrase:

8. Good descriptive phrase:

9. Simile:

10. Good descriptive phrase:

11. Simile:

12. Metaphor:

13. Simile:

14. Good descriptive phrase:

Monitoring Comprehension

Answer these questions with your workshop partner.

1. Florence has been described as "a feast for the eyes." Based on your reading of the article, explain the meaning of the metaphor. In what way is Florence a feast? What things do Florence and a feast have in common? _____

   _____

2. Explain the meaning of this simile: Florence is ringed by hills "as though cupped in the palm of a giant hand." A simile is a creative comparison between two things. The comparison includes the word *like* or *as*. _____

   _____

3. The author writes that Florence's orange roofs and domes are "jumbled like an unruly bunch of marigolds." What two different things is the author comparing through this simile? _____

   _____

   What qualities do these two things share? _____

   _____

4. A limpet is a small, shelled organism that clings to rocks. The author writes, "The tiny jewelers' boutiques that seem stuck to the sides of the bridge like limpets to a rock were once butcher shops." What two different things is the author comparing through this simile? _____

   _____

   What qualities do these two things share? _____

   _____

5. The author writes, "The Pitti Palace crouches like an enormous yellow crab around Pitti Square." What two different things is the author comparing in this simile?

   _____

   _____

   What qualities do these two things share? _____

   _____

6. Describing the domes of the Duomo, the author tells us that they are actually two separate domes, "one on top of the other, like two salad bowls of different sizes." What two different things is the author comparing in this simile? _____

   _____

   What qualities do these two things share? _____

   _____

7. The author writes, "The lights hover like fireflies over the slowly darkening town." What two things is the author comparing in this simile? _____

   _____

   What qualities do these two things share? _____

   _____

8. The author describes the dusk through a metaphor: "At this time the light takes on the gossamer texture of a down powder puff, dusting the roofs and domes a hazy apricot." What two things is the author comparing metaphorically? _____

   _____

   What qualities do these two things share? _____

   _____

9. Longfellow called Giotto's bell tower "the lily of Florence blossoming in stone." What two different things is the author comparing through metaphor? _____

   _____

   What qualities do these two things share? _____

   _____

10. *Critical Thinking Question:* Would you like to travel to Florence and through Italy? Tell your partner why or why not. Then in your notebook, write a paragraph in which you give the reasons for your decision. Be ready to share your paragraph with the class.

Making the Writing Connection

Create a metaphor or simile to complete each of the following:

1. The rocket, posed on the launching pad, looked like a _____.

2. In the winter, the bare branches of the trees looked like _____.

3. Blown by the wind, her hair became _____.

4. The islands of Hawaii are _____.

Playing with Words

Here are the key words from the selection. Draw a very rough picture to go along with each one to show the meaning that word has for you. The first ones will be easy to do; as you progress, use your imagination in picturing meanings.

1. cornerstone

2. gargoyle

3. fresco

4. higgledy-piggledy

5. unruly

6. jostled

7. petulant

8. foray

NARRATION

A narrative is an account of an event or a series of events. It can be fictional (not true) or nonfictional (true). Stories, poems that tell a story, some newspaper reports, history, biography, and autobiography are narrations.

There are four elements in a strategy for successful reading of nonfictional narratives: grasping the time sequence, or chronology, of the events; perceiving cause and effect relationships within the events; relating the events to other similar or different events; and understanding the significance of the events.

Grasping the Chronology

An ability to understand time relationships, or chronology, is important in reading narratives, especially biographies (passages that tell about the life of a person), autobiographies (passages that tell about the life of a person written by that person), and historical accounts (passages that tell about sequences of events). To help you comprehend sequence, authors provide two aids: dates and words that indicate sequence.

First, let us consider how to interpret dates. Start by previewing the following paragraphs by quickly circling the dates. Then read the paragraphs.

Phyllis Wheatley, the first major African-American poet, was born about 1753. She was taken by slavers from Africa to Boston in 1761 and sold there as a slave to John Wheatley, a merchant. Wheatley and his wife recognized Phyllis's quickness of mind and ready wit and provided her with an education far beyond what was typically given to black slaves in America. She learned to read and write, began to read the poetry of English writers, and wrote poems of her own. Freed, she traveled to England, where she was recognized for her poetry and had a collection of poems published in 1773. The volume was titled *Poems on Various Subjects.*

Returning to America, Phyllis Wheatley sent a copy of one of her poems to George Washington during the period of the American Revolution. It expressed her feelings about the War and made reference to the General. This led to the publishing of one of her poems in the *Pennsylvania Magazine* and gradual recognition of her as the Poet of the American Revolution. Despite this recognition, Wheatley died in virtual poverty in 1784.

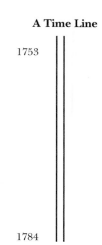

A Time Line

1753

1784

In your preview did you note that the selection is organized chronologically in the order in which events occurred? The first event was the birth of Wheatley in 1753. The last was her death in 1784. The intervening events are presented as they happened, in chronological order. Biographies and historical accounts often are structured chronologically. The writers of such selections typically include dates to give a framework to the account.

Having previewed a selection and discovered a sequence of dates embedded in it, you will find it helpful to visualize a time line in your mind as you read. A time line is simply a line on which dates and related events are labeled in chronological order. As you read, you plot each event on your mental time line.

While reading, you also relate the dates mentioned in the selection to significant dates from the past that function as reference points. You think, "This happened just after the Civil War" or "This happened even before Columbus made his epic journey." Although you should develop your own series of historical reference points that have meaning to you, here are some markers from the past that you may want to use if you have some knowledge of these events:

Reference Points from History

1000 B.C.–A.D. 500	The rise of classical civilizations: Greek, Roman, Indian, Chinese
A.D. 300–400	The collapse of classical civilizations and the beginning of the barbarian invasions of Eurasia
A.D. 600–1000	The rise of Islam
A.D. 1066	The conquest of Britain by William the Conqueror
1300s–1500s	The Renaissance in Europe
1492	Columbus's voyage
1620	Landing of the Pilgrims in Massachusetts
1776	American Declaration of Independence
1787	American Constitution
1803	Louisiana Purchase, which doubled the country's size
1849	Gold Rush
1861–1865	American Civil War
1914–1918	World War I
1939–1945	World War II

Now reread the passage about Phyllis Wheatley. On the vertical time line in the margin, plot the events of her life as well as two key reference points of U.S. history: the Declaration of Independence and the Constitution, 1776 and 1787. In other words, locate each date from the selection on the line and label that date with the event from Wheatley's life. Do the same for the historical reference points.

Based on the time line you have just constructed, answer these questions:

- How old was Phyllis Wheatley when she was enslaved? _____

- How old was she when she died? _____

- Was Wheatley alive when the Constitution was written? _____

Often readers make simple calculations using the dates in a selection. They ask themselves questions similar to the three here; in so doing, they are monitoring their own comprehension.

The strategy you have been applying here has these four elements:

CHRONOLOGY COMPREHENSION STRATEGY

→ In previewing the selection, check dates given to see whether the selection is organized chronologically.

→ In reading a chronologically organized selection, plot times on a mental time line. At times, plot dates sequentially on a time line in the margin.

→ Relate dates to key reference points in history that you know.

→ Make simple calculations based on the dates.

Dates are not the only way a writer expresses time relationships. A writer may use words that signal a passage of time. Here are a few examples of sequence words:

- first, second, third
- for one year, for ten years
- first, next, after that, finally
- yesterday, today, tomorrow
- before, while, as, when, after
- in (in the spring), on (on his birthday), during (during her early years)
- childhood, youth, middle years, old age
- pre- and post-, as in prewar and postwar periods

- then, now
- meanwhile
- soon
- not long after
- later

Preview the following short selection by skimming it and circling words other than dates that communicate time relationships.

A Time Line

1830

Emily Dickinson, considered by many to be one of the greatest American poets, was born in 1830 in Amherst, Massachusetts. Her childhood was a typical one of that day, filled with friends and parties, church and home activities. For about six years, she attended Amherst Academy. Then she attended Mt. Holyoke Female Seminary for a year. "Valentine Extravaganza," her first poem to appear in print, was published in the *Springfield Republican* when she was 22.

Before she was 30, however, Emily withdrew from Amherst society and increasingly applied herself to the writing of poetry. She would not see friends; and with the death of her father in 1874, she became a virtual recluse. During her lifetime, she had only two other poems published, "The Snake" in 1866 and "Success" in 1878. At her death in 1886, her sister discovered more than a thousand poems that Emily Dickinson had written throughout her life. The poems exhibit a directness of expression

1886

and a clarity of image that are apparent even to one who has read little poetry:

> To make a prairie it takes a clover and one
> bee,—
> One clover, and a bee,
> And revery.
> The revery alone will do
> If bees are few.

In this selection, sequence-giving words include *childhood, for about six years, then, for a year, when, before, during,* and *at her death.*

Now reread the Dickinson article. As you read, record key events from Dickinson's life in the margin as a time line. Include a key reference point from history on the line so that you have a general idea of the period in which she lived. Ask as you read, "What do the time-sequencing words tell me about Dickinson's life?"

After reading, answer these questions:

- What are the two major periods in Dickinson's life? _____

  _____

- How do the organization of the selection and the key sequencing words help you

  identify those periods in her life? _____

  _____

Did you identify the two periods? The first is Dickinson's childhood; it is discussed in the first paragraph. The second is the period characterized by her reclusive behavior; it is discussed in the second paragraph. Sometimes when you read chronological material about people and events, it pays to group events into periods or categories: youth, middle years, later years; pre-Darwin, post-Darwin; pre-Reformation, Reformation, post Reformation. Sometimes, as in this case, the way the writer has organized the material into paragraphs helps you to identify patterns in the events.

Here are two more steps in your reading-for-sequence strategy.

CHRONOLOGY COMPREHENSION STRATEGY

→ Watch for sequencing words such as *first, then, finally* and *before, during,* and *after,* which are clues to the passage of time and the sequence of events. Use these words to add events to the time line you visualize during reading.

→ Wherever possible, group events into natural periods or categories, such as childhood, youth, midlife, prewar and postwar, or pre-Constitution and post-Constitution.

In sum, when working with sequence, think about the dates and words that indicate a passage of time, organizing events into a framework to help you remember when things happened. For example, it is easier to remember that an event happened during a person's childhood than to remember that it happened on May 4, 1862.

Analyzing Relationships Within Narratives

A second aspect of reading nonfictional narratives is delving beneath the facts of the account to think about why things happened. Doing this, you are thinking about cause and effect. For example, reading a biography, you must ask, "What were the influences on this person that made him or her do what he or she did? What were the influences that made him or her become the kind of person he or she was?" Reading history, you must ask, "What were the events leading up to this? What were the causes?"

Apply these questions to the lives of Wheatley and Dickinson. What influenced these women to become poets? In the following chart, write down key events from each woman's life that contributed to her becoming a poet.

	Causal Events		
Wheatley			
Dickinson			

Comparing Events with Other Events

A third element of a strategy for reading historical accounts and biographies is to relate events and lives to other events and lives about which you already know. When reading, you say to yourself, "This reminds me of X, Y, and Z that happened several years before." Or "This person's life resembles that of Mr. A." Or "This is just the opposite of what happened when. . . ." Or "This person's life started out the same as Ms. B's, but then took a different turn." Essentially, what you are doing is making comparisons and contrasts with things you already know: You are saying, "This is like. . . . This is different from. . . ."

You can use a Venn diagram made up of two overlapping circles to visualize similarities and differences. In the overlapped central area, record the things that are common to both people or events you are comparing. In the side areas, record the things that are unique.

Think
about . . .

If you were comparing three items (three people, three events, three objects), how would you draw your Venn diagram to lay out your comparisons?

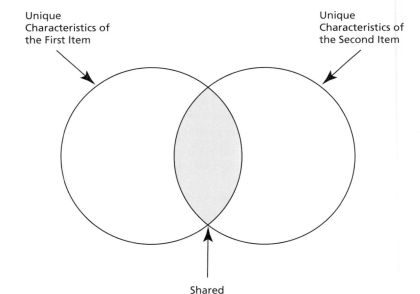

Unique
Characteristics of
the First Item

Unique
Characteristics of
the Second Item

Shared
Characteristics

Now think about the lives of Wheatley and Dickinson. How are the lives of Wheatley and Dickinson similar? How are their lives different?

Use a Venn diagram to make your comparisons and lay out your answers.

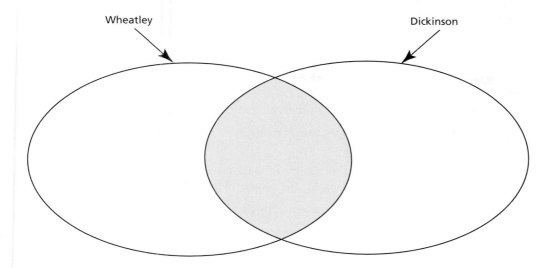

Wheatley   Dickinson

Determining the Significance of Events

A fourth aspect of a strategy for reading historical accounts and biographies is to consider the significance of individuals and events. In thinking about the ultimate meaning of a person's life as you read biography, ask, "What influence did this person have on other persons and events? In what ways did he or she change history and affect the future?" In thinking about the meaning of a series of events or a period of time in history, you ask, "What changes did these events trigger? What were the effects of these events on people and events that were to come?"

Reviewing the Strategy for Reading Narratives

In sum, a strategy for reading nonfictional narrative requires that you ask questions that help you do the following:

NARRATIVE COMPREHENSION
STRATEGY

→ Grasp the sequence of events.

→ Identify causes of events and factors that influenced people's lives.

→ Compare and contrast events and lives to other events and lives.

→ Think about the ultimate meaning or significance of events and people's lives.

Apply this strategy as you read the next selection.

SELECTION 2
Muhammad the Prophet (RELIGION)

A Reading Workshop

Expanding Your Vocabulary for Reading

This selection contains a number of interesting words. Understanding them will help you understand the selection. Read the following sentences and study the italicized terms. Using context clues and word elements, hypothesize a meaning for each term and record it in your reading notebook. Check your hypotheses in the glossary.

1. In those days the king was *preeminent*, far above anyone else in authority. (Note: An eminent person is high in rank or is distinguished. How are the words *eminent* and *preeminent* related?)

2. The convict was *consigned* to the warden to begin his prison sentence.

3. "I appreciate your *forbearance*," said the man. "You have been very patient and understanding as you waited for me to pay my debt."

4. "You promised not to *divulge* the secret to anyone," remarked the lawyer. "Yet as soon as you learned it, you told everyone."

5. The *revelation* that she was a member of the CIA surprised us all. We had not known until then that she was working for the government.

6. In that society the king was *paramount*. His preeminence came as a right of birth.

7. To me that situation was *unique*. I had never seen anything like it before.

8. I had a sense of *impending* trouble as I entered the office and saw the principal behind the desk. Something was about to happen.

9. The *Koran* (or Quran), the sacred scriptures of the Islamic religion, affirms the oneness of God. (Note: See also how the word *Koran* is defined within the sentence by a phrase coming after it and set off by commas. You will find this technique for supplying basic information used a number of times in the selection.)

10. The pagans, who lived in Mecca, believed in many gods. This belief is called *polytheism*. (Remember the meaning of the prefix *poly-*.)

11/12. Muhammad and his *adherents*, or supporters, *migrated* from Medina; they left together because it was unsafe for them there.

13. The leader of the neighboring country tried to *mediate* between the warring parties, but he could do nothing to help them end their struggles.

14. During the *siege* of the city by the enemy, many people were killed.

15. The siege lasted many weeks, yet the results were *inconclusive*. They proved nothing, for nobody came out the victor. (Remember the meaning of the prefix *in-*.)

16. After many hours of work, we looked at what we had done and saw that we had made *negligible* progress. We could hardly see what we had done.

17. Only the most eminent persons were allowed *access* to the party; the rest of us were not allowed to enter.

18. The pagans whom Muhammad fought worshiped *idols*, graven images they held in high regard.

19. The Supreme Court generally adheres to the *precedents* set down in previous decisions. What has been decided in the past is a major factor in present cases.

20. Muhammad made an *alliance* with other tribes, an agreement that bound them together as allies.

21. The queen sent an *envoy* with a message to the emperor. The envoy served as the queen's agent and represented her in official tasks.

Did You KNOW?

The root *medi-* means "middle"; other words with the root are *medium, medial,* and *intermediate*. The prefix *inter-* in *intermediate* means "between."

Did You KNOW?

The prefix *pre-* means "before." Recall that the root *cede-* means "to go or yield." Another word with the prefix is *prefix*. Other words with the root are *intercede, recede,* and *proceed*.

Getting Ready to Read

Preview the selection by glancing over the title, the first and last paragraphs, the headings, and the map. What questions should you ask and answer as you preview?

The part of the world in which the events in this selection take place is the Middle East. You probably recall that the Middle East was the location of the Gulf War, fought in 1991 to free Kuwait from Iraq. You probably heard about Saudi Arabia at that time. Locate these countries on the map in Figure 14.2. Then, talking with a classmate, recall what you remember about the Persian Gulf War of 1991.

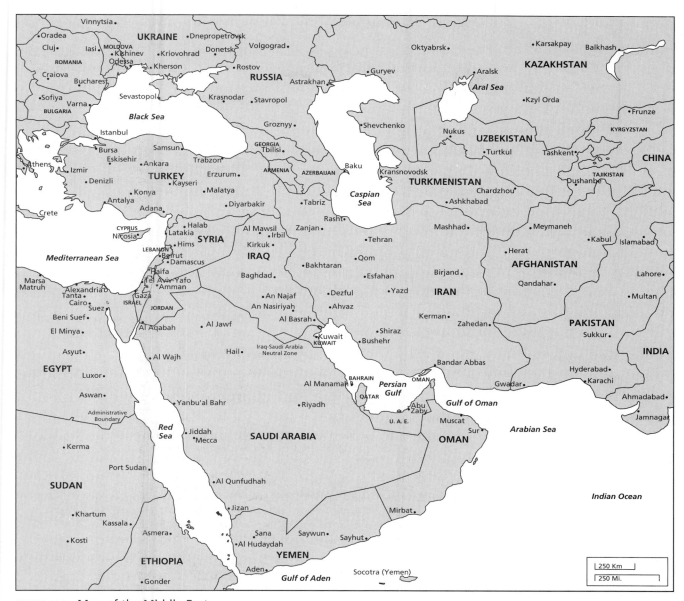

FIGURE 14.2 Map of the Middle East

Reading with Meaning

As you read, make a time line of events in the inner margin. Answer the questions in the outer margin as you go along. Keep thinking, "What were the causes of this? What is the significance of this? What does this remind me of?" It may help to read this selection with a partner, reading several paragraphs alone and then answering the margin questions together.

Muhammad the Prophet

Paul Lunde and John A. Sabini

In or about the year 570 the child who would be named Muhammad and who would become the Prophet of one of the world's great religions, Islam, was born into a family belonging to a clan of Quraysh, the ruling tribe of Mecca, a city in the Hijaz region of northwestern Arabia.

1. Into what kind of family and society was Muhammad born?

2. How might this have affected him?

3. What were key events in Muhammad's early life?

4. How might these events have affected Muhammad?

5. What happened to Muhammad next?

6. How could these events have affected him?

7. What then happened to Muhammad?

8. How could these events have affected him?

9. At first how did Muhammad react?

10. Why did Muhammad react in this way?

11. Why did opposition make him more determined?

12. Predict how the Meccans would react.

13. Of what historical event does this persecution remind you?

Originally the site of the Ka'bah, a shrine of ancient origins, Mecca had with the decline of southern Arabia become an important center of sixth-century trade with such powers as the Sassanians, Byzantines, and Ethiopians. As a result the city was dominated by powerful merchant families among whom the men of Quraysh were preeminent.

Muhammad's Early Life

Muhammad's father, 'Abd Allah ibn'Abd al-Muttalib, died before the boy was born; his mother, Aminah, died when he was six. The orphan was consigned to the care of his grandfather, the head of the clan of Hashim. After the death of his grandfather, Muhammad was raised by his uncle, Abu Talib. As was customary, Muhammad as a child was sent to live for a year or two with a Bedouin family that lived a desert life. This custom, followed until recently by noble families of Mecca, Medina, Tayif, and other towns of the Hijaz, had important implications for Muhammad. In addition to enduring the hardships of desert life, he acquired a taste for the rich language so loved by the Arabs, whose speech was their proudest art, and learned the patience and forbearance of the herdsmen, whose life of solitude he first shared and then came to understand and appreciate.

About the year 590, Muhammad, then in his twenties, entered the service of a widow named Khadijah as a merchant actively engaged with trading caravans to the north. Sometime later Muhammad married Khadijah, by whom he had two sons—who did not survive—and four daughters. During this period of his life Muhammad traveled widely.

The Beginnings of Islam

Then, in his forties, Muhammad began to retire to meditate, or think, in a cave on Mount Hira outside of Mecca, where the first of the great events of Islam took place. One day, as he sat in the cave, he heard a voice, later identified as that of the Angel Gabriel, which ordered him to:

Recite: In the name of thy Lord who created,
Created man from a clot of blood.

Three times Muhammad pleaded his inability to do so, but each time the command repeated. Finally, Muhammad recited the words of what are now the first five verses of the 96th surah or chapter of the Quran—words which proclaim God the Creator of man and the Source of all knowledge.

At first Muhammad divulged his experience only to his wife and immediate circle. But as more revelations directed him to proclaim the oneness of God universally, his following grew, at first among the poor and the slaves, but later also among the most eminent men of Mecca. The revelations he received at this time and those he did so later are all incorporated in the Quran, the Scripture of Islam.

Not everyone accepted God's message transmitted through Muhammad. Even in his own clan there were those who rejected his teachings, and many merchants actively opposed the message. The opposition, however, merely served to sharpen Muhammad's sense of mission and his understanding of exactly how Islam differed from paganism. The belief in the unity of God was paramount in Islam; from this all else followed. The verses of the Quran stress God's uniqueness, warn those who deny it of impending punishment, and proclaim His unbounded compassion to those who submit to His will. Because the Quran rejected polytheism and emphasized man's moral responsibility, it presented a grave challenge to the worldly Meccans.

The Hijrah

After Muhammad had preached for more than a decade, the opposition to him reached such a high pitch that, fearful for their safety, he sent some of his adherents to Ethiopia, where the Christian ruler extended protection to them, the memory of which has been cherished by Muslims ever since. But in Mecca the persecution worsened. Muhammad's followers were abused and even tortured. At last, therefore, Muhammad sent seventy of his followers off to the northern town of Yathrib, which was later to be renamed Medina

("The City"). Later, in the early fall of 622, he learned of a plot to murder him and, with his closest friend, Abu Bakr al-Siddiq, set off to join the emigrants.

In Mecca the plotters arrived at Muhammad's home to find that his cousin, 'Ali, had taken his place in bed. Enraged, the Meccans set a price on Muhammad's head and set off in pursuit. Muhammad and Abu Bakr, however, had taken refuge in a cave where, as they hid from their pursuers, a spider spun its web across the cave's mouth. When they saw that the web was unbroken, the Meccans passed by and Muhammad and Abu Bakr went on to Medina, where they were joyously welcomed by the Medinans as well as the Meccans who had gone ahead to prepare the way.

This was the *Hijrah*—or in English the *Hegira*—usually, but inaccurately translated as "Flight"—from which the Muslim era is dated. In fact, the Hijrah was not a flight but a carefully planned migration which marks not only a break in history—the beginning of the Islamic era—but also, for Muhammad and the Muslims, a new way of life. Henceforth, the organizational principle of the community was not to be mere blood kinship, but the greater brotherhood of all Muslims. The men who accompanied Muhammad on the Hijrah were called the *Muhajirun*—"those that made the Hijrah" or the "Emigrants"—while those in Medina who became Muslims were called the *Ansar* or "Helpers."

Muhammad was well acquainted with the situation in Medina. Earlier, before the Hijrah, the city had sent envoys to Mecca asking Muhammad to mediate a dispute between two powerful tribes. What the envoys saw and heard had impressed them and they had invited Muhammad to settle in Medina. After the Hijrah, Muhammad's exceptional qualities so impressed the Medinans that the rival tribes and their allies temporarily closed ranks as, on March 15, 624, Muhammad and his supporters moved against the pagans of Mecca.

Fighting for Islam

The first battle, which took place near Badr, now a small town southwest of Medina, had several important effects. In the first place, the Muslim forces, outnumbered three to one, defeated the Meccans. Secondly, the discipline displayed by the Muslims brought home to the Meccans, perhaps for the first time, the abilities of the man they had driven from their city. Thirdly, one of the allied tribes which had pledged support to the Muslims in the Battle of Badr, but had then proved lukewarm when the fighting started, was expelled from Medina one month after the battle. Those who claimed to be allies of the Muslims, but really opposed them, were thus served warning: membership in the community imposed the obligation of total support.

A year later the Meccans struck back. Assembling an army of three thousand men, they met the Muslims at Uhud, a ridge outside Medina. After an initial success the Muslims were driven back and the Prophet himself was wounded. As the Muslims were not completely defeated, the Meccans, with an army of ten thousand, attacked Medina again two years later but with quite different results. At the Battle of the Trench, the Muslims scored a signal victory by introducing a new defense. On the side of Medina from which attack was expected they dug a trench too deep for the Meccan cavalry to clear without exposing itself to the archers posted behind earthworks on the Medina side. After an inconclusive siege, the Meccans were forced to retire. Thereafter, Medina was entirely in the hands of the Muslims.

The Growth of Islam

The Constitution of Medina—under which the clans accepting Muhammad as the Prophet of God formed an alliance, or federation—dates from this period. It showed that the political consciousness of the Muslim community had reached an important point; its members defined themselves as a community separate from all others. The Constitution also defined the role of non-Muslims in the community. Jews, for example, were part of the community; they were *dhimmis,* that is, protected people, as long as they conformed to its laws. This established a precedent for the treatment of subject peoples during the later conquests. Christians and Jews, upon a payment of a yearly tax, were allowed religious freedom and, while maintaining their status as non-Muslims, were associate members of the Muslim state. This status did not apply to polytheists, who could not be tolerated within a community that worshipped the One God.

14. Why did the Meccans not investigate the cave?

15. What is the significance of the Hegira?

16. Why was Muhammad acquainted with the situation in Medina?

17. What was the significance of the Battle of Badr?

18. Of what other events do these events remind you?

19. What was the significance of the Constitution of Medina?

20. What do these events tell you about Muhammad's strength at this point?

Ibn Ishaq, one of the earliest biographers of the Prophet, says it was at about this time that Muhammad sent letters to the rulers of the earth—the King of Persia, the Emperor of Byzantium, the Negus of Abyssinia, and the Governor of Egypt among others—inviting them to submit to Islam. Nothing more fully illustrates the confidence of the small community, as its military power, despite the Battle of the Trench, was still negligible. But its confidence was not misplaced. Muhammad so effectively built up a series of alliances among the tribes—his early years with the Bedouins must have stood him in good stead here—that by 628 he and fifteen hundred followers were able to demand access to the Ka'bah during negotiations with the Meccans.

21. In 629, Muhammad reentered Mecca. Why was this act significant?

This was a milestone in the history of the Muslims. Just a short time before, Muhammad had had to leave the city of his birth in fear of his life. Now he was being treated by his former enemies as a leader in his own right. A year later, in 629, he reentered and, in effect, conquered Mecca without bloodshed and in a spirit of tolerance which established an ideal for future conquests. He also destroyed the idols in the Ka'bah, to put an end forever to pagan practices there. At the same time Muhammad won the allegiance of 'Amr ibn al-'As, the future conqueror of Egypt, and Khalid ibn al-Walid, the future "Sword of God," both of whom embraced Islam and joined Muhammad. Their conversion was especially noteworthy because these men had been among Muhammad's bitterest opponents only a short time before.

In one sense Muhammad's return to Mecca was the climax of his mission. In 632, just three years later, he was suddenly taken ill, and on June 8 of that year, with his third wife 'Aishah in attendance, the Messenger of God "died with the heat of noon."

Monitoring Comprehension

Answer these questions based on the selection. Talk out answers with your partner. Refer to the selection and your margin notes for evidence to support your answers.

1. How old was Muhammad when he died?
   a. 20   b. 50   c. 62   d. 72

2. Young Muhammad lost his mother and father at a young age, then his grandfather. Propose what influence these losses might have had in making him the man he became. _____

   _____

3. Muhammad spent a year or two with a Bedouin family in the desert. Propose how this experience may have influenced him as a person. _____

   _____

4. What were two important effects of the Battle of Badr?

   _____

   _____

5. Why was the Hegira significant, or important? _____

   _____

6. Why was the Constitution of Medina significant, or important? _____

   _____

7. *Critical Thinking Question:* What do you believe was Muhammad's most significant contribution to the world? Give reasons to support your belief. _____

   _____

Writing in Response

As you read the selection, did you relate the content to other people, places, or times you know about? Of what other events in history does this account remind you? How are the events similar? How are they different? In your notebook, write a short paragraph or two in which you identify a similar event in history and state the similarities and then the differences. Be ready to talk about relationships.

Playing with Words

Complete these exercises independently as a way to test yourself.

A. Here are the featured words from the selection. Match them with their definitions. Place the correct letter on the line at the left. Use the process of elimination.

Adjectives

_____	1. impending	a. standing out above others
_____	2. inconclusive	b. chief in importance
_____	3. negligible	c. being one of a kind
_____	4. paramount	d. about to occur, threatening
_____	5. preeminent	e. so insignificant that it can be disregarded
_____	6. unique	f. not decisive, without a definite outcome

Verbs

_____	7. consigned	g. handed over, delivered
_____	8. divulged	h. served as go-between, acted to bring agreement between groups
_____	9. mediated	i. moved from one place to settle in another
_____	10. migrated	j. made known to others, told something

Nouns

_____	11. access	k. messenger, diplomatic agent
_____	12. adherents	l. union formed by agreement
_____	13. alliance	m. patience, self-control
_____	14. envoy	n. something made known
_____	15. forbearance	o. the scriptures of Islam
_____	16. Koran	p. belief in many gods
_____	17. idols	q. objects or images worshiped as gods
_____	18. polytheism	r. long effort to overcome resistance
_____	19. precedent	s. entrance, admission
_____	20. revelation	t. case that serves as a model for a later case
_____	21. siege	u. followers, supporters

B. Select the appropriate word from the words just given, and place one in each sentence slot. Do not use a word more than once. Start with the items you know for sure and cross out options as you use them.

Adjectives

1. Graduating from college is of _____ importance to her; all other things are of lesser importance.

2. As a student, her income was _____; she barely had enough money for the basics.

3. The evidence against the prisoner was _____, so they had to release him.

4. He felt a sense of _____ trouble as the test date came closer and closer.

5. The thing that made the house _____ was the way it floated on water.

6. His family held a _____ position in society; they were leaders.

Verbs

7. During the drought, the Bedouins _____ across the desert in search of a new home.

8. He _____ the information to the police when he heard of the seriousness of the crime.

9. The lawyer _____ between the two angry men.

10. As a child she was _____ to the care of a nurse and never saw her parents.

Nouns

11. The two nations signed a new _____ in which they agreed to assist each other in times of war.

12. The president sent an _____ to talk to the prime minister of that country.

13. It was a stunning _____ to learn that the man she had married was a billionaire.

14. As a child, he read the _____; in that way he learned the important principles of Islam.

15. After a lengthy _____, the city surrendered, for it had been without food for many days.

16. _____ is the belief in many Gods.

17. They denied him _____ into the city because he did not believe as they did.

18. Muhammad had many _____ who followed him when he left the city.

19. "I ask your _____ in this case," the hotel manager said. "There will be a long wait before a room is available for you."

20. They worshiped _____, which were golden eagles studded with diamonds.

21. Because there is no _____ that we can follow, we must make up our own minds.

EXTENDING WHAT YOU HAVE LEARNED

Applying Strategies in College and Personal Reading

1. Read a section from a history book that recounts a sequence of events or tells about the events in a person's life. On a card write down

   • The significant events in the order in which they occurred;

   • The factors that brought these events into being;

   • The significance of the events; and

   • Another event that you believe to be similar.

2. Read an article from the travel section of the Sunday newspaper or a travel magazine that describes a place you would like to visit. As you read, visualize what is being described. On an index card, record a few notes about the place. Be ready to tell about the place you have read about.

Building a Knowledge Base for Reading

Circle Florence, Italy, on the map in Figure 14.1 and Mecca in Saudi Arabia on the map in Figure 14.2. Also circle the label for the Mediterranean Sea in Figure 14.2. Decide why the Mediterranean Sea was given that name, based on its two major elements: *medi-* and *terra-*.

Gaining Ownership of Words

Select several words from those featured in this chapter to record in your personal vocabulary list. Include a model sentence for each. Try to use the words you have selected in speaking and writing.

15

Interpreting Style, Tone, and Mood

OBJECTIVE

In this chapter, you will develop strategies for interpreting

1. Style: the author's overall manner of writing;
2. Tone: the way in which an author expresses feelings; and
3. Mood: the expression of feeling in a selection.

You will also have the opportunity to practice strategies you have already learned that help you put together an author's main point and help you infer, compare, judge, and relate.

STYLE

The word *style* means the way in which authors choose and use words, punctuation, sentences, and paragraphs to communicate meanings. Writing can be bare bones, matter-of-fact, and unembellished: An author uses words sparingly and comes directly to the point. Or writing can be flowery and dramatic: An author uses colorful and melodious expressions, painting pictures with descriptive words and providing elaboration. Of course, writing can be somewhere between the plain and the dramatic. And it can be overly matter-of-fact as well as overly dramatic.

Elements of Style

In *Writer's Guide and Index to English,* Porter Perrin identifies elements to consider in thinking about an author's style. Here are those elements as well as questions that you can use to identify an author's style:

1. *Development of ideas:* the way the author develops his or her thought.
   a. Does the writer start with specific information and then develop generalizations? Or does he or she begin with a generalization and then provide details or examples?
   b. Does the writer lay it all out in black and white? Or do you have to infer meanings?
   c. Does the writer present ideas systematically?
   d. Does the writer pack in a lot of details in a short space? Does the writer provide lots of visual detail?

2. *Qualities of sound:* the way the words sound if read aloud.
   a. Do the words flow smoothly? Or is there an awkwardness in the way words flow?
   b. Has the writer effectively used alliteration (the repetition of beginning sounds as in "the forest's ferny floor") or rhyme as in the following poem?

   > Listen, my children, and you shall hear
   > Of the midnight ride of Paul Revere,
   > On the eighteenth of April, in Seventy five;
   > Hardly a man is now alive
   > Who remembers that famous day and year.

   c. Does the writer repeat words for effect?

   d. How has the writer used punctuation to emphasize sound, such as the dash to make you pause in reading or the exclamation mark to lend excitement?

3. *Visual elements:* the way the author uses space and shape.

   a. Is the piece laid out in lines and verses?

   b. Does the author use italic type for emphasis?

4. *Sentences:* the way the author constructs sentences.

   a. Does the author use short sentences or long? A mix of sentence lengths?

   b. Does the author use complicated sentence patterns? Simple, easy-to-read sentences?

5. *Words:* the words the author chooses.

   a. Does the author rely on short words? Long words?

   b. Does the author rely on familiar words? Unfamiliar words?

6. *Imagery:* the pictures the author paints with words.

   a. Does the author paint pictures that you can see in your mind?

   b. Does the author work with ideas that are difficult to picture?

7. *Figures of speech:* metaphors, similes, and unique ways of handling language.

   a. Does the author build unusual relationships through metaphor or simile?

     (1) A simile is a creative comparison that relies on the word *like* or *as* to connect two things. Example: "The branches of the tree stretched heavenward like hands reaching for space."

                   branches = hands

     (2) A metaphor is a creative comparison without *like* or *as*. Example: "The wind is a deadly dragon, slapping the world with its tail."

                  wind = deadly dragon

   b. Does the author use language in unique ways?

8. *Literary allusions:* references to other pieces of literature.

   a. Does the author use words, phrases, or sentences from other authors without quoting directly or telling you their source?

   b. Does the author refer in some way to events from other pieces of literature?

   c. Does the author quote directly (with quotation marks) from other authors?

Read aloud as a class chorus these two stanzas by Alfred, Lord Tennyson, an English poet who lived in the 1880s. As you read, listen for the sounds and rhythm. Consider how Tennyson creatively compares the ending of a year to death.

Ring Out, Wild Bells

> Ring out, wild bells to the wild sky,
>   The flying cloud, the frosty light:
>   The year is dying in the night;
> Ring out, wild bells, and let him die.
>
> Ring out the old, ring in the new,
>   Ring, happy bells, across the snow.
>   The year is going, let him go;
> Ring out the false, ring in the true.

Think
about . . .

If you were writing about New Year's Eve, what things would you talk about? Does New Year's Eve remind you of death?

To describe a new year's beginning, Tennyson uses rhyme and repetition. What repetition of words do you hear? What rhyme? How is the end of a year like the end of a life? In making this connection, Tennyson is working with metaphor—a creative comparison without reliance on the word *like* or *as*. (See Chapter 14 for a discussion of metaphor.) The use of repetition, rhyme, and metaphor are aspects of his style, as is his use of simple, one-syllable words.

Read aloud this piece, which comes from Africa and has a long folk tradition. It has been used as a work chant. Can you infer from context the meaning of "Kum Ba Yah"?

Kum Ba Yah

Kum ba yah, my lord. Kum ba yah!
Kum ba yah, my lord. Kum ba yah!
Kum ba yah, my lord. Kum ba yah!
  Oh lord, Kum ba yah.

I am singing, lord. Kum ba yah!
I am singing, lord. Kum ba yah!
I am singing, lord. Kum ba yah!
  Oh lord, kum ba yah.

I am hoeing, lord. Kum ba yah!
I am hoeing, lord. Kum ba yah!
I am hoeing, lord. Kum ba yah!
  Oh lord, kum ba yah.

I am sowing, lord. Kum ba yah!
I am sowing, lord. Kum ba yah!
I am sowing, lord. Kum ba yah!
  Oh lord, kum ba yah.

- What are the elements of its style? _____
  _____

- Why are these elements important in a work chant, a song that workers chant as they struggle at a difficult job? _____
  _____
  _____

TONE AND MOOD

Tone is simply the manner in which a writer communicates his or her message and feelings; it is closely akin to tone of voice in speaking. The tone of a piece can be sharp and probing, antagonistic and critical, sarcastic, ironic, humorous, or warm and caring. Both in writing and in speaking, tone often reflects the attitude of the author toward his or her subject. To identify the tone of a piece, keep relating it to tone of voice; ask yourself, "If the author were talking to me instead of writing, what tone of voice would he or she be using?"

Mood is the actual feeling communicated. Both tone and style set the mood, which can be happy or sad, positive or negative, calm or excited, or at times just neutral. Within a particular piece, the mood can fluctuate between upbeat and downbeat. Take, for example, the old poem "Casey at the Bat." The mood is down as the Mudville team gets itself into a tight spot. It keeps going down as each batter steps up to the plate and gets nowhere. But when Casey steps up to bat, the mood swings up, for this is the "mighty Casey." The mood keeps swinging up and down as Casey lets one ball after another go by. With the final line—"There is no joy in Mudville./Mighty Casey has struck out"—the mood plummets to an all-time low, and stays there!

You can grasp the mood swings in a piece like this. Put "up-mood" at the top of the vertical axis of a graph, "down-mood" at the bottom. Put "beginning of the piece" on the left side of the horizontal axis and "end of the piece" at the far right side of it. Draw a fluctuating line within the axes to show the mood swings. Your instructor may read "Casey at the Bat" or another narrative poem or short story aloud to you, so that you can listen for mood and create a mood-graph in response.

Now here is a short limerick by Edward Lear to consider in terms of tone and mood. Read it aloud as a class chorus.

The Old Man with a Beard

There was an Old Man with a beard,
Who said: "It is just as I feared!
  Two owls and a hen,
  Four larks and a wren
Have all built their nests in my beard."

What is the tone and mood of the limerick? Lear's poem is humorous—a ridiculous piece of fluff. The feeling is one of outrageousness, more upbeat than downbeat, even though the situation described is far from funny and is not one you would want to happen to you. What does it mean? Perhaps that outrageous things do happen in this world. Perhaps that it helps to face problems with laughing good humor.

Go back now to Chapter 10, pages 192–193. Reread the essay by Robert Fulghum. As you read, ask, "What is the tone of the essay? What kind of mood does the author create?" Write a word or two on this line to describe the tone and mood:

_____

_____

In the next part of this chapter, you will read a series of selections for style, mood, and tone: two literary essays, a speech, and a poem. As you read these, ask, "How do the style, mood, and tone differ from the style, mood, and tone of textbook material?"

SELECTION 1

Fatherhood: Because It's There   (LITERARY ESSAY)

Independent Reading

Expanding Vocabulary for Reading

Use word structure and context clues to determine the meanings of the italicized words. Check the glossary if you are not certain of the meanings. Record the definition of each highlighted term in your notebook.

1. My *reservations* about the project were overcome when I heard that Magic Johnson was involved.

2. *Impregnation* of the female of the species by the male is necessary if the species is to continue.

3. The firefighter's *heroic* deed of going into the burning building to save a child won him recognition.

4. She was *nobly* rewarded for her efforts; she received a splendid trophy and a citation from the president.

Getting Ready to Read

Glance over the title, author's name, and the first paragraph of the selection.

• What is the article about? _____

Did You KNOW?

The adverb *nobly* can be traced to the Latin *nobilis*, meaning "well-known or highborn." Related words are *noble*, *nobility*, and *ignoble*. The prefix *ig-* on *ignoble* means "not."

- What do you already know about this author? What kind of personality does he have? What do you know about his son Ennis? _____

  _____

- What kind of writing do you expect from Cosby? A textbooklike piece? A funny piece? _____

  _____

Set your purpose for reading.

- Write a question you hope to answer by reading the selection. Make it relate to the style, tone, or mood of the writing. _____

  _____

  _____

Reading with Meaning

Read to answer your purpose-setting question.

⁂ Fatherhood: Because It's There
Bill Cosby

It's love, of course, that makes us fathers do it—love for the woman we've married and love for every baby we've ever seen, except the one that threw up on our shoes. And so, in spite of all our reservations about this scary business of reproduction, we must admit that people look happy when they're carrying babies. The male looks especially happy because he has someone to carry it for him, his darling packager.

But his wife is happy too, because she feels she's fulfilling herself as a woman. I've heard so many females say that they became mothers because they wanted to feel like women, as if they felt like longshoremen at all other times. And so many others have said, "I had the baby because I wanted to see if I could," which sounds like a reason for climbing Mount Everest or breaking the four-minute mile. If a chimpanzee can have a baby, the human female should realize that the feat is something less than an entry for the Guinness Book of World Records.

The new father, of course, feels that his mere impregnation of his mate, done every day by otters and apes, is Olympic gold medal stuff. Even if he's afraid of garter snakes, he feels positively heroic. He feels that he and his wife have nobly created something that will last. He never thinks that they may have created one of the top underachievers in their town.   [249 words]

Monitoring Comprehension

Talk about your reaction to the Cosby piece. Then answer the questions.

1. Why do you think Cosby added the phrase, "except the one that threw up on our shoes"? _____

   _____

2. What other phrases does Cosby use for the same reason? _____

   _____

Think about . . .

What thoughts go through your head as you read this article?

3. What is the overall tone of the essay? _____

_____

4. This kind of essay is satire. A satirist talks about a serious issue but uses humor and ridicule. Sometimes this approach is called tongue-in-cheek humor. What other writer—one that you have read in this book—uses a similar approach? _____

_____

_____

5. How does Cosby's style differ from textbook writing? _____

_____

6. What is Cosby's main point, or thesis? What is he saying to you? _____

_____

7. *Critical Thinking Question:* Do you agree or disagree with Cosby's point? Why?

_____

_____

8. *Critical Thinking Question:* How does Cosby's point relate to your life?

_____

_____

9. *Critical Thinking Question:* Cosby wrote this essay before the untimely death of his son. Predict how he might change this article if he were to revise it now.

_____

_____

Reviewing Key Vocabulary

Use the following words in sentences so that the meaning of each is explicit. Try to add a bit of humor to your sentences. Use the sentences in "Expanding Vocabulary for Reading," the selection, and the glossary as models for the sentences you compose.

1. reservations

2. impregnation

3. heroic

4. nobly

SELECTION 2

Address at the Dedication of the Gettysburg National Cemetery (SPEECH)

Independent Reading

Expanding Vocabulary for Reading

Use word elements and context clues to determine the meanings of the italicized words. Check the glossary if you are not certain of the meanings. Record the definition of each highlighted term in your notebook.

1. A *score* of years is twice as long as a decade.

2. He put this *proposition* to me: Every person must do his or her fair share of the work.

3. The priest *consecrated* the site by declaring it a sacred place.

4. "We cannot *hallow* this battlefield; we cannot make it a sacred, or holy place," the president said.

5. Wearing a long skirt does not *detract* from your appearance. It may actually make you look better.

Getting Ready to Read

Read the title, author's name, and introduction to the selection.

- What do you already know about this selection and its author?

  _____

- Setting your purpose for reading: Write one question you hope to answer by reading the selection. _____

  _____

Reading with Meaning

As you read the selection or listen to it as your instructor reads it aloud, pretend you are at Gettysburg and are hearing Lincoln deliver the address. Think how it would have made you feel. What elements of Lincoln's writing style would have led you to feel that way?

Address at the Dedication of the Gettysburg National Cemetery
Abraham Lincoln

Lincoln delivered this address on November 19, 1863, at Gettysburg, Pennsylvania. The prior speaker, Edward Everett, had just presented a very formal two-hour speech to an audience of 100,000 people. Lincoln had made a rough outline of his own address, wrote it out on paper only shortly before, and scribbled the final sentence in pencil after arriving in Gettysburg. The Gettysburg Address, as we know it today, is one of the most quoted speeches of all time.

Four score and seven years ago our fathers brought forth on this continent a new nation, conceived in liberty, and dedicated to the proposition that all men are created equal.

Now we are engaged in a great civil war, testing whether that nation, or any nation so conceived and so dedicated, can long endure. We are met on a great battlefield of

Did You KNOW?

Consecrate is derived from the Latin root *sacr-*, which means "holy." It carries the prefix *con-*, meaning "together." Related words are *sacred* and *sacrament, conspire* and *conscript. Detract* is from the Latin root *tract-*, meaning "to drag or draw." It carries the prefix *de-*, meaning "down." Related words are *retract, contract, tractor; denude, destroy.*

that war. We have come to dedicate a portion of that field as a final resting-place for those who here gave their lives that this nation might live. It is altogether fitting and proper that we should do this.

But, in a larger sense, we cannot dedicate—we cannot consecrate—we cannot hallow—this ground. The brave men, living and dead, who struggled here, have consecrated it far above our poor power to add or detract. The world will little note nor long remember what we say here, but it can never forget what they did here. It is for us, the living, rather to be dedicated here to the unfinished work which they who fought here have thus far so nobly advanced. It is rather for us to be here dedicated to the great task remaining before us—that from these honored dead we take increased devotion to that cause for which they gave the last full measure of devotion; that we here highly resolve that these dead shall not have died in vain; that this nation, under God, shall have a new birth of freedom; and that government of the people, by the people, for the people, shall not perish from the earth.   [353 words]

Monitoring Comprehension and Knowledge of Vocabulary

Complete individually or collaboratively.

1. How did Lincoln's speech make you feel? _____

_____

2. What lines do you particularly like? Write them here and tell why you like the way Lincoln used that particular phrase. _____

_____

3. What words or phrases did Lincoln repeat? Write them here and tell why you think he repeated them. _____

_____

4. How long is four score and seven years? Why did Lincoln not come right out and give the number of years? _____

_____

5. Lincoln used the phrase "gave the last full measure of devotion." What did he mean by that phrase? Why didn't he come out and say it more clearly? _____

_____

_____

6. What is the tone of Lincoln's address?
   a. sarcastic   c. humorous
   b. serious   d. light

7. *Critical Thinking Question:* How does the tone of Lincoln's address differ from the tone of Cosby's essay? _____

_____

8. *Critical Thinking Question:* How do you think Lincoln would have viewed world events since his death? Would he be happy with the world today? Explain. _____

_____

_____

_____

9. How many years are two *score* and five?
   a. 15   b. 25   c. 35   d. 45

10. We are dedicated to the *proposition* that all people have a right to a free education through the twelfth grade. What is the meaning of *proposition* in the sentence?
    a. evil plan   c. dishonorable proposal
    b. statement of basic belief   d. way of doing something

11. *Hallowed* ground is ground that has been
    a. made sacred.   c. talked about.
    b. dug up.   d. used at Halloween for ghostly purposes.

12. When wine has been *consecrated,* it has been
    a. purified chemically.   c. made impure.
    b. consumed.   d. made holy.

13. Behaving that way will *detract* from your reputation. What is the meaning of *detract* in that sentence?
    a. take away from   c. inhibit
    b. increase   d. clear

SELECTION 3

She Sat Still (LITERARY ESSAY)

An In-Text Test

Expanding Vocabulary for Reading

Use word elements and context clues to determine the meanings of the italicized words. Check the glossary if you are not certain of the meanings. Record the definition of each italicized term in your notebook.

1. My friend is an *activist.* She believes it is important to take action and speak out on controversial issues.

2. He was known as a *radical* because of the far-out position he advocated.

3. Martin Luther King was known for the *eloquent* phrases he used in his speeches.

4. In some churches, baptism of the young is a *sacrament.*

5. The young people would *congregate* on the corner in front of the building after school was over for the day.

6. The girl was a living *tribute* to her father, who had sacrificed his life so that she might have an education.

Getting Ready to Read

Glance over the title, author's name, and first paragraph of the selection.

- What is the article about? _____

  _____

- What do you already know about this author? What kind of writing do you expect from him? A textbooklike piece? A funny piece? A serious piece? _____

  _____

  _____

  Set your purpose for reading.

Did You KNOW?

Congregate is from the Latin root *greg-,* which means "flock or herd." It carries the prefix *con-,* which means "together." Related words are *congregation, segregate,* and *segregation.*

Think about . . .

What thoughts go through your head as you preview this article?

- Write a question you hope to answer by reading the selection. Relate your question to the style, tone, or mood of writing. _____

_____

Reading with Meaning

Read to answer your purpose-setting question. Do this on your own.

She Sat Still
Robert Fulghum

"SIT STILL—JUST SIT STILL!" My mother's voice. Again and again. Teachers in school said it, too. And I, in my turn, have said it to my children and my students. Why do adults say this? Can't recall any child ever really sitting still just because some adults said to. That is why several "sit stills" are followed by "SIT DOWN AND SHUT UP!" or "SHUT UP AND SIT DOWN!" My mother once used both versions back to back, and I, smart-mouth that I was, asked her just which she wanted me to do first, shut up or sit down? My mother gave me that look. The one that meant she knew she would go to jail if she killed me, but it just might be worth it. At such a moment an adult will say very softly, one syllable at a time: "Get-out-of-my-sight." Any kid with half a brain will get up and go. Then the parent will sit very still.

Sitting still can be powerful stuff, though. It is on my mind as I write this on the first day of December in 1988, the anniversary of a moment when someone sat still and lit the fuse to social dynamite. On this day in 1955, a forty-two-year-old woman was on her way home from work. Getting on a public bus, she paid her fare and sat down on the first vacant seat. It was good to sit down—her feet were tired. As the bus filled with passengers, the driver turned and told her to give up her seat and move on back in the bus. She sat still. The driver got up and shouted, "MOVE IT!" She sat still. Passengers grumbled, cursed her, pushed at her. Still she sat. So the driver got off the bus, called the police, and they came to haul her off to jail and into history.

Rosa Parks. Not an activist or a radical. Just a quiet, conservative, church-going woman with a nice family and a decent job as a seamstress. For all the eloquent phrases that have been turned about her place in the flow of history, she did not get on that bus looking for trouble or trying to make a statement. Going home was all she had in mind, like everybody else. She was anchored to her seat by her own dignity. Rosa Parks simply wasn't going to be a "nigger" for anybody anymore. And all she knew to do was to sit still.

There is a sacred simplicity in not doing something—and doing it well. All the great religious leaders have done it. The Buddha sat still under a tree. Jesus sat still in a garden. Muhammad sat still in a cave. And Gandhi and King and thousands of others have brought sitting still to perfection as a powerful tool of social change. Passive resistance, meditation, prayer—one and the same.

It works even with little kids. Instead of telling them to sit still, you yourself can sit very still and quiet. Before long they will pay a great deal of attention to you. Students in class are also thrown by silent stillness on the part of a teacher. It is sometimes taken for great wisdom.

And sitting still works with grown-ups. On the very same bus route Rosa Parks used to travel, anybody can sit anywhere on the buses now, and some of the drivers are black—both men and women. The street where she was pulled off the bus has been renamed: Rosa Parks Avenue.

A new religion could be founded on this one sacrament. To belong would be simple. You wouldn't have to congregate on a special day in a special place. No hymns, no dues, no creeds, no preachers, and no potluck suppers. All you have to do is sit still. Once a day, for fifteen minutes, sit down, shut up, and be still. Like your mother told you.

Did You KNOW?

Eloquent carries the Latin root *loqu-*, meaning "to speak," and the prefix *e(x)-*, meaning "out of." Related words are *loquacious*, *elocution*, and *colloquial*, all of which have something to do with speaking.

Think
about . . .

Do you talk to yourself in your mind as you read? What kinds of things do you say to yourself? Why is doing this helpful?

Amazing things might happen if enough people did this on a regular basis. Every chair, park bench, and sofa would become a church.

Rosa Parks is in her seventies now, doing most of her sitting in a rocking chair, living in quiet retirement with her family in Detroit. The memorials to her sitting still are countless, but the best ones are the living tributes in the form of millions of people of every color getting on thousands of buses every evening, sitting down, and riding home in peace.

If there is indeed a heaven, then I've no doubt that Rosa Parks will go there. I imagine the moment when she signs in with the angel at the pearly gates.

"Ah, Rosa Parks, we've been expecting you. Make yourself at home—take any seat in the house."   [800 words]

Monitoring Comprehension and Writing in Response

Answer on your own. Write in complete sentences.

1. Fulghum uses incomplete sentences. They are part of his style. What does this style add to his writing? Why is it acceptable here? _____

_____

2. What is the overall tone of the essay? _____

_____

3. What is the thesis, or main point, of Fulghum's essay? _____

_____

4. *Critical Thinking Question:* Do you agree or disagree with Fulghum's point? Explain.

_____

_____

_____

5. *Critical Thinking Question:* How does Fulghum's point relate to your life?

_____

_____

_____

6. *Critical Thinking Question:* Of all the authors you have read in this chapter, which one's style is closest to Fulghum's? _____

Explain why. _____

_____

_____

Reviewing Key Vocabulary

Use the following words in sentences so that the meaning of each is explicit. Use the sentences in "Expanding Vocabulary for Reading," the selection, and the glossary as models for the sentences you compose.

1. activist

2. radical

3. eloquent

4. sacrament

5. congregate

6. tribute

SELECTION 4

The New Colossus (AMERICAN LITERATURE—POETRY)

A Concluding Thought or Two

Getting Ready to Read

1. Preview by reading the title and the introductory paragraph.

   • What does the adjective *colossal* mean? If you can't give a synonym for the word, check the glossary. _____

   _____

   • Check the glossary (under *colossus*) to find out about the Colossus of Rhodes or check Selection 1, Item 2 on page 101. What was the Colossus of Rhodes? Where did it stand. _____

   _____

   • What was the poet's background? _____

   _____

2. Think about what you already know about the topic. Picture in your mind the New Colossus. What does she hold in her hand? Why does she hold this? What does she have on her head? Why does she have this? How big is she? Ask yourself, "What does the statue mean to people? To me?" Write down what comes to mind.

   _____

   _____

   _____

3. Set your purpose for reading. In writing poetry, authors generally are more concerned about expressing their feelings than providing facts. As a result, your purpose may be

something other than "getting the facts straight." What is your purpose for reading?

_____

Reading with Meaning

Listen as your instructor reads aloud "The New Colossus" or read the poem aloud to yourself or with a partner.

The New Colossus
Emma Lazarus

Emma Lazarus was born in New York City in 1849. Throughout her life, which was short, Lazarus had two major interests: the Jewish people who had come to America and poetry. Her poem "The New Colossus" is engraved on the base of the Statue of Liberty, which is located in New York Harbor near Ellis Island.

> Not like the brazen giant of Greek fame,
> With conquering limbs astride from land to land;
> Here at our sea-washed, sunset gates shall stand
> A mighty woman with a torch, whose flame
> Is the imprisoned lightning, and her name
> Mother of Exiles. From her beacon-hand
> Glows world-wide welcome; her mild eyes command
> The air-bridged harbor that twin cities frame.
> "Keep, ancient lands, your storied pomp!" cries she
> With silent lips. "Give me your tired, your poor,
> Your huddled masses yearning to breathe free,
> The wretched refuse of your teeming shore.
> Send these, the homeless, tempest-tost to me.
> I lift my lamp beside the golden door!"

Monitoring Comprehension and Writing in Response

Answer these questions with a partner or by yourself. Be ready to talk about your answers.

1. Who is the mighty woman with a torch? Why did Emma Lazarus call her Mother of Exiles? Why didn't she come right out and say whom she meant?

   _____

   _____

2. Give some examples of the poet's use of alliteration—the repetition of sounds at the beginnings of words—and her use of rhyme. Hypothesize why she used alliteration and rhyme. Do you like her use of alliteration and rhyme? Tell why or why

   not. _____

   _____

3. Lazarus made the statue speak. What do you think she was trying to achieve by doing

   that? _____

   _____

4. What comparison does the poet build into her first four lines? Why do you think she started with this comparison? _____

_____

5. Lazarus referred to the "huddled masses yearning to breathe free." What did she mean by that phrase? Why didn't Lazarus come right out and say what she meant? _____

_____

6. How do the "huddled masses" feel as they approach the shores of their new land?

_____

_____

7. What does the Statue of Liberty mean to new immigrants? Explain your answer.

_____

_____

8. What meaning does the Statue of Liberty have for you? How does it relate to you and your family?

_____

_____

9. What mood does the poet build into her poem?
   a. despairing
   b. languishing
   c. impassioned
   d. unhappy

10. In the poem, the poet speaks for the Statue of Liberty. In your notebook, write a paragraph or poem in which you pretend you are an inaminate object—a nonliving thing—and speak for it. You might pretend to be the Golden Gate Bridge, the Grand Canyon, Niagara Falls, the Eiffel Tower, the White House, or simply your car as it reacts to your starting it up or reacts to what you make it do. Don't worry about rhyming or alliteration. Just get feelings down on paper.

EXTENDING WHAT YOU HAVE LEARNED

Gaining Ownership of Words

Select several words you have studied in this chapter to record in your personal vocabulary list. Try to use those words in speaking and writing.

Applying the Strategies in Independent Reading

Find a piece you feel you would enjoy reading. It can be anything that appeals to you. Think about the way the author is expressing himself or herself as you read. When you finish, write on a card the name of the author and the title of the selection. Then write down several words, phrases, or sentences that you think are typical of the writer's style, or manner of writing.

Reviewing Elements of Style

When you think of writing style, what elements come to your mind? Record at least three elements that particularly affect your reading enjoyment. Next to each, write down an example.

1. _____

_____

2. _____

_____

3. _____

_____

 ## Summation
Reading with Meaning

What have you learned about reading with meaning? On this page, record words, phrases, sentences, and reading strategies that come to your mind.

What do you see yourself doing in five years? In ten years? How does success in college relate to your goal or dream? Write a paragraph or two in which you explain your goal for yourself and the way in which you hope to get there.

APPENDIX A
AN EXTENDED SECTION OF A COLLEGE TEXT

In most college courses you are required to read lengthy chapters from textbooks. For this reason, Appendix A provides an extended block of material from a chapter of a college text. The chapter is "Chapter 9, Social Stratification," from David Popenoe's *Sociology*, 10th anniversary edition (Prentice Hall, 1995). Dr. Popenoe is a professor of sociology at Rutgers, The State University of New Jersey.

You may read this chapter in a variety of ways and for a variety of purposes, depending on your learning objectives and the goals of the instructor of your course. Because students and instructors will use this material differently, there are no suggested activities at the beginning; rather, the article is provided, followed by study activities from which students and instructors can choose those activities appropriate to their needs. The reading of the chapter and the related activities can take place at any point during the second half of the course. It may be most beneficial to use the material in reference to Chapter 9 of *Reading with Meaning* or during the final weeks of the course as a concluding activity or for assessment purposes. Students may complete some of the activities collaboratively.

CHAPTER
9

SOCIAL STRATIFICATION

- **THE DISTRIBUTION
  OF DESIRABLES**
    Income and Wealth
    Power
    Prestige

- **SOCIAL STATUS AND STATUS
  RANKING**
    Recognizing Social Status
    The Ranking of Social Statuses
    Status Inconsistency

- **HISTORICAL SYSTEMS
  OF STRATIFICATION**
    Slavery
    Caste
    Estate

- **SOCIAL CLASS**
    Class Divisions
    Class Consciousness and False
      Consciousness

- **SOCIAL MOBILITY**
    Open and Closed Societies
    The Conditions of Social Mobility
    The Social Mobility of Women

On the morning of April 15, 1912, what was at the time the world's largest passenger ship sank in the icy North Atlantic on its very first voyage. It took this great ship about three hours to go down. Unfortunately, there were not nearly enough lifeboats to save all the passengers. Afterwards, much was made of the fact that, despite the great loss of life, the passengers aboard the *Titanic* had taken care to observe the social norm of saving "women and children first." Perhaps this claim was necessary so that the British public and government could find some solace in the face of this disaster. Women and children *were* more likely to survive the *Titanic's* sinking; 69 percent of female and child passengers lived, but only 17 percent of male passengers did so.

However, in this case, as in many events that sociologists examine, things were not exactly as they seemed to be. A sociological analysis shows that the first class section of the ship was populated largely by the wealthy; second class was composed largely of middle-class professionals and businesspersons; and third class (and lower) was occupied largely by poor, working-class immigrants coming to the United States. When the survivorship rates aboard the *Titanic* are compared according to sex *and* social class, we see that only 26 percent of third-class passengers survived, compared to 44 percent of second-class passengers and 60 percent of first-class passengers. Male passengers in first class survived at a slightly higher rate than did children in third class. Perhaps it would be more accurate to say that the social norm that applied in the case of the *Titanic* was "first- and second-class women and children first."

The story of the sinking of the *Titanic* is just one illustration of the importance of social class. Desirable things in life are distributed unequally in all societies. In this chapter, we discuss the unequal distribution of desirables, what accounts for this pattern of distribution, and how this inequality both reflects and affects a society's social structure. In the following chapter, we will focus more narrowly on wealth and poverty in the United States.

THE DISTRIBUTION OF DESIRABLES

From birth, people in all known societies face inequality—a lack of equal access to the desirable things offered by their society. What is considered desirable varies from culture to culture, and may include material objects (cattle, gold, fresh food, tickets to the World Series) or nonmaterial valuables (prestige, respect, or fame). No matter what the desired object, though, one thing is certain: It is scarce, meaning that the demand for it exceeds the supply. Not everyone can own large amounts of gold or be

famous. Some people have greater access to the good things in life than others do.

Who are the privileged few in a society? Among animals, it is fairly clear that the rewards go to the physically strong. There is a pecking order among chickens, a ranked organization of hunting packs among wolves and lions, and a dominance hierarchy among many primates, especially certain species of monkeys. In each of these cases, the leaders use their strength to get the other members of the group to cooperate and obey.

Human inequality, in contrast, is based on much more than sheer physical power. In the simplest human societies, personal qualities alone may explain most of the social inequality. The leader of a band of hunter-gatherers, for instance, usually wins that role through bravery, age, and personal strength. But in more complex human societies, personal traits combine with social factors—such as race or the wealth of one's parents—to determine privilege.

Inequality in complex societies is somewhat like the ranking of apartments in an urban high rise, in which the desirable goods include sunlight, distance from street noise, and a scenic view. The best apartments are located in the upper stories, where there is a lot of light, not much noise and pollution, and a good view. Further down, the air is not as clean, the apartments get less direct sun, and the view disappears. The rents also drop, bringing these apartments within reach of less affluent people. Each floor can be thought of as a separate layer, or *stratum*, of privilege. By the time we get to the basement, where the building's maintenance workers have their quarters, we have reached the opposite of the top floor penthouse with its outdoor gardens and pool, unlimited light, and 360° view.

The residents of such a building, like the members of societies, are arranged in a system of **social stratification**—an enduring pattern based on the ranking of groups or categories of people into social positions according to their access to desirables. In an influential analysis that is still the basis for many sociological studies of inequality, Max Weber (1919/1946) identified three key dimensions of social stratification. Using terminology modified somewhat from that employed by Weber, we usually call these dimensions wealth and income (economic status), power (political status), and prestige (social status).

These dimensions are sometimes called the "rewards" of society, but the term *rewards* is misleading because it implies that those who receive them have done something to deserve them. Yet children born to royalty, for instance, are given wealth and prestige at birth and power as soon as they are old enough to exercise it. Often, then, social desirables are given to people who happen to be in a good social position, not only to those who achieve them on the basis of personal merit.

INCOME AND WEALTH

Wealth consists of all the economic assets of a person or group—not only money but also material objects, land, natural resources, and productive labor services. Some of the objects defined as wealth may have value because of the hours of skilled labor that go into making them, some because of their beauty, and some because they will bring future economic rewards. Diamonds have value, for instance, because they are both scarce and beautiful. A letter signed by George Washington has value because it is rare and has historic, patriotic, and sentimental appeal. Land is valued because it can be used to produce other economic assets in the form of crops or minerals.

Closely related to wealth is **income**—the economic gain derived from the use of human or material resources. The concepts of wealth and income should not be confused. *Wealth* refers to the total of all the possessions owned by a person or group. *Income* typically refers to the amount of money that a person or group receives on a regular basis. When we say that a man is "worth three million dollars," we are giving an estimate of his wealth—the sum total of all of his liquid and nonliquid assets: his house, his car, his investments, his bank accounts, and the money in his wallet. When we say that the same man earns $350,000 annually, we are describing his income.

Income is typically expressed as a flow of money per unit of time. But not all income is in the form of money. When family members do their own home repairs and housework, for example, these actions do not produce money. But they do increase the real value of the household. They produce "non-money income": If the members of the family did not do these tasks themselves, they would have to pay someone else to do them.

Although almost all of us would like to possess wealth and income, some people always have more than others. Among nations, too, there is an unequal distribution of economic reward. In Turkey, the per capita *gross national product*—the country's total economic output divided by the number of people living in the country—was $1,360 in 1990. In the United States in the same year, it was $21,100, more than 15 times higher. In Bangladesh, one of the poorest countries in the world, the per capita gross national product is only $180 (Population Reference Bureau, 1991). A nation's wealth is based largely on its natural resources, the strength of its economy, and the kinds of power (military, for example) it can use to obtain resources from other nations.

Wealth passed from one generation to the next has created numerous powerful families in the United States. One such family, the Rockefellers, has been particularly influential in business and politics.

The pattern of the unequal distribution of income in the United States is based on place of residence, race, education, gender, occupation, and other variables. For example, in 1990, Connecticut residents earned an average of $25,358 per capita, which was almost twice the per capita income of Mississippi at $12,735. Looking at the ethnic and racial pattern of income distribution, we see that the median U.S. family income in 1990 was $36,915 for a white family, $23,431 for a Hispanic family, and $21,423 for an African-American family (U.S. Bureau of the Census, 1993). These income differences are even more significant than they may seem at first because the average family size of nonwhites is larger than that of whites. Thus, the lower incomes of nonwhite families must be stretched to meet the needs of more people.

Table 9.1 *Percentage of Private Income Received by Bottom Fifth and Top Fifth of Population, 1989*

	Guatemala	Hong Kong	Hungary	Israel	Ivory Coast	Philippines	Poland	Sri Lanka	United States (1991 data)	Uruguay
Bottom Fifth	6%	5%	11%	6%	5%	6%	10%	5%	3.8%	6%
Top Fifth	55%	47%	32%	40%	53%	48%	35%	56%	46.7%	46%

Source: World Bank, *World Development Report* (New York: Oxford University Press, 1991).

The degree of inequality in the distribution of income in the United States is underscored by other important data. The wealthiest 20 percent of American families receive 46.7 percent of the total national income, while the poorest 20 percent receive only 3.8 percent (U.S. Bureau of the Census, 1993). Table 9.1 shows the percentage of total income received by the bottom and top fifth of the populations in ten countries.

The distribution of wealth in the United States is considerably more unequal than that of income. In 1990, when the top 1 percent of income earners received about 13 percent of all income, the top 1 percent of wealth holders held 31 percent of all net wealth. Indeed, a recent study conducted by the Federal Reserve Board found that the net worth of the top 1 percent of the population exceeds that of the bottom 90 percent (Gilbert & Kahl, 1992)!

In the U.S. economy the poorest people are often those who are the least productive economically. They may be too old or too young to work; they may not be educated enough to get high-paying jobs; they may be discriminated against in finding or advancing in jobs; or they may have to stay home to take care of children. No matter what the reason is, the result is the same: The amount of a family's income is closely tied to how much that family produces, as measured in the economic marketplace.

The pattern of income and wealth distribution in the United States may seem natural, but it is by no means universal. Because the American economy has expanded for most of its history, we often assume that wealth is something a person earns. In a more static economy, however, where the amount of wealth is relatively fixed, wealth is more likely to be something that one inherits rather than something one gains through personal achievement.

In socialist societies, at least ideally, wealth is based on need rather than on what one produces. In other words, "To each according to his needs, from each according to his abilities." A very large family in a socialist country, for example, might receive special payments to help with its additional expenses. People who do not produce through no fault of their own—such as the old and the sick—also receive state support. Even in these societies, however, "productive" people have access to rewards not available to others. In both the People's Republic of China and Cuba, for example, the distribution of income is far from equal (Tsui, 1991; Azicri, 1988).

POWER

Sociologists use the term **power** to refer to the capacity of people or groups to control or influence the actions of others, whether those others wish to cooperate or not. Sociologists study power not only in order to determine who exercises it but also to see why it is exercised and who benefits from its use.

Of the three main types of desirables—wealth and income, power, and prestige—power is the hardest to measure. Most studies of power are nothing more than educated guesses. Many forms of power are so well hidden that they are fully understood only by the power holders themselves. Because it is so hard to measure, and because it is so closely connected to questions of *ideology* (the set of cultural beliefs that is linked to, and helps to maintain, various political, social and class interests), the subject of power—who holds it and how it is used—is much debated in sociology. Some social scientists maintain that power in America is concentrated in the hands of a few people who share a common background and who tend to act together (Domhoff, 1983, 1978; Dye, 1990). For example, C. Wright Mills (1956) suggested that America is run by a "power elite" and calculated its total number at no more than 300 people. Other sociologists disagree strongly, arguing that power in America is divided among many groups and people (Rose, 1967; Riesman, 1961).

Sociologists do agree that real power does not always lie where we think it does. The mayors of some cities, for example, are sometimes mere figureheads while the actual decisions are made by a handful of business leaders who stay behind the scenes. And some decisions are made at lower levels where the work is carried out. Such is often the case with the police officer on the beat or the teacher in the classroom. (The distribution of power in America is discussed further in Chapter 17.)

Clearly, power may exist without wealth: Not all the rich are powerful, and not all the powerful are rich. But the two dimensions are closely related. Wealth can sometimes buy power. In national politics, for instance, candidates for office are often wealthy. The Kennedy brothers, the three Rockefeller governors, and the Roosevelts are only a few men of wealth who have become powerful in politics. Moreover, power is often useful in acquiring wealth. How many lawmakers or generals retire in poverty?

PRESTIGE

The third dimension of social stratification is **prestige**: the favorable evaluation and social recognition that a person receives from others. Prestige comes in many forms: public acceptance and fame, respect and admiration, honor and esteem. Prestige can be gained in many ways: People who are unusually kind, generous, brave, creative, or intelligent are often rewarded with prestige. Money can buy prestige, and power can compel it, or at least its outward appearance. For example, when John D. Rockefeller, Sr., made his first millions in oil, he was publicly despised. Over time, however, he used his great wealth to gain prestige, not only for himself, but also for his heirs, by funding museums, parks, foundations, and charities.

Sometimes the process works in reverse. A person may win prestige first and then translate it into wealth. The novelist and journalist Norman Mailer won prestige as a novelist with his first major work, *The Naked and the Dead*. Since its publication, Mailer has turned out a number of best-selling books.

Most often, however, prestige comes from holding a well-regarded occupational position. In American society, for example, prestige is routinely accorded those who are employed in medicine, science, and law. High prestige can also be attained through success in fields much in the public eye, such as television broadcasting, sports, and the movies.

SOCIAL STATUS AND STATUS RANKING

In general sociological usage, a social status is a socially defined position in a group or society. This us-

age of social status was discussed in Chapter 4. In relation to stratification, however, the term *social status* has a more specialized meaning: a ranked position in a social hierarchy or stratification system. This usage of social status is commonly referred to by sociologists as **socioeconomic status**, or **SES**. SES is a measure of social status that takes into account a person's educational attainment, income level, and occupational prestige. People who share the same socioeconomic status have access to about the same amount of society's desirables.

RECOGNIZING SOCIAL STATUS

Because so much of life is based on social ranking, pinpointing another person's social status is often important. But recognizing status can be difficult in modern urban settings. We often do not personally know many of the people we meet, yet we must make quick judgments about them. Two conditions must exist if we are to recognize an individual's status correctly: We must all be aware of the system used to rank status in our society and there must be some generally understood symbols that let us assess the status level of an unknown person.

In everyday life, one can often accurately determine a person's social status by observing how that individual interacts with others and how other people behave toward him or her. Is the person shown a great deal of respect and treated with formality, or is he or she treated informally? What do people say about and to the person? How does he or she react?

We can also look for what sociologists call status symbols. A **status symbol** can be anything—an obviously cheap or expensive object, a style of dress, a manner of speech—that communicates to others that an individual displaying it occupies a particular level of status.

People on low status levels, of course, do not deliberately display symbols of their low ranking. But people on higher status levels do try to advertise their status and to protect that status from being undervalued. Indeed, the farther up the status ladder people are, the more status symbols they are likely to deliberately display.

Think, for instance, about male attire. The symbolic meanings of a blue work shirt and a dress shirt, tie, and jacket are quite obvious: The man wearing the blue work shirt probably does some kind of physical labor. And the man wearing the tie and jacket probably does "intellectual" work, giving him higher prestige and a larger salary. Many people can also recognize more subtle differences between varieties of suits. A cheap mass-produced polyester suit differs visibly from an expensive wool suit from an exclusive men's store. Within the upper status levels, however, even more subtle distinctions exist that outsiders may not perceive. These distinctions—between a suit from a good men's store, for example, and one that is custom made—are often crucially important to members of high-status groups.

Many other items are used as symbols of status. A house, a neighborhood, a rug, a choice of words, a breed of dog, a car, a painting on the wall—all these things are potential signs of social position to those who know how to read them. And we are all skilled at reading at least the symbols of our own status level, though we may do this without thinking consciously about it.

When people demonstrate their socioeconomic status by blatantly displaying status symbols, they are engaging in **conspicuous consumption** (Veblen, 1899/1967). Examples are ownership of expensive and economically unproductive items such as well-tended lawns and fur coats. People who have recently acquired great wealth sometimes try to demonstrate their new status through conspicuous consumption. These newly wealthy people, referred to as "nouveau riche," buy expensive things—such as polo ponies and yachts—which symbolize the lifestyle of the very wealthy.

Yet status symbols can also mislead. A status symbol may be used fraudulently by people who do not in fact possess the status reflected by the symbol. To present the impression of higher economic status, families may buy pieces of furniture for their living rooms or cars that they can barely afford. Executives in large companies sometime spend money and behave in ways that are more appropriate for the status level above them. In this way, they hope to convince their bosses that they should be promoted. If they get the promotion, they expect that the higher salary that goes along with the new job will cover their costs.

C. Wright Mills (1956) once suggested that "status panic" was widespread in the American middle class, partly because of the spread to the working class of such status symbols as cars and nice clothes. The middle classes, he argued, devote much attention to their choices of where to live and in their pursuit of leisure in order to achieve more exclusive status symbols.

Because most status symbols can be displayed by those outside the appropriate status ranking, the most useful symbols are those that are hardest to fake. Thus, symbols of high status are often costly, and they change frequently. The lower classes, for example, cannot possibly afford to keep up with the changing high fashions in clothing. And many status symbols have a faddish aspect—one year high-status people have Yorkshire terriers, and the next they have sharpeis. Such symbols are especially useful because it takes time for outsiders to notice the changes.

THE RANKING OF SOCIAL STATUSES

Many of the examples of status given so far pertain to occupation, primarily because in modern societies one's occupation is the most important social position a person holds. (Blau & Duncan, 1967). Both income and prestige levels are typically heavily influenced by occupation. The connection is not, however, always as close as it might seem at first. Table 9.2 shows a ranking of occupations by prestige. We can see from the table that jobs that pay the most tend to be highest in prestige and those that pay the least are generally the lowest. But this is not always the case. A justice of the U.S. Supreme Court, one of the highest ranked positions, makes more than $100,000 a year. But a director of a large company or a successful doctor or lawyer who works in a big city like New York or Los Angeles earns even more. The high prestige of the justice is due to the power this position holds and to the years of education and experience required to attain it. The position is also highly selective: There are only nine U.S. Supreme Court justices.

The prestige ranking of various occupations has remained remarkably stable over time. One study found that very little change had occurred in the rankings since 1925 (Hodge, Siefel, & Rossi, 1964; see also Guppy & Goyder, 1984). Another study comparing the prestige rankings of occupations in 1947 and 1963 showed an almost perfect (.99) correlation. There was, however, a slight increase in the prestige of jobs in the sciences and a mild drop for "culturally oriented" occupations such as teaching.

The prestige ranking of occupations is also quite similar in different communities and regions within the United States and among nations. A study of six communities of different sizes in two different regions found that prestige rankings, along with other aspects of the stratification system, were similar from place to place. This seems to reflect a national pattern (Curtis & Jackson, 1977). Another study comparing status rankings in 60 countries, including the United States, also found a high (.83) degree of correlation (Treiman, 1977). An even higher correlation was established by previous studies that focused only on modern, industrial societies (Inkeles & Rossi, 1956).

Still, important differences exist between the United States and other cultures. In the former Soviet Union, for example, working-class occupations were generally accorded higher prestige (and income) than they are in the United States. In fact, the Soviet population consistently placed routine white-collar jobs near the bottom of the prestige ladder, above unskilled manual workers but below skilled

Table 9.2 *Distribution of Prestige Ratings*

Occupation	Rating	Occupation	Rating	Occupation	Rating
Physician	82	Statistician	55	Barber	38
College professor	78	Social worker	52	Jeweler	37
Judge	76	Funeral director	52	Watchmaker	37
Lawyer	76	Computer specialist	51	Bricklayer	36
Physicist	74	Stock broker	51	Airline stewardess	36
Dentist	74	Reporter	51	Meter reader	36
Banker	72	Office manager	50	Mechanic	35
Aeronautical engineer	71	Bank teller	50	Baker	34
Architect	71	Electrician	49	Shoe repairman	33
Psychologist	71	Machinist	48	Bulldozer operator	33
Airline pilot	70	Police officer	48	Bus driver	32
Chemist	69	Insurance agent	47	Truck driver	32
Minister	69	Musician	46	Cashier	31
Civil engineer	68	Secretary	46	Sales clerk	29
Biologist	68	Foreman	45	Meat cutter	28
Geologist	67	Real estate agent	44	Housekeeper	25
Sociologist	66	Fireman	44	Longshoreman	24
Political scientist	66	Postal clerk	43	Gas station attendant	22
Mathematician	65	Advertising agent	42	Cab driver	22
High school teacher	63	Mail carrier	42	Elevator operator	21
Registered nurse	62	Railroad conductor	41	Bartender	20
Pharmacist	61	Typist	41	Waiter	20
Veterinarian	60	Plumber	41	Farm laborer	18
Elementary school teacher	60	Farmer	41	Maid/servant	18
Accountant	57	Telephone operator	40	Garbage collector	17
Accountant	57	Carpenter	40	Janitor	17
Librarian	55	Welder	40	Shoe shiner	9
		Dancer	38		

Note: This table shows the way the American public ranks various occupations. Research has shown these prestige rankings to be relatively constant over time.

Source: James A. Davis and Tom W. Smith, *General Social Survey Cumulative File, 1972–1982* (Ann Arbor, Mich.: Inter-University Consortium for Political and Social Research, 1983).

manual workers (Lane, 1987). This preference in favor of skilled manual occupations continues to be widely held in modern-day Russia. However, it is increasingly challenged as recently unleashed market forces reduce the importance of old and obsolete industries and encourage the development of new enterprises and a middle class (Horn, 1991).

But occupation and income are not the only important factors determining an individual's social status ranking. In the United States, many people base status ranking in part on skin color (Hughes & Hertel, 1990). In fact, cross-cultural studies have suggested that lighter skin colors are preferred not just in the United States but also throughout the world. In Japan, for example, matrimonial ads in newspapers frequently mention light skin as a desirable quality in a prospective spouse. This is why Japanese women looking for husbands frequently use facial powder, parasols, and face hoods to make themselves appear paler (Frost, 1986). Religion is also ranked (in the United States, Protestants have higher status than Catholics and Jews; among Protestants, Episcopalians rank highest), as is education (those who have earned graduate degrees are at the top; those who never went to school are at the bottom).

In most cultures, men have traditionally been ranked higher than women. Also, people who are married generally have a higher status than those who are either single or divorced. Finally, there still exists a ranking based on ethnicity: Descendants of the original Anglo-Saxon settlers rank at the top, and those of foreign-born non-European heritage rank toward the bottom.

STATUS INCONSISTENCY

Although each individual occupies many ranked social statuses, people generally show a marked degree of **status consistency**. That is, people who rank high in one area also usually rank high in other status hierarchies. For example, an individual with high occupational rank usually also has a high income. Furthermore, a high ranking in education, ethnicity, and color often helps a person to achieve high occupational rank. The various status levels may not be exactly equal, but people in any given quartile of one status hierarchy will generally be in the same quartile of the other major status hierarchies. Research has shown that people whose general social position is toward the middle levels of the hierarchy tend to have somewhat lower status consistency than do those at the upper and lower levels (Gilbert & Kahl, 1987).

It is not uncommon, however, especially in the United States, for people to display **status inconsistency**. That is, an individual may rank high in one status area and low in another. Status inconsistency results, for example, when education and personal skill help a person rise above ethnic background or residence to achieve a high-status job. An African-American physician is an example of status inconsistency. Another is Justice Sandra Day O'Connor of the Supreme Court. Occupationally, her status is very high, even though her sex is generally ranked lower.

Some status inconsistency is built into work that has high prestige but low income, such as the ministry. Although they have high occupational prestige, ministers typically make less money than, for example, lower-ranked civil engineers and accountants (see Table 9.2 for prestige ratings). The average minister cannot afford to live in the style that is associated with high occupational status.

People with inconsistent statuses generally attempt to claim the highest one as their "overall" status. For example, royalty from foreign countries often expect to be treated as royalty, even by those who are not their subjects. But others may be inclined to treat them simply as "foreigners" or noncitizens.

HISTORICAL SYSTEMS OF STRATIFICATION

Stratification systems vary in different historical eras and economic structures. Sociologists consider the most significant types of stratification to be slavery, caste, estate, and class systems. Each type is characterized by a different kind of economic relationship between major social groups.

SLAVERY

Freedom or liberty is a highly valued nonmaterial desirable. **Slavery** is an extreme system of stratified inequality in which freedom is denied to one group of people in society. Many societies, including the antebellum South, found it expedient to forcibly import slaves from other societies.

The essential feature of slavery is an economic relationship: Some people own other people. Because they are owned, slaves provide an inexpensive form of labor for their owners. In addition, slaves are themselves commodities that can be sold in the marketplace for a profit (Collins, 1990).

Slavery is most compatible with an economy in which production methods are relatively primitive and require large amounts of human labor. The antebellum South is a good example. It was characterized by an agricultural economy centered around plantations, or very large farms. The major crop was cotton, which required a great deal of human labor to plant, cultivate, harvest, process, and transport.

All stratification systems are justified by an ideology that defends the interests of the higher-ranked individuals and that, more or less successfully, convinces members of the lower-ranked category that their inequality is just and proper. Without such an ideology, it would be difficult or impossible to secure compliance and maintain order among the losers in the struggle for wealth and income, power, and prestige. In the case of American slavery, African-Americans were quite different from those who enslaved them, especially with respect to culture and physical appearance. This facilitated the spread of an ideology that defined those who were enslaved as biologically and culturally inferior, perhaps even subhuman.

Slavery was the most visible feature of stratification in the United States for the first 200 years of its history. It is important to note, however, that this system of stratification required a great deal of repressive social control. Slaves often resisted their condition by revolting or running away. This demonstrates that the ideology that justified slavery, while broadly accepted by the slaveholders, was frequently rejected by the slaves themselves. Although slavery was abolished more than 125 years ago, its effects linger in the form of racism and discrimination against African-American people in the United States today.

CASTE

A **caste system** is a system of stratified inequality in which status is determined at birth and in which people generally cannot change their social position. In a caste system, it is usually very difficult to marry someone from another rank.

The best-known caste system in history was found in traditional India, where there were only four principal castes (*varnas*), but over a thousand subcategories (*jati*). Each *jati* was characterized by its own traditional occupation, place of residence, and rules for dealing with members of other castes. Indians learned early in childhood to recognize the status symbols that identified the members of the various castes. The highest castes were those of priests (*Brahmans*) and warriors (*Kshatriyas*). Many people, however, were not members of any caste. These people, called "untouchables," were considered the lowliest in society, and other caste members were forbidden to come into certain kinds of contact with them.

The caste system in India was justified by an ideology based on the Hindu religion. A principal tenet of Hinduism is the belief in *reincarnation*. After death, souls are reborn into another life on earth. Being born as an untouchable was considered to be the result of not having performed well in one's previous life. The Hindu religion encouraged the untouchables to accept their low social position dutifully (Tumin, 1985).

There have been major changes in India's caste system since the nation achieved independence from Britain after World War II. For example, the Indian constitution bans discrimination against untouchables. However, the Indian caste system is about 4,000 years old, and it has been slow to change.

Some scholars have viewed the situation of African-Americans in the United States as having many caste-like features. One anthropological expert on India (Berreman, 1960, p. 80) found the details of "caste in India and race relations in America . . . [to be] remarkably similar in view of the differences in cultural content."

ESTATE

The **estate system** of stratification is associated with a type of social and economic system called *feudalism*. Agrarian Europe in the Middle Ages was characterized by such a system.

The ideology supporting the European estates granted special privileges to members of the first estate—the priests—and to those of the second estate—the nobles—in contrast to the rights allowed the commoners, including the peasantry, who were classified as the third estate. This ideology was sanctioned by both the Catholic Church and by the laws of the state.

Dominance in the feudal system was maintained by the landowning nobles. On the feudal manor, peasant and lord were bound together in a relationship of *vassalage*: Peasants, or serfs, provided labor and military service in return for protection and material support from the noble.

With the development of extensive trading in late feudalism, a new social group appeared: merchants. The merchants, the first group in the feudal system whose wealth did not depend on inherited land ownership, were instrumental in the decline of feudalism and the rise of capitalism (this major socioeconomic change is discussed in Chapter 18). In effect, the merchants were the first capitalists. As an industrial economic system developed, social class became the dominant form of social stratification.

SOCIAL CLASS

The most common type of stratification in the modern world is the **class system**, a relatively open form of stratification based mainly on economic status. The class system is characterized by boundaries between groups that are less rigidly defined than those in slavery, caste, and estate systems. In a class system, there is considerably more mobility between groups, and achievement (as opposed to ascription) plays a larger role in ranking individuals. Even though a class system allows a relatively high degree of social mobility, however, it also includes strong elements of both stability and hierarchy. Thus, a class system still includes extensive inequality among groups of people.

The ideology that supports modern class systems is wholly secular. In essence, the greater privilege of the elite is justified by the argument that, because a substantial amount of social mobility up or down the class ladder is possible, those who succeed do so largely on the basis of their own merit. This means not only that individual determination and hard work are believed to pay off in the end with wealth and high status (Rossides, 1990; Fallows, 1988) but, more crucially, that the poor are seen as primarily responsible for their poverty. If they had applied themselves more diligently, they would not be poor. Thus, the class system is defended as eminently fair, and both the upper and the lower classes have no one to thank, or to blame, for their fate but themselves.

Sociologists disagree about the nature of social class systems. The major debate revolves around the theories of Karl Marx and Max Weber. For Marx, class is defined by access to the means of production—that is, the sources of wealth. The upper classes (the *bourgeoisie*) own and control the means of production and exploit the labor of the lower classes (the *proletariat*). Marx saw the bourgeoisie and the proletariat as inevitably destined to conflict. This **class conflict**—or struggle between competing classes—takes the form of events such as strikes and revolutions (Marx's views of class are more fully discussed in Chapters 17 and 18).

Weber, in contrast, viewed class systems as having two important dimensions of stratification in addition to economics: power and prestige. According to Marx, power and prestige are ultimately derived from wealth. To Weber, they are relatively independent of economics. Also, according to Weber, the relationship between classes in capitalism is not necessarily conflictful. It can even involve mutual dependence and cooperation.

The term *social class* is somewhat ambiguous because it stands for a very complex social reality. In American sociology, the concept of social class has often been defined broadly enough to include many different economic groupings, as well as groupings based on power and prestige. To the average American, however, "social class" means about the same thing as "social standing" and does not refer to specific groupings (Coleman & Rainwater, 1978).

CLASS DIVISIONS

A society is said to have extensive **class divisions**—perceived and real differences between its classes—when the levels of reward given to members of various classes are very different; when the members of these classes are fully aware of these differences; and when there are only limited opportunities to move from one class to another.

In the United States, the boundaries between the classes are relatively indistinct, awareness of class is low, and movement from one class group to another is fairly common. Class divisions do exist in the United States, however. One of the outstanding contributions of American sociologists in the first half of this century was to point out the major role that class divisions and inequality still play in this nation's life (Page, 1969).

Class divisions are found in cultures throughout the world—not just in advanced, industrialized, or Western nations like the United States. For example, Korea, a country whose class structure was rather poorly defined before World War II, now has four clearly defined classes: a wealthy and powerful capitalist class; a white-collar and small-business class; a working class; and a marginal group at the very bottom of the social ladder (Rossides, 1990).

Determining Class Divisions and Placement

What determines the major class divisions? Who is a member of which social class? Most sociologists today treat these issues as important areas of empirical study. But because class is a very complex concept, there are no easy answers. Universally accepted criteria do not exist for determining who belongs to a social class, as they do for deciding who belongs to a stamp club or football team.

Sociologists have developed three approaches—the objective, the reputational, and the subjective—to assign individuals to particular social classes.

THE OBJECTIVE APPROACH. In this approach, people are assigned by researchers to a social class on the basis of such objective criteria as their amount of income and wealth, type of work, and level of education. Sociologists thus arbitrarily establish class boundaries by defining the "cutoff points" for membership in each social class. Example of social classes formed in this manner are Marx's "capitalists" and "workers," and the modern distinction between the middle (or white-collar) and working (or blue-collar) classes.

Clearly, the use of this method to determine social class placement is not without difficulties. Critics contend that the cutoff points between classes are sometimes illogical. A person whose annual income is $24,999 will be placed by the objective method in a lower class than one whose annual income is $25,000, for example, if an annual income of $25,000 is the cutoff point for membership in the higher class. Furthermore, critics are concerned because the members of these "objective" classes are often unaware of their class membership.

On the positive side, however, the objective method is particularly helpful in allowing sociologists to perform quantitative research. Also, while the lifestyle of a person with an annual income of $24,999 is admittedly no different from that of a person with an annual income of $25,000, both of these individuals probably live quite differently than does a person with an annual income of $100,000.

THE REPUTATIONAL APPROACH. In this method, community members are asked to identify the number and nature of classes in their town or area. These people are also asked to name the class to which community members belong—that is, to place people in classes according to their "reputation." Sociologists who use this approach feel that only "insiders" can understand the social class structure of a given community.

Critics claim that this approach puts too much stress on prestige and not enough on more objective economic and political factors. Moreover, this approach works best in small communities where everyone knows everyone else. It is not as effective in larger communities or for comparing one community with another.

THE SUBJECTIVE APPROACH. Investigators using this approach ask people to place themselves within a social class. The approach thus captures the subjective aspect of social class—how people themselves see the class system and their own positions in it. One problem with using the subjective approach is that some cultures tend to deemphasize the importance of class differences. In the United States, for example, the sociologically important distinction between the middle and working classes is often blurred because the media and politicians routinely characterize everyone who is not rich or destitute as "middle class."

Furthermore, many working-class Americans see themselves as having middle- rather than working-class status, partly as a result of the rise in their economic standard of living since World War II. They can now afford the goods and, to some extent, the lifestyles that were once the mark of the white-collar middle class (Wright & Martin, 1987).

CLASS CONSCIOUSNESS AND FALSE CONSCIOUSNESS

The shared awareness that members of a social class have concerning their common situation and interests is called **class consciousness**. Compared with citizens of other advanced countries, Americans have very little class consciousness. This low level of awareness is especially characteristic, as previously noted, of the American working class.

Marxist sociologists are likely to see this low level of class consciousness in America as an example of **false consciousness**—any situation in which a person's subjective understanding of reality is inconsistent with the objective facts of that situation. False consciousness is clearly promoted by acceptance of the core ideology of equal opportunity that underlies the American class system and also by repeated pronouncements by politicians and other public figures identified with the American upper class that class is not an important feature of American social life. Thus, most Americans do not see their nation's social system as reflecting inequities in the distribution of goods that disproportionately benefit a small elite class.

Low class consciousness in American society is also a result of racial, religious, ethnic, and regional differences that often cut across, and even submerge, class differences. There is so much diversity in American life that social class is only one

way that Americans divide themselves. Instead of thinking about class, Americans tend to focus on inequities in age, sex, education, race, and religion.

The highest degree of class consciousness in American life is probably held by members of this country's upper class, especially those who have been wealthy for generations. This group is sharply aware of being in a unique situation and of sharing a distinct background and common interests (Coleman & Rainwater, 1978).

SOCIAL MOBILITY

Social mobility refers to a change on the part of an individual or a group of people from one status or social class to another. In common usage, "social mobility" means upward movement, or social improvement. But for sociologists, *upward mobility* is only one of several kinds of social mobility. People may also move to a lower status (*downward mobility*). Either upward or downward movement in an individual's status is called *vertical mobility*.

OPEN AND CLOSED SOCIETIES

Stratification systems differ in the ease with which people within them can move from one social status to another. A completely *open* society has never existed. But if it did, people could achieve whatever status their natural talents, abilities, and desires allowed them to attain. An open society would not be a society of equals; unequal social positions would still exist, but these positions would be filled solely on the basis of merit. Therefore, such a system could be described as a perfect *meritocracy*.

In a completely *closed* society everyone would be assigned a status at birth or at a certain age. That status could never be changed. No society has ever been completely closed, although some have been fairly close to this extreme.

The chief distinction between relatively open and relatively closed societies concerns the mix of statuses each contains. Open societies are characterized by greater reliance on *achieved* status than are closed societies; closed societies rely more on *ascribed* status. (Achieved and ascribed statuses were discussed in Chapter 4.) Many studies have shown that industrial, technologically advanced societies such as the United States tend to be relatively open (Hazelrigg & Garnier, 1976). In contrast, preindustrial societies with economies based on agriculture tend to be relatively closed (Eisenstadt, 1971).

India before the time of Gandhi is an example of a relatively closed society. During this era, the rules of the caste system were enforced by law. Yet even in this society, some social mobility was allowed. People could sometimes marry into higher castes, or acquire education and better jobs by obtaining the patronage of higher caste members. Such individuals, or at least their children, were later able to move into those higher castes. Sometimes entire groups were mobile, in which case the hierarchical ranking system of the entire society changed.

THE CONDITIONS OF SOCIAL MOBILITY

Sociologists commonly analyze two types of social mobility: intergenerational and intragenerational. The first type, *intergenerational social mobility*, compares the social position of parents with that attained by their children or grandchildren. In contrast, *intragenerational social mobility* refers to an individual's change in social position within his or her lifetime, as when someone starts out in a lower social class and rises to affluence. Both varieties can, however, entail either upward or downward mobility.

Upward Mobility

One pioneering study uncovered two conditions that seemed especially likely to foster upward mobility within a particular society: advanced industrial development and a large educational enrollment (Fox & Miller, 1965). As societies become more industrialized, the low-salaried, low-status jobs that require few skills are slowly eliminated. These are the jobs most easily performed by machines. At the same time, more jobs are added at the middle and upper levels. The upward mobility that results from such changes in the social or economic system—rather than from individual personal achievement—is called **structural mobility**.

The higher-level jobs will not be filled, however, unless the children of lower-status parents are given the needed knowledge and training. Advanced societies have tried to meet this need with a system of public secondary and higher education. One study concluded that in America "the best readily observable predictor of a young man's eventual status or earnings is the amount of schooling he has had" (Jencks et al., 1979). It is not known, however, whether this is principally because of the knowledge and skills schooling provides or because schooling serves as a kind of filtering system that allocates people to jobs.

Mass communication, urbanization, and geographic mobility are other factors related to high levels of upward mobility (Treiman, 1970). In addition, there is a relationship between upward mobility and a society's form of government. Autocratic governments tend to have a negative effect on upward mobility and income equality, but political democracy

tends to have a positive effect (Tyree, Semyonov, & Hodge, 1979).

Several social conditions can discourage upward mobility. Traditional societies provide few upper-level social positions and therefore few chances for people to move up. In fairly closed societies, such as traditional India, movement from one status to another may be forbidden by tradition or law. Furthermore, industrialization alone does not always ensure upward mobility, because the number of people employed in high-status jobs may remain fairly constant. In India and Egypt, for instance, the professions have expanded very little as these countries have become industrialized, and as a result, many college graduates have had great difficulty finding jobs (Matras, 1984).

In the United States, much individual upward mobility results from what Ralph Turner (1960) calls a contest among equals; in contrast, in England, it is more common for members of the elite to identify promising recruits in the middle classes and to deliberately recruit them for membership in the higher ranks, a process Turner terms *sponsored mobility*.

Downward Mobility

Common sense might suggest that the conditions leading to individual downward mobility are simply the opposites of those leading to upward mobility. To some extent, this is true. Not getting an education, marrying very young, and raising a large family are all related to downward mobility. Being born into a very large family also can lead to downward mobility, if the family cannot provide schooling and other advantages for all the children.

Other conditions leading to downward mobility can be less straightforward. Although living in a city is usually considered to be associated with upward mobility (Lispset & Bendix, 1964), some research has shown that urban living can also promote downward mobility (Fox & Miller, 1965). For instance, downward mobility is typically the lot of newly arrived immigrants to a city (Margolis, 1990). In short, city life promotes mobility of all kinds. Small-town and rural life, however, are definitely associated with lower rates of mobility.

Downward mobility has received surprisingly little attention from sociologists, in part because so many opportunities for upward structural mobility have existed throughout American history that downward mobility may not have seemed like a very important topic. However, recent changes in the American economy, to be discussed in the next chapter, suggest that we may be on the brink of a new era in which downward mobility may become more common than it ever was before, a trend that could have a variety of negative consequences for both individuals and the society as a whole.

THE SOCIAL MOBILITY OF WOMEN

Until recently, most studies of social mobility have focused exclusively on men, typically comparing sons with their fathers. Studies of the mobility of women, which have turned up some important findings, have become increasingly common as more and more women have entered the labor market. These studies also have had to consider some interesting methodological questions. Should a daughter's job be compared with that of her father or her mother, or both? Doesn't a woman achieve mobility through marriage as well as through the job market?

One study showed that a woman's occupational mobility is affected by the occupational status of *both* of her parents (Rosenfeld, 1978). Whether or not the mother works outside the home and the occupational position she holds are important factors that must be considered in studies of female mobility. Increasingly, of course, these will have to be considered in studies of male mobility as well. According to one such study, there seems to be a positive correlation between working mothers and the job status of their sons, but not that of their daughters (Sewell, Hauser, & Wolf, 1980).

Another researcher found that women may achieve greater social mobility through marriage than men do through their jobs (Chase, 1975). This study determined that in his first job a man tends to "inherit" the occupational status of his father. A woman, however, often marries a man with an occupational status quite different from that of her father and becomes associated more with her husband's status. Marriage may not always involve upward mobility; one study concluded that mobility through marriage is as often downward as it is upward (Glenn, Ross, & Tully, 1974).

In general, research has suggested that the process of gaining an education and getting a job has become very similar for both working men and working women (Treiman & Terrell, 1975). The qualifications needed for a job are the same for both sexes, and the route to a higher-status job is typically through education. Women, however, are still heavily concentrated in "pink-collar" clerical and service-oriented jobs, which tend to be low in pay and prestige (Bernard, 1981).

SUMMARY WITH KEY TERMS

1. All societies display some system of **social stratification**, an enduring pattern based on the ranking of groups or categories of people into social positions according to their access to desirables. Three principal dimensions of social stratification have been identified: wealth, power, and prestige.

2. **Wealth** consists of all the economic assets of a person or group—not only money but also material objects, land, natural resources, and productive labor services. **Income** is the economic gain derived from the use of human or material resources. Both income and wealth are distributed very unequally in our society, the latter much more than the former. Such factors as religion, race, education, occupation, and sex affect the distribution of wealth and income.

3. **Power** refers to the capacity of people or groups to control or influence the actions of others, whether those others wish to cooperate or not. Sociologists disagree on the nature of power in America. C. Wright Mills held that power is concentrated in the hands of a few people—the "power elite." Others believe that power is divided among many groups and people. Power and wealth are closely associated; wealth can sometimes buy power, and power is often used to acquire wealth.

4. **Prestige**, the favorable evaluation and social recognition that a person receives from others, is a more subjective aspect of social stratification. Prestige comes in such forms as fame, respect, honor, and esteem. Although money can buy prestige and power can command it, prestige usually comes from a person's holding a high occupational position.

5. **Socioeconomic status**, or **SES**, is a measure of social status that takes into account a person's educational attainment, income level, and occupational prestige. Correctly identifying an individual's social status depends on two things: general awareness of the character of a society's system of status ranking and widely understood signals that let us assess the status of an individual. A surprising level of agreement exists in America concerning the ranking of most social positions, although people's backgrounds can affect the way they rank others. A **status symbol** is anything that communicates to others that an individual displaying it occupies a certain level of status. When people demonstrate their socioeconomic status by displaying status symbols blatantly, they are engaging in **conspicuous consumption**.

6. The most important determinant of social status in modern societies is occupation, although skin color, religion, marital status, age, sex, and many other factors are also important. The prestige ranking of occupations has remained relatively stable over time. In general, people who rank high in one area will also rank high in other status hierarchies, exhibiting **status consistency. Status inconsistency** occurs when a person ranks high in one dimension of status and low in another.

7. There are four major historical types of stratification: slavery, caste, estate, and class systems. **Slavery** is an extreme system of stratified inequality in which freedom is denied to one group of people in society who are owned by another and may be regarded as subhuman. A **caste system** is an elaborate and rigid stratification system in

which status is determined at birth and in which people generally cannot change their social position. In the **estate system** of stratification, which is associated with a type of agrarian society called feudalism, the ownership of land gives power to the nobles, and peasants are bound to the nobles' land in a vassal relationship.

8. The most common system of stratification in the modern world is the **class system**, a relatively open form of stratification based mainly on economic status. According to Marx, class is defined by access to the means of production or sources of wealth, and the two basic social classes in capitalism are the workers (proletariat) and the owners (bourgeoisie). Marx saw these two classes as being in a state of continual **class conflict**, or struggle between competing classes. Unlike Marx, Weber viewed class systems as having two dimensions of stratification in addition to economics: power and prestige.

9. Class divisions are the perceived and real differences between a society's classes. Sociologists determine class divisions using three approaches: the objective, the reputational, and the subjective. The level of shared awareness that members of a social class have concerning their common situation and interests, called **class consciousness**, is relatively low in the United States. This is in part because of **false consciousness**—any situation in which a person's subjective understanding of reality is inconsistent with the objective facts of that situation.

10. Social mobility refers to a change on the part of an individual or a group of people from one status or social class to another. This movement can be upward or downward. In an open society, status can be gained by the direct efforts of the individual. In a closed society, status is bestowed at birth or at a certain age and is almost impossible to change. Although no society is either completely open or completely closed, industrialized societies tend to be more open, and agricultural societies tend to be more closed.

11. Sociologists analyze two varieties of social mobility: intergenerational mobility, which compares the social position of parents with that attained by their children or grandchildren, and intragenerational mobility, which refers to an individual's change in social position within his or her lifetime. Upward social mobility is encouraged at the national level by industrial development and a large educational enrollment. Upward mobility that results from changes in the social or economic system—rather than from individual personal achievement—is called **structural mobility**. Upwardly mobile people tend to be those who are well educated. Downwardly mobile people often come from large families, do not get an education, marry very young, and have large families.

12. Recent studies have stressed that the occupational status of both parents may be relevant to a child's achievement. Women and men must meet the same qualifications for a job, but in many cases women are still concentrated in low-paying and low-prestige jobs.

ACTIVITIES FOR MAKING MEANING WITH THE CHAPTER

1. Preview the chapter by scanning the introductory outline of topics and subtopics, the introductory matter, the headings and subheadings, and the summary points.

   - What is the main topic of the chapter?
   - What kind of material does Dr. Popenoe present at the beginning of the chapter?
   - What is his system of headings and subheadings? How does his system help you see the organization of the chapter?
   - Predict what Dr. Popenoe means by his first heading "The Distribution of Desirables": What "desirables" will he explain? How do you know?
   - What will the author talk about under the heading "Historical Systems of Stratification"? How do you know?
   - What kind of material does Dr. Popenoe provide in conclusion? How do you know this is the conclusion? How does his use of numbers and boldface type help you at this point?

2. Based on a preview of the chapter, make a data chart in which you lay out the major headings, your prediction as to what Popenoe will talk about under each major heading, and your prior knowledge of each of these subtopics. Use the chart on page 7 of *Reading with Meaning* as a guide.

3. Read the introductory three paragraphs of the chapter, especially the vignette about the *Titanic*'s sinking. What is the main idea Popenoe is trying to get across? What does he say he is going to cover in the chapter? Bracket the vignette. Put a star at the point where Popenoe tells you what he is going to cover in the chapter.

4. Read the section under the heading "The Distribution of Desirables," including the material under the three subheadings: "Income and Wealth," "Power," and "Prestige." Make in-text notes after you read each paragraph. For example, underline main ideas, circle key points, itemize points in the margin, and draw arrows if appropriate. Then compare your in-text notes with a partner's. Explain to one another why you highlighted the points as you did.

5. For one of the subsections of the section titled "The Distribution of Desirables," make a web of the main ideas and supporting details. For example, if you choose to web the matter under "Prestige," put that term and its definition at the core of your web. Show supporting details on branches extending from the core.

6. Use SQ3R to study the section under the main heading "Social Status and Status Ranking." Remember to preview to see what the section is about and to think about what you already know about status. Then create questions based on the main headings and subheadings, and read with your questions in mind. After reading each subsection, see whether you can tell yourself the answers to your questions. If you cannot, reread until you can tell yourself in your head the main ideas of the subsection. When you have done this, review by talking about your questions and answers with a workshop partner. Do this with the expectation that you may be tested on the points covered and that you may be asked to explain main ideas and provide supporting details.

7. According to Dr. Popenoe in the section titled "Social Status and Status Ranking," a number of factors determine an individual's social status in the United States. Web the factors. Then write a summary paragraph in which you start with a topic sentence and go on to enumerate the factors.

8. Write a paragraph in which you give your opinion as to the factor that is most unfair in determining a person's status. In this paragraph, include reasons to support your opinion. You may want to coauthor the paragraph with a workshop partner if your instructor concurs. Write a second paragraph in which you give your opinion of the factor that is the fairest determinant of status.

9. Working in a three-person team, discuss the historical systems of stratification: slavery, caste, and estate. Start by clarifying the essential aspects of each system. Then develop a three-oval Venn diagram in which you lay out similarities and differences among the three systems. Let one member of your team take the lead as you talk about each system.

10. Read the introduction to the section titled "Social Class." With a partner, decide how this system differs from the prior three systems: slavery, caste, and estate? Together write a sentence or two expressing the differences. Then make a visual showing the differences.

11. Popenoe explains three approaches for determining class divisions and placements. How does this author help you see that he will be talking about three approaches? What kind of information does he give you about each approach?

12. Make a graph showing some of the data in Table 9.1 on page 295. What conclusions can you draw from the chart and your graph?

13. Read the section titled "Social Mobility," including the three major subsections under it. Then develop an opinion: In which kind of society would you prefer to live, an open or a closed one? Write your opinion at the central hub of a web. Give your supporting reasons as branches going out from the hub.

14. Review the subsection "The Conditions of Social Mobility." Explain these points to a partner:

   • The difference between intergenerational social mobility and intragenerational mobility;

- The meaning of structural mobility;
- The difference between upward and downward mobility;
- Factors that encourage upward mobility;
- Factors that discourage upward mobility;
- The relationship between educational level and mobility; and
- Factors affecting the social mobility of women.

Be ready to answer multiple-choice questions on the material in this subsection.

15. Talk about the following questions in three-person teams. Be ready to share your ideas with the class in a discussion that will follow. Being able to discuss ideas in class is important to your success in college. As you discuss the first three questions, each team member should in turn take the lead in discussing a question. Before talking about the last question, each team member should jot down his or her opinion and supporting reasons.

    - What is meant by the phrase "status symbol"? List several things that are symbols of status to you. What status symbols do you associate with the instructor of this course? With some of your course mates?

    - What is meant by the phrase "class consciousness"? How class-conscious are you? Be ready to give reasons in support of your judgment of yourself.

    - What is meant by the phrase "conspicuous consumption"? What are some things you associate with conspicuous consumption? How do you feel when you see someone blatantly displaying evidence of his or her high level of status? Why do you think you feel that way?

    - Do you believe that inequalities within society will eventually disappear? Or do you believe that inequalities will always be with us? Be ready to give evidence in support of your opinion.

16. Study summary items 1–12 on pages 304–305. How can you best use this kind of material? When should you read it? Reread it? How should you handle it? Highlight it? Make notes on it?

17. Select six words new to you from the chapter. Pronounce the words by breaking them into syllable parts. Then, using the context and word elements as clues, write a definition for each of your words. Turn to a partner and share your definitions so that your partner also understands the meaning of each one.

APPENDIX B
CALCULATING YOUR READING RATE:
READING RATE TABLES AND EXPLANATIONS

To calculate your reading rate:

1. Record your starting time in hours, minutes, and seconds; for example, you might have started at

| 10 o'clock | 55 minutes | 31 seconds |

2. Read the selection and record your ending time; for example, you might have finished reading at

| 11 o'clock | 5 minutes | 10 seconds |

3. Subtract your starting time from your ending time to find the time it took you to read the selection:

11 o'clock	5 minutes	10 seconds
10 o'clock	55 minutes	31 seconds
	9 minutes	39 seconds

4. Convert your time to a decimal by rounding up to the nearest quarter of a minute, as follows:

$$60 \text{ seconds} = 1 \text{ minute}$$
$$45 \text{ seconds} = .75 \text{ minute}$$
$$30 \text{ seconds} = .50 \text{ minute}$$
$$15 \text{ seconds} = .25 \text{ minute}$$

In this case, 9 minutes and 39 seconds becomes 9.75 minutes.

5. To find your reading rate, divide the number of words in the selection by your reading time given in minutes; for example,

$$\frac{750 \text{ words}}{9.75 \text{ minutes}} = 77 \text{ reading rate (words per minute)}$$

Or use the tables on pages 310–311 to find your reading rate. To use the tables,

- Locate your reading time in the far left column.
- Locate the number of words in the selection in the top row.
- Find your reading rate at the intersection of the selected column and the row on the chart.

NUMBER OF WORDS

TIME IN DECIMAL MINUTES	100	150	200	250	300	350	400	450	500	550	600	650	700	750	800	850	900	950	1000	1050	1100	1150	1200
2.0	50	75	100	125	150	175	200	225	250	275	300	325	350	375	400	425	450	475	500	525	550	575	600
2.5	40	60	80	100	120	140	160	180	200	220	240	260	280	300	320	340	360	380	400	420	440	460	480
3.0	33	50	67	83	100	117	133	150	167	183	200	217	233	250	267	283	300	317	333	350	367	383	400
3.5	29	43	57	71	86	100	114	129	143	157	171	186	200	214	229	243	257	271	286	300	314	329	343
4.0	25	38	50	63	75	87	100	113	125	138	150	163	175	188	200	213	225	238	250	263	275	288	300
4.5	22	33	44	56	67	78	89	100	111	122	133	144	156	167	178	189	200	211	222	233	244	256	267
5.0	20	30	40	50	60	70	80	90	100	110	120	130	140	150	160	170	180	190	200	210	220	230	240
5.5	18	27	36	45	55	64	73	82	91	100	109	118	127	136	145	155	164	173	182	191	200	209	218
6.0	17	25	33	42	50	58	67	75	83	92	100	108	117	125	133	142	150	158	167	175	183	192	200
6.5	15	23	31	38	46	54	62	69	77	85	92	100	108	115	123	131	138	146	154	162	169	177	185
7.0	14	21	29	36	43	50	57	64	71	79	86	93	100	107	114	121	129	136	143	150	157	164	171
7.5	13	20	27	33	40	47	53	60	67	73	80	87	93	100	107	113	120	127	133	140	147	153	160
8.0	13	19	25	31	38	44	50	56	62	69	75	81	87	94	100	106	113	119	125	131	138	144	150
8.5	12	18	24	29	35	41	47	53	59	65	71	76	82	88	94	100	106	112	118	124	129	135	141
9.0	11	17	22	28	33	39	44	50	56	61	67	72	78	83	89	94	100	106	111	117	122	128	133
9.5	11	16	21	26	32	37	42	47	53	58	63	68	74	79	84	89	95	100	105	111	116	121	126
10.0	10	15	20	25	30	35	40	45	50	55	60	65	70	75	80	85	90	95	100	105	110	115	120
10.5	10	14	19	24	29	33	38	43	48	52	57	62	67	71	76	81	86	90	95	100	105	110	114
11.0	9	14	18	23	27	32	36	41	45	50	55	59	64	68	73	77	82	86	91	95	100	105	109
11.5	9	13	17	22	26	30	35	39	43	48	52	57	61	65	70	74	78	83	87	91	96	100	104
12.0	8	13	17	21	25	29	33	38	42	46	50	54	58	62	67	71	75	79	83	87	92	96	100
12.5	8	12	16	20	24	28	32	36	40	44	48	52	56	60	64	68	72	76	80	84	88	92	96
13.0	8	12	15	19	23	27	31	35	38	42	46	50	54	58	62	65	69	73	77	81	85	88	92
13.5	7	11	15	19	22	26	30	33	37	41	44	48	52	56	59	63	67	70	74	78	81	85	89
14.0	7	11	14	18	21	25	29	32	36	39	43	46	50	54	57	61	64	68	71	75	79	82	86
14.5	7	10	14	17	21	24	28	31	34	38	41	45	48	52	55	59	62	66	69	72	76	79	83
15.0	7	10	13	17	20	23	27	30	33	37	40	43	47	50	53	57	60	63	67	70	73	77	80
15.5	6	10	13	16	19	23	26	29	32	35	39	42	45	48	52	55	58	61	65	68	71	74	77
16.0	6	9	13	16	19	22	25	28	31	34	38	41	44	47	50	53	56	59	62	66	69	72	75
16.5	6	9	12	15	18	21	24	27	30	33	36	39	42	45	48	52	55	58	61	64	67	70	73
17.0	6	9	12	15	18	21	24	26	29	32	35	38	41	44	47	50	53	56	59	62	65	68	71
17.5	6	9	11	14	17	20	23	26	29	31	34	37	40	43	46	49	51	54	57	60	63	66	69
18.0	6	8	11	14	17	19	22	25	28	31	33	36	39	42	44	47	50	53	56	58	61	64	67
18.5	5	8	11	14	16	19	22	24	27	30	32	35	38	41	43	46	49	51	54	57	59	62	65
19.0	5	8	11	13	16	18	21	24	26	29	32	34	37	39	42	45	47	50	53	55	58	61	63
19.5	5	8	10	13	15	18	21	23	26	28	31	33	36	38	41	44	46	49	51	54	56	59	62
20.0	5	8	10	13	15	18	20	23	25	28	30	33	35	38	40	43	45	48	50	53	55	58	60
20.5	5	7	10	12	15	17	20	22	24	27	29	32	34	37	39	41	44	46	49	51	54	56	59
21.0	5	7	10	12	14	17	19	21	24	26	29	31	33	36	38	40	43	45	48	50	52	55	57
21.5	5	7	9	12	14	16	19	21	23	26	28	30	33	35	37	40	42	44	47	49	51	53	56
22.0	5	7	9	11	14	16	18	20	23	25	27	30	32	34	36	39	41	43	45	48	50	52	55
22.5	4	7	9	11	13	16	18	20	22	24	27	29	31	33	36	38	40	42	44	47	49	51	53
23.0	4	7	9	11	13	15	17	20	22	24	26	28	30	33	35	37	39	41	43	46	48	50	52
23.5	4	6	9	11	13	15	17	19	21	23	26	28	30	32	34	36	38	40	43	45	47	49	51
24.0	4	6	8	10	12	15	17	19	21	23	25	27	29	31	33	35	37	40	42	44	46	48	50
24.5	4	6	8	10	12	14	16	18	20	22	24	27	29	31	33	35	37	39	41	43	45	47	49
25.0	4	6	8	10	12	14	16	18	20	22	24	26	28	30	32	34	36	38	40	42	44	46	48
25.5	4	6	8	10	12	14	16	18	20	22	23	25	27	29	31	33	35	37	39	41	43	45	47
26.0	4	6	8	10	11	13	15	17	19	21	23	25	27	29	31	33	34	36	38	40	42	44	46
26.5	4	6	7	9	11	13	15	17	19	21	22	24	26	28	30	32	34	36	37	39	41	43	45

NUMBER OF WORDS

TIME IN DECIMAL MINUTES	1250	1300	1350	1400	1450	1500	1550	1600	1650	1700	1750	1800	1850	1900	1950	2000	2050	2100	2150	2200	2250	2300	2350
2.0	625	650	675	700	725	750	775	800	825	850	875	900	925	950	975	1000	1025	1050	1075	1100	1125	1150	1175
2.5	500	520	540	560	580	600	620	640	660	680	700	720	740	760	780	800	820	840	860	880	900	920	940
3.0	417	433	450	467	483	500	517	533	550	567	583	600	617	633	650	667	683	700	717	733	750	767	783
3.5	357	371	386	400	414	429	443	457	471	486	500	514	529	543	557	571	586	600	614	629	643	657	671
4.0	313	325	338	350	363	375	388	400	412	425	437	450	462	475	487	500	512	525	537	550	562	575	588
4.5	278	289	300	311	322	333	344	356	367	378	389	400	411	422	433	444	456	467	478	489	500	511	522
5.0	250	260	270	280	290	300	310	320	330	340	350	360	370	380	390	400	410	420	430	440	450	460	470
5.5	227	236	245	255	264	273	282	291	300	309	318	327	336	345	355	364	373	382	391	400	409	418	427
6.0	208	217	225	233	242	250	258	267	275	283	292	300	308	317	325	333	342	350	358	367	375	383	392
6.5	192	200	208	215	223	231	238	246	254	262	269	277	285	292	300	308	315	323	331	338	346	354	362
7.0	179	186	193	200	207	214	221	229	236	243	250	257	264	271	279	286	293	300	307	314	321	329	336
7.5	167	173	180	187	193	200	207	213	220	227	233	240	247	253	260	267	273	280	287	293	300	307	313
8.0	156	163	169	175	181	188	194	200	206	213	219	225	231	238	244	250	256	263	269	275	281	288	294
8.5	147	153	159	165	171	176	182	188	194	200	206	212	218	224	229	235	241	247	253	259	265	271	276
9.0	139	144	150	156	161	167	172	178	183	189	194	200	206	211	217	222	228	233	239	244	250	256	261
9.5	132	137	142	147	153	158	163	168	174	179	184	189	195	200	205	211	216	221	226	232	237	242	247
10.0	125	130	135	140	145	150	155	160	165	170	175	180	185	190	195	200	205	210	215	220	225	230	235
10.5	119	124	129	133	138	143	148	152	157	162	167	171	176	181	186	190	195	200	205	210	214	219	224
11.0	114	118	123	127	132	136	141	145	150	155	159	164	168	173	177	182	186	191	195	200	205	209	214
11.5	109	113	117	122	126	130	135	139	143	148	152	157	161	165	170	174	178	183	187	191	196	200	204
12.0	104	108	113	117	121	125	129	133	138	142	146	150	154	158	163	167	171	175	179	183	188	192	196
12.5	100	104	108	112	116	120	124	128	132	136	140	144	148	152	156	160	164	168	172	176	180	184	188
13.0	96	100	104	108	112	115	119	123	127	131	135	138	142	146	150	154	158	162	165	169	173	177	181
13.5	93	96	100	104	107	111	115	119	122	126	130	133	137	141	144	148	152	156	159	163	167	170	174
14.0	89	93	96	100	104	107	111	114	118	121	125	129	132	136	139	143	146	150	154	157	161	164	168
14.5	86	90	93	97	100	103	107	110	114	117	121	124	128	131	134	138	141	145	148	152	155	159	162
15.0	83	87	90	93	97	100	103	107	110	113	117	120	123	127	130	133	137	140	143	147	150	153	157
15.5	81	84	87	90	94	97	100	103	106	110	113	116	119	123	126	129	132	135	139	142	145	148	152
16.0	78	81	84	87	91	94	97	100	103	106	109	113	116	119	122	125	128	131	134	138	141	144	147
16.5	76	79	82	85	88	91	94	97	100	103	106	109	112	115	118	121	124	127	130	133	136	139	142
17.0	74	76	79	82	85	88	91	94	97	100	103	106	109	112	115	118	121	124	126	129	132	135	138
17.5	71	74	77	80	83	86	89	91	94	97	100	103	106	109	111	114	117	120	123	126	129	131	134
18.0	69	72	75	78	81	83	86	89	92	94	97	100	103	106	108	111	114	117	119	122	125	128	131
18.5	68	70	73	76	78	81	84	86	89	92	95	97	100	103	105	108	111	114	116	119	122	124	127
19.0	66	68	71	74	76	79	82	84	87	89	92	95	97	100	103	105	108	111	113	116	118	121	124
19.5	64	67	69	72	74	77	79	82	85	87	90	92	95	97	100	103	105	108	110	113	115	118	121
20.0	63	65	68	70	73	75	78	80	83	85	88	90	93	95	97	100	103	105	108	110	113	115	118
20.5	61	63	66	68	71	73	76	78	80	83	85	88	90	93	95	98	100	102	105	107	110	112	115
21.0	60	62	64	67	69	71	74	76	79	81	83	86	88	90	93	95	98	100	102	105	107	110	112
21.5	58	60	63	65	67	70	72	74	77	79	81	84	86	88	91	93	95	98	100	102	105	107	109
22.0	57	59	61	64	66	68	70	73	75	77	80	82	84	86	89	91	93	95	98	100	102	105	107
22.5	56	58	60	62	64	67	69	71	73	76	78	80	82	84	87	89	91	93	96	98	100	102	104
23.0	54	57	59	61	63	65	67	70	72	74	76	78	80	83	85	87	89	91	93	96	98	100	102
23.5	53	55	57	60	62	64	66	68	70	72	74	77	79	81	83	85	87	89	91	94	96	98	100
24.0	52	54	56	58	60	62	65	67	69	71	73	75	77	79	81	83	85	87	90	92	94	96	98
24.5	51	53	55	57	59	61	63	65	67	69	71	73	76	78	80	82	84	86	88	90	92	94	96
25.0	50	52	54	56	58	60	62	64	66	68	70	72	74	76	78	80	82	84	86	88	90	92	94
25.5	49	51	53	55	57	59	61	63	65	67	69	70	72	74	76	78	80	82	84	86	88	90	92
26.0	48	50	52	54	56	57	59	61	63	65	67	69	71	73	75	77	79	80	82	84	86	88	90
26.5	47	49	51	52	54	56	58	60	62	64	66	67	69	71	73	75	77	79	81	82	84	86	89

GLOSSARY

EXPLANATION

- The guide words at the top of each page indicate which words are located on that page. For example, the guide words for the first page are *aa* and *articulation*. Words that come alphabetically after *aa* but before *articulation* are found on the page.

- Within parentheses after each entry, the word is marked to show pronunciation. Use the marks (called diacritical marks) to help you pronounce the words.

ă	act, cat	o͞o	ooze
ā	ace, cape	ou	out, cloud
â	air, care	ŭ	up
ä	arm	ü	use, flute
ĕ	egg, fed	û	urn, turn
ē	equal, feed	ə	occurs in unaccented
ĭ	it, lit		syllables and is
ī	ice, line		pronounced as follows:
ŏ	fox, lot	a	aloud
ō	over, so	e	item
ô	order	i	pencil
oi	oil, toy	o	atom
o͝o	took, put	u	circus

The symbol (′) as in **fre′dəm** marks the primary stress, or accent. The syllable preceding it is pronounced with greater emphasis than other syllables. The symbol (′) as in **tel′ əfon′** marks the secondary stress, or accent. The syllable preceding the secondary accent (′) is pronounced with less emphasis than the one marked (′).

A

a•a (ä′ä′), *noun,* a blocky, angular lava. Some Hawaiian lava fields are made of *aa.* (Chap. 7)

ab•hor (ăb hôr′), *verb,* loathe; feel disgust for. The talented artist *abhorred* the cheap copies of his paintings. (Chap. 8)

ab•nor•mal•i•ties (ăb′nôr măl′ ə tēs), *noun,* the features, acts, or happenings that differ from the ordinary or the standard. The child was born with severe *abnormalities* that made his survival unlikely. (Chap. 2)

ac•cess (ăk′sěs), *noun,* an approach to something or somebody; admittance. The reporters were unable to gain *access* to the private meeting. (Chap. 14)

ac•ti•vist (ăk′tə vǐst), *noun,* one who supports political or national interests by every means, including force. The *activists* stormed into the hall and shouted the speaker down. (Chap. 15)

ad•her•ent (ăd hǐr′ ənt), *noun,* a supporter or follower of a cause or leader. Jesse Jackson had many *adherents* during his presidential campaign. (Chap. 14)

aes•thet•ic (ěs thĕt′ǐk), *adjective,* artistic; having a sense of beauty. The graceful ballet appealed to her *aesthetic* sensitivity. (Chap. 2)

af•firms (ə fĕrms′), *verb,* declares to be true; maintains firmly or positively. Each day he *affirms* that he is innocent. (Chap. 7)

af•flu•ent (ăf′ lū ənt′), *adjective or noun,* having an abundance of wealth, wealthy; those with wealth. If you are *affluent,* you can afford the finer things in life. (Chap. 4)

a•gil•i•ty (ə jǐl′ ə tē), *noun,* the ability to move quickly and easily. The horse showed its *agility* as it jumped over the wall. (Chap. 2)

a•grar•i•an (ə grer′ ē ən), *adjective,* related to farming of the land. America was an *agrarian* nation in the early days; now the country has become industrialized. (Chap. 4)

a•kin (ə kǐn′), *adjective,* related; similar. We like Dixieland; our tastes in music are *akin* to one another. (Chap. 6)

al•le•vi•ate (ə lē′vē āt′), *verb,* lessen; mitigate; make easier to bear. The rescue squad was able to *alleviate* the patient's pain. (Chap. 2)

al•li•ance (ə lī′ əns), *noun,* a connection or agreement between nations or parties for some special purpose. During World War I, the United States made an *alliance* with Great Britain and France against Germany. (Chap. 14)

al•loy (ăl′oi), *noun,* a composition of two or more metals melted together. Stainless steel is an *alloy* of steel and chromium that resists rust. (Chap. 7)

am•ni•o•cen•te•sis (ăm′ nē ō cĕn tē sǐs), *noun,* a technique for testing a fetus for abnormalities. Early in their pregnancies, many women undergo *amniocentesis* to determine whether their babies may be born with an abnormal genetic characteristic. (Chap. 2)

a•nat•o•my (ə năt′ə mē), *noun,* the structure of a plant, an animal, or its parts. The biology class studied the *anatomy* of the heart. (Chap. 13)

an•ec•dote (ăn′ ǐk dōt), *noun,* short and generally interesting account of an event. The after-dinner speaker opened her remarks with an *anecdote* that caught our attention. (Chap. 2)

a•non•y•mous (ə nŏn′ ə məs), *adjective,* without an acknowledged or known name. My friend preferred to be an *anonymous* donor; he did not want anyone to know that he had contributed to the scholarship fund at the university.

an•tag•o•nist (ăn tăg′ ə nǐst), *noun,* an opponent in any kind of contest. The candidate for office had several *antagonists* running against him. (Chap. 9)

an•te•date (ăn′tə dāt′), *verb,* be an older date than; happen before in time. The arrival of Columbus in the New World *antedates* that of the pilgrims in Plymouth. (Chap. 3)

an•thro•pol•o•gist (ăn′thrə pŏl′ə jǐst), *noun,* one who studies the origins, development, cultures, and beliefs of human beings. The *anthropologist* was able to rebuild a clay bowl from the fragments she unearthed. (Chap. 3)

an•ti•bi•ot•ic (ăn′tī bī ŏt′ǐk), *noun,* a substance produced by molds, yeast, or bacteria that kills or weakens germs. The *antibiotic* was put directly on the infection to kill the bacteria. (Chap. 3)

an•ti•war (ăn′tē wôr′), *adjective,* against or opposed to war. Pacifists are *antiwar.* (Chap. 3)

an•to•nym (ăn′ tə nǐm), *noun,* a word that means the opposite of another word. The word *large* is an *antonym* for the word *small.* (Chap. 3)

aq•ua•pho•bi•a (ăk′wə fō′bǐ ə), *noun,* a fear of water. His *aquaphobia* prevented him from learning to swim. (Chap. 3)

arch (ärch), *adjective,* most important; sly, cunning. Among several, he was the *arch* rival. (Chap. 13)

ar•chae•ol•o•gy (är′kē ŏl′ə jē), *noun,* the study of customs, life, and things of ancient times by excavating the remains of structures and cities. Because she wanted to know more about Greek buildings, she studied *archaeology.* (Chap. 3)

ar•id (är′ ǐd), *adjective,* dry, lacking moisture, having little rainfall. Deserts are *arid* places. (Chap. 4)

ar•tic•u•la•tion (är tǐk′yə lā′shən), *noun,* a jointed state; state of being connected. The House and Senate committees worked smoothly together; they had good *articulation.* (Chap. 3)

as•pire (ə spīr′), *verb,* seek; aim for. We *aspire* to achieve our dreams. (Chap. 8)

as•so•ci•ate (ə sō′shē āt′), *verb,* join as partner; bring together; connect with other parts. The dog *associated* his leash with going out for a walk. (Chap. 14)

a•ssump•tion (ə sŭmp′ shən), *noun,* something taken for granted; supposition. The customer's *assumption* was that the goods would be ready on the date promised. (Chap. 6)

asth•ma•tic (ăz mǎt′ĭk), *adjective,* having a respiratory disorder including difficult breathing, with gasping or coughing. The *asthmatic* patient was using an oxygen mask. (Chap. 14)

as•tro•nom•i•cal (ăs′ trə nŏm′ək əl), *adjective,* having to do with astronomy; very high. Galileo made *astronomical* measurements with his telescope. The price was *astronomical;* there was no way I could pay. (Chap. 3)

at•tri•butes (ăt′ trə byüts), *noun,* the qualities considered belonging to a person or thing; characteristics. Her ability to put people at ease is one of her *attributes.* (Chap. 7)

au•ra (ôr′ə), *noun,* a distinctive character or manner. The procession had an *aura* of beauty and dignity. (Chap. 12)

au•then•tic (ô thĕn′tĭk), *adjective,* worthy of belief; not copied or imitation; genuine. The ten-dollar bill was not *authentic;* it was counterfeit. (Chap. 12)

au•to•crat (ô tə krăt′), *noun,* a ruler who holds absolute power. Some kings were *autocrats* who thought their power was a given right. (Chap. 7)

au•to•crat ic (ô′ tə krăt′ĭk), *adjective,* acting with unrestricted authority. *Autocratic* kings and queens had unlimited power over the people. (Chap. 4)

au•top•sy (ô′ tŏp sē), *noun,* procedure after death to determine cause of death; a postmortem examination of a body. Bruce died under strange circumstances; as a result, the medical examiner performed an *autopsy* on his body. (Chap. 2)

av•id (ăv′ ĭd), *adjective,* extremely eager; keen. Many writers start out as *avid* readers. (Chap. 13)

awe•some (ô′səm), *adjective,* bringing a feeling of power, dread, terror, or reverent wonder and respect. The sight of Niagara Falls was *awesome.* (Chap. 7)

B

banned (bǎnd), *verb,* forbidden or not allowed by law or social pressure. The law *banned* the use of the dangerous pesticide. (Chap. 11)

ben•e•fit (bĕn′ ə fĭt), *noun,* something for the good or well-being. The special assistance was given to him for his *benefit.* (Chap. 3)

be•nev•o•lent (bə nĕv′ə lənt), *adjective,* kindly, intended to help others. The woman was known for her *benevolent* deeds; she had a heart of gold. Related word: **benevolence,** *noun,* wish to help others, charitableness. (Chap. 5)

bi•cam•er•al (bī kăm′ ər əl), *adjective,* having two chambers. The U.S. Congress is *bicameral.* (Chap. 4)

bi•cen•ten•ni•al (bī sĕn tĕn′ ē əl), *noun,* a 200th anniversary. In 1977 the United States celebrated the *bicentennial* of the Constitution. (Chap. 3)

binge (bĭnj), *noun,* a drunken spree; out-of-control self-indulgence. The next day, they regretted what they had done on the previous night's *binge.* (Chap. 8)

bi•sect (bī′ sĕkt), *verb,* to divide into two equal parts. We *bisected* the apple so that we each got a half. Related word: **dissect,** *verb,* to cut apart to examine, to analyze. (Chap. 4)

blan•ket (blăng′ kĭt), *adjective,* covering everything. Because the student's plans were still incomplete, the advisor could not give him *blanket* approval for what he wanted to do. (Chap. 5)

brac•ing (brās′ ĭng), *verb,* preparing; putting oneself in readiness. They were *bracing* the tent against the expected winds. (Chap. 2)

brood (brüd), *verb,* dwell moodily in thought; ponder at length. He had the tendency to *brood* about his errors, but he could not bring himself to correct them. (Chap. 2)

C

cam•ou•flage (kăm′ ə fläzh′), *verb,* color or screening objects so that they blend into their background. The spots on the bird's eggs *camouflaged* them so that the predator walked by without seeing them. (Chap. 13)

ca•price (kə prēs′), *noun,* a change of mind with no apparent reason. Because directions were given by *caprice,* not by reason, the workers did not know what to do next. (Chap. 13)

car•ni•vore (kär′nə vōr′), *noun,* an animal that eats meat. The eagle is a *carnivore* that eats fish. (Chap. 3)

cas•cade (kă skād′), *noun,* a series of waterfalls over rocks. We carried our canoe around the dangerous *cascade* for we were afraid to try to paddle it over the waterfalls. (Chap. 4)

cen•ten•ni•al (sĕn tĕn′ē əl), *noun,* a 100th anniversary. A parade and fireworks marked the town's *centennial.* (Chap. 3)

cha•os (kā′ŏs′), *noun,* a state of confusion and disorder. The *chaos* in the village after the battle was terrible. (Chap. 4)

cir•cum•nav•i•gate (sûr´kəm năv´ ə gāt´), *verb,* sail around. In the early 1400s, Chinese ships *circumnavigated* Southeast Asia and sailed to India and the Persian Gulf. (Chap. 3)

ci•vil•i•ty (sə vĭl´ ə tē), *noun,* courteous behavior, act of politeness. Given the animosity that had existed so long between them and us, I was impressed by the *civility* with which they received us. (Chap. 5)

clar•i•fy (klăr´ ə fī), *verb,* make clear. His summary will *clarify* what he said. (Chap. 3)

cleave (klēv), *verb,* split open; split or cut with a blow. The cook will *cleave* the chops off the roast one by one. (Chap. 2)

co•hab•it (kō hăb´ĭt), *verb,* live together; live together as husband and wife. Fred and Jane will *cohabit* after they marry. (Chap. 3)

co•los•sal (kə lŏs´əl), *adjective,* huge; gigantic. The pyramids of Egypt are *colossal* structures. (Chap. 15)

co•los•sus (kə lŏs´əs), *noun,* anything huge or gigantic. The legendary statue of Apollo, known as the *Colossus* of Rhodes, was one of the seven wonders of the world. (Chap. 15)

com•pen•sa•tory (kəm pĕn´ sə tôr´ ē), *adjective,* making up for; compensating for. The accident victim asked for *compensatory* payments because of his inability to hold a job. (Chap. 7)

com•pla•cent (kŏm plā´ sənt), *adjective,* satisfied with one's advantages. *Complacent* citizens may find that their rights will become limited if they ignore the self-serving acts of officials. (Chap. 12)

com•plex•i•ties (kəm plĕk´ sə tēs), *noun,* intricacies, involved aspects. I could not understand the *complexities* of the case, for there were so many factors involved in it. (Chap. 5)

con•cen•tra•tion (kŏn´ sən trā´shən), *noun,* the amount of a substance in a given area or volume. His soft drink had a high *concentration* of sugar. (Chap. 13)

con•cep•tion (kən sĕp´ shən), *noun,* a thought or idea; point at which a female becomes pregnant. Her *conception* of geology is poorly developed. At *conception,* the egg and sperm unite to form a new being. (Chap. 2)

con•cep•tu•al (kən sĕp´ chōō əl), *adjective,* pertaining to concepts. He arranged his thoughts into a *conceptual* scheme. (Chap. 7)

con•di•tioned (kən dĭsh´ ənd), *adjective,* produced by a learned response; trained to exhibit a response. His behavior over the years was *conditioned* by what was accepted in his family. (Chap. 8)

con•fig•u•ra•tion (kən´ fĭg yə rā´ shən), *noun,* a form; manner of arrangement; shape. The *configuration* of the petals on the flower reminded me of a star. (Chap. 7)

con•gre•gate (kŏng´grə gāt´), *verb,* come together; gather; assemble. The students *congregated* in the schoolroom. (Chap. 15)

con•se•crate (kŏn´sə krāt´), *verb,* declare sacred; dedicate for a purpose. The ceremony *consecrated* the new temple. (Chap. 15)

con•sign (kən sīn´), *verb,* hand over; deliver. His arrest forced him to *consign* his expensive car to the courts. (Chap. 14)

con•sis•tent•ly (kən sĭs´ tənt lē), *adverb,* without wavering from the same course of action; in agreement with. The judge *consistently* expressed a liberal point of view. (Chap. 7)

con•sti•tute (kŏn´ stə tüt), *verb,* make up; form. The Senate and the House of Representatives *constitute* the Congress of the United States. (Chap. 2)

con•tempt (kən tĕmpt´), *noun,* the feeling one has about something or someone regarded as unworthy or mean; scorn; disdain. She felt *contempt* for the selfish people who thought only of themselves. (Chap. 2)

con•ti•nen•tal di•vide (kŏn´tə nən´təl dĭ vīd´), *noun,* a line of mountaintops across a continent that separates stream flows to oceans on either side. The pioneers found passes across the *continental divide.* (Chap. 6)

con•tra•dic•tion (kŏn trə dĭk´shən), *noun,* an act or statement of disagreement or direct opposition; inconsistency. The sloppy paper was a direct *contradiction* of the careful work she always had done. (Chap. 6)

con•verge (kən vûrj´), *verb,* tend to meet in a point, come together; tend to common result. Their efforts *converged* to get the job done. (Chap. 8)

con•vey (kən vā´), *verb,* carry; transport; make known. This paper will *convey* the message to the president. (Chap. 2)

cor•ner•stone (kôr´nər stōn´), *noun,* a stone built into the corner of an important building and usually hollowed out to contain documents. Before it was cemented in place, newspapers and pictures were placed in the *cornerstone.* (Chap. 14)

coun•ter•part (koun´tər pärt´), *noun,* a person or thing that closely resembles another; thing that corresponds to another. The executive had to consult with her *counterpart* in the central office. (Chap. 4)

coup (kōō), *noun,* an unexpected achievement. It was a *coup* to achieve an A in that difficult course. (Chap. 8)

cue (kyōō), *noun,* a signal; prompt; hint. The raised hand was a *cue* that the children should be quiet. Related word: **queue,** *noun,* line. (Chap. 13)

cul•prit (kŭl´ prĭt), *noun,* person who is guilty of an offense. The FBI caught the *culprit* responsible for setting the fires. (Chap. 2)

cul•tur•al (kŭl′ chər əl), *adjective,* having to do with culture; related to social behavior patterns, arts, beliefs, customs, of a people. The sociologist was investigating the *cultural* life of the village. (Chap. 9)

cur•ren•cy (kûr′ ən sē), *noun,* money; medium of exchange. The *currency* he tried to deposit was counterfeit. (Chap. 12)

D

dazz•le (dăz′ əl), *verb,* overpower with bright light; excite the imagination. His description of traveling in the Grand Canyon *dazzled* the audience. (Chap. 2)

de•ba•cle (dĭ bä′kəl), *noun,* a rout; sudden collapse or overthrow. The battle turned into a complete *debacle:* Everything went wrong for the invading armies. (Chap. 6)

de•cen•tral•ize (dē sĕn′ trə līz), *verb,* spread the power among various groups. The businessperson decided to *decentralize* power among three vice-presidents. Related word: **decentralization,** *noun,* the act of dispersing power among several people or groups. (Chap. 3)

de•hy•dr•ation (dē hī drā′ shən), *noun,* the loss of water or moisture; taking away of moisture. I suffered from *dehydration* after spending hours in the desert. (Chap. 2)

dé•jà vu (dā zhä voo′), *French noun,* the feeling of having previously experienced something that one is actually experiencing for the first time. I was overcome with *déjà vu* when I entered the school. (Chap. 2)

del•e•gate (dĕl′ ə gāt), *verb,* give authority to another. The president will *delegate* authority to the committee chairperson. (Chap. 4)

de•lib•er•ate (dĭ lĭb′ər ĭt), *adjective,* carefully considered; done on purpose. His *deliberate* noise spoiled the performance. (Chap. 2)

dem•o•crat (dĕm′ ə krăt), *noun,* one who believes that government should be run by the people, for the people, of the people. My friend is a true *democrat* and does all he can to support democratic ideologies. Note: from the Greek words, *dēmos,* meaning "people," and *kratos,* meaning "rule." (Chap. 5)

de•plore (dĭ plôr′), *verb,* regret deeply, express regret. I really *deplore* the way my friends treat their parents. (Chap. 4)

dep•re•ca•tion (dĕp′rə kā′shən), *noun,* a disapproval of; protestation against. No one likes his or her work to be subject to *deprecation* by others. (Chap. 12)

de•rive (di rīv′), *verb,* obtain from some source. The musician will *derive* pleasure from the concert. (Chap. 7)

der•ma•tol•o•gy (dûr′ mə tŏl′ə jē), *noun,* the science of the skin and its diseases. The *dermatologist* gave him an antibiotic for his rash. (Chap. 3)

des•ig•na•tion (dĕz′ ĭg nā′ shən), *noun,* the appointment to a position or duty, the pointing out of something. She took her *designation* as lookout person for the explorers seriously because she knew that their lives depended on her actions. Related word: **designate,** *verb,* to point out or to appoint to a position or duty. (Chaps. 2 and 4)

des•o•late (dĕz′ə lĭt), *adjective,* deserted; sorrowful; lifeless; gloomy. I was *desolate* after learning of the disaster. (Chap. 2)

de•tract (dē trăkt′), *verb,* take away; withdraw value or reputation. All the nasty remarks did not *detract* from his fine reputation. (Chap. 15)

dev•as•tate (dĕv′ ə stāt), *verb,* overwhelm, cause to be overwhelmed, lay waste to. The family was *devastated* to learn that their home had been destroyed in the flood. The flood *devastated* the land. Related word: **devastation,** *noun,* the act or result of laying waste to. (Chaps. 4 and 6)

de•vise (dĭ vīz′), *verb,* invent; form in the mind new applications of ideas. He was able to *devise* a new part to repair the machine. (Chap. 13)

di•a•lect (dī′ ə lĕkt′), *noun,* a variety of a language. Their *dialect* had special words we did not understand. (Chap. 12)

dif•fu•sion (dĭ fū′zhən), *noun,* a spreading widely, scattering. The leak caused the *diffusion* of the fluid throughout the lake. (Chap. 13)

di•gest•ive (dī jĕs′tĭv), *adjective,* relating to the process of breaking down foods into simpler chemical forms. The stomach is part of the *digestive* tract. (Chap. 13)

di•min•ish (dĭ mĭn′ ĭsh), *verb,* make smaller; reduce. You cannot *diminish* my enthusiasm with your negative comments; I will persist. (Chap. 12)

dis•crep•an•cy (dĭs krĕp′ən sē′), *noun,* a difference; inconsistency. There was a large *discrepancy* between what she said and what she meant. (Chap. 12)

dis•crim•i•na•tion (dĭs krĭm′ ə nā′ shən), *noun,* different, often negative attitude or actions against a group of people; ability to make fine distinctions. *Discrimination* still exists in the nation. The man acted with *discrimination,* making small changes in the original plan. Related word: **discriminate,** *verb,* to treat a group of people in a different manner, to distinguish. (Chap. 5)

disk (dĭsk), *noun,* a flat circular object. The sun looks like a bright yellow *disk* even though we know it is a sphere. (Chap. 7)

dis•sent (dĭ sĕnt′), *noun,* difference in opinion, often strong disagreement with what is. After a time the monarch could not quell the *dissent* in the country. Also as a *verb,* to differ in opinion. The right to *dissent* from the majority view is an important feature of a democracy. (Chap. 5)

di•vulge (dĭ vŭlj´), *verb,* reveal; make known. The mechanic cannot *divulge* her technique for repairing the special part. (Chap. 14)

dom•i•nant (dŏm´ ə nənt), *adjective,* most influential or important; determining. Jim's father played a *dominant* role in his life and the decisions he made about college. (Chap. 2)

du•el (dōō´əl), *noun,* a fight or contest between two persons, usually prearranged. Alexander Hamilton was killed by Aaron Burr in a *duel* on the bluffs of Weehawken, New Jersey. (Chap. 8)

du jour (də jôr), *adjectival expression from French,* of the day, special variety. We decided to have the soup *du jour,* the soup that was the special that day at my favorite restaurant. (Chap. 5)

dy•nam•ic (dī năm´ ĭk), *adjective,* energetic, forceful. I was very impressed with the *dynamic* personality of the Senate candidate. (Chap. 5)

E

e•clipse (ē klĭps´), *noun or verb,* the moving into the shadow of a planet or moon; to darken; hide; obscure. The *eclipse* of the sun frightened the people of some ancient cultures. (Chap. 7)

e•co•nom•ic (ē´kə nŏm´ ĭk), *adjective,* having to do with production, distribution, and use of wealth. Adam Smith formulated *economic* principles in the 1700s. (Chap. 12)

ed•i•fice (ĕd´ə fĭs), *noun,* a large or imposing building. The Lincoln Memorial in Washington is a grand *edifice.* (Chap. 7)

e•ject (ĭ jĕkt´), *verb,* expel; force out. The unruly were *ejected* from the meeting. (Chap. 7)

e•lab•or•ate (ĭ lăb´ ə rāt´), *verb,* add details. Dickens could *elaborate* on all the characters in his novels. (Chap. 12)

el•o•quent (ĕl´ə kwənt), *adjective,* having fluent, expressive, forceful speech. The preacher's *eloquence* held the audience in rapt attention. (Chap. 15)

e•mas•cu•late (ĭ măs´kyə lāt´), *verb,* castrate; remove testes or ovaries; weaken. Steers are bulls that have been *emasculated.* The governor was *emasculated* by the overwhelming vote of no confidence. (Chap. 7)

em•bod•ied (ĕm bŏd´ ēd), *verb,* represented in a definite form, personified. The little children *embodied* innocence. (Chap. 4)

em•bo•lus (ĕm´bəl əs), *noun,* a clot or undissolved mass carried in the circulatory system. Sometimes the body can dissolve an *embolus* in the bloodstream. (Chap. 13)

em•bry•o (ĕm´brē ō´), *noun,* an organism in early stages of development. The organs of the *embryo* were not yet developed. (Chap. 13)

e•mi•gre´ (ĕm´ĭ grā), *noun,* a person who leaves or flees a country for political reasons. Sometimes *emigrés* are called political refugees. Members of the nobility became *emigrés* during the French Revolution. (Chap. 4)

em•phy•se•ma (ĕm´f ə sē´ mə), *noun,* a condition in which there is a great increase in the size of the air sacs in the lungs and breathing becomes difficult. Because Martha had been a heavy smoker in her youth, she developed *emphysema* when she was sixty. (Chap. 2)

en•dorse (ĕn dôrs´), *verb,* approve; support. The politician *endorsed* his friend during the primaries. (Chap. 2)

en•sure (en shür´), *verb,* to make certain. "The hard work of every member of the brigade will *ensure* our success," said the leader. Related word: **insure,** *verb,* Many people *insure* their lives; they take out an *insurance* policy that will pay their heirs upon death. (Chap. 5)

en•ti•tle (ĕn tī´ tl), *verb,* to give one the right or title to. Winning the award will *entitle* me to free membership in the association for life. Related word: **entitlements,** the right to. Many *entitlements* came with the award. (Chap. 5)

en•vis•age (ĕn vĭz´ ĭj), *verb,* picture in one's mind. It was difficult to *envisage* things happening as he suggested. (Chap. 4)

en•voy (ĕn´voi), *noun,* a diplomatic representative. An *envoy* is next in rank below an ambassador. (Chap. 14)

e•qual•i•ty (ĕ kwŏl´ ə te), *noun,* the state of being equal; sameness in number, size, rank. When rewarding people for work done, showing *equality* between the sexes is important. (Chap. 3)

e•volve (ĭ vŏlv´), *verb,* develop or change gradually. Fossils indicate that horses *evolved* from ancestors the size of dogs. (Chaps. 3 and 13)

ex•pec•ta•tion (ĕk spĕk tā´shən), *noun,* an anticipation; something looked forward to. The child's *expectation* was for far more than Santa would bring. (Chap. 6)

ex•plic•it (ĕk splĭs´ ĭt), *adjective,* clearly stated; definite. Her directions were *explicit;* no one misunderstood. (Chap. 2)

ex•tinc•tion (ĭk stĭngk´shən), *noun,* a dying out of a biological line. We have caused the *extinction* of many plant and animal species. (Chap. 8)

F

fe•tus (fē´ təs), *noun,* an animal embryo, especially a human embryo more than eight weeks old. The *fetus* was only ten weeks old when the woman miscarried. (Chap. 2)

flaunt (flônt), *verb,* show off; display boastfully. The boys skated very close to the girls to *flaunt* their skills. (Chap. 2)

flick•er (flĭk′ər), *verb,* flutter; waver; give off unsteady light. The lamp lights *flickered* during the electrical storm. (Chap. 7)

flor•id (flôr′ĭd), *adjective,* ruddy in cheeks or complexion. Their faces were *florid* from exposure to the intense sun. (Chap. 12)

for•ay (fôr′ā), *noun,* a raid for plunder. The horse troop made a *foray* through the town to take food and livestock. (Chap. 14)

for•bear•ance (fôr bâr′əns), *noun,* the quality of being patient. The mother had *forbearance* as the child struggled to dress himself without help. (Chap. 14)

fore•saw (fôr sô′), *verb past tense,* saw into the future. The economist *foresaw* many monetary problems in the months ahead. (Chap. 3)

fore•sight (fôr′sīt), *noun,* a forward view; ability to foresee. She had the *foresight* to carry her umbrella because the weather prediction was rain. (Chap. 12)

fre•quent (frē′kwənt), *verb,* go often to or regularly. He *frequents* the arcade to play the game machines. (Chap. 8)

fres•co (frĕs′kō), *noun,* a picture painted in wet plaster. *Frescoes* allow the paint to become embedded in the plaster. (Chap. 14)

friv•o•lous (frĭv′ə ləs), *adjective,* with lack of sense; trivial; of little importance. His objections were *frivolous;* people paid no attention. (Chap. 12)

fu•ror (fyoor′ôr), *noun,* an outburst of excitement; rage. The referee's poor decision caused a *furor* in the grandstand. (Chap. 2)

G

gar•goyle (gär′goil), *noun,* a rainspout on a roof gutter often made in the shape of an ugly animal or human head. When it rained, the *gargoyles* spouted water from their mouths. (Chap. 14)

gen•er•ate (jĕn′ə rāt′), *verb,* produce; bring into existence. Their kindness will *generate* a lot of good will. (Chap. 2)

ge•net•ic (jə nĕt′ĭk), *adjective,* dealing with genetics, the science of heredity. Mendel worked with *genetic* traits but did not use the word *gene.* (Chap. 3)

ge•ol•o•gy (jē ŏl′ə jē), *noun,* the science that deals with the earth, the rocks that compose it, and its changes. In *geology* class, we identified rocks that we collected. (Chaps. 2, 3)

graph•ic (grăf′ĭk), *adjective,* lifelike; vivid; pertaining to drawing or painting. The *graphic* description of the scene was so realistic, we felt we were actually there viewing the scene ourselves. (Chap. 3)

gross na•tion•al prod•uct (grōs′ năsh′ ən əl prŏd′ əkt), *noun,* the total market value of all the goods and services produced by a nation in a given period of time. Because the economy of the United States is growing, the *gross national product* this year will be greater than it was last year. (Chap. 11)

H

hal•low (hăl′ ō), *verb,* make holy; consecrate. Lincoln did not think he could *hallow* a battlefield. (Chap. 15)

hand•some•ly (hăn′səm lē), *adverb,* generously; impressively; skillfully. The artist *handsomely* crafted a beautiful silver bowl. (Chap. 2)

hap•haz•ard (hăp′hăz′ ərd), *adjective,* at random; by chance. His notes were *haphazard;* he had trouble organizing them for study. (Chap. 13)

hard-liner (härd-lī′nər), *noun,* a person taking a very conservative or orthodox view, usually in politics. The *hard-liners* did their best to obstruct democratic moves in China. (Chap. 7)

haz•ard (hăz′ ərd), *noun,* peril, risk, possible source of harm. The fire chief had overlooked a possible fire *hazard* in the dorm. (Chap. 2)

he•mo•sta•sis (hē′mə stā′sĭs), *noun,* the condition of blood stoppage. Two Greek words meaning "blood" and "standing" are put together to make the word *hemostasis.* (Chap. 13)

herb•i•vore (hūr′bĭvôr), *noun,* an animal that eats plants. Cows and horses are *herbivores.* (Chap. 3)

her•o•ic (hĭ rō′ĭk), *adjective,* of or suitable to a hero; having qualities of a hero. With *heroic* effort, the men lifted the car off the child. (Chap. 15)

het•er•o•sex•u•al (het′ ə rō sĕk′ shoo əl), *adjective,* having to do with different sexes; having to do with sexual feeling for persons of the opposite sex. His feelings toward others were *heterosexual.* (Chap. 3)

hi•er•o•glyph•ic (hī′ər ə glĭf′ĭk), *adjective,* pertaining to a picture writing system where symbols stand for words. Egyptian *hieroglyphic* writing includes pictures of birds and tools. (Chap. 9)

hig•gle•dy-pig•gle•dy (hĭg′əl dē-pĭg′əl dē), *adverb,* confused jumble. After the crowd left, the chairs were left scattered *higgledy-piggledy* around the room. (Chap. 14)

hor•rif•ic (hô rif′ĭk), *adjective,* causing horror. Being caught in a fire is a *horrific* experience. (Chap. 6)

hy•per•ac•tive (hī pər ak′tĭv), *adjective,* overactive; easily excited. The *hyperactive* child was constantly moving about. (Chap. 3)

hy•po•thet•i•cal (hī′pə thĕt′ə kəl), *adjective,* not well supported by evidence; conditional; supposed. His argument was *hypothetical;* it was not based on fact. (Chap. 2)

I

i•de•ol•o•gy (ī dē ŏl′ ə jē), *noun; plural,* **ideologies,** body of ideas that reflect the beliefs of a group or person. I could not accept the *ideology* of that political party, so I changed my affiliation. Related word: **ideological,** of an ideology. (Chap. 5)

i•dol (ī′dəl), *noun,* an image representing a deity. Some *idols* are worshiped, fed, and clothed as if they were alive. (Chap. 15)

ig•ne•ous (ĭg′nĭ əs), *adjective,* fire-formed; produced under intense heat. *Igneous* rocks form from molten material. (Chap. 7)

im•bibe (ĭm bīb′), *verb,* absorb; drink. The man *imbibes* as a blotter soaks up ink. (Chap. 8)

im•paired (ĭm pârd′), *verb,* injured; damaged; harmed; weakened. Because his vision has been *impaired* since the accident, he cannot drive. (Chap. 2)

im•pend•ing (ĭm pĕn′dĭng), *adjective,* about to happen. We ran inside to avoid the *impending* thunderstorm. (Chap. 14)

im•preg•na•tion (ĭm prĕg nā′shən), *noun,* the process of making pregnant; fertilization. The *impregnation* resulted in twins. (Chap. 15)

im•prov•i•sa•tion (ĭm′prəv ĭ zā′shən), *noun,* something provided on the spur of the moment. The musician did an *improvisation* when the song title was announced. (Chap. 2)

in•al•ien•a•ble (ĭn ā′ lyə nə bəl), *adjective,* not able to be taken or given away. Some rights are *inalienable,* according to the American Constitution. (Chap. 5)

in•au•di•ble (ĭn ô′də bəl), *adjective,* not capable of being heard. The machinery was so quiet that it was *inaudible* to the workers. (Chap. 2)

in•con•clu•sive (ĭn′kən klōō′sĭv), *adjective,* not settled. The experiment did not settle anything; it had *inconclusive* results. (Chap. 14)

in•cor•rig•i•ble (ĭn kor′ə jə bəl), *adjective,* uncorrectable, unmanageable. His lengthy criminal record indicated he was *incorrigible.* (Chap. 11)

in•cum•bent (ĭn kŭm′bənt), *noun,* the holder of an office. The newcomer challenged the *incumbent* president in the election. (Chap. 6)

in•dict•ment (ĭn dīt′mənt), *noun,* formal, generally written accusation, especially a charge handed down by a grand jury. I was stung by her *indictment;* I had not realized that she thought so badly of me. The grand jury handed down an *indictment* that indicated that there was enough evidence to charge the businessperson with fraud. (Chap. 2)

in•dis•crim•in•ate•ly (ĭn′dĭs krĭm′ə nĭt lē), *adverb,* not discriminately; not making a distinction; not observing a difference. The madman fired his gun *indiscriminately,* hitting bystanders as well as his intended target. (Chap. 8)

in•dulge (ĭn dŭlj′), *verb,* give in to one's desires and pleasures. They *indulged* in double cheeseburgers even though they knew the fat was bad for them. (Chap. 8)

in•fla•tion (ĭn flā′shən), *noun,* a sharp increase in prices resulting from a too fast increase in the amount of paper money. In a period of *inflation,* the dollar loses value. (Chap. 4)

in•no•va•tion (ĭn′ə vā′shən), *noun,* something new or different that is introduced. The invention of the transistor was an *innovation* that made modern computers possible. (Chap. 3)

in•sur•rec•tion (ĭn′sə rĕk′shən), *noun,* a revolt; open resistance against civil authority. Shay's Rebellion in 1676 was an *insurrection* by farmers to prevent debt judgments against them. (Chap. 7)

in•ten•si•ty (ĭn tĕn′sə tē), *noun,* a great strength; power; violence. The heat *intensity* of the furnace burned their faces. (Chap. 2)

in•ter•ac•tion (ĭn′tər ăk′shən), *noun,* an action on each other. The *interaction* of the members of the team showed fine team spirit and cooperation. (Chap. 6)

In•ter•net (ĭn′ tər nĕt′), *noun,* web of computers interconnected via telephone and other forms of electronic communication. Today, many students depend on the *Internet* for information as they write term papers. (Chap. 3)

in•ter•state (ĭn′tər stāt′), *adjective,* between states. The railroad carrying goods from Missouri to California was involved in *interstate* commerce. (Chap. 3)

int•er•val (ĭnt′ər vəl), *noun,* a period between events; pause; space between objects. The game had fifteen-minute *intervals* between quarters. (Chap. 4)

in•tim•i•date (ĭn tĭm′ ə dāt′), *verb,* make timid; cow. The others were *intimidated* by his outspoken sureness. (Chap. 12)

in•tra•state (ĭn′trə stāt′), *adjective,* within one state. The inspector's duties were *intrastate;* he took water samples only in Georgia. (Chap. 3)

in•tu•it (ĭn tōō′ ĭt), *verb,* sense or know by intuition. Try to *intuit* the relationship between the cause and the effect. (Chap. 4)

in•un•date (ĭn′ ən dāt′), *verb,* overflow; flood; overwhelm. The water broke through the dam and *inundated* the valley below. (Chap. 6)

in•vin•ci•bil•i•ty (ĭn vĭn′sə bĭl′ə tē), *noun,* the status of not being able to be conquered or overcome. The ignorant soldiers thought that their *invincibility* protected them against bullets. (Chap. 12)

ir•re•press•i•ble (ĭr ĭ prĕs′ə bəl), *adjective,* impossible to control or restrain. The team had an *irrepressible* spirit that carried them to victory. (Chap. 12)

isth•mus (ĭs′məs), *noun,* a narrow neck of land connecting two larger land areas. The *isthmus* of Suez connects Asia and Africa. (Chap. 6)

J

jos•tle (jŏs′əl), *verb,* push or shove rudely against. The pickpocket *jostled* the victim to draw his attention away from the thieving action. (Chap. 15)

K

keen (kēn), *verb,* wail for the dead. They *keened* loudly and made everyone aware of the tragedy. (Chap. 8)

Ko•ran (Kō rän′), *noun,* Islamic sacred scripture. The *Koran* is believed by Muslims to contain revelations by Allah. (Chap. 14)

L

leg•end•ar•y (lĕj′ən dĕ rē), *adjective,* in regard to a story handed down by tradition. Although *legendary* exploits have no proof of truth, they are often accepted as having happened. (Chap. 8)

le•gions (lē′jəns), *noun,* large numbers, multitudes, armies. There were *legions* who followed his great leadership. (Chap. 12)

leg•is•la•tive (lĕj′ ĭs lā′tĭv), *adjective,* having the function of making laws. Our national *legislative* body sits in Washington. (Chap. 4)

lei•sure•ly (lē′zhər lē), *adjective,* without haste; taking plenty of time. The couple took a *leisurely* stroll along the beach. (Chap. 2)

leth•al (lēth′ əl), *adjective,* capable of killing; causing death. He was arrested for carrying a *lethal* weapon. (Chap. 3)

life•style (līf′ stīl), *noun,* a characteristic way of life; manner of life that reflects values and attitudes. Their reckless *lifestyle* showed they cared nothing of other people's needs or feelings. (Chap. 3)

lit•e•rar•y (lĭt′ə rĕr′ē), *adjective,* relating to books, literature, writing. It was a *literary* family; they enjoyed reading books and writing stories. (Chap. 12)

lounge (lounj), *verb,* stand, sit, or lie at ease and lazily. I love to *lounge* in the sun; it relaxes me. (Chap. 4)

lu•cra•tive (lōō′krə tĭv), *adjective,* profitable, yielding gain. Selling goods in heavy demand is *lucrative* work. (Chap. 2)

lure (lŭr), *noun,* attraction, temptation. The *lure* of the sea beckoned to him, so he became a sailor. (Chap. 4)

M

man•date (mân′dāt), *noun,* a formal order or command. They had no choice; the order to vacate was a *mandate* from the court. (Chap. 12)

man•u•script (măn′yə skrĭpt′), *noun,* something handwritten, typewritten, or in computer rough draft as opposed to final printed copy. Some libraries have collections of *manuscripts* written by famous authors. (Chap. 12)

mar•i•tal (măr′ ə təl), *adjective,* relating to marriage. Their *marital* relationship was a happy one. (Chap. 3)

mar•ket (mär′kĭt), *verb,* buy or sell; deal. The tradesman *markets* his wares at the mall. (Chap. 2)

mass (măs), *noun,* a lump or large blob. The doctor discovered a *mass* of fatty tissue in the woman's leg. (Chap. 5)

mec•ca (mĕk′ə), *noun,* a place many people want to visit or the goal of one's ambitions. The word comes from the city of *Mecca,* which is a center for Islamic pilgrims. (Chap. 4)

me•di•ate (mē′dĭ āt′), *verb,* try to bring agreement between disputing groups or persons. The mediator was called to *mediate* the differences between labor and management. (Chap. 14)

mem•o•ra•ble (mĕm′ ər ə bəl), *adjective,* worthy of remembering; notable. For the Pearl Harbor survivor, December 7 is a *memorable* day. (Chap. 3)

merge (mĕrj), *verb,* combine; consolidate; gradually absorb. The small computer company *merged* with a larger business organization. (Chap. 3)

met•a•mor•phic (mĕt′ə môr′fĭk), *adjective,* having change in form or structure. Heat and pressure can change sedimentary rocks into *metamorphic* rocks. (Chap. 7)

mi•grate (mī′grāt), *verb,* move from one country or region to settle in another. Many of us have ancestors who *migrated* here from another country. (Chap. 14)

mil•len•ni•um (mĭ lĕn′ ē əm), *noun,* one thousand years. There are trees that have lived more than a *millennium.* (Chap. 3)

min•i•mize (mĭn′ ə mīz), *verb,* make the least out of, reduce to the smallest amount. Do not *minimize* your own contribution to the cause; you have worked very hard. Related word: **minimal,** *adjective,* very small (Chap. 5)

mire (mīr), *verb,* sink in soft, deep mud or slushy snow. Spinning the wheels only *mired* the car more deeply. (Chap. 6)

mod•er•a•tion (mŏd ər ā′ shun), *noun,* a state of being moderate; reasonableness; restraint. People help to maintain their health by eating and drinking in *moderation.* (Chap. 8)

mod•est (mŏd′ ĭst), *adjective,* not too great, not expensive or showy. The couple bought a *modest* house even though they were very wealthy. (Chap. 5)

mo•men•tous (mō mĕn′ təs), *adjective,* very important, outstanding. World leaders at times must make *momentous* decisions. (Chap. 4)

mor•tal (môr′ tl), *adjective,* sure to die sometime; human. Some people do very risky things. They forget that they are *mortal.* (Chap. 8)

mor•tal•i•ty (môr tăl′ ə tē), *noun,* death rate, mortal nature. The *mortality* from smoking is increasing among women. (Chap. 2)

mul•ti•tude (mŭl′tə tōōd), *noun,* a crowd; a great many. The hungry *multitude* gathered around the food truck. (Chap. 3)

mus•ter (mŭs′tər), *verb,* summon; gather together. The new miners *mustered* their courage before entering the deep mine shaft. (Chap. 6)

N

nas•cent (năs′ ənt), *adjective,* just coming into existence, just beginning to develop. Bruce had a *nascent* idea, which eventually developed into a full-blown plan of action. (Chap. 4)

nat•ur•al•ist (năch′ər ə lĭst), *noun,* a person who studies plants and animals. John Muir was a *naturalist* who crusaded for national parks and nature reservations. (Chap. 7)

neg•li•gi•ble (nĕg′lə jə bəl), *adjective,* not worth considering; insignificant. Because their differences were *negligible,* they agreed on the contract. (Chap. 14)

neu•tral (nōō′trəl), *adjective,* not taking either side. The fans were not *neutral;* they cheered for their own teams. (Chap. 13)

niche (nĭch), *noun,* in ecology, the role or position and function of an animal or plant in the natural community. The monkey's *niche* was to live and feed in the tops of trees. (Chap. 3)

no•bly (nō′blē), *adverb,* in a noble manner; splendidly. The musician stood in front of a very critical audience and performed *nobly.* (Chap. 15)

non•com•mu•nist (nŏn′ kŏm′ yə nĭst), *noun,* one who does not believe in communism, the political system in which all property is owned by the state. As an American, I am a *noncommunist.* (Chap. 3)

nov•ice (nŏv′ ĭs), *noun,* one without experience; one new to the position. He was a *novice* with hammer and saw, but the carpenter would train him. (Chap. 2)

O

ob•jec•tive (əb jĕk′tĭv), *adjective* or *noun,* unbiased; free from personal feelings; something toward which effort is directed. While interpreting the data, the chemist made an effort to be *objective.* The pioneers' *objective* was to get the shelter finished before winter arrived. (Chap. 8)

ob•liv•i•on (ə blĭv′ ĭ ən), *noun,* the condition of being forgotten by the world. Some early civilizations have passed into *oblivion.* (Chap. 7)

ob•scu•ri•ty (əb skyōōr′ə tē), *noun,* the condition of being unknown; dimness. The original meanings of the markings on the monument have fallen into *obscurity.* (Chap. 9)

ob•sessed (əb sĕssd′), *verb,* holding an idea or feeling to an intense degree. Churchill was *obsessed* with the idea of defending Britain from the Nazis. (Chap. 12)

ob•ses•sion (əb sesh′ ən), *noun,* a persistent idea or dominating influence that a person cannot escape. Columbus was driven by an *obsession* to reach India by sailing westward. (Chap. 9)

o•men (ō′ mən), *noun,* an occurrence believed to be a sign of a future event. Early peoples saw the appearances of certain animals as *omens* of good hunting. (Chap. 7)

om•nip•o•tent (ŏm nĭp′ə tənt), *adjective,* having unlimited power or authority. Many ancient kings were *omnipotent* in their kingdoms. (Chap. 3)

om•ni•pres•ent (ŏm′nə prĕz′ ənt), *adjective,* all present; being or existing everywhere. In many religions, God is thought to be *omnipresent.* (Chap. 3)

op•er•a•tive (ŏp′ ər â′tĭv), *adjective,* exerting influence; being in effect. The rules *operative* when he played the game have since been changed. (Chap. 2)

o•ver•all (ō′vər ôl′), *adjective,* from one extreme of a thing to the other. The *overall* length of the car was fifteen feet. (Chap. 2)

o•vert (ō′ vĕrt), *adjective,* not hidden; open; public. The spy took no *overt* actions to avoid being the object of attention. (Chap. 7)

P

pa•ho•e•ho•e (pä hō′ ā hō′ ā), *noun,* lava that looks like coils of heavy rope. Some Hawaiian lava fields are made of *pahoehoe.* (Chap. 7)

pair (pâər), *verb,* to arrange two parts for use together. He *paired* the two straps so that together they held the case firmly on his back. (Chap. 13)

pan•the•on (păn′thĭ ŏn′), *noun,* a temple dedicated to the gods. Hadrian erected a domed *pantheon* that today is used as a church. (Chap. 12)

par•a•mount (păr′ə mount′), *adjective,* above all; superior in authority. His *paramount* concern was to make his car payment. (Chap. 14)

par•tial (pär′ shəl), *adjective,* relating to a part or piece of the whole. The money she earned made only a *partial* payment for her coat. (Chap. 7)

pas•sive (păs′ ĭv), *adjective,* inactive; submissive. The child was so *passive* that we knew something was wrong. (Chap. 2)

sed•i•men•ta•ry (sĕd′ə mĕn′tər ē), *adjective,* formed from deposits of sediment. Some *sedimentary* rocks show layers of different colors. (Chap. 7)

seem•ing•ly (sē′ming lē), *adverb,* apparently; at first sight or view. *Seemingly* they were very pleasant, but in reality they were two-faced. (Chap. 14)

siege (sēj), *noun,* the surrounding of a fortified place to capture it by cutting off supplies or help. The army kept bombarding the fort while keeping it under *siege.* (Chap. 14)

sig•nif•i•cant (sĭg nĭf′ ə kənt), *adjective,* important; meaningful. Beth knew that her graduation from college was a *significant* event for her family. (Chap. 3)

sig•ni•fy (sĭg′nə fī′), *verb,* be a sign of. The arrow in the road sign *signifies* a curve. (Chap. 8)

sit•u•a•tion (sĭch′ə wā′shən), *noun,* a state of affairs, or plight, at any given time. In winter camp at Valley Forge, Washington's men were in a desperate *situation.* (Chap. 6)

slo•gan (slō′ gən), *noun,* motto, word, or expression used to advertise a group or business. The business adopted the *slogan* "We try harder." (Chap. 5)

soar (sôr), *verb,* climb; rise; fly upward. When crude oil prices *soar,* gasoline prices quickly follow. (Chap. 2)

sov•er•eign (sŏv′ĭ rĭn), *noun,* monarch; king or queen. The *sovereign* had her portrait put on all the coins and stamps. (Chap. 12)

spate (spāt), *noun,* a sudden onset or outpouring. Desert flowers bloom after a *spate* of rain. (Chap. 7)

spec•ter (spĕk′tər), *noun,* a ghost; visible spirit. In Dickens's *A Christmas Carol,* Scrooge was frightened by a series of *specters.* (Chap. 7)

spew (spū), *verb,* discharge contents; vomit. Old Faithful geyser *spewed* water and steam into the air. (Chap. 2)

squa•lor (skwôl′ ər), *noun,* filthy, wretched condition. I was aghast at the *squalor* I saw when I visited the poor country. Related word: **squalid,** *adjective,* dirty, wretched. (Chap. 4)

sta•ble (stā′ bəl), *adjective,* not likely to fall; firm; steady. The economy seems *stable* at this point; therefore, I think I will risk a job change. (Chap. 7)

sta•tis•tics (stə tĭs′ tĭks), *noun,* mathematical facts and figures; also a branch of mathematics. The sociologist provided some *statistics* to prove his point. My friend studied *statistics* because she wanted to become a psychologist. (Chap. 2)

stim•u•lus (stĭm′ yə ləs), *noun,* something that excites or arouses. A scratch on the frog's nose was the *stimulus* that made him jump. (Chap. 14)

struc•tur•al (strŭk′chər əl), *adjective,* having to do with structure; pertaining to how parts are put together.

Structural steel made up the framework of the building. (Chap. 3)

sub•sist (səb sĭst′), *verb,* be kept alive; just exist. During the potato famine, the Irish *subsisted* on almost nothing. (Chap. 2)

sub•tle (sŭt′l), *adjective,* delicate; likely to avoid perception. The mouse never noticed the *subtle* movements of the owl. (Chap. 2)

suc•cess•ive (sək sĕs′ĭv), *adjective,* following in order without interruption. The medicine was to be taken for ten *successive* days. (Chap. 14)

su•per•in•ten•dent (soo′pər ĭn tĕn′dənt), *noun,* one who directs or oversees an institution or enterprise. The *superintendent* was in charge of the blueprints for the new bridge. (Chap. 3)

su•per•high•way (sū′ pər hī′ wā), *noun,* major road, especially one having limited access. We decided to use the country roads on our motoring trip of Europe rather than the *superhighways.* (Chap. 3)

sup•press (sə prĕs′), *verb,* stop, often by force; hold back. The autocrat tried to *suppress* religious expression. Related word: **suppression,** putting down by force. When the *suppression* of dissent became intense, the people rose up and overthrew the government. (Chap. 5)

sus•cep•ti•ble (sə sĕp′ tə bəl), *adjective,* easily affected by; open to, as a disease. Having had a flu shot, I was less *susceptible* to catching the "bug" that was going around. (Chap. 5)

sym•bol•ic (sĭm bŏl′ ĭk), *adjective,* functioning to represent something else. In the novel, the sea was *symbolic* of family and security. Related word: **symbolize,** *verb,* to represent something else. (Chap. 4)

syn•the•sis (sĭn′thə sĭs), *noun,* a building of simpler parts into a complex organization. Plants make sugar by *synthesis* of small molecules. (Chap. 7)

syn•thet•ic (sĭn thĕt′ ĭk), *adjective,* made by putting components together; made, rather than formed naturally. *Synthetic* fabrics take the place of cotton and wool. (Chaps. 5 and 12)

T

te•di•ous (tē′dĭ əs), *adjective,* lengthy and tiresome. Westward pioneers made *tedious* journeys. (Chap. 7)

tel•e•graph (tĕl′ə grăf), *noun,* a device for sending coded messages over long distances. Marconi invented a wireless *telegraph* and was the first to send a message across the Atlantic Ocean. (Chap. 3)

ter•rain (tər rān′), *noun,* the surface of the land with reference to its natural features. The *terrain* before us was arid and uninviting. (Chap. 4)

ter•ror•ize (tĕr′ər īz), *verb,* to create fear; coerce violently. The volcanic eruption *terrorized* the people living on the mountain slopes. (Chap. 7)

the•o•ret•i•cal (thē′ ə rĕt′ ək əl), *adjective,* dealing with theories; not practical. *Theoretical* knowledge of the universe is obtained from examining changes in stars. (Chap. 3)

ther•a•py (thĕr′ ə pē), *noun,* treatment for physical disorders or disabilities. After I had been in an automobile accident, I had to go for *therapy* to overcome a slight limp I had acquired (Chap. 5)

throm•bus (thrŏm′ bəs), *noun,* a blood clot. Fibrin molecules of the plasma together with blood cells make a clot called a *thrombus.* (Chap. 13)

till (tĭl), *verb,* cultivate, often by plowing. The farmer *tilled* the fields late into the night. Readers should *till* the text before beginning to read. (Chap. 1)

tox•ic (tŏk′ sĭk), *adjective,* poisonous; caused by poison. She experienced a *toxic* reaction to seafood. (Chap. 2)

tra•di•tions (trə dĭsh′ ĕns), *noun,* elements of a culture or modes of thought or behavior passed on from one generation to the next. Having traveled extensively in the Far East, the man, became impressed with the *traditions* associated with the Hindu religion. Related word: **traditional,** handed down by tradition, customary. (Chap. 5)

trans•con•ti•nen•tal (trăns′kŏn tə nən′təl), *adjective,* extending across a continent. When tracks from the Pacific coast and from Omaha were joined near Ogden, Utah, in 1869, the first *transcontinental* railroad was completed. (Chap. 3)

trans•form (trăns fôrm′), *verb,* change in form, character, appearance. The dirty travelers were *transformed* by their hot bath and change into fresh clothes. (Chap. 2)

trans•mis•sion (trăn smĭsh′ ən), *noun,* a sending, a passing along. The *transmission* of data from the primary health insurance plan to a secondary one is very slow. (Chap. 3)

trau•ma (trô′mă), *noun,* violent bodily injury; shock. The word *trauma* can mean physical harm or severe shock to mental well-being. (Chap. 12)

trea•tise (trē′tĭs), *noun,* a formal book or paper on some subject. Asa Gray wrote a *treatise* on plant identification. (Chap. 6)

trends (trĕnds), *noun,* general directions of activity or movement, tendencies. The economist studied monetary *trends* in the country and determined that people typically were carrying higher debts than previously. (Chap. 2)

trib•ute (trĭb′ūt), *noun,* an offering of gratitude or esteem; a forced gift or valuable paid in submission. In *tribute,* the people laid hundreds of flowers at their leader's feet. (Chap. 15)

tri•lat•er•al (trī lăt′ ər əl), *adjective,* having three sides or parties. The three electric companies have a *trilateral* agreement to share power when one company has a shortage. (Chap. 3)

triv•i•al (trĭv′ ĭ əl), *adjective,* unimportant; commonplace. His problems were *trivial;* he soon forgot them. (Chap. 7)

trust (trŭst), *noun,* a monopoly; organization in restraint of trade. Antitrust laws now regulate the powers of *trusts.* (Chap. 12)

tur•moil (tûr′moil), *noun,* a state of disturbance, commotion, agitation. The attack came from two directions and put the defenders in *turmoil.* (Chap. 8)

U

u•nan•i•mous (ūnăn′ə məs), *adjective,* all in agreement; in complete accord. They all agreed; the vote was *unanimous.* (Chap. 4)

u•nique (ū nēk′), *adjective,* sole; the only one of its kind. Because something *unique* has no like or equal, we should not say something is *very* unique. (Chap. 14)

un•mar•ried (ŭn măr′ēd), *adjective,* not joined as husband and wife. The *unmarried* young people hoped to find friends who would become possible wives or husbands. (Chap. 3)

un•prec•e•den•ted (un prĕs′ə dĕn′tid), *adjective,* never known or done before. The record high jump was *unprecedented.* (Chap. 8)

un•ru•ly (un rü′lē), *adjective,* difficult to control; not conforming to rule. The chairperson had difficulty in maintaining order when the members became *unruly.* (Chap. 14)

un•sta•ble (ŭn stă′ bəl), *adjective,* not steady or firm, likely to change. The *unstable* conditions after the revolution made people uneasy. (Chap. 3)

V

ver•i•ta•ble (vĕr′ə tə bal), *adjective,* genuine; real; true. He was a *veritable* jack-of-all-trades; there was nothing he could not do. (Chap. 7)

ves•i•cle (vĕs′ə kəl), *noun,* a cavity; sac; small bladder. The sponge was filled with *vesicles.* (Chap. 7)

vice ver•sa (vī′sə vûr′sə), *adverb,* the other way around. She was going first to Denmark and then to Norway, or *vice versa.* (Chap. 8)

vir•tu•al (vûr′chōō əl), adjective, in force or in effect but not actually expressed as such. The general was the *virtual* power behind the throne; he told the king what to do. (Chap. 6)

vis•cous (vĭs′kəs), adjective, sticky; gummy. The *viscous* grease dripped from the roasting pan. (Chap. 7)

vis•i•bil•i•ty (vĭz ə bĭl′ ə tē), noun, the capacity of being seen. The fog made the *visibility* very poor. (Chap. 2)

W

wrest (rĕst), verb, pull away by force. The thief tried to *wrest* the jewelry from the woman. (Chap. 2)

Glossary compiled by George and Dorothy Hennings

CREDITS

Reading on page

8–9
Henry Graff, *The Great Nation,* © 1985 by Riverside Publishing Company. Reprinted with permission of the publisher.

12–13
Pat Sleem, "For Heaven's Sake, Choose a Job You Enjoy!" Reprinted with permission from *Careers and the College Grad* (Holbrook, MA: Bob Adams, Inc.), p. 16.

15–16
Adapted from Helena Curtis and N. Sue Barnes, *Invitation to Biology,* © 1985 by Worth Publishers. Reprinted by permission of the publisher.

18–19, 169–170
Fergus Hughes, Lloyd Noppe, and Illene Noppe, *Child Development,* © 1996. Reprinted by permission of Prentice Hall, Inc., Upper Saddle River, New Jersey.

26–27
Adapted from Leo Fay et al., *Riverside Reading Program, Level 15.* © 1989 by Riverside Publishing Company. Reprinted with permission of the publisher.

27–29
Selected excerpt from *Physical Geology: Principles, Processes, and Problems* by Charles Cazeau, Robert Hatcher, and Francis Siemankowski, Copyright © 1976 Charles Cazeau, Robert Hatcher, and Francis Siemankowski. Reprinted by permission of Charles Cazeau.

29–31, 87
David Krogh, *Biology: A Guide to the Natural World.* © 2000, pp. 8–9, 496. Reprinted by permission of Prentice Hall, Inc., Upper Saddle River, New Jersey.

33–34, 243–244, 247–248
Charles G. Morris, *Psychology: An Introduction,* 6th ed., © 1988. Reprinted by permission of Prentice Hall, Inc., Englewood Cliffs, New Jersey.

50–51, 127–129
Kathryn Kelley and Donn Byrne, *Exploring Human Sexuality.* © 1992 by Prentice Hall. Reprinted by permission of Prentice Hall, Inc., Englewood Cliffs, New Jersey.

53–54
David Popenoe, *Sociology,* 11th ed. © 2000, pp. 90–91. Reprinted by permission of Prentice Hall, Inc., Upper Saddle River, New Jersey.

77, 152–153, 171–172
John Macionis, *Sociology,* 6th ed., © 1997. Reprinted by permission of Prentice Hall, Inc., Upper Saddle River, New Jersey.

79–80
John Mack Faragher, et al., *Out of Many: A History of the American People,* 3rd ed. © 2000, pp. 237–238. Reprinted by permission of Prentice Hall, Inc., Upper Saddle River, New Jersey.

84–85
Elizabeth Romanaux, "Give Them a Rude Awakening," from the "Perspectives" section of the *Sunday Star-Ledger* (Newark, NJ), January 23, 2000. © 2000. All rights reserved. Reprinted by permission of the publisher.

90–92
Stephen Robbins, *Management,* 2nd ed., © 1988, pp. 199–201. Reprinted by permission of Prentice Hall, Inc., Englewood Cliffs, New Jersey.

95–96
Thomas Dye, *Politics in America,* 3rd ed. © 1999, pp. 12, 15. Reprinted by permission of Prentice Hall, Inc., Upper Saddle River, New Jersey.

103
John Macionis, *Sociology,* 3rd. ed., © 1991. Reprinted by permission of Prentice Hall, Inc., Englewood Cliffs, New Jersey.

104–105
Karl Case and Ray Fair, *Principles of Economics,* 2nd ed., © 1992, pp. 538–539. Reprinted by permission of Prentice Hall, Inc., Englewood Cliffs, New Jersey.

107–111
George Cruys, "The Dream of Panama," *Skald* (Spring/Summer 1986), pp. 2–7. Copyright 1986 by Royal Viking Line. Reprinted by permission of Royal Viking Line.

117–125
The seven paragraphs on pages 117–125 are adapted from Chester R. Longwell, Adolph Knopf, and Richard Flint, *Physical Geology* (New York: John Wiley, 1948), pp. 347–348.

135–137
The four paragraphs on pages 135–137 are from Jay Pasachoff, Naomi Pasachoff, Roy Clark, and Marlene Westermann, *Physical Science Today.* © 1987 by Prentice Hall, Inc. Reprinted by permission of the publisher.

141
Philip Kotler and Gary Armstrong, *Principles of Marketing.* © 1994. Reprinted by permission of Prentice Hall, Inc.

142
Jean Berko Gleason, *The Development of Language.* © 1985 by Charles E. Merril. Reprinted by permission of the publisher.

145–146	Excerpt from "Primary Lessons" by Judith Ortiz-Cofer is reprinted with permission from the publisher of *Silent Dancing: A Partial Remembrance of a Puerto Rican Childhood* (Houston: Arte Publico Press, University of Houston, 1990).
149–150	From *The Star-Ledger* (Newark, NJ), May 27, 1994, a column by L. Hall. Reprinted by permission of the editor of *The Star-Ledger.*
156–158	From *American Indian Myths and Legends* by Richard Erdoes and Alfonso Ortiz. Copyright ©1984 by Richard Erdoes and Alfonso Ortiz. Reprinted by permission of Pantheon Books, a division of Random House, Inc.
174–176	Daniel Politoske, *Music,* 4th ed. © 1988, pp. 510–512. Reprinted by permission of Prentice Hall, Inc., Englewood Cliffs, New Jersey.
177–178	From *Hunger of Memory* by Richard Rodriguez. Copyright © 1982 by Richard Rodriguez. Reprinted by permission of David R. Godine, Publisher.
182	Nila Smith and H. Alan Robinson, *Reading Instruction for Today's Children,* 2nd ed. © 1980 by Prentice Hall, Inc. Reprinted by permission of the publisher.
186	Thomas Brock, David Smith, and Michael Madigan, *Biology of Microorganisms,* 4th ed. © 1984 by Prentice Hall, Inc. Reprinted by permission of the publisher.
187–188	Eudora Welty, *One Writer's Beginnings* (Cambridge, Mass.: Harvard University Press, 1984), pp. 29–30. Copyright 1983, 1984 by Eudora Welty. Reprinted by permission of the publisher.
189–190	Robert Wiggins, "Complex Insecurity: Big Brother Is Watching You," *MacUser,* 4 (April 1988), p. 47. Copyright © 1988 Ziff Communications Company.
191	Alan Mandell, *The Language of Science.* Copyright 1974 by the National Science Teachers Association. Reprinted by permission of the National Science Teachers Association.
192–193	From *All I Really Need to Know I Learned in Kindergarten* by Robert Fulghum. Copyright © 1986, 1988 by Robert Fulghum. Reprinted by permission of Villard Books, a division of Random House, Inc.
220–222	Harry Truman, "The 8 Best Presidents—and Why," *Parade Magazine,* April 3, 1988, pp. 4–5. From *More Plain Speaking,* by Harry S. Truman, edited by Margaret Truman and Scott Meredith. Reprinted by permission of the author and Scott Meredith Literary Agency, Inc., 845 Third Avenue, New York, NY 10022 and with permission from *Parade.* Copyright © 1988.
225–226	From *The Star-Ledger* (Newark, NJ), April 12, 1991, a column by Lawrence Hall. Reprinted by permission of the publisher.
228–230	From *I Know Why the Caged Bird Sings* by Maya Angelou. Copyright © 1969 by Maya Angelou. Reprinted by permission of Random House, Inc.
233–235, 236, 237–238, 241	Excerpts from John W. Hole, Jr., *Human Anatomy and Physiology.* Copyright 1979 by William C. Brown. Reprinted by permission of the publisher.
239–240	Jeffrey Slater and John Tobey, *Basic College Mathematics,* © 1991, p. 3. Reprinted by permission of Prentice Hall, Inc., Englewood Cliffs, New Jersey.
255	William Tracy, "Middle West Meets Middle East," *ARAMCO World Magazine,* 38:5 (September–October 1987), p. 3. Used with permission.
258–259	Anne Marshall Zwack, "Florence the Magnificent," *Travel and Leisure,* 17:4 (April 1987), pp. 103–114, 162. Reprinted by permission of *Travel and Leisure* and the author.
269–272	Paul Lunde and John A. Sabinin. *ARAMCO and Its World: Arabia and the Middle East.* Copyright 1980 by Arabian American Oil Company. Reprinted by permission of ARAMCO.
280	From *Fatherhood* by Bill Cosby. Copyright © by William H. Cosby, Jr. Used by permission of Doubleday, a division of Bantam Doubleday Dell Publishing Group, Inc.
285–286	From *It Was on Fire When I Lay Down on It* by Robert Fulghum. Copyright © 1989 by Robert Fulghum. Reprinted by permission of Villard Books, a division of Random House, Inc.
293–306	David Popenoe, *Sociology,* 10th ed., Copyright © 1995. Reprinted by permission of Prentice Hall, Inc., Upper Saddle River, New Jersey.
296	The International Bank for Reconstruction and Development/World Bank, Table from *World Development Report 1991* © 1991. Reprinted by permission of Oxford University Press, Inc.
299	James A. Daves and Tom W. Smith, *General Social Survey Cumulative File, 1972–1982,* Inter University Consortium for Political and Social Research, © 1983. Reprinted by permission of Tom W. Smith.

INDEX

Names of authors of selections are given in italics. Names of selections are in bold.

A

Achievement of Desire, 177–78
Activating what you know before reading, 2, 4
Aesop, 184–85
Affixes, 39–48
African-American Folk Music, 174–76
Age at First Marriage, 209–10
Alliteration, 276
Allusions, literary, 277
Anatomy and Physiology, 235
Angelou, Maya, 228–30
Antonyms, using to unlock the meaning of words, 23–25
Apply ideas to one's life, 140–41
Approximations, making, 99–100
Assigned reading, dealing with, 2
Author's purpose, 2
Autobiography, reading of, 70, 145, 177–78, 187–88, 228–30

B

Ballpark figure, 99–100
Bar graphs, 206–8
Because It's There, 280–81
Bias in writing, detecting, 217–18
Big Brother Is Watching You, 189–200
Biographies, reading, 262–66
Brock, Thomas, 186
Byrne, Donn, 50–51

C

Can Chimpanzees Learn to Speak?, 142–43
Case, Karl, 104–5
Cause/effect, recognizing, 124–26
Cazeau, Charles, 27–29
Cell Membrane, 236
Chance Event or Not? Anecdote, Common Sense, and Statistics in Science, 29–31
Charts and tables, interpreting, 195–203
Charts for gathering data, 172–73
Charts for predicting before reading, 7, 15
Child Development, 17–20
Child's Experience of Divorce, 169–70
Chiras, Daniel, 55–56
Chronology, comprehending, 262–65

Chunks of meaning, 182–85
Circle graphs, 204–6
Cloud, Jenny Leading, 156–58
Clue words, following, 115–39, 240–41
Cofer, Judith, 145–46
Cohabitation, 49–51
College: A Transition Point in My Life, 70–71
Color of Money, 76–77
Comparing, strategy for, 141–43, 266
Comparisons and contrasts, recognizing, 121–22
Compound words, 39, 48
Concentrating while reading, 181
Concluding, 146–47
Conditional relationships, recognizing, 122–24
Connotation, 218–19
Context clues to unlock the meaning of words, 23–38
Context/Dictionary/Context strategy, 24–25
Cosby, Bill, 280
Critical thinking, 140–62
Cruys, George, 107–11
Cultural Change, 171–72
Curtis, Helena, 15–16

D

Data chart, recording opinions with, 219
Data charts as a before reading strategy, 7, 15
Data-gathering chart, 172–73
Daydreaming, 247–48
Deductive paragraphs, 66–67
Definitions, comprehending, 233–40
Definitions, using to unlock the meaning of words, 23–25
Denotation, 218–19
Descriptions, comprehending, 253–62
Details, comprehending, 98–114
Diacritical marks, 312
Dickinson, Emily, 256 (See also **Emily Dickinson**)
Dictionary, using to unlock the meaning of words, 24
Diffusion and Osmosis, 237–38
Directional changes, recognizing, 118–22

Distractions and reading, 181
Doing Something About Osteoporosis While You Are Young, 87
Drawings, line, 211–12
Dream at Panama, 105–11
Dye, Thomas, 95–96

E

Eagle, 255
Early Presidents of the United States, 66–70
Eat, Drink, but the Dietary Doom-Sayers Won't Let You Be Merry, 148–51
Education of Richard Rodriguez, 177–78
Eight Best Presidents and Why, 220–24
Elements Known to Ancient Civilizations, 134–38
Emily Dickinson, 264–65
Enumeration, paragraphs of, 115–16
Equations, using for interpreting definitions, 234
Erdoes, Richard, 156–58
Essay questions, 166–67
Examinations, preparing for (See test taking)
Examples, recognizing, 116–18
Explanations, comprehending, 240–52
Explanations, using to unlock the meaning of words, 23–25

F

Fables, reading, 184–85
Fact versus opinion, 217–18
Faragher, John, 78–80
Fatherhood: Because It's There, 280
Fifty States of the United States, 199–203
Figures of speech, 277
Fix-up strategies, 70
Florence, the Magnificent, 257–59
Food Chains, 55–56
Footnotes, 3
For Heaven's Sakes, Choose a Job You Enjoy, 12–13
Forming a Friendship, 127–29
Fulghum, Robert, 192–93, 285–86

G

General versus specific, 62–66
Genius of Mark Twain, 224–26
Getting ready to read, 1–21
Gettysburg Address, 282–83
**Give Them a Rude Awakening:
    Be Polite to Pushy
    People,** 84–85
Gleason, Jean, 142
Glossary, using to unlock the
    meaning of words, 312–26
Graff, Henry, 6, 8–9
Graphs:
    bar, 206–8
    circle, 204–6
    line, 209–12
    pictograph, 203–4
    pie, 204–6
Great Constructions of the World,
    100–102
Grids, interpreting (See charts and
    tables)
Guide words, 312

H

Hall, Lawrence, 149–50, 225–26
Headings and subheadings, 2
Hennings, George, 115–16, 131–32
He's My Son!, 102–4
Highlighting a text, 170–71
Hole, John, 235, 236, 237–38
Hughes, Fergus, 17–19, 169–70
Hypothetical Cell, 235

I

I Know Why the Caged Bird
    Sings, 228–30
Idea, main (See Main idea)
Idea mapping, 71, 113, 250
Idea webbing, 10, 13, 172
If-then relationships, 122–24
Illustrations, use of in previewing, 3
Imagery, 277
Immigration to the United States,
    207–9
Implied meanings, 143–46
Inductive paragraphs, 67
Inferring,
    main idea, 68–70
    making inferences, 143–46
**Internet in Postindustrial
    Society,** 52–54
Introductory sections of a
    chapter, 2–4

J

James, Michener, 98–99
Judging, 147
Judgments, assessing the validity
    of, 219

K

Kelly, Kathryn, 50–51, 127–29
Kotler, Philip, 141
Krogh, David, 29–31, 87
Kum ba yah, 278

L

Land Views, 255–56
Language and Communication, 191
Lazarus, Emma, 288
Lear, Edward, 279
Limericks, 279
Lincoln, Abraham, 282–83
Line graphs, 209–12
Linear paragraphs, 69
Love Isn't Easy, 192–93
Lunde, Paul, 269–72

M

Macionis, John, 77, 103, 152–53
Main idea, 61–97
Mandell, Alan, 191
Map of
    Central America and the
        Caribbean, 114
    Italy, 258
    Little Big Horn region, 162
    Middle East, 269
    northeastern United States, 11
    United States, 202
mapping ideas for writing, 112, 250–51
mapping a summary for writing,
    182–83
Marketing in a Changing World, 141
Marriage Customs, 63–66
**Maya Angelou's School
    Thoughts,** 228–30
Meaning of Democracy, 95–96
Metacognition, 20
Metaphor, 254–55, 277–78
**Microscope and
    Microorganisms,** 185–87
Mind talk as part of reading, 64,
    241–42
Mood, definition of, 278
Moon, 256
Moral Power or Gun Power, 152–53
Morris, Charles, 33–34, 243–44,
    247–48
Muhammad the Prophet, 267–72

N

Narratives, comprehending, 262–75
Nation on the Move, 8–9
**Native American Myths and
    Legends,** 154–61
New Colossus, 287–88
Newspaper columns,
    149–50, 225–26
Noppe, Lloyd, 17–19, 174–76

Note taking in a text (See
    Highlighting)
Numerical detail, 99–100

O

Old Man with a Beard, 279
On Geology, 27–29
One Writer's Beginnings, 187–88
Opinions, comprehending, 217–32
O/P/O Strategy, 219
Outlines of chapters, 17–18, 173

P

Paragraph, structure of (See
    Structure of a paragraph)
Paragraphs, writing, 250–51
Paraphrasing, 234
**Partial Remembrance of a Puerto
    Rican Childhood,** 145–46
Pasachoff, Jay, 135–38
**Pavlov's Conditioning
    Experiments,** 243–44
Personal reading, 2
Persuasive writing, 217–32
Phyllis Wheatley, 262–63
Pictographs, interpreting, 203–4
Pie graphs, 204–6
Politoske, Daniel, 174–76
Popenoe, David, Appendix A, 53–54,
    291–307
Populations on the Land, 195–96
Predicting based on clue
    words, 115–39
Predicting before reading, 2–3
Prefixes, 39–47
Prenatal Development, 33–34
Previewing before reading, 2–4
Primary Lessons, 145–46
Punctuation and sound effects, 176
Purpose, author's, 2
Purpose, reader's, 2, 5

Q

Question types, examination, 163–67
Questioning before reading, 2–5

R

Rate of reading, see Reading rate
Reader's purpose, 2, 3
Reading, definition of, 1
Reading rate,
    calculating, 309–11
    charts for finding, 310–11
Reasons, recognizing, 124–26
Reciting as part of reading, 168
Recognizing
    how many items will be
        discussed, 115–16
    whether a comparison or contrast
        is coming, 120–22

whether a conditional relationship is being established, 122–24
whether an example is coming, 116–18
whether a reason is going to be given, 124–26
whether there will be a change in direction, 118–20
Reference points from history, 263
Relating events, 265–67
Remembering for tests, 178–79
Reviewing after reading, 168
Rhyme, 266, 267
Ring Out, Wild Bells, 277
Robbins, Stephen, 90–92
Rodriguez, Richard, 177–78
Romanaux, Elizabeth, 84–85
Root words, 39

S

Sabini, John, 269–72
Satire, 281
Schwa, 51
Self-monitoring, 70
Semantic webbing (See Idea webbing)
Sentence, topic (See Topic sentence)
Setting a purpose for reading, 5
She Sat Still, 285–86
Short-answer questions, 164–67
Significance of events, determining, 267
Signs of Life, 15–16
Simile, 254, 255, 277
Slater, Jeffrey, 239–40
Sleem, Pat, 12–13
Smith, Nila, 182
Social Stratification, Appendix A, 292–307
Sound, repetitive use of, 276–77
SQ3R, 167–68
Strategy for
    comparing, 141
    comprehending chronology, 262–65
    comprehending definitions, 233–40
    comprehending descriptions, 253–62
    comprehending explanations, 240–52
    comprehending narratives, 262–75
    comprehending opinions and judgments, 217–32
    concluding, 146–47
    detecting bias, 217–18
    differentiating fact from
        opinion, 219
    distinguishing between general and specific, 62–63
    fixing up, 70
    getting at implied meanings, 143–46
    getting ready to read, 1–5
    grasping chronology, 262–65
    inferring, 68–70, 143–46
    interpreting charts and tables, 195–203
    interpreting graphs, 203–11
    interpreting line drawings, 211–12
    judging, 147
    making main ideas while reading, 66
    preparing for a test, 164–67
    recognizing cause and effect, 124–26
    recognizing conditional relationships, 122–24
    remembering, 178–79
    sorting significant from less significant details, 98–99
    studying, 174–80
    summarizing, 176
    surveying before reading, 2–4
    thesis-making, 83–98
    topic finding, 62
    unlocking the meaning of unfamiliar words, 59
    visualizing, 234, 241
    working with details, 98–114
Structure of a paragraph, 63–69
Style
    definition of, 276
    elements of, 276–277
    reading to determine, 277–78
Suffixes, 39, 47–48
Summaries, writing after reading, 176, 250–51
Sun Disappears: A Solar Eclipse, 129–34
Surveying before reading, 2–4
Syllable segments, 48–49
Synonyms, using to unlock the meaning of words, 23–25

T

Tables, interpreting, 195–203
Television Viewing, Reading, and School Achievement, 213–15
Tennyson, Alfred, 255, 277
Test taking, 163–67
Tests, objective and subjective, 163–67
Thesis of an article, 83–98
Thinking along, 64, 241–42
Thinking aloud, 64, 241–42

Thomas Jefferson and His Presidency, 79–80
Thoreau, Henry David, 254
Three Classes of Rocks, 115–16
Three States of Matter, 138
Three States of the United States: Florida, Nevada, and Illinois, 71–74
Time, words signaling passage of, 264–65
Time lines, using for comprehending chronology, 263
Time Management, 90–92
Tone, definition of, 278
Topic, determining, 61–62
Topic sentence, 61, 66–67
Tortoise and the Hare, 184–85
Truman, Harry S., 220–24
Two-parent and Single-parent Families in the United States, 205

U

Understanding Whole Numbers, 239–40

V

Venn diagrams, 142–43, 266
Vertere derivatives, 41
Visualizing, 234, 241, 254
Vocabulary, developing, 23–59
Volcanic Action on Hawaii, 120

W

Walden Pond, 254
Weather in New Delhi and Santiago, 210–11
Webbing (See Idea webbing)
Welty, Eudora, 187–88
What Does McDonald's Pay? 104–5
What's Involved in Rapid Reading? 182–83
Wiggins, Robert, 189–200
Word elements, 39–59
Word element clues, 39–59
Word tower and wheel, 40–41
World Energy Production and Consumption, 206–7
Writing
    creating summaries, 176
    mapping a selection before writing, 71, 113, 250–51
    using clue words, 138–39

Z

Zwack, Anne, 258–59

ROOTS AND COMBINING FORMS

ELEMENT	MEANING	SAMPLE WORDS
ann(u)-, enni-	year	annual, millennium
astr-	star	astronomical
bene-	good	benefit
bi-, bin-	two, twice	bicycle, binary
bio-	life	biology
cede-	to go or yield	secede
cent-	hundred	century
clos-, claus-, clus-	to close	disclose, claustrophobia
cred-	to believe	creditable
dict-	to write	dictate
dino-	terrible	dinosaur
duct-	to lead	conduct
duo-	two	duet
eco-	home, abode, habitat	ecology
equi-	equal	equate
fac-	to make	manufacture
fid-	faith	infidel
firm-	firm, strong	infirm
flu-, flux, fluv, fluor	to flow	fluid, fluctuate
fort-	strong	fortitude
geo-	earth	geology
grand-	great	grandeur
-graph, -gram, -graphy	writing	telegraph, telegram, orthography
grav-	heavy	gravity
greg-	flock or herd	congregate
hab-	to have, hold as customary	habit
hem-	blood	hemoglobin
hetero-	other	heterogeneous
igni-	fire	ignite
ject-, jac-	to throw	reject
jur-, just-	right, law, to take an oath	jury, perjury
-logy	study or science of	geology
loqu-, locut-	to speak	loquacious, elocution
macro-	large	macromanage
mal-	bad	malicious
manu-	hand	manuscript
matr-	mother	maternal
medi-	middle	mediator
meta-	change	metamorphic
micro-	small	microscope
migra-	to move	migrate, immigrate, emigrate
mill-	thousand	millennium
mit-, mis-	to let go or send	mission
mono-	one	monotonous
morph-	form or shape	morphology
mort-	death	mortal
mult-	many	multitude
nasc-, nat-	to be born	prenatal
nobl-	well-known, highborn	noble
-nomy	study or science of	economy
oct-	eight	octagon
paleo-	old	paleontology
pan-	all, every	panacea